COMBINED MARTIAL ART

실전무예
합도술 교본

오성출판사

Combined Martial Art

합도술 창시자 곽웅쾌 박사 ▶

Dr. Tom Gwak, Creator of Hap Do Sool

◀ 미국 캘리포니아 본관 사범들

Main School Instructors (U.S.A.)

- Mr. John Klopping (1st Deg. Blk-Blt)
- Mr. Jim Cipolla (Assistant Instructor 2nd Deg. Blk-Blt)
- Mr. Jhon Gwak (Master 5th Deg. Blk-Blt)
- Dr. Tom Gwak (Grand Master 9th Deg. Blk-Blt)
- Dr. Darold Simms (Instructor 4th Deg. Blk-Blt)
- Mr. Kevin Simms (2nd Deg. Blk-Blt)
- Mr. Khalil Daneshvar (2nd Deg. Blk-Blt)

◀ 캐나다 벤쿠버 댈타 사범들
Canada School Instructors

- **Instructor Mr. Murray Wallace**
  (Delta, B.C., Canada)
- **Instructor Mr. Tony Pentland**
  (Surrey, B.C., Canada)

합도술 창시자 곽웅쾌 박사 ▶
20세 때 상체의 모습
Master Tom Gwak at the age of 20.

◀ 20m 높이에서 중심을 잡고 가볍게 뛰어
내리는 합도술 창시자 곽웅쾌 박사.
Master Tom Gwak jumps off the side of
a mountain and drops 20 meters to
land without injury.

Combined Martial Art

권투시합: 1969년 한국 라이트급 1인자 아세아 올림픽 출전 김성출 선수와 합도술 창시자 곽웅쾌 박사 시합에서 4라운드에 KO승.
Professional Boxing Match: Tom Gwak Vs. 1969 Asian Olympic Light Weight Contender Number 1, Kim Sung Chool. Tom Gwak won by KO in the 4th Round.

◀ 영화: 1969년 합도술 창시자 곽웅쾌 박사 "금문의 결투" 한 장면
Tom Gwak in a Scene from the movie "The Golden Gate Fight" 1969

▲ 합도술 창시자 곽웅쾌 박사 상단 앞차기
Master Tom Gwak executes a High Front Kick.

▲ 합도술 창시자 곽웅쾌 박사 차력시범을 보이는 장면.
Create of Hapdosool Dr. Tom Gwak Demonstration of Cha Ryuk Sool.

◀ 한국 서울 본관에서 합도술 창시자 곽웅쾌 박사가 학생들 공중 후방 낙법을 가르치는 장면.
Master Tom Gwak is shown here teaching his students Flying Back Nak Bubs at his studio in Seoul, Korea.

시범: 미국 시카고 시청 광장에서 못 판위에 누워 세멘트 10장을 가슴위에 올려놓고 수사관이 햄머로3번을 내려쳐 모두 부수는 장면. ▶
A demonstration held at the Chicago Civic Center in Chicago, Illinois, U.S.A. Master Tom Gwak is lying on a bed of nails with a total of 10 concrete slabs placed on his abdomen. A sledge hammer was used to break the concrete slabs on Master Gwak's abdomen. A total of three powerful blows were necessary to smash through the stack of slabs. The person swinging the hammer was an Investigation Detective for the Evenston, Illinois Police Department.

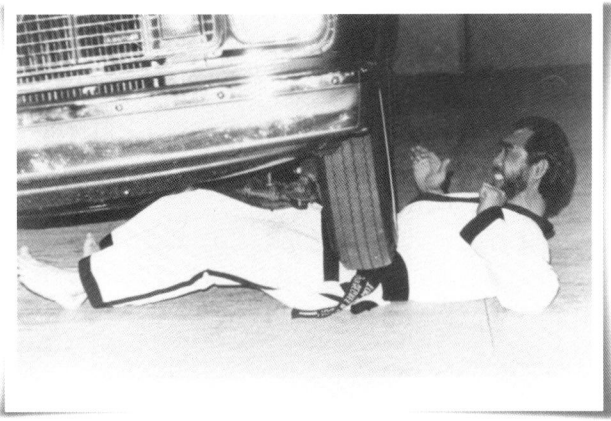

◀ 차력 시범: 합도술 창시자 곽웅쾌 박사 배위로 자동차가 넘어가는 장면.
Demonstration of Ki power : vehicle drives over Master Gwak's stomach.

머리말

천지를 창조하신 조물주는 인간을 만물의 연장으로 우주를 지배할 수 있는 능력을 부여하였지만 7척 단신의 체구에는 힘의 한계가 있는 것이다. 그러나 무술을 통달하고 심신을 단련하면 인간은 누구나 체력의 한계를 초월할 수 있는 불가사리의 경지를 이룩할 수 있다.

본인은 임진왜란 때 사비로 군대를 만들어 왜군을 물리치신 문무를 겸한 사학자 곽재우 옹(호: 홍표) 홍의장군의 18대 손이며 고종 대원군의 섭정(攝政)때 산수화가 정삼품 곽석규 옹(호: 석강) 증조부 만석 군의 3대 손으로 중국 흑룡강성 목단강(黑龍江省 牧丹江) 에서 태어나서 1년을 지난 후 부모님과 한국 경북 영일군 청하면 고현리 392번지 한가옥 안에 대지가 3,400평이고 12채의 집이 있는 할아버지의 본가(本家)로 돌아 왔다.

아버지는 내가 3살 때 연못이 있고 작은 동산이 있는 공원 같은 넓은 집에 운동을 할 수 있는 여러 시설들을 만들어 주셨으며 평행봉, 철봉대, 펀칭백 (Punching Bag), 역기, 역기는 기차 바퀴로 만들었으며 역기 대는 바위를 들어 올리는 지렛대로 만들었고 펀칭백(Punching Bag)은 일본 군인들이 사용하던 니꾸삭꾸(배낭) 자루 백에 톱밥과 헌옷들을 가늘게 잘라 혼합시켜 넣어서 큰 나무 가지에 매어 달아 주셨다.

일본 통치 국 이였기에 우리 무술의 도장은 아무데도 없었고 젊은 남자들은 모두 일본 강제 의용병으로 끌려갔고 군데군데 일본 군인들이 한국 부녀자들을 넓은 공간에서 병정 훈련들을 가르치곤 했으며 우리 마을에서는 우리 집 바깥마당에서 훈련을 가르쳤고 내가 자라오면서 할아버지와 아버지 형님께 기초 무술들을 배웠다.
처음 입산한 동기는 초등학교 6 학년 때 친구들과 여름 방학 때 산으로 캠핑(Camping)을 가서 수련을 하게 되었다. 야생초, 야생과일, 개구리,

뱀, 가재등을 잡아먹으면서 바위틈에서 흘러나오는 생수를 마시면서 목욕을 하고 정신통일 연습을 했다. 신비롭게도 정신 집중을 하려고 해도 잘 안되던 것이 쉽게 할 수 있게 되었다. 그때부터 정신통일을 하는 법을 터득했고, 힘도 솟아나고 정신이 맑아지니 매일매일 새 사람이 된 기분으로 운동을 할 수 있었다. 약 3주정도 친구들과 있다가 머루, 다래, 버섯, 더덕, 칡뿌리 산에서 나는 약초와 과일들을 많이 가지고 집에 왔다. 방학 때면 항상 친구들과 또는 혼자서도 입산하여 집에서 풀지 못한 기술들을 모아 입산하여 풀고 축지법도 혼자서 연구하고 단련하며 터득했다.

고등학교를 가기위해 대구 신암동 제1 육군병원 앞 과수원집으로 옮겼으며 무술을 더욱 연구하기 위하여 과수원 창고에 체육관을 만들어 관원들을 모집했다. 관원들은 일순간에 수십 수백 명이 몰려왔다. 내가 연구하기 위해 모집하는 관원들이니 입관 비와 회비는 물론 없었다. 운동을 잘하는 관원들에게는 과수원에서 떨어지는 과일들을 공짜로 먹게 했고 가끔씩 밤에 밤참을 만들어 주면서 밤샘을 하며 연구와 연습을 하기도 했다.

한국전쟁(6.25사변)이 끝나고 휴전을 하고 있을 때 이니 먹을 것이 부족하였고 배를 채우기 위하여 더욱 관원들이 몰려왔다. 수백 명씩 모여 운동을 했지만 그땐 우리 체육관에 기존 무술의 이름도 없었다. 어떤 날은 권투와 당수 다음날은 유도와 씨름 또 그 다음날은 레스링 과 야와라 계속 바꾸어 가면서 짜임새도 없이 오합지졸로 순서 없는 잡탕 무술 이였다. 종합무술을 찾기 위해 사방으로 수소문하여 사부님들을 찾아 기술을 배워 보았지만 만족하지 못하고 좋은 기술들을 찾지 못했다.

일본정부는 한국에서 36년간 일본통치 국으로 있으면서 한국의 각종고유 무술들을 말소 시켰고 한국에서 각종 고유 무술을 하신 Grand

Master들은 모두 돌아 가셨고 도사님 들은 깊은 산 속 암자에 들어가서 여생을 마감 하셨고 한국의 고유 무술의 비술은 결국 전수되지 못했었다. 실질 종합무술이 없으니 그간 오합지졸로 무술을 익히든 기술들을 집대성하기로 마음먹고 그때부터 틈틈이 입산하여 연습했든 각종무술들을 하나씩 정립하기 시작했다. 입산하여 무술을 정립하여 만들기까지 4년 반 세월동안 많은 실제경험을 통하여 만들었다. 그간 실제경험을 통하여 만들기까지 많은 이야기가 있었지만 사람들이 합도술을 알게 될 때 그때 하기로 하겠다.

본인은 권투, 씨름, 유도, 태권도, 야와라, 합기도, 레슬링, 기계체조, 차력, 요가까지 배워온 여러 무술의 기술을 연결 동작으로 권술, 족술, 낙법술, 막기술, 스텝술, 유술, 공중제비술, 차력술을 혼합하여 형을 만들었고, 고정술, 호신술, 급소 지압술을 혼합시켜 더 연구하여 실전 종합 무술로 만들었으며 기초부터 고수들 까지도 배울 수 있는 연결 동작으로 드디어 1968년 4월 19일 합도술 이름으로 협회를 서울 중구 을지로 3가에서 결성했다.

실전(實戰) 무술을 세상에 인정받기 위하여 미국에 있는 세계 프로 권투 Heavy급 Champion 무하메드 알리와 일본에 있는 세계 프로 레슬링 Heavy 급 Champion 안토니오 이노끼 에게 진짜 보내기(Knock Out)를 하자고 도전장을 두 사람 에게 각각 보내면서 한국일보 본사 4층 Hall에서 16개 언론사 기자들에게 공식 공개 발표회를 가졌다. 권투와 레슬링은 내가 오랫동안 전문으로 하였기에 장단점을 더욱 연구 개발하여 각 무술의 기술들을 총 집대성 하여 만들었기에 자신을 가지고 먼저 두 사람에게 공식 도전장을 보냈다. 각 신문에 기사와 각 방송국에 시범 출연을 하였고, 극동 영화사에선 금문의 결투란 영화에 무술감독과 주연을 동시에 맡아 하였다. 체육관에서 제자들과 연구한 기술들을 다지던 중 한국의 협객인 김두한씨가 나를 찾아 직접 기술을 Testing하시고 합도술에 매료되어 후원 인으로 정릉 유원지에 종합무술관을 만들어 한국의 모던 우수 무술인 들을 한곳에 집합시켜 수련시킬 계획을 세워 합도술 Center를 건축할 부지를 주셨고, 정부에 건축 시설비로 3,000만원의 지원금을 신청하셨다. 김두한씨의 금전적 도움을 받아 협회를 운영하였으며 자동차도 구입하여 활동하게 하여 주셨고 본관 관장들은 정릉 유원지 수영장에서 경비를 보게 하였다. 당시 공화당 박정희 대통령에게 정릉 유원지에 30만평을 30년간 무상 임대를 받아 여러 시설들을 하는 도중 이였다. 정릉 유원지가 완성되면 정릉 유원지 내에 합도술 센터에 있는 관원들이 모든 경비를 맡도록 계획을 세웠다.

정릉 김두한씨의 자택에서 같이 많은 계획을 세워 결정하고 활동하다가 김두한씨의 경제 사정이 좋지 않아 월남 대통령 경호원 사범으로 초청을 받고 잠시 출국 하였다가 한국에 돌아오니 김두한씨는 운명을 달리 하셨기에 한국의 활동을 중단하고 더 큰 넓은땅 미국 진출을 결심 알 카폰의 고장인 Chicago에서 활동하기로 마음먹고 Illinois Evanston에 정착하여 숲 미국에 생소한 합도술을 주정부 및 연방정부에 사단 법인으로 신청하여 많은 어려움 속에서 결국 미국 사상 최초로 종합무술의 합도술 협회를 1977년 3월 9일 Illinois주정부 사단법인 허가 #.7255 를 받고, 1978년 4월 20일 연방정부 사단법인 36-3000674 로 허가를 받았다.

한국인으론 미국에서 최초로 미국 중부지역 웰터급 프로 권투 License 02-10381-B 도 받았다. 많은 미국 프로 권투 흥행주(Promoter)들이 만불 ($10,000.00)씩 주겠다고 시합 제의가 여러 번 들어왔다. 그때 세계 헤비급 챔피온 시합이 백만 불 정도 였으며 그때 처음 시합엔 많은 돈 이였다. 미국에서 합도술의 뿌리를 내리는 데는 권투시합은 좋지 않을 것 같아서 미국에서 권투 코치로만 하기로 했다.

ATF(American Taekwondo Federation)의 주체로 1974년 숲 Illinois 태권도 선수권 시합을 하던 날 관객들과 선수들이 약 3천명이 모인 대학교 강당에서 미국 사범들이 한국 Master와 실전 대련을 하자고 시합 주최 석에 도전을 해왔다고 한다. 황당한 일이였다. 만약 실수를 했을 땐 치명적인 체육관 Business에 지장이 있으니 도전을 받겠다는 한국 관장님들은 아무도 없었다. 나에겐 좋은 기회였다. 다행히 먼저 도전을 해왔으니 속으로는 좋았다.

미국에서 미국관장들과 무술로 실전격투(實戰格鬪)로 겨루워 보기를 얼마나 고대했던가 한국에서는 실전격투 경험은 많이 했지만 서구인들은 보통 6척이 넘는 거구들이라서 어른과 아이와 대련하는 격이니 우선 체격에서 압도적으로 불리하지만 내가 상대 하겠다고 쾌히 승낙 을 했다. 대담하게 도전을 받겠다고 했더니 상대편에서 그만 취소하겠다고 하여 그날 그들의 도전이 좌절 되어 나에겐 아쉽게 되었다.

많은 무술의 고수들이 입산하여 자기 나름대로 무술을 연구하여 실전(實戰) 무술이라고 하지만 실력이 발표되지 않았기에 나는 세상에 실전 합도술(實戰合道術)의 기술을 알리고 싶었다. 많은 사람들은 실전 합도술로 연구하며 다져온 나를 믿지를 않았다. 첫째 나이도 어리고 또 최고의 단수인 9단이라고 하니 한국 Master들도 믿지를 않았다. 체육관 간판에도 세계 최고의 Grand Master라고 선전했다. 많은 한국 관장들도 중상과 모략 시기와 질투로 신문에다 투고도 했다.

미국이란 나라는 실력이 있으면 인정되는 나라이기에 체구가 큰 서구민족을 상대로 체육관에서 학생들을 Sparring Partner로 생각하고 열심히 가르치며 연구를 했다. 그동안 체육관으로 많은 도전의 전화가 왔고 체육관 유리벽에 나를 그린 그림에다 종종 총구멍을 내기도 했다. 갱이 가장많은 "알카폰"의 고장이라 처음부터 각오는 하고 정착을 했지만 한편으론 불안도 했다. Grand Master와 대련을 하고 싶다고 전화도 수없이 걸려왔다.

한번은 키가 2m 정도 체중은 300파운드가 넘어 보이는 거구가 일주일 동안 매일 찾아와서 학생들을 가르치는 기술들을 다보고 우리 학생(Larry Bordam)을 통하여 Master와 대련을 하고 싶다고 도전을 해왔다. 합도술은 일주일 동안 가르치는 기술이 다르기에 일주일을 보아야 합도술의 맥을 알수있다. 우리 학생을 통해 도전을 해왔으니 거절 할 수도 없어 다음날 낮 12시에 다시 체육관에 오라고 했다. 그 시간엔 체육관 문을 열지 않을 시간이고 단 둘이만 있으니 혹 실수를 해도 적당히 하려고 했지만 우리 관원들이 10명 이상이 Master의 실력을 보기위하여 체육관에 찾아왔기에 놀라지 않을수가 없었다.

우리 학생에게 각서를 작성 하도록 지시했다. 서로 몸을 다치든지 죽더라도 상대의 잘못이 아닌 본인의 책임으로 서로 Signature을 하고 Judo Uniform 6호를 주고 입으라고 했다. 몸이 거구라 도복이 반소매였지만 입게했고 체육관 가운데서 서로 견제하며 대치하고 섰다. 상대는 나의 기술과 정보를 많이 알고 있었지만 나는 상대가 어떤 무술을 했는지 아무런 정보도 없었다. 그러나 상대가 양손을 올려 얼굴에 붙이고 대치하고 있는 Form이 권투 자세 였기에 손이 무기인줄 짐작을 하고 발을 먼저 사용하기로 했다.

몸을 왼쪽으로 돌면서 먼저 왼쪽 Jab으로 가볍게 던져 보았다. 상대는 내가 발의 기술을 사용하는 줄을 알고 있었던 것 같았다. 당황하며 뒤로 몸을 빼는 순간 위로 뛰면서 몸을 시계방향으로 돌아 오른발 이단 뒤돌려 뒤축 차기로 상대의 오른쪽 관자놀이(Temple)을 차고 양발을 바닥에 닿는 동시 오른쪽 정권 Hook으로 상대의 왼쪽 늑골을 치고 왼쪽 정권 Uppercut으로 명치(Solar plexus)를 치니 윽! 하며 앞으로 숙이는 순간에 오른쪽 정권 Hook으로 상대의 왼쪽 턱을 치니 상대는 아래로 무릎을 접으면서 앞으로 쓰러졌다. 상대는 잠깐사이 4번 연결동작 공격을 받았다. 불과 1-2초 정도였다.

한참 후에 무릎을 세워 꿇어앉으며 나에게 졌다고 했다. 체육관 관원들은 순간 박수를 치며 기뻐했다. 자기는 Golden Group에서 Pro Boxer 무하메드 알리의 Sparring Partner이며 다른 체육관에서 돈을 받고 관장들을 Knock out 시켜 체육관 문을 닫게하는 Knockout contractor 이라고 했다. 같은 City에 있는 미국 체육관에서 보내서 왔다고 하면서 합도술의 기술을 배우겠다고 하여 Application을 쓰고 현금 $60.00을 내고 체육관에 입관을 했다. 깨끗한 무사 같은 사나이 였다.

그후부터 미국 Chicago에서 미국 체육관에서 실전 격투기는 합도술 뿐이라고 소문이 나기 시작했다. NBC TV에서 합도술 차력시범을 했으며 각 매스컴과 세계 5대 신문중의 하나인 TIMES, TRIBUNE과 지방신문에도 합도술의 기사와 차력 소개를 했고 뉴욕에서 물리학 박사가 비행기를 타고 와서 차력의 힘으로 작은 체구에서 어떻게 그 무서운 파괴력의 힘을 낼 수 있는 냐고 하면서 힘은 무게에 비례 한다고 했다 과학적으로 입증되는 충분한 설명을 해주었다.

California Culver City에 있는 한국 태권도 미들급 Champion (한국 박정희 대통령에게 표창장을 받음) 이관장과 California Riverside City에 있는 태권도 8단의 김관장(한국 첩보부대 출신) 신게임(실전)을 하자고 해왔다. 2명의 관장이 모두 코뼈와 왼쪽 늑골 3개가 부러지고 무릎을 끓었다. 그 이후에도 몇 관장으로부터 도전을 받아 왔지만 다행히 한 번도 실수 한 적이 없었다. 그때부터 합도술 창시자에게 Master Killer 라는 별명이 붙었다.

혼자서도 모든 기술을 배워 연결 동작으로 사용할 수 있는 대학의 교육 과정으로 Curriculum program과 Syllabus들을 만들어 1987년도 미국 California 주정부 교육청에 Vocational School로 Hapdosool College of Health Science 대학으로 No. 20320 허가를 받아 미국학생들을 가르쳤다.

1998년 Canada Vancouver에서 World Ultimate Warrior Challenge(세계 무술인 최후의 도전) 이라는 격투기 시합에 합도술 사범 Light급 (Shervin Tehranchi) 와 Middle급 (Robert Dowell) 두 사범을 보내어 모두 Knock Out을 시켜 이겼고 1999년에 Middle급 (Robert Dowell) 사범이 또 Canada에서 두 번째 세계 격투기 시합에서도 Knock Out으로 또 승리를 했다. 세계 시합에서 실전 합도술의 기술이 완전 인정이 되었으며 시합도중 심판석 해설자가 실전 합도술의 기술 호평도 해주었다.

본인이 수십 년 동안 산 경험으로 기술을 보강 정립시켜 만든 기술이기에 무술을 배우시는 분들에게 도움이 되었으면 하는 마음 입니다. 실전 합도술의 참뜻은 자기방어 (Self Defense) 남으로 부터 공격을 막기 위하여 차고, 때리고, 받고, 꺽고, 던지고, 조르고, 차력으로 힘을 발육 시키고, 급소를 누르고, 근육과 인대를 뻗어 혈액 순환을 촉진시켜 지압과 호흡으로 긴장을 풀어주고 장기의 기능을 강화 시켜 건강을 회복시키는 기술인 것이다.

무술 학위를 줄수 있는 종합 무예대학 academic degree program의

curriculum을 만들기 위해 미국 학위 System을 좀 더 알고 신체경락 혈 자리를 정확히 잡는 과목을 만들기 위하여 지압대학을 졸업하고 한의과대학에서 학사, 석사, 박사(Ph.D.) 학위를 받고 중국에 유학을 가서 동양의 주역과 침술, 본초학을 강도 높게 연구하여 동양무술과 동양의술이 일맥상통 하고 모든 경락혈이 급소 혈맥이며 책에 없는 급소와 오묘한 비술들을 배우고 연구 개발하여 완성시켰다.

서양의술은 symptom(증상) 조절이고 동양의 의술은 function(기능) 조절이기에 서양 의학을 공부하고 동, 서양의 의학을 모두 마치고, 국제 교육법을 좀더 연구 분석하고 미국에서 UCI (University of California Irvine) 의과 대학에서 인체에 관한 과목 anatomy, neurobiology, respiratory, digestive, cardiovascular, pelvic, kidney, urinary, extremities를 더 공부하고 시체를 직접 해부하면서 동, 서양의 의술을 결합시켜 무술의 급소와 연결된 장기의 신경조직을 치명적 파괴 또는 보호하는 기술들을 연구 개발 하였고 무술인들이 공부를 해야하는 syllabus들도 일일이 자신의 경험으로 만들었다.

1997년 Yuin University of Hawaii 대학교와 합도술 대학이 합병하여 무예학 학사, 석사, 박사(Ph.D.)학위 curriculum을 만들어 교육을 시켜왔다. 동양무술은 공격목적이 아니고 즉 수명연장, 건강, 평화를 목적에 본이 되는 것을 학술로 인하여 더욱 알게 되어 인체 내부 속에 작은 우주를 만들어 음양오행(陰陽五行)으로 상호 연결하여 동, 서양의 의술과 무술을 결합하여 활용하는 기술을 정립하였고, 그동안 본인이 직접 배우고 연구 단련한 기술인 권술, 족술, 던지기기술, 낙법술, 꺽기술, 고정술, 지압술, 차력술, 스텝을 혼합시켜 강약으로 호흡과 힘을 조화시켜 기술을 하나로 체계화하여 본인이 직접 수십년 동안 동, 서양 사람들을 상대로 실제 산 경험으로 기술들을 보강하여 실전 종합무예(실전합도술)의 책을 정립시켜 만든 기술이기에 무술을 배우시는 분들에게 도움이 되었으면 하는 마음입니다.

실전합도술의 참뜻은 첫째, 자기방어(Self Defense) 외부로부터 공격을 막기 위하여 차고, 때리고, 받고, 꺽고, 던지고, 조르고, 차력으로 힘을 발육시켜 급소를 공격하고 모든 기술을 사용하여 자기를 보호하는 기술. 둘째, 건강 관리(Health Control) 신진대사를 촉진시켜 몸의 기능과 면역성(Immune)을 강화시키고 소멸되는 뇌의 세포를 재생시켜 모든 병을 예방하고 몸의 균형을 잡아주며 단전에 氣(기)를 모아 발육시켜 약한 장기에 옮겨 사용하게 하는 기술. 셋째, 정신수양(Mental Discipline) 호흡을 통하여 무아상태로 만들어 긴장을 풀어주고 자아를 찾아 고귀한 생을 연장 하므로 자신의 귀중한 존재를 알고 편안하고 평화로운 마음을 만드는 기술들을 만들었습니다.

실전합도술 창시자
곽웅쾌 박사

HAP DO SOOL

THE COMBINED MARTIAL ART

Written By

Dr. Tom Woong Qwai Gwak

October 2004

Los Angeles, California

U.S.A

PREAMBLE

The Creator of heaven and earth made humankind the masters of the universe. Unfortunately, humans possessed physical limitations. A six-foot tall man does not have the eagles eyesight, the cats reflexes, the rabbits speed or the apes strength. Even so, by mastering martial arts and training the mind and heart human beings can overcome these limitations. I was born in the Mok Dan Gang Province of Huk Long Gang Sung, China. A year later. I moved to my father's home in the Yung Il Goon Province of Kyungbuk Korea. My father provided me with many sports equipment and I began my training at the age of three. I was supplied equipment including parallel bars, iron bars, and punching bags. The weights were made with train wheels train wheels. One of the bars was made with a lever for lifting up rocks lifting up rocks. The punching bag was made with a knapsack bag used by Japanese soldiers and was filled with worn-out clothes, finely shredded sawdust and hung on a tree.

At the time, because Korea was a colony of Japan, no schools for our martial arts training existed, and all the young men were dragged away as involuntary soldiers. There were Japanese soldiers training Korean women military drills here and there in wide, open areas. In my hometown, the training took place in my front yard, and as I grew older I learned basic martial arts from my father and grand father.

My first motive for living in mountainous areas was when I went on a camping trip with friends in the sixth grade during a summer break.

By eating wild plants and fruits, frogs, snakes, crawfish, and drinking spring water, I practiced mental concentration. I attained mental concentration even though it had previously been difficult, and from that time onward I practiced my training daily feeling like a person reborn with invigorated power and a refreshed spirit. After staying there for about three weeks with friends, I returned home with many wild grapes, hardy kiwi (actinidia arguta), mushrooms, todok roots (Colonopsis lanceolata), arrowroots, wild herbs and other fruits. During school breaks, I always entered the mountains either with friends or alone. Techniques that I could not understand while training at home I took to the mountains and practiced and perfected them such as Chuk Ji Bub, a technique to cover distance in a short amount of time.

To enroll in high school, I moved to an orchard house near the Armed Forces Hospital located at Shinam-dong, Daegu City. In order to research more about the martial arts, I built a martial arts school inside the orchard storage facility and opened it to the public. Immediately thereafter, individuals joined the school in large numbers but because it was for my own research, I charged no membership fees. For those doing well in exercise, I allowed them to eat the fruit that fell in the orchards, and sometimes I even held night practices providing students with evening snacks.

It was the time when the war between North and South Korea had ended and a truce was signed. There was little food and more members came in just to fill up their stomachs. Many hundreds gathered and practiced but, at the time, there was no name for the martial arts school. Some days we practiced boxing, Dang Soo Do and Gong Soo Do (Karate), and on other days Judo and Ssirum (Korean Sumo), and on the following days wrestling, Hap Ki Do and Yawara. Though we continued our practice, there was no structure or form to our martial arts training, which was of a disorderly fashion.

Even though I searched for a combined martial art, I could not find one I considered acceptable.

During that time, Korea had been a Japanese colony for 36 years. All of the Grand Masters of the native Korean martial arts had passed away, and most of the Dosa (monks) finished the remainder of their lives in their hermitage; therefore, the traditional methods of the native Korean martial arts could not be handed down. I made up my mind to compile those skills, which were practiced in a disorganized fashion. I resolved to enter the mountains for four years and to create step-by-step one combined martial arts system. When I returned from the mountains, I began to teach people Hap Do Sool, the combined martial arts system I had formulated during my training and research.

After learning martial art skills such as boxing, Ssirum, Judo, Tae Kwon Do, Hap Ki Do, wrestling, gymnastics, Cha Ryuk (developing extraordinary strength and focus through concentration) and even yoga, I formed a connection among the many types of martial skills such as punching, kicking, falling, blocking, footwork, leverage, tumbling, Cha Ryuk, self-defense, pressure points, choking and pinning techniques and others needed to create an authentic combined martial arts system for actual fighting. Finally on April 19th, 1968, I declared the name of Hap Do Sool, a combined martial arts system that could be learned by beginners and masters alike.

To have Hap Do Sool acknowledged throughout the world as an actual fighting martial arts system, I mailed letters of challenge to two persons respectively: Muhammad Ali, World Heavyweight Boxing Champion of the United States, and Antonio Inoki, World Professional Wrestling Champion of Japan. On the fourth floor in the main hall of the Korea Times, I made formal announcements to 16 mass media companies that I was challenging these two individuals to a contest where the victor would win by knocking out the other opponent. Because I had been involved with boxing and wrestling and had evaluated the strong and weak aspects of many martial arts, I confidently challenged them to a duel; however, I did not receive a reply from either of them.

While I was laying the foundation of techniques that would later become Hap Do Sool, I continued my research into combining the martial arts, choreographed and acted in martial arts movies by Korean movie company Guk Dong, and provided interviews and demonstrations to television, radio and newspaper companies. Doo Han Kim, a legendary Korean freedom fighter, personally called me to test my skills. He was so impressed by my skill and knowledge of the healing arts that he provided me a site to build a Hap Do Sool martial arts institute. His plan was to attract and train outstanding students in the martial arts at this site in Korea. He then applied for a support fund of 30 million Won (est. $268,000) to the Korean government. With the monetary support of Doo Han Kim, I operated the Hap Do Sool association, purchased a car for its activities, and employed the instructors to work as security guards at the Jungreung Recreation Park swimming pool.

I was very much active with Doo Han Kim at his home in Jungreung for several years; however, because of the financial burden caused by the Recreation Park, Doo Han Kim was no longer able to support the Hap Do Sool operations. I decided to leave Korea and work as a martial arts instructor for the bodyguards of the president of Vietnam. When I returned to Korea a few years later, Doo Han Kim had passed away and I decided to move to the United States to the city of Evanston, Illinois, a suburb of Chicago. I applied for a charter to teach Hap Do Sool, which was a martial arts style unfamiliar to America. The Hap Do Sool Association of Combined Martial Arts was incorporated on April 20, 1978 (#36-3000674) and registered with the federal government and the State of Illinois as a non-profit organization.

I obtained a Professional Boxers license (#02-104381-B) in the welterweight division, the only Korean in the central region of the United States to receive one at the time. Although many professional boxing promoters in the United States were interested in signing me to matches at $10,000 each, I decided that my professional boxing career would not assist the growth of Hap Do Sool in the United States so I decided to concentrate only on coaching boxing in the United States.

In 1974, the All-Illinois Tae Kwon Do Tournament was sponsored by the American Tae Kwon Do Federation (ATF). About 3,000 people were in attendance. I was informed by the chairman of the ATF about a challenge match from the instructors of the United States to a contest against the Korean masters. It was an absurd and embarrassing matter because this tournament was for the students and not the masters but there were no Korean masters willing to take the challenge due to the fact that the Korean martial arts community would be adversely affected in the case of any mistake. However, this was a good opportunity for me to display my skills. My heart felt good that the challenge initially came from the United States. How long had I been waiting for a match of an actual martial arts fight against masters from the United States! I had many real fighting experiences in Korea, but this match was likened to that of a child versus an adult considering the giant bodies of the six-foot tall Westerners. I gladly accepted the challenge. Unfortunately, the match never took place and was never rescheduled because the American instructors declined to fight and pleaded no contest.

Many martial arts masters had entered the mountains and tried to master the actual fighting skills developed by them but none of this power was made known because they did not fight or issue challenges to people on the outside and kept the techniques solely to themselves, so I wanted to let the actual fighting skills of Hap Do Sool be seen by all. Many people disbelieved my actual fighting abilities, and others from established systems felt I was too young to hold the ninth degree black belt rank. Even the Korean masters were skeptical and many Korean martial arts masters sent slanderous letters to newspapers to discredit my name.

In the US, I eagerly studied and taught the physically larger Americans, viewing them as my sparring partners at the martial arts school. During the meantime, I received many telephone calls asking for challenges to the Grand Master, and from time to time gunshots were fired on posters with my picture on it. Although I was prepared for the challenge of succeeding in this mafia- abundant place of Al Capone, I became apprehensive as I settled in because of the numerous threats and gunshots.

Once, a very large individual who looked to be over 300 pounds and 6.6 feet tall visited my place everyday for an entire week and watched the techniques I was teaching the students, requested a challenge match with the Master through our student Larry Bordam. Hap Do Sool encompasses different skills that are taught daily during a one-week period so it takes at least a week to comprehend the core teachings of Hap Do Sool. Since I was requested the challenge match through my student I could not refuse, and I told the individual to visit the school again at noon on the following day. I had believed that only the two of us would be in attendance, but I was surprised when I saw about ten people, mostly comprised of my students, come to see the match.

I directed our students to write down an agreement. I secured signatures from the both of us to confirm that even though we might get hurt or die, the responsibility would be our own and we would not blame the opponent. My opponent knew a lot about my techniques since he had studied them for a whole week, but I had no information whatsoever of his fighting style or ability. Looking at the form of his boxing position having placed his two fists near his face, I estimated that his hands were the weapons.

Turning my body lightly to the left, I initiated the first attack by a light left jab. The opponent seemed to believe that I used only my feet. At the moment he tried to move, I turned my body clockwise jumping up and kicking the opponents right temple with my right foot and then followed with a double swing kick. Coming down from my jump attack and touching the ground at the same time, I hit his left rib with a right fist hook, at which he shouted Wook! As he fell, within that short moment as his body lowered downward, I hit his solar plexus with a left fist uppercut. Following that moment, with a right fist hook I hit his left jaw, and then he fell to his knees. The entire encounter lasted Only a couple Seconds.

He bowed his knees down and said that he lost. Those who witnessed the contest burst into applause. He informed me that he was a former sparring partner of professional boxer Muhammad Ali in the Golden Gloves competitions and that he was now a hired tough paid to close down other martial arts schools after knocking the masters out, and that he was sent by another school in the same city to close down my school. After the match, he joined our school paying $60.00 in cash after filling out an application because he wanted to learn Hap Do Sool. He was a fine gentleman, like a knight.

Thereafter, rumors about Hap Do Sool being the only martial arts institute to teach authentic hand-to-hand fighting began to spread. I gave demonstrations on Cha Ryuk (developing extraordinary strength and focus through concentration) to NBC Television, the Chicago Times, the Chicago Tribune, local newspapers and many other mass media companies, who introduced articles about Hap Do Sool and the art of hand-to-hand fighting. A doctor of physics arrived all the way from New York by airplane and asked how a person with a small body structure could dispense out an incredible amount of power. He said that power is proportional to weight but I gave him a satisfactory explanation that was scientifically proven.

On another occasion, middleweight Korean Tae Kwon Do champion Master Lee, who received a letter of recommendation from Korean President Park Jung Hee, and eight-degree black belt Tae Kwon Do Master Kim each challenged me to actual fighting duels on two different occasions. The two masters both suffered broken noses and broken ribs and had surrendered to me. Thereafter, I received and won many challenges and, fortunately, I have not made even one mistake. From that time on, the nickname of Master Killer was affixed to the founder of Hap Do Sool.

In 1998 at the Mixed Martial Art Raw Combat Competition held in Vancouver, Canada in a raw combat hand-to-hand fighting match, Shervin Tehranchi, a lightweight instructor of Hap Do Sool, and

Robert Dowell, a middleweight instructor of Hap Do Sool, both competed and won their matches by knock-out. In 1999, Robert Dowell won by knock-out for the second time in a row at another mixed martial art competion called the Ultimate Warrior Challenge Warrior Challenge held in Vancouver the following year. The judges gave favorable comments during the match on the Hap Do Sool techniques, and Hap Do Sools perfect record was acknowledged in these international tournaments.

This skill was formed by strengthening and refining the techniques through real-life experiences for many decades, and I hope this benefits seekers of the martial arts. The true meanings of Hap Do Sool are; firstly, self-defense (protecting oneself from attacks by others), implementing arts of kicking, punching, head bashing, breaking, throwing, choking, applying pressure points, and protecting oneself by applying all types of self-defense skills; secondly, to practice health control by enhancing the metabolism and strengthening the function and immunity system of the body, preventing disease, balancing the body, concentrating ki (energy) in the lower abdomen, and the skill of using the power to transfer strength to other body parts; and thirdly, to release tension and stress by achieving the state of perfect mental discipline, and also to attain and extend the noble life by attaining self-realization, a way for a comfortable and peaceful mind.

Tom Gwak, Ph.D.
Creator of Hap Do Sool

Combined Martial Art

CONTENTS

목 차

01. 준비 운동: Warm Up Sequence ········· **030**
02. 합도 술 本: Fundamental Exercise Sequence ········· **046**
03. 자세: Stance Technique ········· **100**
04. 급소 술: Vital Point Technique ········· **124**
05. 스탭 술: Steps Technique ········· **136**
06. 권 술: Punching Technique ········· **150**
07. 족 술: Kicking Technique ········· **182**
08. 막기 술: Blocking Technique ········· **232**
09. 형: Forms Technique ········· **258**
10. 공중제비 술: Tumbling Technique ········· **410**
11. 낙법 술: Nak Bub Technique ········· **418**
12. 던지기 술: Yu Sool Technique ········· **438**
13. 고정 술: Go Jung Sool Technique ········· **454**
14. 호신 술: Ho Shin Sool Technique ········· **464**
15. 기공요가 술: Yoga Sool Technique ········· **482**
16. 지압 술: Acupressure Technique ········· **522**

Warming Up Sequences

준|비|운|동

01. 한팔 돌리기: Single Arm Circles

02. 양팔 돌리기: Double Arm Circles

03. 가슴 벌리기: Chest Expansions

04. 무릎 반동: Knee Bounces

05. 허리 틀기: Trunk Twists

06. 옆구리 숙이기: Side Bends

07. 허리 숙이기: Front & Back Bends

08. 허리 돌리기: Hip Circles

09. 모둠발 뛰기: Modified Jumping Jacks

10. 목 팽창: Neck Tensions

11. 목 돌리기: Neck Relaxations

12. 한다리 뻗기: Single Leg Stretch

13. 양다리 뻗기: Double Leg Stretch

14. 손목 돌리기: Wrist Circles

15. 발목 돌리기: Ankle Circles

16. 손가락 발가락 뻗기: Finger & Toe Stretch

항상 준비 운동을 할 때는 긴장을 풀고 몸의 근육을 이완시킬다.

1. 한팔 돌리기

허리를 똑바로 펴고 선 자세에서 양다리를 어깨 넓이로 벌리고 양팔과 양손을 앞으로 똑같이 뻗고 손바닥은 아래로 하고 오른발 뒤꿈치를 들면서 오른팔을 시계 방향으로 한바퀴 돌리고 왼발 뒤꿈치를 들면서 왼팔을 반시계 방향으로 한바퀴 돌리고 반대로 오른발 뒤꿈치를 들면서 반시계 방향으로 돌리고 왼발 뒤꿈치를 들면서 왼팔은 시계 방향으로 돌린다.

Single Arm Circles:

Start_Stand with your legs comfortably apart and position your arms out in front of you.
Description_Begin with your left arm. Keep your arms straight and swing your arm forward by rotating at the shoulder in a windmill motion. As your left arm revolves over, alternate to your right arm. Continue this motion until you have completed at least 10 revolutions for each arm. Then reverse the motion by swinging your arm backwards in the same reversed motion for at least 10 revolutions for each arm.

2. 양팔 돌리기

허리를 똑바로 펴고 선 자세에서 양다리를 어깨 넓이로 벌리고 양팔과 양손을 앞으로 똑같이 뻗고 손바닥은 아래로 하고 양발뒤꿈치를 들면서 양팔을 동시에 아래로 내려 뒤로 한바퀴 돌리고 다시 반대로 양발뒤꿈치를 들면서 양팔을 반대로 뒤로 한바퀴 동시에 돌린다.

Double Arm Circles:

Start_ Stand with your legs comfortably apart and position your arms out in front of you.
Description_ Keep your arms straight and swing your arms forward at the same time by rotating at the shoulder in a windmill motion. After completing one full circular forward revolution, reverse the motion by swinging your arms backwards. Continue this process of rotating your arms forward, then backwards for at least 10 times.

3. 가슴 벌리기

허리를 똑바로 펴고 선 자세에서 양다리를 어깨 넓이로 벌리고 양팔과 양손을 앞으로 똑같이 뻗고 양손바닥은 서로 반대로 틀어 양팔을 뒤로 돌려 뒤에서 손뼉을 친다.

Chest Expansion:

Start_Stand with your legs comfortably apart and position your arms out in front of you.
Description_Bend both of your arms and jerk your elbows back behind you. Expand your chest and try to stretch your arms back behind you in a breast stroking motion. Expand your chest and try to clap your hands behind you. Continue this sequence for at least 10 times.

4. 무릎 반동

허리를 똑바로 펴고 선 자세에서 양다리를 어깨 넓이로 벌리고 양팔과 양손을 앞으로 똑같이 뻗고 손바닥은 아래로 하고 양팔과 양무릎을 아래로 내리면서 무릎 반동으로 반을 굽혔다가 일어난다.

Knee Bounce:

Start_Stand with your legs comfortably apart and position your arms out in front of you
Description_ Keep your back and arms straight. Squat down by bending at the knees and sway both of your arms back. Come back up at about half way then squat back down. Then sway both of your arms forward as you stand back up. Continue 10 times.

01

5. 허리 틀기

허리를 똑바로 펴고 선 자세에서 양다리를 어깨 넓이로 벌리고 손바닥을 아래로 하고 양팔을 옆 수평으로 벌리고 오른손을 왼쪽 어깨에 대고 왼손등은 등 뒤 허리에 붙이고 왼쪽 어깨를 밀면서 왼쪽으로 허리를 틀어 3번 반동으로 허리를 틀고 다시 양팔을 옆 수평으로 벌렸다가 왼손은 오른쪽 어깨에 대고 오른손등은 등 뒤 허리에 붙이고 오른쪽 어깨를 밀면서 오른쪽으로 허리를 틀어 3번 반동으로 허리를 튼다.

Trunk Twist:

Start_Stand with your legs comfortably apart. Place your right hand on the front of your left shoulder, and position the back of your left hand behind your lower back.

Description_Turn your upper body clockwise by twisting at the waist. Apply a slight amount of pressure to your right shoulder with your left hand to help assist the twisting. Then rotate back and twist your upper body counter clockwise in the opposite direction. At the same time, switch your arms and apply a slight amount of pressure with your right hand to your left shoulder to help assist the twisting in the opposite direction. Continue this process twisting in both directions for at least 10 times.

준비운동: Warming Up Sequences 035

6. 옆구리 숙이기

허리를 똑바로 펴고 선 자세에서 양다리를 어깨 넓이로 벌리고 오른손가락 끝을 오른쪽 겨드랑이에 붙이고 왼손바닥을 펴고 무릎을 펴고 왼팔을 아래로 내리면서 왼쪽 옆구리를 옆으로 2번 반동으로 굽혔다가 다시 반대로 왼손가락 끝을 왼쪽 겨드랑이에 붙이고 오른손바닥을 펴고 무릎을 뻗어 오른팔을 아래로 내리면서 오른쪽 옆구리를 옆으로 2번 반동으로 굽혔다가 제자리에 온다.

Side Bend:

Start_Stand with your feet wide apart and stretch your arms straight out sideways. Your legs should be based out at lest far enough so that your feet are directly underneath your elbows.
Description_ Beginning with the left side, place your left hand on the side of your right hip and extend your right arm straight up. Bend your right knee while extending your left leg. Lean your body sideways into your left leg and reach your right arm over your head so that you are stretching the right side of your body. Reset your body back to the starting position and continue the same motion but on the opposite side. Repeat 10 times on each side.

7. 허리 숙이기

허리를 똑바로 펴고 선 자세에서 양다리를 어깨 넓이로 벌리고 두 무릎을 뻗어 팔을 똑바로 아래로 내려 땅바닥에 양손가락 끝을 대었다가 반동으로 굽혀 양손바닥을 땅에 대고 일어나서 양손바닥을 엉덩이에 대고 허리를 뒤로 제쳤다가 손등을 등뒤 허리에 대고 뒤로 넘겼다가 다시 제자리에 온다.

Front Back Bend:

Start_Stand with your legs comfortably apart and place your hands on your thighs.
Description_Slap your thighs and bend your body forward while keeping a straight back. Try to bring your chest as close as possible to your knees. Stretch your arms towards the ground try to touch the floor with both of your hands. Make sure to keep your legs straight so you are stretching the back of your hamstrings. Then stand back up and slap your thighs once more. Place both your hands behind your lower back and bend your body back. Arch your back and stretch backwards as far as possible while using your hands to support your lower back. Repeat this sequence 10 times.

준비운동: Warming Up Sequences

8. 허리 돌리기(왼쪽, 오른쪽)

왼쪽-허리를 똑바로 펴고 선 자세에서 양다리를 어깨 넓이로 벌리고 왼손등을 허리 뒤에 대고 오른손바닥은 앞 복부에 대고 앞으로 굽혀 왼쪽으로 한바퀴 돌렸다가 다시 되돌려 제자리에 온다.

오른쪽-허리를 똑바로 펴고 선 자세에서 양다리를 어깨 넓이로 벌리고 오른손등을 허리 뒤에 대고 왼손바닥은 앞 복부에 대고 앞으로 굽혀 오른쪽으로 한바퀴 돌렸다가 다시 되돌려 제자리에 온다.

Hip Circle:

Start_Stand with your legs wide apart. Your feet should be spread apart wider then the width of your shoulders. Grab the knot of your belt with your left hand, and tuck your right hand behind the back of your belt.

Description_ Keep your legs straight. Lean your upper body towards the left and then revolve your body at the waist in a clockwise motion. Circle your hips as wide as you can. Circle your hips 10 times and reverse the direction for 10 more times.

9. 모둠발 뛰기

허리를 똑바로 펴고 양다리를 붙이고 똑바로 서서 손가락을 서로 붙이고 손바닥을 양 허벅지에 붙여 점핑하면서 다리를 어깨넓이로 벌리고 양팔을 어깨 수평으로 벌렸다가 다시 점핑하면서 양손바닥을 양 허벅지에 치고 다시 점핑하면서 양다리를 벌리고 양팔을 머리위로 올려 양 손벽을 치고 다시 점핑하면서 양다리를 붙이고 양손바닥으로 양허벅지를 친다.

Modified Jumping Jacks:

Start_Stand straight up with your feet together and your arms at your side.
Description_Spread your legs out to shoulder width as you hop up and swing your arms straight out sideways. Then bring your feet and arms back together as you hop again. Hop once more and spread your feet out to shoulder width apart. But now swing your arms from the side up above your head. Repeat this sequence 10 times.

10. 목 팽창

허리를 똑바로 펴고 선 자세에서 양다리를 어깨 넓이로 벌리고 양손을 양 허리띠에 대고 목을 오른쪽 반동으로 2번숙이고 왼쪽 반동으로 2번숙이고 앞 반동으로 2번숙이고 머리 뒤 반동으로 2번을 숙인다.

Neck Tension:

Start_Stand with your legs comfortably apart and place your hands on your hips.
Description_Tilt your head toward the left while trying to touch your left ear to your left shoulder and sinking your right shoulder down. Switch to the opposite side. Repeat 10 times one each side.

11. 목 돌리기

허리를 똑바로 펴고 선 자세에서 양다리를 어깨 넓이로 벌리고 양손을 양 허리띠에 대고 목을 앞으로 숙여 왼쪽으로 한 바퀴 돌렸다가 다시 반대로 오른쪽으로 한 바퀴 돌린다.

Neck Relaxation:

Start_Tilt your head down. Stand with your legs comfortably apart and place your hands on your hips. Description_Rotate your neck slowly counter-clockwise in a circular motion for 10 revolutions. Then repeat in the opposite direction.

준비운동: Warming Up Sequences

12. 한 다리 뻗기

양다리를 많이 벌리고 양손바닥을 양 허벅지에 대고 왼쪽 무릎 자세를 낮추고 오른손으로 오른쪽 무릎을 반동으로 3번 누르고 반대로 오른쪽 무릎 자세를 낮추고 왼손으로 왼쪽 무릎을 반동으로 3번을 누른다.

Single Leg Stretch:
Start_Have your legs slightly wider then the width of your shoulders, and keep your legs slightly bent. Slightly crouch down, and place your hands on your knees.
Description_Extend your left leg straight, and bend your right knee. Crouch down, and try to touch your butt to the ground, while leaning your body towards your extended left leg. Switch to the opposite side.

13. 양다리 뻗기

선 자세에서 양다리를 어깨 넓이로 벌리고 허리를 굽혀 양손으로 무릎을 반동으로 2번 누르고 아래로 자세를 낮추어 그대로 무릎을 짚고 똑바로 앉아 반동으로 2번을 아래로 누른다.

Double Leg Stretch:
Start_Spread your feet apart so they are slightly wider then the width of your shoulders. Keep your legs straight. Bend your body forward and rest with your hands on your knees.
Description_Keep your legs locked straight and lean your body into your legs. Try to bring your chest as close to your knees as possible and stretch out the back of your hamstring. Then bend your legs and crouch down while keeping your back straight. Extend both of your arms straight out in front of you and try to sit your butt to the ground as far as possible.

14. 손목 돌리기

무릎을 접고 앉은 자세에서 오른손으로 왼 손등을 잡고 아래위로 접었다 폈다 하여 손목을 풀고 다시 반대로 왼손으로 오른 손등을 잡고 아래위로 접었다 폈다 하여 손목을 풀고 다음은 양 팔꿈치를 접어 양팔 겨드랑이를 위로 들어 양 손목을 아래로 내려 힘을 빼고 양 손목을 앞 뒤 옆으로 흔들어 푼다.

Wrist Circles:

Start_Stand with your legs comfortably apart and position your arms out in front of you. Have your palms face out with your fingers pointed up.
Description_Rotate your wrists outward in a circular motion for 10 revolutions. Then reverse the direction.

15. 발목 돌리기(왼쪽, 오른쪽)

왼쪽-무릎을 접고 앉은 자세에서 오른손으로 오른 발목을 잡고 왼손으로 오른발가락을 하나씩 잡아당기고 발가락을 전부 모아 아래위로 접었다 폈다 하다가 발목을 좌우로 돌리고 반대로 왼손으로 왼 발목을 잡고 오른손은 왼발가락을 하나씩 잡아당기고 발가락을 전부모아 아래위로 접었다 폈다 하다가 발목을 좌우로 돌린다.

오른쪽-무릎을 접고 앉은 자세에서 왼손으로 왼발 목을 잡고 오른손으로 왼발가락을 하나씩 잡아당기고 발가락을 전부 모아 아래위로 접었다 폈다 하다가 발목을 좌우 로 돌리고 반대로 오른손으로 오른 발목을 잡고 왼손은 오른발가락을 하나씩 잡아당기고 발가락을 전부모아 아래위로 접었다 폈다 하다가 발목을 좌우로 돌린다.

Ankle Circles:

Start_Stand with your left leg on the ball of its foot with your left heel up.
Description_Rotate your ankle in a circular motion counter-clockwise for 5 revolutions. Then reverse the motion clockwise. Repeat the sequence on the other ankle.

16. 손가락, 발가락 뻗기

허리를 똑바로 펴고 선 자세에서 다리를 어깨 넓이로 벌리고 양손가락을 깍지를 끼고 앞으로 쭉 뻗고 다음은 팔을 구부려 왼 주먹을 살짝 쥐고 오른손으로 왼손가락 마디를 하나씩 누르고 다시 반대로 오른 주먹을 살짝 쥐고 왼손으로 오른손가락 마디를 하나씩 누르고 다음은 왼손가락을 하나씩 잡아당겨 흔들고 다시 반대 손가락을 하나씩 잡아당겨 흔들고 다음은 왼발가락을 모두 위로 들고 발을 들어 땅바닥에 앞-축을 내리치기를 하고 다시 오른발가락을 모두 위로 들어올리고 오른발을 들어 땅 바닥에 앞-축으로 내리쳐 발가락을 뻗치게 한다.

Finger and Toe Stretch:

Start_Have your left arm straight out, and your right leg straight back with your heel up.
Description_Pull the fingers of your left hand back with your right hand while leaning forward and lifting your left heel up high so you are stretching your toes. Then push your left wrist down with your right hand. Keep your left leg back, and flop your foot over so that the top of your foot is resting on the ground. Lean back so you are stretching your instep. Repeat all of the above, but on the opposite side.

합도술

Fundamental Exercise Sequences

합 | 도 | 술 | 본

01. 중간 다리-뻗기 (왼쪽, 오른쪽):
    Middle leg-extension (L. R.)
02. 하단 앞-차기 (왼쪽, 오른쪽):
    Low front-kick (L. R.)
03. 하단 옆-차기 (왼쪽, 오른쪽):
    Low side-kick (L. R.)
04. 하단 돌려-차기 (왼쪽, 오른쪽):
    Low roundhouse-kick (L. R.)
05. 하단 반대 돌려-차기 (왼쪽, 오른쪽):
    Low reverse roundhouse-kick (L. R.)
06. 중단 앞-차기 (왼쪽, 오른쪽):
    Middle front-kick (L. R.)
07. 중단 옆-차기 (왼쪽, 오른쪽):
    Middle side-kick (L. R.)
08. 중단 돌려-차기 (왼쪽, 오른쪽):
    Middle roundhouse-kick (L. R.)
09. 중단 바깥 뒤축 훅-차기 (왼쪽, 오른쪽):
    Middle outside heel hook-kick (L. R.)
10. 앞무릎-차기 (왼쪽, 오른쪽):
    Front knee-kick (L. R.)
11. 상단 앞-차기 (왼쪽, 오른쪽):
    High front-kick (L. R.)
12. 상단 앞다리-올리기 (왼쪽, 오른쪽):
    High leg-extension (L. R.)
13. 하단 X-막기:
    Low X-block
14. 하단 옆-막기 (왼쪽, 오른쪽):
    Low side-block (L. R.)
15. 중단 옆-막기 (왼쪽, 오른쪽):
    Middle side-block (L. R.)
16. 상단 옆-막기 (왼쪽, 오른쪽):
    High side-block (L. R.)
17. 상단 팔뚝 얼굴-막기 (왼쪽, 오른쪽):
    High forearm face-block (L. R.)
18. 상단 X-막기:
    High X-block
19. 둘 연합-펀치 (왼쪽, 오른쪽):
    Two combination-punches (L. R.)
20. 팔꿈치-훅 (왼쪽, 오른쪽):
    Elbow-hook (L. R.)
21. 옆 둘 잽 직선-펀치 (왼쪽, 오른쪽):
    Side double jab straight-punches (L. R.)
22. 앞 박치기 (왼쪽, 오른쪽):
    Front head-butt (L. R.)
23. 밭 다리 후려치기 (왼쪽, 오른쪽):
    Outside leg hook-throw (L. R.)
24. 안 다리 후려치기 (왼쪽, 오른쪽):
    Inside leg hook-throw (L. R.)
25. 빼치기 (왼쪽, 오른쪽):
    Sweep-throw (L. R.)
26. 엉덩이-업어치기 (왼쪽, 오른쪽):
    Hip-throw (L. R.)
27. 어깨-업어치기 (왼쪽, 오른쪽):
    Shoulder-throw (L. R.)
28. 기합 단련:
    Vocalized-willpower
29. 차력-술:
    Cha Ryuk-Sool
30. 앞-당기기:
    Front-pulls
31. 제자리-뛰기 (왼쪽, 오른쪽):
    Hop-steps (L. R.)
32. 10 선-자세 :
    Ten stance-form

1. 중간 다리-뻗기(왼쪽, 오른쪽)

· 기본자세-똑바로 선 자세에서 양다리를 어깨 넓이로 벌린다.

왼쪽-양 엄지(첫째 손가락)를 양옆 허리띠 위에 걸어 띠를 잡고 오른발을 한발 앞으로 옮기고 왼발을 앞으로 뻗어 허리까지 다리 중간 뻗기를 하고 왼발을 오른발 뒤로 놓고 오른발을 한발 뒤로 놓는다.

Middle Leg Extension:

Begin with your feet shoulder width apart and your hands placed on your hips. Step forward with your right leg towards 12:00 and shift your weight to your right leg.

· 기본자세-똑바로 선 자세에서 양다리를 어깨 넓이로 벌린다.

오른쪽-양 엄지(첫째 손가락)를 양옆 허리띠 위에 걸어 띠를 잡고 왼발을 한발 앞으로 옮기고 오른발을 앞으로 뻗어 허리까지 다리 중간 뻗기를 하고 오른발을 왼발 뒤로 놓고 왼발을 한발 뒤로 놓는다.

While keeping your left leg straight, slowly swing your left leg up to waist level while keeping your toes pointed.

2. 하단 앞-차기 (왼쪽, 오른쪽)

· 기본자세-똑바로 선 자세에서 양다리를 어깨 넓이로 벌린다.

왼쪽-양 팔꿈치를 겨드랑이에 붙이고 양손은 살짝 주먹을 쥐고 양 옆 턱 5cm 정도 가까이까지 올려놓고 양 옆 턱을 막고 고개를 약간 숙이고 상대의 양 눈동자를 주시하면서 오른쪽 한발을 앞으로 옮기고 왼발로 하단 앞 차기를 하고 왼발을 오른발 뒤로 놓고 오른발을 한발 뒤로 놓으며 자세를 아래로 내리면서 하단 앞 막기를 한다.

Low Front Kick:

Begin with your feet shoulder width apart and both your fists guarding your face with both your elbows protecting your ribs. Step forward towards 12:00 with your right leg. Lift your left knee up and extend straight out with your leg at a 45-degree angle downward aiming towards your opponent's low section. Ensure your toes are back so that you are kicking with the ball of the foot.

· 기본자세-똑바로 선 자세에서 양다리를 어깨 넓이로 벌린다.
오른쪽-양 팔꿈치를 겨드랑이에 붙이고 양손은 살짝 주먹을 쥐고 양옆턱 5cm 정도 가까이까지 올려놓고 양 옆 턱을 막고 고개를 약간 숙이고 상대의 양 눈동자를 주시하면서 왼쪽 한발을 앞으로 옮기고 오른발로 하단 앞 차기 를 하고 오른발을 왼발 뒤로 놓고 왼발을 한발 뒤로 놓으며 자세를 아래로 내리면서 하단 앞 막기를 한다.

After executing the low front kick, step back to the stand stance and bend both your knees while keeping your back straight. Cross both your forearms and extend both your arms straight down in front of your groin. Ensure you keep your chin down. Execute a Low X Block with your forearms.

3. 하단 옆-차기 (왼쪽, 오른쪽)

· 기본자세–똑바로 선 자세에서 양다리를 어깨 넓이로 벌린다.
왼쪽–양 팔꿈치를 겨드랑이에 붙이고 양손은 살짝 주먹을 쥐고 양 옆 턱 5cm 정도 가까이까지 올려놓고 양 옆 턱을 막고 고개를 약간 숙이고 상대의 양 눈동자를 주시하면서 오른쪽 한발을 앞으로 옮기고 왼발로 하단 옆차기를 한다.

Low Side Kick:

Begin with your feet shoulder width apart and both your fists guarding your face with both your elbows protecting your ribs. Step forward with your right leg towards 12:00 with your right foot facing 3:00 while turning your body clockwise so your chest is also facing 3:00. Lift up your left knee and bring it in towards you. Extend your left leg straight out sideways towards 12:00 with your leg at a 45-degree angle downward aiming towards your opponent's low section.

Chapter 03~04

· 기본자세-똑바로 선 자세에서 양다리를 어깨 넓이로 벌린다.
오른쪽-양 팔꿈치를 겨드랑이에 붙이고 양손은 살짝 주먹을 쥐고 양 옆 턱 5cm 정도 가까이까지 올려놓고 양 옆 턱을 막고 고개를 약간 숙이고 상대의 양 눈동자를 주시하면서 왼쪽 한발을 앞으로 옮기고 오른발로 하단 옆차기를 한다.

Ensure you are kicking with the knife edge heel of the foot, and you are keeping your rear end aligned with your back. Keep your guard up and both elbows at your side while kicking.

4. 하단 돌려-차기(왼쪽, 오른쪽)

· 기본자세-똑바로 선 자세에서 양다리를 어깨 넓이로 벌린다.

왼쪽-양 팔꿈치를 겨드랑이에 붙이고 양손은 살짝 주먹을 쥐고 양 옆 턱 5cm 정도 가까이까지 올려놓고 양 옆 턱을 막고 고개를 약간 숙이고 상대의 양 눈동자를 주시하면서 오른쪽 한발을 앞으로 옮기고 왼발로 하단 돌려차기를 한다.

Low Roundhouse Kick:

Begin with your feet shoulder width apart and both your fists guarding your face with both your elbows protecting your ribs. Step forward with your right leg towards 12:00 with your right foot facing 2:00 while turning your body clockwise, so your chest is also facing 2:00. Lift up your left knee so your knee is pointed towards 2:00.

·기본자세-똑바로 선 자세에서 양다리를 어깨 넓이로 벌린다
오른쪽-양 팔꿈치를 겨드랑이에 붙이고 양손은 살짝 주먹을 쥐고 양 옆 턱 5cm 정도 가까이까지 올려놓고 양 옆 턱을 막고 고개를 약간 숙이고 상대의 양 눈동자를 주시하면서 왼쪽 한발을 앞으로 옮기고 오른발로 하단 돌려차기를 한다.

 Extend your left leg so it is at a 45degree angle downward, and pull your toes back so you are kicking with the ball of your left foot aiming towards your opponent's low section. Ensure your left foot is pointing towards 3:00 and you are keeping your rear end aligned with your back. Keep your guard up and both elbows at your side while kicking.

5. 하단 반대 돌려-차기(왼쪽, 오른쪽)

· 기본자세-똑바로 선 자세에서 양다리를 어깨 넓이로 벌린다.
왼쪽-양 팔꿈치를 겨드랑이에 붙이고 양손은 살짝 주먹을 쥐고 양 옆 턱 5cm 정도 가까이까지 올려놓고 양 옆 턱을 막고 고개를 약간 숙이고 상대의 양 눈동자를 주시하면서 오른쪽 한발을 앞으로 옮기고 왼발로 하단 반대 돌려차기를 한다.

Low Reverse Roundhouse Kick:

Begin with your feet shoulder width apart and both your fists guarding your face with both your elbows protecting your ribs. Step forward with your right leg towards 12:00 with your right foot facing 2:00 while turning your body clockwise, so your chest is also facing 2:00. Then turn your body counter-clockwise, and lift up your left knee. Bring your left foot in towards you while your left knee is pointing towards 10:00.

Chapter 05~06

· 기본자세-똑바로 선 자세에서 양다리를 어깨 넓이로 벌린다.
오른쪽-양 팔꿈치를 겨드랑이에 붙이고 양손은 살짝 주먹을 쥐고 양 옆 턱 5cm 정도 가까이까지 올려놓고 양 옆 턱을 막고 고개를 약간 숙이고 상대의 양 눈동자를 주시하면서 왼쪽 한발을 앞으로 옮기고 오른발로 하단 반대 돌려차기를 한다.

Extend your left leg, and kick out towards 12:00 aiming for your opponent's low section. Pull your toes back so you are kicking with the ball of the foot. Keep your guard up and both elbows at your side while kicking.

6. 중단 앞-차기(왼쪽, 오른쪽)

· 기본자세-똑바로 선 자세에서 양다리를 어깨 넓이로 벌린다.

왼쪽-양 팔꿈치를 겨드랑이에 붙이고 양손은 살짝 주먹을 쥐고 양 옆 턱 5cm 정도 가까이까지 올려놓고 양 옆 턱을 막고 고개를 약간 숙이고 상대의 양 눈동자를 주시하면서 오른쪽 한발을 앞으로 옮기고 왼발로 중단 앞 차기 를 하고 왼발을 오른발 뒤로 놓고 오른발을 한발 뒤로 놓으며 무릎을 약간 굽히면서 중단 앞 막기를 한다.

Middle Front Kick:

Begin with your feet shoulder width apart and both your fists guarding your face with both your elbows protecting your ribs. Step forward towards 12:00 with your right leg. Lift your left knee up and extend straight out at a 90degree angle aiming towards your opponent's mid section. Ensure your toes are back so that you are kicking with the ball of the foot.

Chapter 06~07

· 기본자세-똑바로 선 자세에서 양다리를 어깨 넓이로 벌린다.
오른쪽-양 팔꿈치를 겨드랑이에 붙이고 양손은 살짝 주먹을 쥐고 양 옆 턱 5cm 정도 가까이까지 올려놓고 양 옆 턱을 막고 고개를 약간 숙이고 상대의 양 눈동자를 주시하면서 왼쪽 한발을 앞으로 옮기고 오른발로 중단 앞 차기를 하고 오른발을 왼발 뒤로 놓고 왼발을 한발 뒤로 놓으며 무릎을 약간 굽히면서 중단 앞 막기를 한다.

After executing the middle front kick, step back to the stand stance and slightly bend both your knees while keeping your back straight. Cross both your forearms and extend both your arms out in front of your solarplex at a 45degree angle downward. Execute a middle x block with your forearms.

7. 중단 옆-차기(왼쪽, 오른쪽)

· 기본자세-똑바로 선 자세에서 양다리를 어깨 넓이로 벌린다.

왼쪽-양 팔꿈치를 겨드랑이에 붙이고 양손은 살짝 주먹을 쥐고 양 옆 턱 5cm 정도 가까이까지 올려놓고 양 옆 턱을 막고 고개를 약간 숙이고 상대의 양눈동자를 주시하면서 오른쪽 한발을 앞으로 옮기고 왼발로 중단 옆차기를 한다.

Middle Side Kick:

Begin with your feet shoulder width apart and both your fists guarding your face with both your elbows protecting your ribs. Step forward with your right leg towards 12:00 with your right foot facing 3:00 while turning your body clockwise, so your chest is also facing 3:00. Lift up your left knee and bring it in towards you.

Chapter 07~08

· 기본자세-똑바로 선 자세에서 양다리를 어깨 넓이로 벌린다.
오른쪽-양 팔꿈치를 겨드랑이에 붙이고 양손은 살짝 주먹을 쥐고 양 옆 턱 5cm 정도 가까이까지 올려놓고 양 옆 턱을 막고 고개를 약간 숙이고 상대의 양 눈동자를 주시하면서 왼쪽 한발을 앞으로 옮기고 오른발로 중단 옆차기를 한다.

Extend your left leg straight out sideways towards 12:00 with your leg at a 90-degree angle aiming towards your opponent's mid section. Ensure you are kicking with the knife-edge heel of the foot, and you are keeping your rear end aligned with your back. Keep your guard up and both elbows at your side while kicking.

8. 중단 돌려-차기(왼쪽, 오른쪽)

· 기본자세-똑바로 선 자세에서 양다리를 어깨 넓이로 벌린다.

왼쪽-양 팔꿈치를 겨드랑이에 붙이고 양손은 살짝 주먹을 쥐고 양 옆 턱 5cm 정도 가까이까지 올려놓고 양 옆 턱을 막고 고개를 약간 숙이고 상대의 양눈동자를 주시하면서 오른쪽 한발을 앞으로 옮기고 왼발로 중단 돌려차기를 한다.

Middle Roundhouse Kick:

Begin with your feet shoulder width apart and both your fists guarding your face with both your elbows protecting your ribs. Step forward with your right leg towards 12:00 with your right foot facing 2:00 while turning your body clockwise, so your chest is also facing 2:00. Lift up your left knee so your knee is pointed towards 2:00.

Chapter 08~09

· 기본자세-똑바로 선 자세에서 양다리를 어깨 넓이로 벌린다.

오른쪽-양 팔꿈치를 겨드랑이에 붙이고 양손은 살짝 주먹을 쥐고 양 옆 턱 5cm 정도 가까이까지 올려놓고 양 옆 턱을 막고 고개를 약간 숙이고 상대의 양 눈동자를 주시하면서 왼쪽 한발을 앞으로 옮기고 오른발로 중단 돌려차기를 한다.

Extend your left leg so it is at a 90degree angle, and pull your toes back so you are kicking with the ball of your left foot aiming towards your opponent's mid section. Ensure your left foot is pointing towards 3:00, and you are keeping your rear end aligned with your back. Keep your guard up and both elbows at your side while kicking.

9. 중단 바깥 뒤축 훅-차기(왼쪽, 오른쪽)

· 기본자세-똑바로 선 자세에서 양다리를 어깨 넓이로 벌린다.
왼쪽-양 팔꿈치를 겨드랑이에 붙이고 양손은 살짝 주먹을 쥐고 양 옆 턱 5cm 정도 가까이까지 올려놓고 양 옆 턱을 막고 고개를 약간 숙이고 상대의 양 눈동자를 주시하면서 오른쪽 한발을 앞으로 옮기고 왼발로 중단 바깥 뒤축 훅 차기를 한다.

Middle Outside Heel Kick:

Begin with your feet shoulder width apart and both your fists guarding your face with both your elbows protecting your ribs. Step forward with your right leg towards 12:00 with your right foot facing 3:00 while turning your body clockwise, so your chest is also facing 3:00. Lift up your left knee and bring it in towards you. Extend your left leg straight out sideways towards 1:00 at a 90-degree angle.

· 기본자세-똑바로 선 자세에서 양다리를 어깨 넓이로 벌린다.
오른쪽-양 팔꿈치를 겨드랑이에 붙이고 양손은 살짝 주먹을 쥐고 양옆턱 5cm 정도 가까이까지 올려놓고 양 옆 턱을 막고 고개를 약간 숙이고 상대의 양 눈동자를 주시하면서 왼쪽 한발을 앞으로 옮기고 오른발로 중단 바깥 뒤축 훅 차기를 한다.

Then hook your left foot across horizontally from right to left. Ensure you are hooking with the knife-edge heel of the foot towards your opponent's back or area of the kidney and you are keeping your rear end aligned with your back. Keep your guard up and both elbows at your side while kicking.

10. 앞 무릎-차기(왼쪽, 오른쪽)

· 기본자세-똑바로 선 자세에서 양다리를 어깨 넓이로 벌린다.

왼쪽-양 팔꿈치를 겨드랑이에 붙이고 양손은 살짝 주먹을 쥐고 양 옆 턱 5cm 정도 가까이까지 올려놓고 양 옆 턱을 막고 고개를 약간 숙이고 상대의 양 눈동자를 주시하면서 오른쪽 한발을 앞으로 옮기면서 양손으로 상대의 양옷깃을 잡고 앞으로 당겨 내리면서 왼쪽 무릎으로 앞 무릎차기를 한다.

Front Knee Kick:

Begin with your feet shoulder width apart and both your fists guarding your face with both your elbows protecting your ribs. Step forward with your right leg towards 12:00 with your right foot facing 1:00. Reach out and grab with both arms towards 12:00.

· 기본자세-똑바로 선 자세에서 양다리를 어깨 넓이로 벌린다.

오른쪽-양 팔꿈치를 겨드랑이에 붙이고 양손은 살짝 주먹을 쥐고 양 옆 턱 5cm 정도 가까이까지 올려놓고 양 옆 턱을 막고 고개를 약간 숙이고 상대의 양 눈동자를 주시하면서 왼쪽 한발을 앞으로 옮기면서 양손으로 상대의 양 옷깃을 잡고 앞으로 당겨 내리면서 오른쪽 무릎으로 앞 무릎차기를 한다.

Lift your left knee and point it towards 1:00. Thrust your left knee up and out towards 1:00 while pulling in with your arms and bending your body forward in a crunching motion. Ensure your toes are pointed towards the ground on your left foot. Repeat on the opposite side.

11. 상단 앞-차기(왼쪽, 오른쪽)

· 기본자세-똑바로 선 자세에서 양다리를 어깨 넓이로 벌린다.
왼쪽-양 팔꿈치를 겨드랑이에 붙이고 양손은 살짝 주먹을 쥐고 양 옆 턱 5cm 정도 가까이까지 올려놓고 양 옆 턱을 막고 고개를 약간 숙이고 상대의 양 눈동자를 주시하면서 오른쪽 한발을 앞으로 옮기고 왼발로 상단 앞 차기를 하고 왼발을 오른발 뒤로 놓고 오른발을 한발 뒤로 놓으며 앞으로 상단 앞 막기를 한다.

High Front Kick:

Begin with your feet shoulder width apart and both your fists guarding your face with both your elbows protecting your ribs. Step forward towards 12:00 with your right leg. Lift your left knee up and extend your leg straight out at a 135degree angle upward aiming towards your opponent's high section. Ensure your toes are back so that you are kicking with the ball of the foot.

· 기본자세-똑바로 선 자세에서 양다리를 어깨 넓이로 벌린다.
오른쪽-양 팔꿈치를 겨드랑이에 붙이고 양손은 살짝 주먹을 쥐고 양 옆 턱 5cm 정도 가까이까지 올려놓고 양 옆 턱을 막고 고개를 약간 숙이고 상대의 양 눈동자를 주시하면서 왼쪽 한발을 앞으로 옮기고 오른발로 상단 앞 차기를 하고 오른발을 왼발 뒤로 놓고 왼발을 한발 뒤로 놓으며 앞으로 상단 앞 막기를 한다.

After executing the high front kick, step back to the stand stance and slightly bend both your knees while keeping your back straight. Cross both your forearms and extend both your arms out in front of your solarplex at a 45degree angle downward. Execute a middle x block with your forearms.

12. 상단 앞다리-올리기(왼쪽, 오른쪽)

· 기본자세-똑바로 선 자세에서 양다리를 어깨 넓이로 벌린다.
왼쪽-양 팔꿈치를 겨드랑이에 붙이고 양손은 살짝 주먹을 쥐고 양 옆 턱 5cm 정도 가까이까지 올려놓고 양 옆 턱을 막고 고개를 약간 숙이고 오른쪽 한발을 앞으로 옮기고 왼쪽 다리높이 올리기를 한다.

High Leg Extension:

Begin with your feet shoulder width apart. Have both your fists guarding your face with both your elbows protecting your ribs just for practice. Step forward with your right leg towards 12:00 and shift your weight to your right leg.

· 기본자세-똑바로 선 자세에서 양다리를 어깨 넓이로 벌린다.
오른쪽-양 팔꿈치를 겨드랑이에 붙이고 양손은 살짝 주먹을 쥐고 양 옆 턱 5cm 정도 가까이까지 올려놓고 양 옆 턱을 막고 고개를 약간 숙이고 왼쪽 한발을 앞으로 옮기고 오른쪽 다리 높이 올리기를 한다.

While keeping your left leg straight, swing your left leg straight up while trying to touch your left knee to your left shoulder. Ensure you are keeping your toes pointed.

합도술본: Fundamental Exercise Sequences

13. 하단 X-막기

· 기본자세-똑바로 선 자세에서 양다리를 어깨 넓이로 벌린다.
양 팔꿈치를 겨드랑이에 붙이고 양손은 살짝 주먹을 쥐고 양 옆 턱 5cm 정도 가까이까지 올려놓고 양 옆 턱을 막고 고개를 약간 숙이고 상대의 양 눈동자를 주시하면서 허리를 똑바로 펴고 양 무릎을 45도 정도 내리면서 동시에 양팔을 아래로 내려 하단 X 막기를 한다.

Low X Block:

Begin with your feet slightly wider than the width of your shoulders, and both your fists guarding your face with both your elbows protecting your ribs. Bend both your knees while keeping your back straight. While keeping a fist, cross both your forearms and extend both your arms straight down in front of your groin. Ensure you keep your chin down and you are blocking with your forearms. Repeat on the opposite side.

14. 하단 옆-막기(왼쪽, 오른쪽)

· 기본자세–똑바로 선 자세에서 양다리를 어깨 넓이로 벌린다.

왼쪽–양 팔꿈치를 겨드랑이에 붙이고 양손은 살짝 주먹을 쥐고 양 옆 턱 5cm 정도 가까이까지 올려놓고 양 옆 턱을 막고 고개를 약간 숙이고 상대의 양 눈동자를 주시하면서 오른발을 들어 발 앞 끝을 오른쪽으로 돌려 놓으면서 왼발을 들어 앞으로 뒤꿈치를 들고 한발 옮기며 중심은 뒷다리에 두고 왼손바닥은 앞으로 아래로 하고 오른손바닥은 위로하며 허리를 왼쪽으로 틀면서 동시에 쌍수도로 하단 옆 막기를 한다.

· 기본자세–똑바로 선 자세에서 양다리를 어깨 넓이로 벌린다.

오른쪽–양 팔꿈치를 겨드랑이에 붙이고 양손은 살짝 주먹을 쥐고 양 옆 턱 5cm 정도 가까이까지 올려놓고 양 옆 턱을 막고 고개를 약간 숙이고 상대의 양 눈동자를 주시하면서 왼발을 들어 발 앞 끝을 왼쪽으로 돌려놓으면서 오른발을 들어 앞으로 뒤꿈치를 들고 한발 옮기며 중심은 뒷다리에 두고 오른손바닥은 앞으로 아래로 하고 왼손바닥은 위로하며 허리를 오른쪽으로 틀면서 동시에 쌍수도로 하단 옆 막기를 한다.

Low Side Block:

Begin with your feet shoulder width apart and both your fists guarding your face with both your elbows protecting your ribs. Turn your body counter-clockwise so you are facing towards 9:00 in a left side Back Stance. Most of your weight should be on your right leg, and your right leg should be slightly bent. Your left leg should be out and bent with your left heel up, and on the ball of your left foot. Ensure your back is straight. Then extend your fingers straight, and together. Tuck your thumb in, and slightly bend your middle finger to make an even length between your index, middle, and ring finger. Extend your left arm downward past your left thigh with your knife hand facing down. Your left arm should only be slightly bent, and you should be blocking with your left forearm. Keep your right knife hand at belt level with your palm face up.

15. 중단 옆-막기(왼쪽, 오른쪽)

· 기본자세-똑바로 선 자세에서 양다리를 어깨 넓이로 벌린다.

왼쪽-양 팔꿈치를 겨드랑이에 붙이고 양손은 살짝 주먹을 쥐고 양 옆 턱 5cm 정도 가까이까지 올려놓고 양 옆 턱을 막고 고개를 약간 숙이고 상대의 양 눈동자를 주시하면서 오른발을 들어 발 앞 끝을 오른쪽으로 돌려놓으면서 왼발을 들어 앞으로 한발 옮기며 중심은 양다리에 두고 왼 주먹은 눈높이로 손가락은 얼굴 쪽으로 오른 주먹은 왼 팔꿈치에 붙이며 허리를 왼쪽으로 틀면서 동시에 양주 먹으로 중단 옆 막기를 한다.

· 기본자세-똑바로 선 자세에서 양다리를 어깨 넓이로 벌린다.

오른쪽-양 팔꿈치를 겨드랑이에 붙이고 양손은 살짝 주먹을 쥐고 양 옆 턱 5cm 정도 가까이까지 올려놓고 양 옆 턱을 막고 고개를 약간 숙이고 상대의 양 눈동자를 주시하면서 왼발을 들어 발 앞 끝을 왼쪽으로 돌려놓으면서 오른발을 들어 앞으로 한발 옮기며 중심은 양다리에 두고 오른 주먹은 눈높이로 손가락은 얼굴 쪽으로 왼 주먹은 오른 팔꿈치에 붙이며 허리를 오른쪽으로 틀면서 동시에 양 주먹으로 중단 옆 막기를 한다.

Middle Side Block:

Begin with your feet shoulder width apart and both your fists guarding your face with both your elbows protecting your ribs. Turn your body counter-clockwise, and step out with your left leg towards 8:00 into a left side Middle Stance. You should be facing towards 9:00. Bend both your legs so your weight is distributed equally between both legs. While keeping a fist, bring your left arm out towards 9:00 with your left arm bent at a 90degree angle so you are blocking with your left forearm. Ensure your chin is down, and your left fist is at eye level. Place your right fist in your inside left elbow for support.

16. 상단 팔뚝 옆-막기(왼쪽, 오른쪽)

· 기본자세–똑바로 선 자세에서 양다리를 어깨 넓이로 벌린다.

왼쪽–양 팔꿈치를 겨드랑이에 붙이고 양손은 살짝 주먹을 쥐고 양 옆 턱 5cm 정도 가까이까지 올려놓고 양 옆 턱을 막고 고개를 약간 숙이고 상대의 양 눈동자를 주시하면서 왼발을 들어 발 앞 끝을 왼쪽으로 돌리며 허리를 틀어 중심은 앞다리에 두고 왼팔은 얼굴을 스쳐 5cm정도 머리위에 올려놓고 오른 주먹은 오른쪽 눈 꼬리 옆에 눈과 주먹사이는 5cm 정도 띄우고 동시에 양팔뚝 상단 옆막기를 한다.

· 기본자세–똑바로 선 자세에서 양다리를 어깨 넓이로 벌린다.

오른쪽–양 팔꿈치를 겨드랑이에 붙이고 양손은 살짝 주먹을 쥐고 양 옆 턱 5cm 정도 가까이까지 올려놓고 양 옆 턱을 막고 고개를 약간 숙이고 상대의 양 눈동자를 주시하면서 오른발을 들어 발 앞 끝을 오른쪽으로 돌리며 허리를 틀어 중심은 앞 다리에 두고 오른팔은 얼굴을 스쳐 5cm정도 머리위에 올려놓고 왼 주먹은 왼쪽 눈 꼬리 옆에 눈과 주먹사이는 5cm 정도 띄우고 동시에 양주먹으로 상단 옆막기를 한다.

High Side Forearm Block:

Begin with your feet shoulder width apart and both your fists guarding your face with both your elbows protecting your ribs. Turn your body counter-clockwise, and step out with your left leg towards 8:00 into a left side Forward Stance. You should be facing towards 9:00. Bend your left leg so most of your weight is on your front leg, and keep your right leg aligned with your back. While keeping a fist, extend your left arm up over your head at a 45degree angle so you are deflecting with your forearm. Keep your chin down while looking up towards your left forearm. Ensure your right fist is guarding the right side of your face.

17. 상단 팔뚝 얼굴-막기(왼쪽, 오른쪽)

· 기본자세-똑바로 선 자세에서 양다리를 어깨 넓이로 벌린다.
왼쪽-양 팔꿈치를 겨드랑이에 붙이고 양손은 살짝 주먹을 쥐고 양 옆 턱 5cm 정도 가까이까지 올려놓고 양 옆 턱을 막고 고개를 약간 숙이고 상대의 양 눈동자를 주시하면서 허리를 오른쪽으로 틀면서 왼 팔뚝으로 정면 얼굴막기를 한다.

· 기본자세-똑바로 선 자세에서 양다리를 어깨 넓이로 벌린다.
오른쪽-양 팔꿈치를 겨드랑이에 붙이고 양손은 살짝 주먹을 쥐고 양 옆 턱 5cm 정도 가까이까지 올려놓고 양 옆 턱을 막고 고개를 약간 숙이고 상대의 양 눈동자를 주시하면서 허리를 왼쪽으로 틀면서 오른 팔뚝으로 정면 얼굴막기를 한다.

Forearm Face Block:

Begin with your feet shoulder width apart and both your fists guarding your face with both your elbows protecting your ribs. Lean towards the left, and pivot off your left leg while slightly turning your body clockwise. At the same time you are dodging towards the left, make a fist and bring your left forearm across your face so you are blocking with your forearm. Ensure your right fist is guarding your face, and keep your chin down.

18. 상단 X-막기

· 기본자세-똑바로 선 자세에서 양다리를 어깨 넓이로 벌린다.

양 팔꿈치를 겨드랑이에 붙이고 양손은 살짝 주먹을 쥐고 양 옆 턱 5cm 정도 가까이까지 올려놓고 양 옆 턱을 막고 고개를 약간 숙이고 상대의 양 눈동자를 주시하면서 허리를 똑바로 펴고 양 무릎을 45도 정도 내리면서 동시에 양팔을 위로 올려 상단 X 막기를 한다.

High X Block:

Begin with your feet shoulder width apart and both your fists guarding your face with both your elbows protecting your ribs. While keeping your back straight, slightly bend both your legs. Extend both your arms over your head so they are slightly bent, and cross both your fists so the backs of your knuckles are touching. Ensure you are looking up towards your fists and you are deflecting with your forearms.

19. 둘 연합-펀치(왼쪽, 오른쪽)

· 기본자세–똑바로 선 자세에서 양다리를 어깨 넓이로 벌린다.

왼쪽–양 팔꿈치를 겨드랑이에 붙이고 양손은 살짝 주먹을 쥐고 양턱 옆 5cm 정도 가까이 올려놓고 양 옆턱을 막고 고개를 약간 숙이고 상대의 양 눈동자를 주시하면서 주먹은 모지(둘째손가락)와 장지(셋째 손가락)에 힘을 주고 상대 인중을 향해 손가락을 아래로 향하게 주먹을 쥐고 왼쪽 오른쪽으로 번갈아 직선 펀치를 한다.

Two Combination Punches:

Begin with your feet shoulder width apart and both your fists guarding your face with both your elbows protecting your ribs. Turn your body clockwise while pushing off with your left leg. While making a fist, extend your left arm straight out towards 12:00 so you are punching with your first two knuckles. Ensure your right fist is guarding your face.

· 기본자세–똑바로 선 자세에서 양다리를 어깨 넓이로 벌린다.
오른쪽–양 팔꿈치를 겨드랑이에 붙이고 양손은 살짝 주먹을 쥐고 양 턱 옆 5cm 정도 가까이 올려놓고 양 옆 턱을 막고 고개를 약간 숙이고 상대의 양 눈동자를 주시하면서 주먹은 모지(둘째손가락)와 장지(셋째손가락)에 힘 을 주고 상대 인중을 향해 손가락을 아래로 향하게 주먹을 쥐고 오른쪽 왼쪽으로 번갈아 직선 펀치를 한다.

As you bring your left hand back to guard, turn your body counter-clockwise while pushing off with your right leg, and extend your right arm out towards 12:00 so you are punching with your first two knuckles. Ensure your chin is down, and you Ki-hap on your right punch.

20. 팔꿈치-훅(왼쪽, 오른쪽)

· 기본자세-똑바로 선 자세에서 양다리를 어깨 넓이로 벌린다.

왼쪽-양 팔꿈치를 겨드랑이에 붙이고 양손은 살짝 주먹을 쥐고 양 옆 턱 5cm 정도 가까이까지 올려놓고 양 옆 턱을 막고 고개를 약간 숙이고 상대의 양 눈동자를 주시하면서 허리를 오른쪽으로 틀면서 상대 오른쪽 턱을 왼쪽 팔꿈치로 훅을 친다.

Elbow Hook:

Begin with your feet shoulder width apart and both your fists guarding your face with both your elbows protecting your ribs. Turn your body clockwise while pushing off with your left leg. Hook your left elbow straight across your face horizontally. Ensure your right fist is guarding your face, and your right elbow is by your side.

· 기본자세-똑바로 선 자세에서 양다리를 어깨 넓이로 벌린다.
오른쪽-양 팔꿈치를 겨드랑이에 붙이고 양손은 살짝 주먹을 쥐고 양 옆 턱 5cm 정도 가까이까지 올려놓고 양 옆 턱을 막고 고개를 약간 숙이고 상대의 양 눈동자를 주시하면서 허리를 왼쪽으로 틀면서 상대 왼쪽 턱을 오른쪽 팔꿈치로 훅을 친다.

As you are bringing your left hand back to guard, turn your body counter-clockwise while pushing off with your right leg. Hook your right elbow straight across your face horizontally. Ensure your left fist is guarding your face, and your left elbow is by your side. Keep your chin down.

21. 옆 둘 잽 직선-펀치(왼쪽, 오른쪽)

· 기본자세-똑바로 선 자세에서 양다리를 어깨 넓이로 벌린다.

왼쪽-몸과 발을 왼쪽으로 돌려 권투 자세로 앞에 주먹은 30cm 정도 앞으로 간격을 두고 오른쪽 팔꿈치를 겨드랑이에 붙이고 턱과 주먹의 거리는 5cm 정도 거리에 두고 양손은 살짝 주먹을 쥐고 고개를 약간 숙이고 상대의 양눈동자를 주시하면서 상대의 인중을 향해 왼쪽 주먹으로 2번의 정권 잽을 주고 오른발을 돌려 발가락에 힘을 주고 몸을 왼쪽으로 틀어 오른발을 밀면서 오른쪽 주먹으로 정권 직선 펀치를 한다.

Side Double Jab Straight Punch:

Begin with your feet shoulder width apart in a left side stance. Keep your right fist guarding the right side of your face, and have your left hand about 6 inches in front of your face at eye level. Extend your left arm straight out towards 9:00, executing a left jab with your fist.

· 기본자세-똑바로 선 자세에서 양다리를 어깨 넓이로 벌린다.
오른쪽-몸과 발을 오른쪽으로 돌려 권투 자세로 앞에 주먹은 30cm 정도 앞으로 간격을 두고 왼쪽 팔꿈치를 겨드랑이에 붙이고 턱과 주먹의 거리는 5cm 정도 거리에 두고 양손은 살짝 주먹을 쥐고 고개를 약간 숙이고 상대의 양 눈동자를 주시하면서 상대의 인중을 향해 오른쪽 주먹으로 2번의 정권 잽을 주고 왼발을 돌려 발가락에 힘을 주고 몸을 오른쪽으로 틀어 왼발을 밀면서 왼쪽 주먹으로 정권 직선 펀치를 한다.

As you bring your left fist back to guard, extend your left arm out once more, straight out towards 9:00, executing another left jab with your fist. Turn your body counter-clockwise, as you bring your left fist back to guard. Push off with your right leg, and lean slightly forward while extending your right arm straight out towards 9:00, executing a right cross with your fist. Ensure your guard is up with your chin down.

22. 앞 박치기(왼쪽, 오른쪽)

· 기본자세–똑바로 선 자세에서 양다리를 어깨 넓이로 벌린다.

왼쪽–왼쪽으로 몸을 돌려 양 팔꿈치를 겨드랑이에 붙이고 양손은 살짝 주먹을 쥐고 양 옆 턱 5cm 정도 가까이까지 올려놓고 양 옆 턱을 막고 고개를 약간 숙이고 상대의 양눈동자를 주시하면서 양손으로 상대의 머리를 잡고 앞으로 당겨 기합을 넣으면서 순간 이마로 상대의 정면 박치기를 한다.

Front Head Butt:

Begin with your feet shoulder width apart and both your fists guarding your face with both your elbows protecting your ribs. Step forward with your left leg towards 12:00.

· 기본자세-똑바로 선 자세에서 양다리를 어깨 넓이로 벌린다.
오른쪽-오른쪽으로 몸을 돌려 양 팔꿈치를 겨드랑이에 붙이고 양손 은 살짝 주먹을 쥐고 양 옆 턱 5cm 정도 가까이까지 올려놓고 양 옆 턱을 막고 고개를 약간 숙이고 상대의 양 눈동자를 주시하면서 양손으로 상대의 머리를 잡고 앞으로 당겨 기합을 넣으면서 순간 이마로 상대의 정면 박치기를 한다.

Reach out and grab with both hands towards 12:00. While keeping your chin down, push off with your left leg and thrust your head forward, hitting your opponent's nose with your forehead.

23. 밭 다리 후려치기(왼쪽, 오른쪽)

· 기본자세–똑바로 선 자세에서 양다리를 어깨 넓이로 벌린다.
왼쪽–양 팔꿈치를 겨드랑이에 붙이고 양손은 살짝 주먹을 쥐고 양 옆 턱 5cm 정도 가까이까지 올려놓고 양 옆 턱을 막고 고개를 약간 숙이고 상대의 양 눈동자를 주시하면서 오른발을 앞으로 한발 옮기면서 양손으로 상대의 양 옷깃을 잡고 왼발로 상대의 뒷다리를 걸어 양손으로 상대를 밀면서 밭다리 후리기를 한다.

Outside Hook Throw:

Begin with your feet shoulder width apart and both your fists guarding your face with both your elbows protecting your ribs. Step out with your right leg towards 1:00, and shift your weight to your right leg.

· 기본자세-똑바로 선 자세에서 양다리를 어깨 넓이로 벌린다.
오른쪽-양 팔꿈치를 겨드랑이에 붙이고 양손은 살짝 주먹을 쥐고 양 옆 턱 5cm 정도 가까이까지 올려놓고 양 옆 턱을 막고 고개를 약간 숙이고 상대의 양 눈동자를 주시하면서 왼발을 앞으로 한발 옮기면서 양손으로 상대의 양 옷깃을 잡고 오른발로 상대의 뒷다리를 걸어 양손으로 상대를 밀면서 받다리 후 리기를 한다.

Pick up your left leg and hook with your left foot in a counter-clockwise, circular motion so you are hooking with the knife-edge heel of the foot.

합도술본: Fundamental Exercise Sequences

24. 안 다리 후려치기(왼쪽, 오른쪽)

· 기본자세-똑바로 선 자세에서 양다리를 어깨 넓이로 벌린다.
왼쪽-양 팔꿈치를 겨드랑이에 붙이고 양손은 살짝 주먹을 쥐고 양 옆 턱 5cm 정도 가까이까지 올려놓고 양 옆 턱을 막고 고개를 약간 숙이고 상대의 양 눈동자를 주시하면서 오른발을 앞으로 한발 옮기면서 양손으로 상대의 양 옷깃을 잡고 왼발로 상대의 안다리를 걸어 양손으로 상대를 밀면서 안다리 후리기를 한다.

Inside Hook Throw:
Begin with your feet shoulder width apart and both your fists guarding your face with both your elbows protecting your ribs. Step forward towards 12:00 with your right leg, and shift your weight to your right leg.

· 기본자세–똑바로 선 자세에서 양다리를 어깨 넓이로 벌린다.
오른쪽–양 팔꿈치를 겨드랑이에 붙이고 양손은 살짝 주먹을 쥐고 양 옆 턱 5cm 정도 가까이까지 올려놓고 양 옆 턱을 막고 고개를 약간 숙이고 상대의 양 눈동자를 주시하면서 왼발을 앞으로 한발 옮기면서 양손으로 상대의 양 옷깃을 잡고 오른발로 상대의 안다리를 걸어 양손으로 상대를 밀면서 안다리 후리기를 한다.

Pick up your left leg and hook with your left foot in a clockwise, circular motion so you are hooking with the knife-edge heel of the foot.

25. 빼치기(왼쪽, 오른쪽)

· 기본자세-똑바로 선 자세에서 양다리를 어깨 넓이로 벌린다.

왼쪽-양 팔꿈치를 겨드랑이에 붙이고 양손은 살짝 주먹을 쥐고 양 옆 턱 5cm 정도 가까이까지 올려놓고 양 옆 턱을 막고 고개를 약간 숙이고 상대의 양 눈동자를 주시하면서 오른발을 앞으로 한발 옮기면서 양손 으로 상대의 양 옷깃을 잡고 오른손은 밀고 왼손은 당기며 왼발을 들어 상대의 오른발 빼치기를 한다.

Side Sweep Throw:

Begin with your feet shoulder width apart and both your fists guarding your face with both your elbows protecting your ribs. Step forward with your right leg towards 1:00. Reach out and grab with both hands towards 12:00. Turn your body counter-clockwise while pulling with your left arm down and towards your left side.

· 기본자세-똑바로 선 자세에서 양다리를 어깨 넓이로 벌린다.
오른쪽-양 팔꿈치를 겨드랑이에 붙이고 양손은 살짝 주먹을 쥐고 양 옆 턱 5cm 정도 가까이까지 올려놓고 양 옆 턱을 막고 고개를 약간 숙이고 상대의 양 눈동자를 주시하면서 왼발을 앞으로 옮기면서 양손으로 상대의 양 옷깃을 잡고 왼손은 밀고 오른손은 당기며 오른발을 들어 상대의 왼발 빼치기를 한다.

At the same time, push straight out towards 12:00 with your right arm, and sweep your left foot across towards 1:00. Ensure you are sweeping with the inner side of your left foot.

합도술본: Fundamental Exercise Sequences

26. 엉덩이-업어치기(왼쪽, 오른쪽)

· 기본자세-똑바로 선 자세에서 양다리를 어깨 넓이로 벌린다.

왼쪽-양 팔꿈치를 겨드랑이에 붙이고 양손은 살짝 주먹을 쥐고 양 옆 턱 5cm 정도 가까이까지 올려놓고 양 옆 턱을 막고 고개를 약간 숙이고 상대의 양 눈동자를 주시하면서 왼발을 앞으로 옮기면서 양손으로 상대의 양 옷깃을 잡고 왼쪽 엉덩이를 상대의 사타구니에 대면서 오른발을 들어 뒤로 한발 옮기며 양 무릎을 굽혀 상대의 몸을 들어 올려 왼쪽으로 업어치기를 한다.

Hip Throw:

Begin with your feet shoulder width apart and both your fists guarding your face with both your elbows protecting your ribs. Step out with your left leg towards 1:00, and hook around your opponent's waist with your left arm. Step back with your right leg towards 11:00 so both feet are square, and so you are facing 6:00.

・기본자세–똑바로 선 자세에서 양다리를 어깨 넓이로 벌린다.
오른쪽–양 팔꿈치를 겨드랑이에 붙이고 양손은 살짝 주먹을 쥐고 양 옆 턱 5cm 정도 가까이까지 올려놓고 양 옆 턱을 막고 고개를 약간 숙이고 상대의 양 눈동자를 주시하면서 오른발을 앞으로 옮기면서 양손으로 상대의 양 옷깃을 잡고 오른쪽 엉덩이를 상대의 사타구니에 대면서 왼발을 들어 뒤로 한발 옮기며 양 무릎을 굽혀 상대의 몸을 들어 올려 오른쪽으로 업어치기를 한다.

Bend both your legs and crouch slightly forward. Extend both your legs while having your left hip slightly sticking out. Turn your body clockwise, and throw your opponent over your left hip while guarding your face with your right hand.

합도술본: Fundamental Exercise Sequences

27. 어깨-업어치기(왼쪽, 오른쪽)

· 기본자세-똑바로 선 자세에서 양다리를 어깨 넓이로 벌린다.

왼쪽-양 팔꿈치를 겨드랑이에 붙이고 양손은 살짝 주먹을 쥐고 양 옆 턱 5cm 정도 가까이까지 올려놓고 양 옆 턱을 막고 고개를 약간 숙이고 상대의 양 눈동자를 주시하면서 왼발을 앞으로 옮기면서 양손으로 상대의 양 옷깃을 잡고 왼쪽 엉덩이를 상대의 사타구니에 대면서 오른발을 들어 뒤로 한발 옮기며 양 무릎을 굽혀 상대의 몸을 들어 올려 왼쪽으로 어깨 업어치기를 한다.

Shoulder Throw:

Begin with your feet shoulder width apart and both your fists guarding your face with both your elbows protecting your ribs. Step with your left foot towards 1:00 while grabbing your opponent's lapel with both hands.

· 기본자세-똑바로 선 자세에서 양다리를 어깨 넓이로 벌린다.

오른쪽-양 팔꿈치를 겨드랑이에 붙이고 양손은 살짝 주먹을 쥐고 양 옆 턱 5cm 정도 가까이까지 올려놓고 양 옆 턱을 막고 고개를 약간 숙이고 상대의 양 눈동자를 주시하면서 오른발을 앞으로 옮기면서 양손으로 상대의 양 옷깃을 잡고 오른쪽 엉덩이를 상대의 사타구니에 대면서 왼발을 들어 뒤로 한발 옮기며 양 무릎을 굽혀 상대의 몸을 들어 올려 오른쪽으로 어깨 업어치기를 한다.

Then step back with your right leg towards 11:00, and bend both your legs. Bring your left elbow in so your shoulder is caught under your opponent's lapels, and pick up your opponent with your legs. Turn your shoulders clockwise, and throw your opponent over your left shoulder.

28. 기합 단련

· 기본자세—똑바로 선 자세에서 양다리를 어깨 넓이로 벌린다.

양손가락을 벌리고 양손은 겨드랑이 높이에서 10cm 간격을 앞으로 하고 숨을 들어 마신 후 숨을 멈추고 단전에 힘을 넣어 양 뒷축을 들었다가 내리면서 단전의 힘으로 양 손날에 기를 모아 순간 애! 소리를 지르며 양손가락을 쥐면서 턱 밑까지 들어 올린다.

Vocalized Willpower:

Begin with your hands out at shoulder level, and your palms facing down with your elbows up. Slightly bend both your legs while you vocalize, and thrust both knife hands downward, harnessing your Ki. Bend your elbows so your thumbs are pointed up, and explode upward while extending your legs up.

29. 차력-술

· 기본자세-똑바로 선 자세에서 양다리를 어깨 넓이로 벌린다.

양팔을 들어 양 손날은 양 눈높이에 두며 숨을 들어 마신 후 숨을 멈추고 정신통일을 하며 입으로 기합소리를 고르게 내면서 입으로 호흡조절을 하며 자세를 내려앉으면서 온 몸속에 힘을 앉은 자세까지 힘을 발육 시켰다가 그 힘을 모아들고 일어나서 팔을 옆으로 완전히 뻗은 다음 숨을 천천히 내쉬며 팔을 아래로 내리면서 몸에 힘을 이완시킨다.

Cha Ryuk-Sool:

The purpose of this exercise is to develop your Ki. Begin with your hands out at eye level, and your palms facing down with your elbows up. Take a deep breath through your nose and hold it. Then exhale all of your air through your mouth evenly as you vocalize and lower yourself down squeezing all of the air out of your body by contracting your abdomen. Try to harness your Ki. Next, hold your breath and raise your body up slowly while contracting every muscle in your body and transferring your Ki to specific parts of your body. Stand all the way back up, and extend your arms straight out sideways. Once you fully extend your arms out, inhale through your nose and relax.

30. 앞-당기기

· 기본자세-똑바로 선 자세에서 양다리를 어깨 넓이로 벌린다.
자세를 내리면서 중심을 잡고 양손으로 상대의 양 옷깃을 잡고 앞으로 당긴다.

Front Pulls:

Begin with your feet shoulder width apart and both your fists guarding your face with both your elbows protecting your ribs. Reach out and grab with both your hands towards 12:00. Bend both your legs while pulling your arms towards you. Ensure you keep your back straight.

31. 제자리-뛰기(왼쪽, 오른쪽)

· 기본자세-똑바로 선 자세에서 양다리를 어깨 넓이로 벌린다.
왼쪽-왼발을 들어 중심을 잡고 제자리 뛰기를 한다.

Hop Steps:

Begin with your left knee up above your belt, and both your fists guarding your face with both elbows protecting your ribs. Hop up and down with your right leg while you extend your left leg towards 12:00, kicking out in front of you. Pull your toes back on your left foot, and keep your back straight.

32. 10-선 자세

· 기본자세-똑바로 선 자세에서 허리를 펴고 무릎을 45도 내려 기마자세를 만든 후에 중심 을 잡는다. 양 주먹을 양 허리에 붙이고 손가락은 위쪽으로 한다.

1, 허리를 틀어 왼쪽 주먹으로 정권 직선 펀치(기마자세)
2, 허리를 틀어 오른쪽 주먹으로 정권 직선 펀치(기마자세)
3, 왼쪽 팔꿈치 훅 펀치(선 자세)
4, 오른쪽 팔꿈치 훅 펀치(선 자세)
5, 오른쪽 3시 방향 양 손날 하단 옆 막기(후방자세)

Basic Stance Form:

Begin in a Horse Stance with both arms at your side and fists at belt level.
01) Left Straight Punch
02) Right Straight Punch (Ki-hap)
03) Left Elbow Hook.
04) Right Elbow Hook
05) Right Side Low Side Block.

6, 오른쪽 3시 방향 양 팔뚝 중단 옆 막기(후방자세)
7, 오른쪽 3시 방향 양 팔뚝 상단 옆 막기(후방자세)
8, 왼쪽 9시 방향 양 손날 하단 옆 막기(후방자세)
9, 왼쪽 9시 방향 양 팔뚝 중단 옆 막기(후방자세)
10, 왼쪽 9시 방향 양 팔뚝 상단 옆 막기(후방자세)

· 차렷

똑바로 선 자세로 허리와 무릎을 세우면서 양 주먹은 양 허리에 붙이며 양 주먹을 살짝 쥐고 똑바로 부동자세로 선다.

· 경례

똑바로 선 부동자세에서 눈동자를 아래로 내려다보면서 양손을 마주잡고 허리를 45도 각도로 숙여 절을 하고 다시 부동자세로 선다.

06) Right Side Middle Side Block
07) Right Side High Side Forearm Block
08) Left Side Low Side Block.
09) Left Side Middle Side Block
10) Left Side High Side Block.

Stance
자 | 세

01 차렷: Attention

02 경례: Salute

03 쉬어: At Ease

04 기마자세: Horse Stance

05 전방자세 (왼쪽, 오른쪽): Forward Stance (Left, Right)

06 중방자세 (왼쪽, 오른쪽): Middle Stance (Left, Right)

07 후방자세 (왼쪽, 오른쪽): Back Stance (Left, Right)

08 선 자세: Front stance

09 공격 자세 (왼쪽, 오른쪽): Fight Stance (Left, Right)

1. 차렷

허리를 똑바로 펴고 양 발 뒤꿈치를 붙이며 무릎을 펴고 양팔은 양 다리에 붙이고 주먹은 힘을 빼며 살짝 쥐고 부동자세를 한다.

Attention:

Stand straight with your hands by your sides. Stand with the heels of your feet together and the front of your feet apart to form a V shape for better stability. Maintain a good posture by keeping your neck, back, and legs straight while looking forward.

2. 경례

허리를 똑바로 펴고 양 발 뒤꿈치를 붙이며 무릎은 펴고 양손을 서 로 잡고 턱밑으로 가까이까지 올려 허리와 머리를 45도 각도 아래로 숙여 인사를 한다.

Salute:

Begin by standing at attention with your feet together and your hands by your sides. Keep your legs, neck, and back straight and while looking forward. Bow by cupping your hands together and bending your upper body forward at the hips. Bend your body over to about a 90 degree angle and bow your head while looking towards the ground. When you bow your head, verbally say "hap do" aloud as a gesture of respect. After bowing, lift your head and look forward. Bring your hands back to your sides and stand straight up back to attention.

(Frount)

(Side)

자세: Stance

3. 쉬어
허리를 똑바로 펴고 양 다리를 어깨 넓이로 벌리고 양손을 등 뒤에 서 손짐을 짓고 편안하게 선 자세.

At Ease:
Stand with your feet apart and parallel to each at a distance slightly wider than the width of your shoulders. Keep your back straight and clasp your hands together behind your back.

4. 기마자세
허리를 똑바로 펴고 양다리를 어깨 넓이 1.5배로 벌리고 중심은 양다리에 두고 양 무릎을 45도정도 앞으로 굽히고 양 주먹을 양 허 리 띠에 붙이기.

Horse Stance:
Stand with your feet parallel to each other. Then step out with a leg so that your stance is wide. Keep your back straight and bend your knees at about 90 degree angles. Your feet should be positioned directly under your knees; and if they are not, reposition them until they are. Imagining yourself sitting on an invisible chair might help you to keep a good posture. Make a fist with your hands and place them by your sides just above your hips. Rotate your fists so that the under sides of your wrists are facing upward.

5. 전방자세 (왼쪽, 오른쪽)

허리를 똑바로 펴고 양다리를 어깨 넓이로 벌리고 몸을 옆으로 돌 려 중심은 앞다리에 두고 뒷발 뒤꿈치를 45도정도 들고 앞다리에 힘을 주고 서기.

Forward Stance:

(Left)
Stand sideways with your left leg forward and your right leg back. Take a large step forward slightly toward the left upper corner with your left leg and shift your weight into it. Bend your left knee until it is directly above your left foot. Straighten your right leg and position your right foot horizontally so that it is facing the right. Slightly tilt your chin down and look straight ahead. Guard by positioning your right hand by the corner of your right temple. Keep your right elbow tucked into your side. Then position your left hand out at about 6 to 8 inches directly in front of the corner of your left temple and keep your left elbow pointing downward. Both of your hands should be at eyebrow level.

(Right)
Stand sideways with your right leg forward and your left leg back. Take a large step forward slightly toward the right upper corner with your right leg and shift your weight into it. Bend your right knee until it is directly above your right foot. Straighten your left leg and position your left foot horizontally so that it is facing the left. Slightly tilt your chin down and look straight ahead. Guard by positioning your left hand by the corner of your left temple. Keep your left elbow tucked into your side. Then position your right hand out at about 6 to 8 inches directly in front of the corner of your right temple and keep your right elbow pointing downward. Both of your hands should be at eyebrow level.

6. 중방자세 (왼쪽, 오른쪽)

허리를 똑바로 펴고 양다리를 어깨 넓이로 벌리고 몸을 옆으로 돌려 중심은 양다리에 두고 무릎을 45도 정도 내려서 기마 자세와 같이 옆으로 몸을 돌려 서기.

Middle Stance:

(Left)
Stand sideways so that your left foot is forward and your right foot is back. Take a medium size step forward slightly towards the upper left corner with your left leg. Position your right foot horizontally so that it is pointing towards the right side. Position your left foot slightly diagonally so that it is pointing towards the upper right corner. Bend both your of legs equally and center your balance between your legs. Slightly tilt your chin down and look straight ahead. Guard by positioning your right hand by the corner of your right temple. Keep your right elbow tucked into your side. Then position your left hand out at about 6 to 8 inches directly in front of the corner of your left temple and keep your left elbow pointing downward. Both of your hands should be at eyebrow level.

(Right)
Stand sideways so that your right foot is forward and your left foot is back. Take a medium size step forward slightly towards the upper right corner with your right leg. Position your left foot horizontally so that it is pointing towards the left side. Position your right foot slightly diagonally so that it is pointing towards the upper left corner. Bend both your of legs equally and center your balance between your legs. Slightly tilt your chin down and look straight ahead. Guard by positioning your left hand by the corner of your left temple. Keep your left elbow tucked into your side. Then position your right hand out at about 6 to 8 inches directly in front of the corner of your right temple and keep your right elbow pointing downward. Both of your hands should be at eyebrow level.

7. 후방자세 (왼쪽, 오른쪽)

허리를 똑바로 펴고 양다리를 어깨 넓이로 벌리고 몸을 옆으로 돌려 중심은 뒷다리에 두고 앞발 뒤꿈치를 45도 정도 들고 뒷다리에 힘을 주고 서기.

Back Stance:

(Left)
Stand sideways so that your left foot is forward and your right foot is back. Look towards your left. Position your right foot horizontally and position your left foot diagonally so that it is pointing towards the right front corner. Your feet should not be aligned straight with each other, but your left foot should be placed more towards the left. To make sure your feet are at good angles to each other, imagine a line on the ground that begins at your left big toe and travels back towards your right foot. That line should run into the back edge of your right heel. Position your shoulders at a slight angle towards the left. Your shoulders should be aligned with your feet. Bend your right leg and slightly lean back. Do not limbo your body backwards. Keep your back semi straight and shift most of your balance into your right leg. Elevate the heel of your left foot up while keeping the ball of your foot on the ground. Slightly tilt your chin down and look straight ahead. Guard by positioning your right hand by the corner of your right temple. Keep your right elbow tucked into your side. Then position your left hand out at about 6 to 8 inches directly in front of the corner of your left temple and keep your left elbow pointing downward. Both of your hands should be at eyebrow level.

(Right)
Stand sideways so that your right foot is forward and your left foot is back. Look towards your right. Position your left foot horizontally and position your right foot diagonally so that it is pointing towards the left front corner. Your feet should not be aligned straight with each other, but your right foot should be placed more towards the right. To make sure your feet are at good angles to each other, imagine a line on the ground that begins at your right big toe and travels back towards your left foot. That line should run into the back edge of your left heel. Position your shoulders at a slight angle towards the right. Your shoulders should be aligned with your feet. Bend your left leg and slightly lean back. Do not limbo your body backwards. Keep your back semi straight and shift most of your balance into your left leg. Elevate the heel of your left foot up while keeping the ball of your foot on the ground. Slightly tilt your chin down and look straight ahead. Guard by positioning your left hand by the corner of your left temple. Keep your left elbow tucked into your side. Then position your right hand out at about 6 to 8 inches directly in front of the corner of your right temple and keep your right elbow pointing downward. Both of your hands should be at eyebrow level.

자세: Stance

8. 선 자세

허리를 똑바로 펴고 양다리를 어깨 넓이로 벌리고 중심은 양다리 에 두고 몸에 힘을 빼며 부드러운 자세로 서기.

Front Stance:

Stand with your feet parallel to each other and position them at a distance slightly wider than the width of your shoulders. Then very slightly angle your feet a few degrees outward so that your heels are slightly inward. Bend your legs a little bit while slightly leaning your upper body forward to counter-balance your hips. You should be well balanced in this position while having your weight evenly distributed between both legs. Guard up by positioning your hands by your face towards the corners of your temples. Your hands should be at about eyebrow level. Keep your elbows tucked into your body and relax your shoulders. Slightly tilt your chin down and look straight ahead.

9. 공격 자세 (왼쪽, 오른쪽)

(왼쪽)

허리를 똑바로 펴고 양다리를 어깨 넓이로 벌리고 몸을 왼쪽 옆으로 돌려 중심은 앞다리에 두고 뒷발 뒤꿈치를 45도정도 들고 몸에 힘을 빼고 부드러운 자세로 서서 왼쪽 주먹은 왼쪽 눈높이에 두고 오른쪽 주먹은 오른쪽 턱에 붙이고 서기.

(오른쪽)

허리를 똑바로 펴고 양다리를 어깨 넓이로 벌리고 몸을 오른쪽 옆으로 돌려 중심은 앞다리에 두고 뒷발 뒤꿈치를 45도정도 들고 몸에 힘을 빼고 부드러운 자세로 서서 오른쪽 주먹은 오른쪽 눈높이에 두고 왼쪽 주먹은 왼쪽 턱에 붙이고 서기.

Fight Stance:

(Left)

Stand sideways so that your left foot is forward and your right foot is back. Look towards your left. Position your right foot horizontally and position your left foot diagonally so that it is pointing towards the right front corner. Your feet should not be aligned straight with each other, but your left foot should be placed more towards the left. To make sure your feet are at good angles to each other, imagine a line on the ground that begins at your left big toe and travels back towards your right foot. That line should run into the back edge of your right heel. Position your shoulders at a slight angle towards the left. Your shoulders should be aligned with your feet. Slightly bend your knees and distribute your balance evenly amongst both legs. Also slightly tilt your chin down and look straight ahead. Guard by positioning your right hand by the corner of your right temple. Keep your right elbow tucked into your side. Then position your left hand out at about 6 to 8 inches directly in front of the corner of your left temple and keep your left elbow pointing downward. Both of your hands should be at eyebrow level.

(Right)

Stand sideways so that your right foot is forward and your left foot is back. Look towards your right. Position your left foot horizontally and position your right foot diagonally so that it is pointing towards the left front corner. Your feet should not be aligned straight with each other, but your right foot should be placed more towards the right. To make sure your feet are at good angles to each other, imagine a line on the ground that begins at your right big toe and travels back towards your left foot. That line should run into the back edge of your left heel. Position your shoulders at a slight angle towards the right. Your shoulders should be aligned with your feet. Slightly bend your knees and distribute your balance evenly amongst both legs. Also slightly tilt your chin down and look straight ahead. Guard by positioning your left hand by the corner of your right temple. Keep your left elbow tucked into your side. Then position your right hand out at about 6 to 8 inches directly in front of the corner of your right temple and keep your right elbow pointing downward. Both of your hands should be at eyebrow level.

자세: Stance

합도술

Upper Body Parts Used for Striking

상 단 치 기 종 류

01 정권: Fist knuckle
02 등뒤주먹: Back fist
03 수도: Knife hand
04 수장: Palm
05 가위손끝: Tips of the Scissor Fingers
06 간수: Spear hand
07 안 팔굽: Interior forearm
08 바깥팔뚝: Exterior forearm
09 밤알: Chestnut Fist
10 팔굽: Elbow
11 이마: Forehead

1. 정권

모지(둘째손가락), 장지(셋째손가락) 상단 관절 끝마디 부위.

Fist knuckle:
The tip of the index and middle knuckle.

2. 등뒤주먹

모지(둘째손가락), 장지(셋째손가락) 상단 관절 윗 부위.

Back fist:
The top of the index and middle knuckle.

3. 수도
세끼손가락(다섯째손가락), 상단 밑 손바닥 근육 부위.

Knife hand:
The outer edge of the hand.

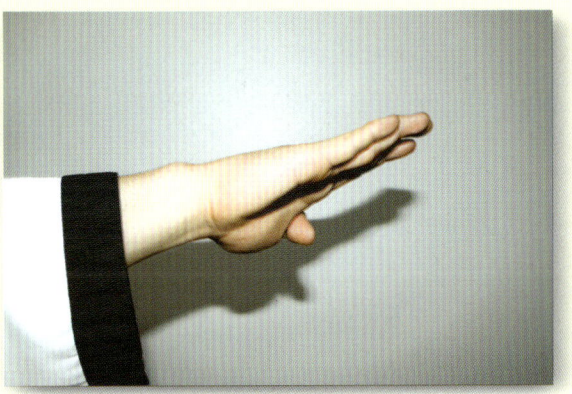

4. 수장
손목 끝에 있는 손바닥뼈 부위.

Palm:
The palm of the hand.

5. 가위손끝

모지(둘째손가락), 장지(셋째손가락)끝 부위.

Tips of the Scissor Fingers:
The tip of the index and middle finger.

6. 간수

엄지와 새끼손가락(첫째손가락과 끝 손가락)을 손바닥에 붙이고 셋 손가락(모지, 장지, 검지)끝을 가지런히 붙여 모은 손끝부위.

Spear hand:
Place your index, middle and ring finger together so that they are equal in length.

7. 안 팔굽
요골 쪽에 있는 부위.

Interior forearm :
Inner forearm of the radius.

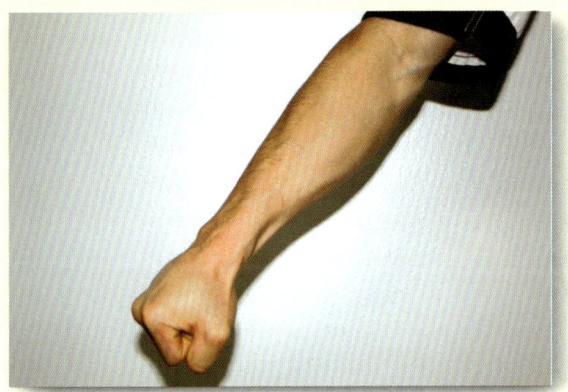

8. 바깥팔뚝
척골 쪽에 있는 부위.

Exterior forearm:
Outer forearm of the ulna.

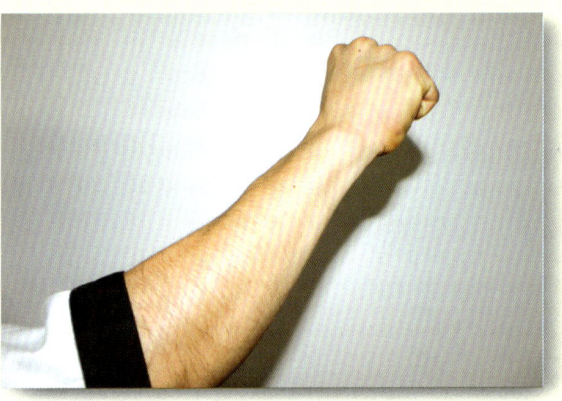

9. 밤알

손가락 가운데 관절 끝을 내밀어 나온 관절부위.

Chestnut Fist

The tip of the second knuckle on the middle finger.

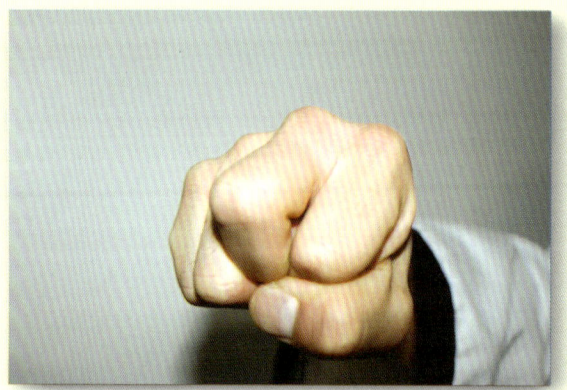

10. 팔굽

팔의 위아래 관절이 이어진 곳의 바깥쪽 관절 부위.

Elbow:

Bend the elbow. The front part of the tip of the elbow.

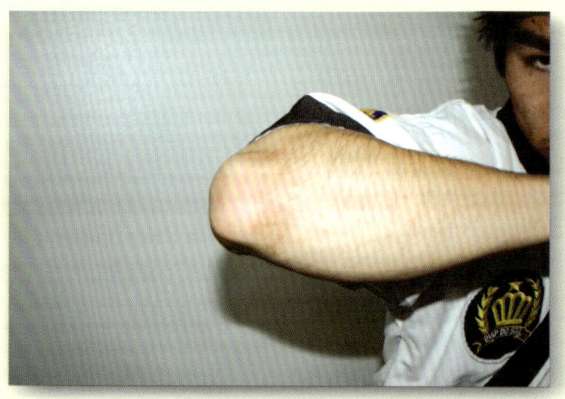

11. 이마
눈썹 위로부터 머리털이 난 부분까지의 사이 부위.

Forehead :
The front portion of the forehead just below the hair line.

합도술

Lower Body Parts Used for Striking
하 단 치 기 종 류

01 앞 축: Ball of the foot
02 옆 축: Side of the foot
03 뒤 축: Heel of the foot
04 무릎 위: Upper part of the knee
05 무릎 아래: Lower part of the knee
06 발바닥: Sole of the foot

1. 앞 축
발가락을 위로 제쳐 올리고 발가락 상단 관절부위.

Ball of the foot:
Pull your toes back and expose the ball of the foot.

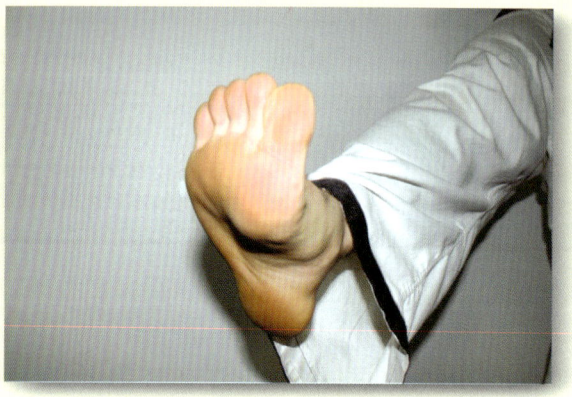

2. 옆 축
발뒤축 복사뼈 쪽 옆 부위.

Side of the foot:
The outer edge of the foot.

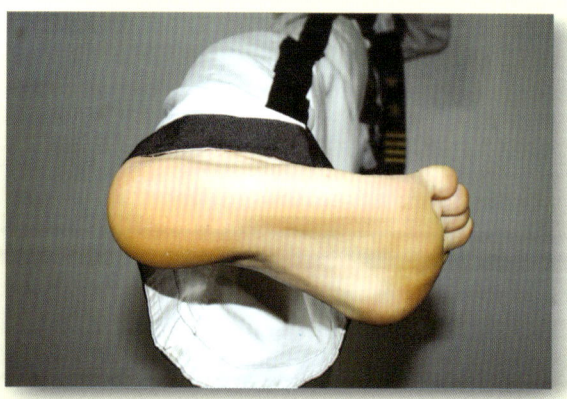

3. 뒤 축
발뒤꿈치 상단 뼈끝 부위.

Heel of the foot:
The heel of the foot.

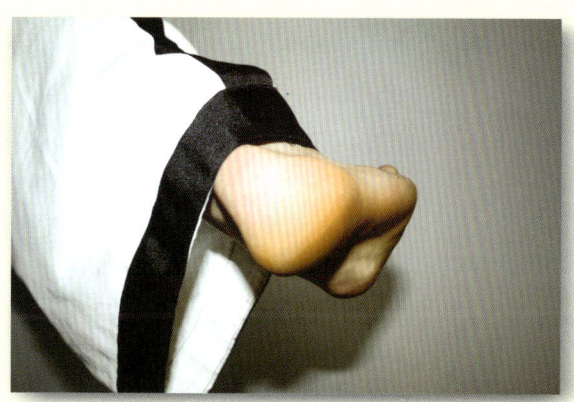

4. 무릎 위
다리를 구부릴 때 튀어나오는 관절 상단 무릎부위.

Upper part of the knee:
The upper part of the knee.

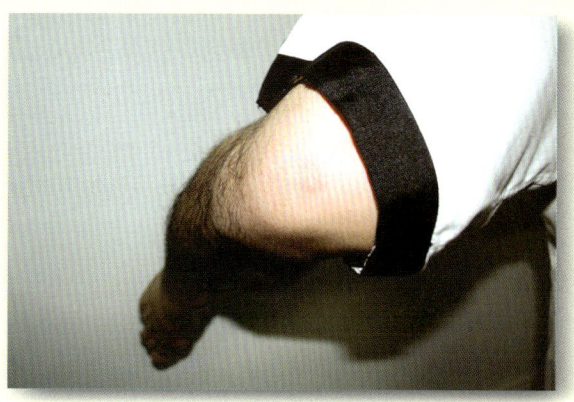

하단치기종류: Lower Body Parts Used for Striking

5. 무릎 아래
관절 하단 무릎부위.

Lower part of the knee:
The lower part of the knee.

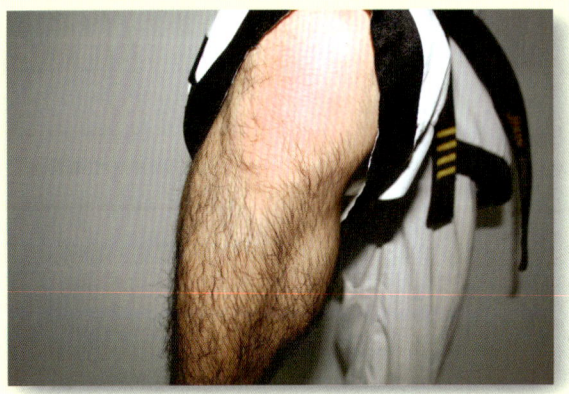

6. 발바닥
발바닥 부위.

Sole of the foot:
The bottom sole of the foot.

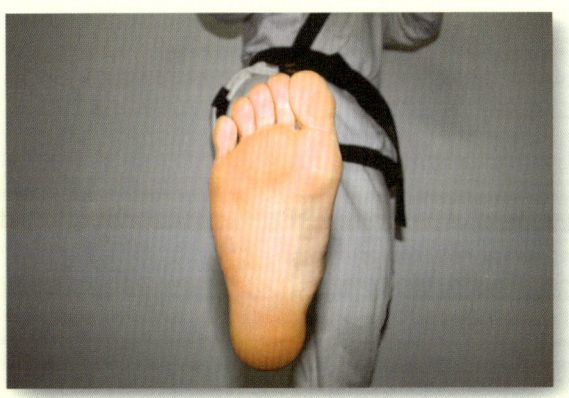

7. 정강이
앞쪽 무릎에서 앞쪽 발목까지 경골 부위

Lower part Shin:
The lower part of the Tibia Bone.

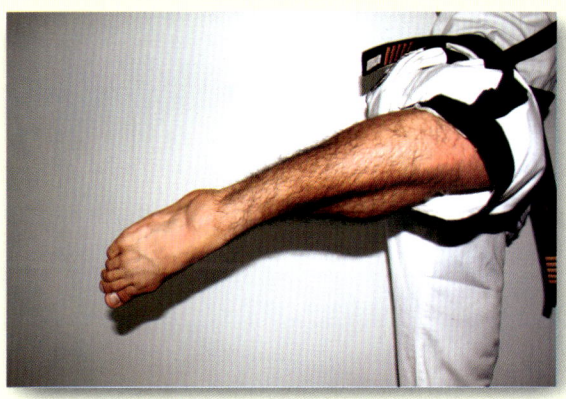

Vital Point Techniques
급 | 소 | 술

01. 내정명 (內睛明): Nae Jung Myung
02. 동자료 (瞳子髎): Dong Jah Ryoh
03. 태양 (太陽): Tae Yang
04. 청궁 (聽宮): Chung Goong
05. 예풍 (翳風): Yeh Poong
06. 인중 (人中): In Joong:
07. 협거 (頰車): Hyup Guh
08. 승장 (承漿): Seung Jang
09. 아문 (啞門): Ah Moon
10. 지합 (地合): Ji Hap
11. 편도선 (扁桃腺): Tonsils
12. 천용 (天容): Chun Yong
13. 인영 (人迎): In Young
14. 견정 (肩井): Gyun Jung
15. 심하 (心下): Solar plexus
16. 장문 (章門): Jang Moon
17. 음낭 (陰囊): Um Nang
18. 장강 (長强): Jang Gang
19. 독비 (犢鼻): Doke Be

1. 내정명(內睛明)

코 쪽 눈 꼬리 안을 엄지로 코 쪽을 향하여 누르기.

Nae Jung Myung:

Place the tip of your thumb at the inner corner of the eye, next to the bridge of the nose. Apply pressure by pushing in towards the bridge of the nose.

2. 동자료(瞳子髎)

귀 쪽 눈 꼬리를 엄지로 눈쪽 누르기.

Dong Jah Ryoh:

Place the tip of your thumb at the outer corner of the eye near the ear. Apply pressure by pushing in towards the eyes.

3. 태양(太陽)

눈썹 끝에 외측으로 오목한곳을 엄지로 누르기.
(정권 훅 펀치, 상단 돌려차기)

Tae Yang:

Place the tip of your thumb at the temple, on side of the head about 1cm past the outer corner of the eye. Apply Pressure by pushing in. (fist / knuckle hook punch, high roundhouse kick)

4. 청궁(聽宮)

귀 가운데 앞쪽 오목한 부위를 엄지로 얼굴쪽 누르기.
(정권 훅 펀치, 상단 돌려차기)

Chung Goong:

Place the tip of your thumb just above the conch of the ear. Apply pressure by pushing in towards the face. (fist / knuckle hook punch, high roundhouse kick)

5. 예풍(翳風)

귓밥 뒤 오목한 부위를 엄지로 귓쪽 누르기.
(정권 직선 펀치, 정권 훅 펀치, 상단 돌려차기)

In Joong:

Place the tip of your thumb just above the middle of the upper lip directly below the tip of the nose. Apply pressure by pushing in and upwards into the nose. (straight punch, fist / knuckle hook punch, high roundhouse kick)

6. 인중(人中)

코밑과 입술 가운데 약간위에 엄지로 콧쪽 누르기.
(정권 직선 펀치, 정권 훅 펀치, 상단 돌려차기)

In Joong:

Place the tip of your thumb just above the middle of the upper lip directly below the tip of the nose. Apply pressure by pushing in and upwards into the nose. (straight punch, fist / knuckle hook punch, high roundhouse kick)

7. 협거(頰車)

턱 모서리 뼈 3cm 옆 엄지로 입 쪽으로 누르기.
(정권 훅 펀치, 상단 돌려차기)

Hyup Guh:

Place the tip of your thumb about 1cm next to the side corner of the jaw bone. Apply pressure by pushing in and of the mouth. (fist / knuckle hook punch, high roundhouse kick)

8. 승장(承漿)

아랫입술 가운데 밑 오목한 부위를 엄지로 누르기.
(정권 직선 펀치, 상단 돌려차기)

Seung Jang:

Place the tip of your thumb just above the chin and directly below the middle of the lower lip. Apply pressure by pushing in. (fist / knuckle hook punch, high roundhouse kick)

9. 아문(啞門)

뒤 머리카락 끝 가운데 약간 올라가서 오목한 부위 3cm 위쪽에 엄지로 머리 위쪽을 향해 누르기.
(정권 훅 펀치, 팔꿈치 훅 지르기, 상단 돌려차기)

Ah Moon:

Place the tip of your thumb at the center of the back of neck, approximately 3cm below the hair line. Apply pressure by pushing in and up towards the head.
(fist / knuckle hook punch, elbow hook punch, high roundhouse kick)

10. 지합(地合)

턱 중앙 끝 부위.
(정권 어퍼컷 펀치, 앞차기)

Ji Hap:

Tip of the chin; the very center tip of the chin.
(fist / knuckle uppercut punch, high front kick)

11. 편도선(扁桃腺)

턱 모서리 뼈와 턱 중앙 끝 중간 사이에 엄지로 윗쪽으로 누르기.
(정권 직선편치, 상단 옆차기)

Tonsils:

Place the tip of your thumb midway from the tip of the chin and the ear lobe under the side of the jaw next to the tonsils. Apply pressure by pushing in & up towards the head.
(fist straight punch, side kick)

12. 천용(天容)

턱 모서리 뼈 밑 흉쇄돌근 앞 부위를 엄지로 누르기.
(정권 훅 펀치, 상단 돌려차기)

Chun Young:

Place the tip of your thumb directly on the tonsils just below the point where the side jaw bone angles. Apply pressure by pushing in.
(Fist Hook, Roundhouse Kick)

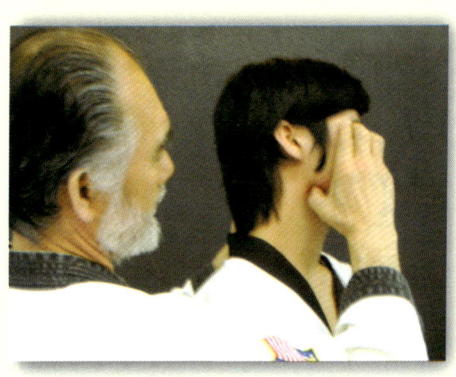

13. 인영(人迎)

목 가운데 튀어나온 목젖 옆 부위에 엄지와 검지로 목젖을 잡고 누르며 당기기.
(정권 직선 펀치, 정권 훅 펀치, 팔굽 훅 펀치, 상단 돌려차기)

In Young:

Grab the sides of the adam's apple with your thumb and index finger. Apply pressure by squeezing your fingers together and pulling.
(fist / knuckle straight punch, fist knuckle hook punch, elbow uppercut, high roundhouse kick)

14. 견정(肩井)

어깨 쇄골의 높은 곳 7번째 목뼈 이은선의 중간부위.
(수도치기, 상단 뒷축 내려찍기)

Gyun Jung:

Midway point of the 7th cervical vertebra and the highest part of the shoulder.
(knife cut, chop down high heel kick)

15. 심하(心下)

가슴뼈 아래 가운데 오목하게 들어간 곳.
(정권 어퍼컷 펀치, 중단 앞차기)

Solar plexus:
The solar plexus is located directly below the sternum at the point where both the bottom rib cages meet. (Fist Uppercut, Middle Front Kick)

16. 장문(章門)

제 11늑골 아래.
(정권 훅 펀치, 팔 굽 훅 펀치, 중단 돌려차기)

Jang Moon:
The point directly at the very bottom of the rib cage at the 11th floating rib.
(fist knuckle hook punch, elbow hook punch, middle roundhouse kick)

17. 음낭(陰囊)

사타구니 사이에 있는 불알을 손으로 잡고 누르면서 당기기
(하단 앞차기, 무릎 앞차기)

Um Nang:

From behind, reach between your opponent's legs and grab their scrotum with one hand. Apply pressure to the scrotum by squeezing and pulling towards you.
(Low front kick, front knee kick)

18. 장강(長强)

항문 위쪽 미골 끝(꼬리뼈)
(정권 어퍼컷 펀치, 무릎 앞차기)

Jang Gang:

The very tip of the perineum bone located just above the anus.
(fist knuckle uppercut punch, front knee kick)

19. 독비(犢鼻)

무릎 뼈 아래 양쪽 외측 오목한 부위.
(무릎 관절에 하단 옆차기)

Doke Be:

The inner knee directly below the knee cap.
(Low side kick to front knee joint)

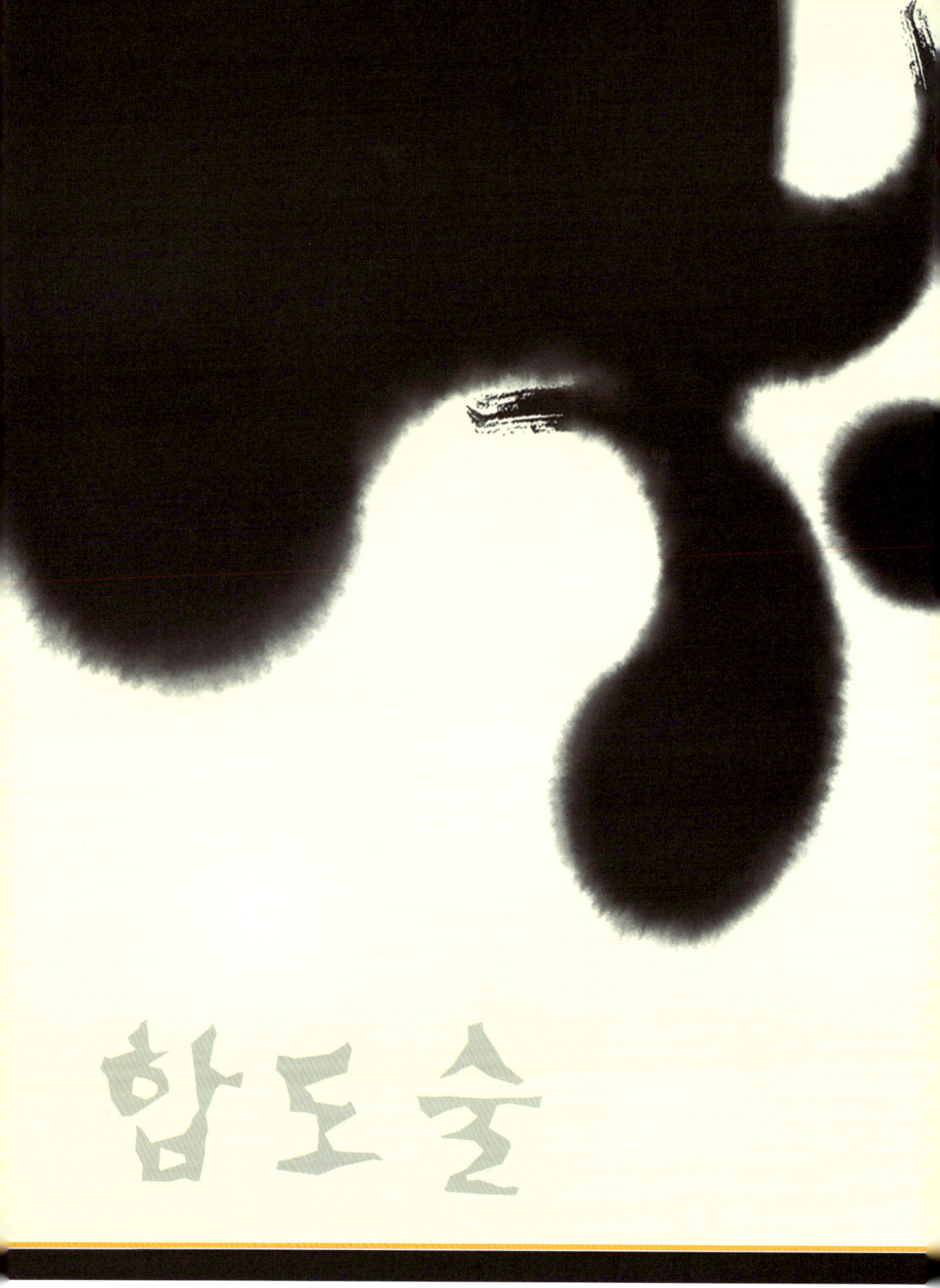

Stepping Techniques
스 | 탭 | 술

01. 한발 들고 뜀뛰기 (왼쪽, 오른쪽): Hop Kick Step
02. 이중 스탭 (왼쪽, 오른쪽): Front Toe Step
03. 양발 왕복 스탭 (왼쪽, 오른쪽): Front to Back Step
04. 양발 이중 왕복 스탭 (왼쪽, 오른쪽): Front to Back Double Step
05. 양발 옆 스탭 (왼쪽, 오른쪽): Side to Side Step
06. 양발 이중 옆 스탭 (왼쪽, 오른쪽): Side to Side Step Double Step
07. 양발 앞뒤 교환 (왼쪽, 오른쪽): Switch Step
08. 양발 이중 앞뒤 교환 (왼쪽, 오른쪽): Switch Double Step

1. 한발 들고 뜀뛰기 (왼쪽, 오른쪽)

선 자세에서 양발을 어깨넓이로 벌려 양손은 살짝 주먹을 쥐고 주먹 간격으로 양턱에 올려붙이고 오른발은 땅을 딛고 왼발은 위로 들어 오른발에 중심을 잡고 깡충 깡충 반복하며 위로 뛰면서 왼발은 차기를 하며 반복 뛰기.

Hop Kick Step:

(Left)

Begin in a left Fight Stance.

Raise your left knee up to about waist level and stand on your right leg. Slightly bend your right leg to maintain better balance. Begin by bouncing on your right leg. While bouncing, ensure that your weight is primarily balanced on the ball of your foot and slightly raise the heel with each bounce. While keeping your left knee in the air, kick to your opponent's midsection with your left leg on each bounce. Repeat for 10 left side hop kick and return to a left Fight Stance.

(Right)
Begin in a right Fight Stance.

Keep your guard up with your hands.   Raise your right knee up to about waist level and stand on your left leg. Slightly bend your left leg to maintain better balance. Begin by bouncing on your left leg. While bouncing, ensure that your weight is primarily balanced on the ball of your foot and slightly raise the heel with each bounce. While keeping your right knee in the air, kick to your opponent's midsection with your right leg on each bounce. Repeat for 10 right side Hop Kick Steps and return to a right Fight Stance.

2. 이중 스탭 (왼쪽, 오른쪽)

선 자세에서 양발을 어깨넓이로 벌려 양손은 살짝 주먹을 쥐고 주먹 간격으로 양턱에 올려붙이고 오른발은 위로 뛰어 반복튀기를 하고 다시 왼발을 위로 뛰었다가 반복튀기를 번갈아 한다.

Front Toe Step:

(Left)

Begin in a left Fight Stance.

Shift most of your weight into your right leg and get into a left Back Stance. Slightly bend your right leg to maintain better balance. Lift the heel of your left foot in a raised position and balance on the ball of your left foot. Then begin by hopping on your right leg while bouncing your left foot up and down as you hop. Time the bounce so that you land on your right leg before your left foot hits the ground. Maintain the heel of your left foot lifted in a raised position as you bounce up and down on the ball of your left foot. Repeat for 10 left side Bounce Steps and return to a left Fight Stance.

(Right)
Begin in a right Fight Stance.
Shift most of your weight into your left leg and get into a right Back Stance. Slightly bend your left leg to maintain better balance. Lift the heel of your right foot in a raised position and balance on the ball of your right foot. Then begin by hopping on your left leg while bouncing your right foot up and down as you hop. Time the bounce so that you land on your left leg before your right foot hits the ground. Maintain the heel of your right foot lifted in a raised position as you bounce up and down on the ball of your right foot. Repeat for 10 right side Bounce Steps and return to a right Fight Stance.

스탭술: Stepping Techniques

3. 양발 왕복 스탭 (왼족, 오른쪽)

선 자세에서 양발을 어깨넓이로 벌려 양손은 살짝 주먹을 쥐고 왼쪽 주먹은 눈높이에서 손 한 뼘 간격에 올려놓고 오른쪽 주먹은 오른쪽 옆 턱에 주먹 간격에 올려붙이고 왼발을 앞에 오른발은 뒤에 놓고 양발은 어깨 넓이로 벌리고 중심은 양 앞발에 두고 양발을 동시에 앞뒤로 반발씩 왕복 뛰기를 한다.

Front to Back Step:

(Left)

Begin in a left Fight Stance.

Slightly bend your legs and shift some of your weight into your right leg. Then push off your right leg and hop forward while maintaining a guard. Land into a Fight Stance and land with both of your feet simultaneously. Next, slightly bend your legs and shift your weight into your left leg. Then push off your left leg and hop backwards back to your original location. Land into a Fight Stance and land with both of your feet simultaneously. Repeat 10 left Front to Back Steps.

(Right)
Begin in a right Fight Stance.

Slightly bend your legs and shift some of your weight into your left leg. Then push off your left leg and hop forward while maintaining a Fight Stance. Land into a Fight Stance and land with both of your feet simultaneously. Next, slightly bend your legs and shift your weight into your right leg. Then push off your right leg and hop backwards back to your original location. Land into a Fight Stance and land with both of your feet simultaneously. Repeat 10 right side Front to Back Steps.

스탭술: Stepping Techniques

4. 양발 이중 왕복 스탭 (왼족, 오른쪽)

선 자세에서 양발을 어깨넓이로 벌려 양손은 살짝 주먹을 쥐고 한손은 눈높이 한 뼘 간격에 두고 다른 손은 옆 턱 반 주먹 사이로 벌려 붙이고 양발은 앞뒤 어깨 넓이로 벌리고 동시에 앞뒤 이중으로 뛰어 반발씩 왕복 반복 뛰기.

Front to Back Double Step:

(Left)

Begin in a left Fight Stance.

Slightly bend your legs and shift some of your weight into your right leg. Then push off your right leg and hop forward while maintaining a guard. Take a step forward with your left foot during your hop and land with the ball of your foot. Once you have settled your balance into your left foot, bring your right foot in and place in on the ground so you return to a left Fight Stance. Next, slightly bend your legs and shift some of your weight into your left leg. Then push off your left leg and hop backwards while maintaining a guard. Take a step backwards towards the original position of your right foot with your right foot during your hop and land with the ball of your foot. Once you have settled your balance into your right foot, also return your left foot back into its original position. You should finish the step back in your original position while maintaining a guard and left Fight Stance. Repeat 10 times in a left Fight Stance.

(Right)
Slightly bend your legs and shift some of your weight into your left leg. Then push off your left leg and hop forward while maintaining a guard. Take a step forward with your right foot during your hop and land with the ball of your foot. Once you have settled your balance into your right foot, bring your left foot in and place in on the ground so you return to a right Fight Stance. Next, slightly bend your legs and shift some of your weight into your right leg. Then push off your right leg and hop backwards while maintaining a guard. Take a step backwards towards the original position of your left foot with your right foot during your hop and land with the ball of your foot. Once you have settled your balance into your left foot, also return your right foot back into its original position. You should finish the step back in your original position while maintaining a guard and right Fight Stance. Repeat 10 times in a right Fight Stance.

5. 양발 옆 스탭 (왼족, 오른쪽)

선 자세에서 양발을 어깨넓이로 벌려 양손은 살짝 주먹을 쥐고 양손은 양턱 주먹 간격으로 붙이고 동시에 옆으로 양쪽 반발씩 반복 뛰기.

Side to Side Step:

Begin in a Front Stance.

Slightly bend your right leg and shift your weight into it. Then push off your right leg and hop sideways towards the left of your current position while maintaining a guard. Land into a Front Stance but to the left of your original location, and land with both of your feet simultaneously. Next, slightly bend your left leg and shift your weight into it. Then push off your left leg and hop towards the right and return back to your original location. Land into a Front Stance and land with both of your feet simultaneously. Repeat 10 times hopping from the right to the left and back. Then repeat 10 more times but hopping from the left to the right and back.

6. 양발 이중 옆 스탭 (왼족, 오른쪽)
선 자세에서 양발을 어깨넓이로 벌려 양손은 살짝 주먹을 쥐고 양손은 양턱 한주먹 간격으로 붙이고 양발은 옆으로 어깨 넓이로 벌리고 동시에 옆으로 이중으로 반발씩 반복 뛰기.

Side to Side Double Step:
Slightly bend your right leg and shift your weight into it. Lift the heel of your left foot in a raised position while balancing on the ball of your left foot. Push off your right leg and hop sideways towards the left while maintaining a guard. Land with your left foot first then let your right foot follows. Land into a Front Stance. Next, slightly bend your left leg and shift your weight into it. Lift the heel of your right foot in a raised position while balancing on the ball of your right foot. Push off your left leg and hop sideways towards the right while maintaining a Front Stance. Land with your right foot first then let your left foot follow. Land into a Front Stance. Make sure when you are stepping that your feet land at separate times so you are doing a double step.

Repeat 10 times hopping from the right to the left and back. Then repeat 10 more times but hopping from the left to the right and back.

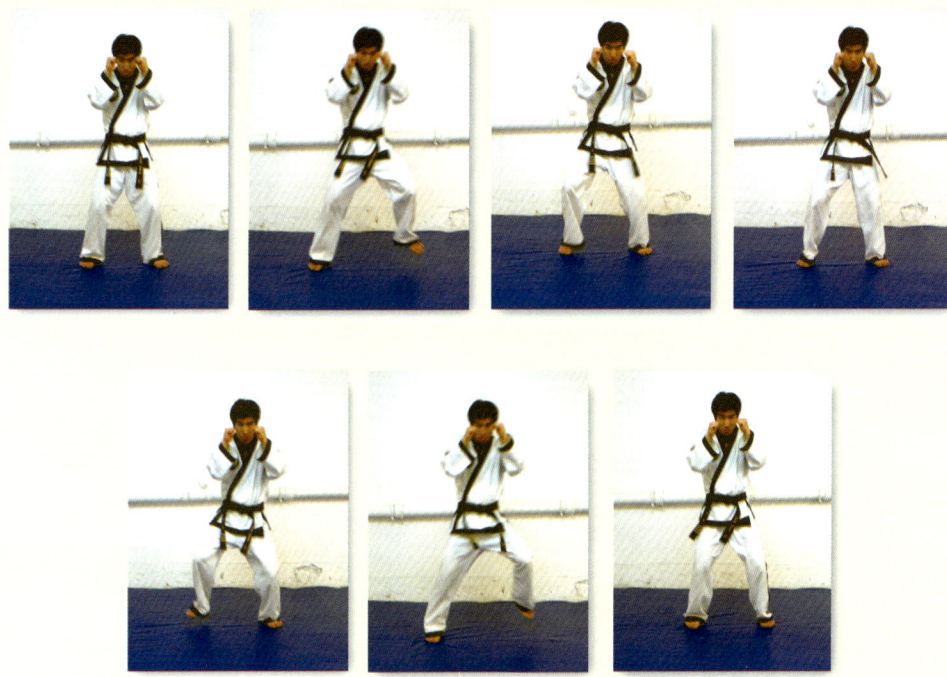

스탭술: Stepping Techniques

7. 양발 앞뒤 교환 (왼족, 오른쪽)

선 자세에서 양발을 어깨넓이로 벌려 양손은 살짝 주먹을 쥐고 한손은 눈높이 한 뼘 간격에 두고 다른 손은 옆 턱 반 주먹 사이로 벌려 붙이고 양발을 어깨 넓이로 벌리고 동시에 몸을 뛰어 양쪽으로 몸을 돌려 양발을 교환하며 자세를 바꾸어 반복 뛰기.

Switch Step:

Begin in a left Fight Stance.
Slightly bend your legs. Then hop up and twist your upper body and hips 180 degrees towards the left. Land simultaneously with both feet and into a switched stance so that your right foot is now forward and your left foot is back. You should end up in a right Fight Stance. Now in a right Fight Stance, slightly bend your legs. Then hop up and twist your upper body and hips 180 degrees towards the right. Land simultaneously with both feet and into your original stance in a left Fight Stance. In this position, your left foot should be forward and your right foot should be back. Repeat 10 times while starting in a left Fight Stance. Then repeat 10 times while starting in a right Fight Stance.

8 양발 이중 앞뒤 교환 (왼족, 오른쪽)

선 자세에서 양발을 어깨넓이로 벌려 양손은 살짝 주먹을 쥐고 한손은 눈높이 한 뼘 간격에 두고 다른 손은 옆 턱 반 주먹 사이로 벌려 붙이고 양발을 어깨 넓이로 벌리고 동시에 몸을 뛰어 양발을 양쪽으로 이중 교환하며 자세를 바꾸어 반복 뛰기.

Switch Double Step:

Begin in a left Fight Stance.

Slightly bend your legs and shift your weight into your right leg. Then hop up and twist your upper body and hips 180 degrees towards the left. Land onto your left leg and put your balance into it. Once you have landed with your left foot, set your right foot down onto the floor. You should end up in a right Fight Stance.

Now in a right Fight Stance, slightly bend your legs and shift your weight into your leftg leg. Then hop up and twist your upper body and hips 180 degrees towards the right. Land onto your right leg and put your balance into it. Once you have landed with your right foot, set your left foot down onto the floor. You should end up back into a left Fight Stance. Repeat 10 times while starting in a left Fight Stance. Then repeat 10 times while starting in a right Fight Stance.

Punching Techniques
권 | 술

01. 직선 잽 (왼쪽, 오른쪽): Straight Jab (Left, Right)

02. 직선 주먹치기 (왼쪽, 오른쪽): Straight Cross (Left, Right)

03. 주먹 훅 (왼쪽, 오른쪽): Fist Hook (Left, Right)

04. 주먹 어퍼컷 (왼쪽, 오른쪽): Fist Uppercut (Left, Right)

05. 주먹 스윙 (왼쪽, 오른쪽): Swing Punch (Left, Right)

06. 정권 손등치기 (왼쪽, 오른쪽): Back Knuckle Strike (Left, Right)

07. 수도 치기 (왼쪽, 오른쪽): Knife Hand Chop (Left, Right)

08. 간수 찌르기 (왼쪽, 오른쪽): Spear Hand Stab (Left, Right)

09. 수장 치기 (왼쪽, 오른쪽): Palm Strike (Left, Right)

10. 밤알 지르기 (왼쪽, 오른쪽): Chestnut Fist Punch (L. R.)

11. 팔꿈치 훅 (왼쪽, 오른쪽): Elbow Hook (L. R.)

12. 팔꿈치 어퍼컷 (왼쪽, 오른쪽): Elbow Uppercut (L. R.)

13. 2번–10번 연결 펀치: 2-10 Punch Combination

1. 잽 펀치

공격 자세에서 왼쪽 주먹은 눈높이로 눈에서 손 한뼘 간격으로 띄우고 오른쪽 주먹은 오른쪽 턱 주먹 간격으로 올려놓고 오른쪽 팔굽은 옆구리에 붙이고 왼쪽 앞발에 중심을 두고 왼쪽 정권을 직선으로 가볍게 친다.

Straight Jab:

Guard up and stand ready in a fighting stance. Keep both of your elbows pointing down and protect the vital areas of your body. Apply pressure into the ball of your lead foot. Remain relaxed and quickly strike your opponent with the lead arm by extending your arm straight out at your target in a snapping motion. During your attack, quickly twist your hips and shoulders into your strike while pivoting on the ball of your lead foot. Also during the extension of your jab, slightly twist the arm and rotate the fist inward until your knuckles are horizontal. Align your middle knuckle, wrist, arm, and shoulder straight as you fully extend your jab. At the moment of contact with your target, clench your fist and deliver tension into your arm, wrist, and shoulder. Your intent should be to deliver your attack in a snapping motion and hitting your target with the front of the index and middle knuckle of your fist. Immediately after you hit your target, relax your arm and quickly retract it back into the guard.

2. 정권 직선펀치

공격 자세에서 왼쪽 주먹은 눈높이로 눈에서 손 한뼘 간격으로 띄우고 오른쪽 주먹은 오른쪽 턱 주먹 간격으로 올려놓고 오른쪽 팔굽은 옆구리에 붙이고 오른쪽 뒷발에 중심을 두고 뒷발을 앞으로 밀며 왼쪽으로 허리를 틀면서 오른쪽 정권을 직선으로 친다.

Straight Cross:

Guard up and stand ready in a fighting stance. Keep both of your elbows pointing down and protect the vital areas of your body. Slightly bend your legs and apply pressure into the ball of your back foot. Remain relaxed and propel your body forward by pushing off the ground with your back leg. At the same time, strike your opponent with your rear hand by extending your punching arm straight out at your opponent while rotating your hips and shoulders into your attack. Slightly pivot on the balls of your feet during the rotation of your body. As you extend your arm out to punch, slightly twist your arm and rotate your fist inward until your knuckles are horizontal. At the moment of contact with your target, clench your fist and deliver tension into your arm, wrist, and shoulder. Your intent should be to deliver your attack in a whipping motion and hit your target with the front of the index and middle knuckle of your fist. Immediately after you hit your target, relax your arm and quickly retract it back into the guard while rotating your body back into a fighting stance.

3. 주먹 훅

공격 자세에서 양쪽 주먹은 턱 높이로 턱에서 주먹 간격으로 띄우고 양쪽 팔굽은 옆구리에 붙이고 왼발에 중심을 두고 밀며 오른쪽으로 허리를 틀면서 왼쪽 정권으로 훅을 친다.

Fist Hook:

Guard up and stand ready in a fighting stance. Apply pressure into the ball of the foot of the side you intend to hook with while slightly shifting your weight into that leg. Slightly twist your body towards that side. Position the fist of your hooking arm level with your nose and extend it out until your arm is half way bent. Keep your wrist straight. Raise the elbow of your hooking arm out to the side until your forearm is horizontal, and rotate your fist until your knuckles are vertical and the back of your hand is facing out.

Tighten your abdominal while keeping the rest of your body relaxed. Strike your target with your fist by hooking your arm at a horizontal angle while at the same time, rotating your hips and shoulders into your attack. Pivoting on the ball of your foot of the side you are hooking off of. Your intent should be to deliver your attack in a twisting motion and hit your target with the front of the index and middle knuckle of your fist. Immediately after you hit your target, relax your arm and quickly retract it back into the guard while rotating your body back into a fighting stance.

권술: Punching Techniques

4. 어퍼컷 펀치

공격 자세에서 양쪽 주먹은 턱 높이로 턱에서 주먹 간격으로 띄우고
양쪽 팔굽은 옆구리에 붙이고 왼발에 중심을 두고 무릎을 접었다 세우면서 오른쪽으로 허리를 틀어 왼쪽 정권으로 어퍼컷을 친다.

Fist Uppercut:

Guard up and stand ready in a fighting stance. Keep both elbows pointing down and remember to protect the vital areas of your body. Apply pressure into the ball of your lead foot. Remain relaxed and slightly bend both of your legs while shifting your weight to your lead leg. Slightly dip your lead shoulder and extend your lead arm out in a 90-degree angle so that your forearm is vertical. Twist your fist and wrist until your index knuckle and thumb is facing out while pivoting on the balls of your feet and rotating your hips and shoulders inward.

As you are rotating your body, extend your legs and push off the ball of your lead foot while extending your back and chest while driving your fist straight up and through your target. Your goal should be to hit your target with the front of your index and middle knuckle of your fist. Clench your fist and deliver tension into your arm, wrist, and back at the moment of contact with your target. As soon as you hit your target, quickly retract your arm back into the guard and rotate your body back into a fighting stance.

권술: Punching Techniques

5. 스윙 펀치

공격 자세에서 양쪽 주먹은 턱 높이로 턱에서 주먹 간격으로 띄우고 양쪽 팔굽은 옆구리에 붙이고 왼발에 중심을 두고 밀며 오른쪽으로 허리를 틀면서 왼쪽 정권을 길게 내어 스윙 펀치를 한다.

Swing Punch:

Guard up and stand ready in a fighting stance. Apply pressure into the ball of your lead foot and slightly lean your body towards your backside. Extend your lead arm semi straight and twist your wrist inward until your fist is at a downward angle. At the same time, tighten your abdominals while keeping the rest of your body relaxed and quickly rotate your hips and shoulders inward while pivoting on the ball of your lead foot.

Swing your lead arm straight across horizontally and through your target at the same time you rotate your body. Your goal should be to hit your target with the top corner of the index knuckle of your fist. Clench your fist and deliver tension into your arm, chest, and waist at the moment of contact with your target. As soon as your swinging arm hits your target, quickly retract your arm back into the guard.

권술: Punching Techniques

6. 정권 손등펀치

공격 자세에서 양쪽 주먹은 턱 높이로 턱에서 주먹 간격으로 띄우고 양쪽 팔굽은 옆구리에 붙이고 왼발에 중심을 두고 몸을 앞으로 옆으로 뒤로 틀면서 팔굽 인대를 당겨 손등정권 편치를 한다.

Back Knuckle Punch:

Guard up and stand ready in a fighting stance. Apply pressure into the ball of your lead foot and slightly lean your body inward towards your chest. Extend your lead arm semi straight and move your lead forearm across your face. At the same time, tighten your abdominals while keeping the rest of your body relaxed and quickly rotate your hips and shoulders outward while pivoting on the balls of your feet. Snap your fist back towards your target.

Your goal should be to hit your target with the back of the index and middle knuckle of your fist. Clench your fist and deliver tension into your arm, chest, and waist at the moment of contact with your target. As soon as your swinging arm hits your target, quickly retract your arm back into the guard.

7. 수도 치기
공격 자세에서 양발에 중심을 두고 왼손엄지를 안으로 오므려 검지에 붙이고 나머지 손가락도 붙이며 아래 앞 양옆 뒤로 손 옆날(척골)에 기를 모아 수도 치기를 한다.

Knife Hand Chop:
Guard up and stand ready in a fighting stance. Apply pressure into the ball of the foot of the side you intend to hook with while slightly shifting your weight into that leg. Slightly twist your body towards that side. Lock the fingers of your left hand straight and together so that your hand is rigid. Position the palm of your hand up and extend your arm until your arms is half way straight.

Twist your torso inward while moving your hand horizontally across in a chopping motion. Strike your target from the using the outer edge of your hand. Tighten your abdomen, chest, forearm, and wrist at the moment of impact. After you chop your target, quickly retract your hands and body back into a fighting stance.

8. 간수 찌르기

공격 자세에서 양발에 중심을 두고 왼쪽 엄지를 안으로 오므려 검지에 붙이고 검지 장지 약지를 가지런히 붙이고 새끼지는 약지에 붙여 아래 앞 양옆 뒤로 손끝에 기를 모아 간수 찌르기를 한다.

Spear Hand Stab:

Guard up and stand ready in a fighting stance. Open your attacking hand and stiffen your fingers straight. Touch the tip of your index and ring finger together and rest your middle finger on top. Curve tip of your middle finger so that the ends of your index, middle, and ring finger are of equal length and the tips conjoin at one point. Bend the thumb and tuck it under the palm of the hand. Keep your fingers tight and together.

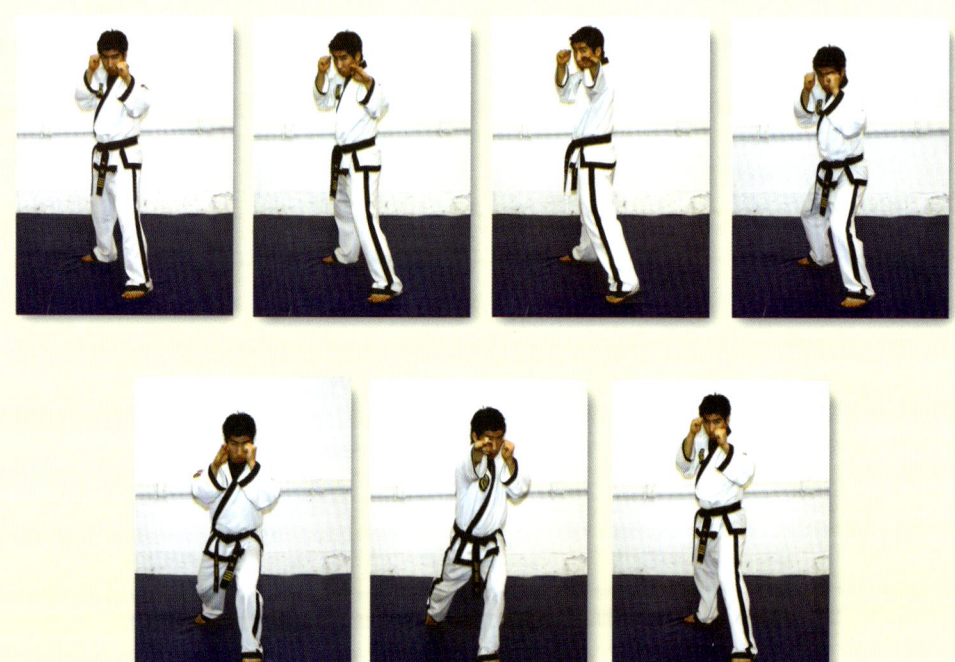

This finger arrangement is called the spear hand. Keep your wrist and fingers straight with your forearm and strike your target in a jabbing motion. Hit your intended target with the combined tips of your index, middle, and ring finger. This strike is most effective when striking your opponent's eye or throat.

권술: Punching Techniques

9. 수장 펀치

공격 자세에서 양발에 중심을 두고 왼쪽 손목을 뒤로 제쳐 손바닥과 팔목 관절에 기를 모아 아래 앞 양옆으로 수장 펀치를 한다.

Palm Strike:

Guard up and stand ready in a fighting stance. Apply pressure into the balls of your feet. Open and expose the palm of your hand you will intend to strike with. Curl your thumb and fingers and bend your wrist back. Remain relaxed and propel your body forward by pushing off the ground with your legs.

At the same time, rotate your hips and shoulders into your attack while pivoting on the balls of your feet. Extend your striking arm and hit your target with the bottom center of the palm of your hand while you rotate your body. As soon as you strike your opponent, quickly retract your hand back into the guard while rotating your body back into a fighting stance.

권술: Punching Techniques

10. 밤알 지르기

장지 손가락을 접어 검지와 약지 손가락 둘째 관절마디에 장지의 첫째 관절 마디를 붙이고 장지의 둘째 관절 마디를 돌출시켜 주먹을 쥐고 밤알을 만들어 지르기를 한다.

Chestnut Fist Punch :

Guard up and stand ready in a fighting stance. Apply pressure into the balls of your feet. Clench your punching hand into a fist but have the middle knuckle of your middle finger protruding out. Roll the tips of your fingers into your fist and squeeze your fingers together.

Tuck your thumb under your fist and across your index finger to reinforce the fist. Strike your opponent in the center of their sternum using the tip of the middle knuckle of your middle finger. Turn your hips and body into your punch.

권술: Punching Techniques

11. 팔꿈치 훅

공격 자세에서 양발에 중심을 두고 양 주먹을 양 턱에 붙이고 허리를 시계 방향으로 돌리면서 왼쪽 팔 굽 관절로 몸을 옆으로 틀어 팔꿈치로 훅을 친다.

Elbow Hook:

Guard up and stand ready in a fighting stance. Apply pressure into the ball of your leading feet. Flex your abdomen while turning your body and hips inward while pivoting on the balls of your leading foot. Raise your arm up and bend it so that the point of your elbow is sharp.

Keep your chin down while maintaining a guard with your right fist. Hook your elbow and hit your target by whipping your upper body with your hips. Hit your target with the front corner of your elbow.

권술: Punching Techniques

12. 팔꿈치어퍼컷

공격 자세에서 양발에 중심을 두고 양 주먹을 양 턱에 붙이고 허리를 시계 방향으로 돌리면서 왼쪽 팔 굽 관절로 몸을 옆으로 틀어 팔꿈치를 위로 들어올려 어퍼컷을 친다.

Elbow Uppercut:

Guard up and stand ready in a fighting stance. Slightly bend your knees and apply pressure into the ball of your leading feet. Slightly dip your upper body downward and move your lead hand across

your face. Keep your arm bent tightly and raise the point of your striking elbow upward to your target as you flex your abdomen and push off the ground with your lead leg. Extend your lead leg and body while turning your hips and body inward.

권술: Punching Techniques

13. 2번-10번 연결 펀치: **2-10 Punch Combination**

장소: 얼굴
Target: Face

2번 연속: 왼쪽 쨉 / 왼쪽 직선 펀치
2 Punch Combination: L. Jab / L. Straight Punch

3번 연속: 왼쪽 쨉 / 왼쪽 직선 펀치 / 오른쪽 직선 펀치
3 Punch Combination: L. Jab / L. Straight Punch / R. Straight Punch

4번 연속: 왼쪽 잽 / 왼쪽 직선 펀치 / 오른쪽 직선 펀치 / 왼쪽 훅
4 Punch Combination: L. Jab / L. Straight Punch / R. Straight Punch / L. Hook

5번연속: 왼쪽 잽 / 왼쪽 직선 펀치 / 오른쪽 직선 펀치 / 왼쪽 훅 / 오른쪽 훅
5 Punch Combination: L. Jab / L. Straight Punch / R. Straight Punch / L. Hook / R. Hook

권술: Punching Techniques

6번 연속: 왼쪽 쨉 / 왼쪽 직선 펀치 / 오른쪽 직선 펀치 / 왼쪽 훅 / 오른쪽 훅 / 왼쪽 어퍼컷
6 Punch Combination: L. Jab / L. Straight Punch / R. Straight Punch / L. Hook / R. Hook / L.Uppercut

7번 연속: 왼쪽 잽 / 왼쪽 직선 펀치 / 오른쪽 직선 펀치 / 왼쪽 훅 / 오른쪽 훅 / 왼쪽 어퍼컷 / 오른쪽 어퍼컷

7 Punch Combination: L. Jab / L. Straight Punch / R. Straight Punch / L. Hook / R. Hook / L. Uppercut / R. Uppercut

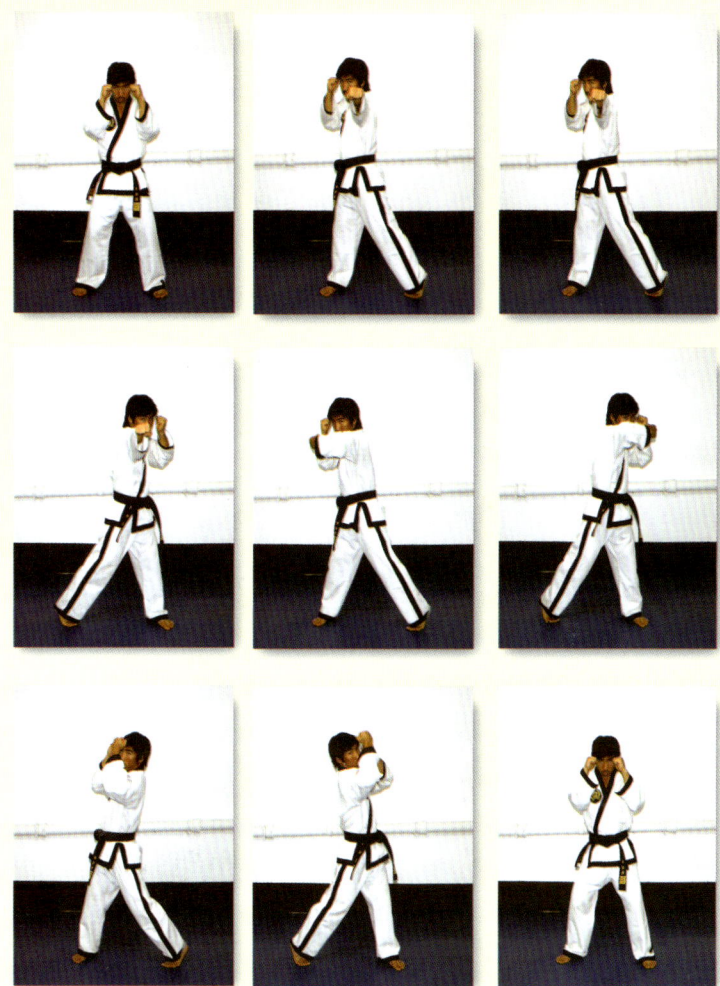

권술: Punching Techniques

Chapter 13

8번 연속: 왼쪽 잽 / 왼쪽 직선 펀치 / 오른쪽 직선 펀치 / 왼쪽 훅 /
오른쪽 훅 / 왼쪽 어퍼컷 / 오른쪽 어퍼컷 / 왼쪽 훅
8 Punch Combination: L. Jab / L. Straight Punch / R. Straight Punch /
L. Hook / R. Hook / L. Uppercut / R. Uppercut / L. Hook

9번 연속: 왼쪽 잽 / 왼쪽 직선 펀치 / 오른쪽 직선 펀치 / 왼쪽 훅 / 오른쪽 훅 / 왼쪽 어퍼컷 / 오른쪽 어퍼컷 / 왼쪽 훅 / 왼쪽 직선 펀치
9 Punch Combination: L. Jab / L. Straight Punch / R. Straight Punch / L. Hook / R. Hook / L. Uppercut / R. Uppercut / L. Hook / L. Straight Punch

권술: Punching Techniques

10번 연속: 왼쪽 잽 / 왼쪽 직선 펀치 / 오른쪽 직선 펀치 / 왼쪽 훅 /
오른쪽 훅 / 왼쪽 어퍼컷 / 오른쪽 어퍼컷 / 왼쪽 훅 / 왼쪽 직선 펀치 / 오른쪽 직선 펀치
10 Punch Combination: L. Jab / L. Straight Punch / R. Straight Punch / L. Hook /
R. Hook / L. Uppercut / R. Uppercut / L. Hook / L. Straight Punch / R. Straight

권술: Punching Techniques

Kicking Techniques
족 | 술

01. 앞 차기 (하단, 중단, 상단) (왼쪽, 오른쪽):
    Front Kick (Low, Middle, High) (Left, Right)

02. 앞 뒤축 차기):
    High Front Heel Kick

03. 옆 차기 (하단, 중단, 상단) (왼쪽, 오른쪽):
    Side Kick (Low, Middle, High) (Left, Right)

04. 돌려차기 (하단, 중단, 상단) (왼쪽, 오른쪽):
    Roundhouse Kick (Low, Middle, High) (Left, Right)

05. 반대 돌려차기 (하단, 중단) (왼쪽, 오른쪽):
    Reverse Roundhouse Kick (Low, Middle) (Left, Right)

06. 바깥 뒤축 훅 차기 (중단, 상단) (왼쪽, 오른쪽):
    Heel Hook Kick (Low, Middle) (Left, Right)

07. 앞 무릎차기 (왼쪽, 오른쪽):
    Forward Thrusting Knee Kick

08. 뒤축 앞 내려찍기 (왼쪽, 오른쪽):
    Chop Axe Kick (Left, Right)

09. 이중 앞차기 (왼쪽, 오른쪽):
    Jumping Fake Front Kick (Left, Right)

10. 가위 발 앞차기 (왼쪽, 오른쪽):
    Jumping Front Split Kick (Left, Right)

11. 회전 돌려차기 (왼쪽, 오른쪽):
    Spinning Heel Hook Kick (Left, Right)

12. 초승달 뒤축 안 찍기 (왼쪽, 오른쪽):
    Inward Crescent Kick (Left, Right)

13. 초승달 뒤축 밭 찍기 (왼쪽, 오른쪽):
    Outward Crescent Kick (Left, Right)

14. 아래 뒤축 회전차기 (왼쪽, 오른쪽):
    Low Spinning Heel Kick (Left, Right)

15. 뒤 뒤축 차기 (왼쪽, 오른쪽):
    Back Heel Kick (Left, Right)

16. 뛰며 한발 옆차기 (왼쪽, 오른쪽):
    Jumping Side Kick (Left, Right)

17. 이단 한발 앞차기 (왼쪽, 오른쪽):
    Jumping Front Kick (Left, Right)

18. 이단 한발 돌려차기 (왼쪽, 오른쪽):
    Jump Spinning Heel Hook Kick (Left, Right)

19. 이중 돌려차기 (왼쪽, 오른쪽):
    Jump Spinning Roundhouse Kick (Left, Right)

1. 앞 차기 (하단, 중단, 상단)

선 자세에서 양 주먹을 턱까지 올려놓고 오른쪽 발가락을 앞으로 하고 한발 앞으로 옮겨 놓으면서 중심은 오른쪽 다리에 두고 왼쪽 다리를 들어 앞 차기를 한다.

Front Kick:

(Left)

Begin in a Front Stance.

Take a step forward with your right leg. Lift your left knee up to your target's level. Extend your left leg in a kicking motion towards your target. Ensure that your toes are curled back and your foot is flexed when you kick and strike your target using the balls of your left foot. Return your left leg back to its original position after kicking your target. Then step back with your right leg and return back to a Front Stance.

Low

Middle

High

족술: Kicking Techniques

(Right)
Begin in a Front Stance.
Take a step forward with your left leg. Lift your right knee up to your target's level. Extend your right leg in a kicking motion towards your target. Ensure that your toes are curled back and your foot is flexed when you kick and strike your target using the balls of your left foot. Return your right leg back to its original position after kicking your target. Then step back with your left leg and return back to a Front Stance.

Low

Middle

High

족술: Kicking Techniques

2. 앞 뒤축 차기

선 자세에서 양 주먹을 턱까지 올려놓고 오른쪽 발가락을 앞으로 하고 한발 앞으로 옮겨 놓으면서 중심은 오른쪽 다리에 두고 왼쪽 다리를 들어 뒤축으로 앞 차기를 한다.

High Front Heel Kick:

(Left)

Begin in a Front Stance.

Take a step forward with your right leg and shift your weight into that leg. Lift and bend your left leg and bring that knee in toward your body. Then kick with your left leg straight up vertically and pull the left foot back so that you strike under your opponent's chin using the heel of the foot. Maintain your balance and guard. After kicking with the left leg, step with your left leg, then right leg back to your original Front Stance position.

(Right)
Begin in a Front Stance.
Take a step forward with your left leg and shift your weight into that leg. Lift and bend your right leg and bring that knee in toward your body. Then kick with your right leg straight up vertically and pull the right foot back so that you strike under your opponent°Øs chin using the heel of the foot. Maintain your balance and guard. After kicking with the right leg, step with your right leg, then left leg back to your original Front Stance position.

3. 옆 차기 (하단, 중단, 상단)

선 자세에서 양 주먹을 턱 까지 올려놓고 오른쪽 발가락을 오른쪽으로 돌려 한발 앞으로 옮겨 놓으면서 중심은 오른쪽 다리에 두고 왼쪽 다리를 들어 다리와 허리를 일직선으로 옆 차기를 한다.

Side Kick:

(Left)

Begin in a Front Stance.

Take a step forward with your right foot in a side position by twisting your foot 90 degrees in a clockwise direction. By doing so, your right foot should be perpendicular to your left foot. Simultaneously, turn your hips and torso with your foot towards the right in a clockwise direction until your body is sideways. Lift your left knee and bring it in towards your stomach and align your left heel with the side of your left hip. Extend your left leg out while keeping your hips and back straight and aligned with each other. Curve your left ankle back and tilt your foot down so that the side of your left heel pointed and exposed to your target. At the moment of impact with your target and heel, flex your ankle and foot while keeping your heel aligned with your leg, hips, and back. Return your left leg back to its original position after kicking your target. Then step back with your right leg and return back to a Front Stance.

Low

Middle

High

족술: Kicking Techniques

(Right)
Begin in a Front Stance.
Take a step forward with your left foot in a side position by twisting your foot 90 degrees in a counter-clockwise direction. By doing so, your left foot should be perpendicular to your right foot. Simultaneously, turn your hips and torso with your foot towards the left in a counter-clockwise direction until your body is sideways. Lift your right knee and bring it in towards your stomach and align your right heel with the side of your right hip. Extend your right leg out while keeping your hips and back straight and aligned with each other. Curve your right ankle back and tilt your foot down so that the side of your right heel pointed and exposed to your target. At the moment of impact with your target and heel, flex your ankle and foot while keeping your heel aligned with your leg, hips, and back. Return your right leg back to its original position after kicking your target. Then step back with your left leg and return back to a Front Stance.

Low

Middle

High

족술: Kicking Techniques

4. 돌려차기 (하단, 중단, 상단)

선 자세에서 양 주먹을 턱 까지 올려놓고 오른쪽 발가락을 오른쪽으로 돌려 한발 앞으로 옮겨 놓으면서 중심은 오른쪽 다리에 두고 왼쪽 다리를 들어 허리를 오른쪽으로 돌리면서 돌려차기를 한다.

Roundhouse Kick:

(Left)

Begin in a Front Stance.

Take a step forward with your right foot in a side position by twisting your foot 90 degrees in a clockwise direction. By doing so, your right foot should be perpendicular to your left foot. Lift your left knee while turning your hips towards the right in a clockwise direction so that your body is sideways. Align your left thigh with your hips. Raise your left foot level with your left knee so that your shin is horizontal and parallel with the ground. Curl the toes of your left foot and curve your ankle so that your foot is at a 90 degree angle with your leg. Extend your left leg and kick your target at a side angle. During your kick, simultaneously pivot on the ball of your right foot while twisting your hips with your kick and twist your upper body counter-clockwise in the opposite direction as your kick. Flex your ankle and foot at the moment of impact and strike your target using the ball of your foot in a twisting and whipping motion. Return your left leg back to its original position after kicking your target. Then step back with your right leg and return back into a Front Stance.

Low

Middle

High

족술: Kicking Techniques

Chapter 03

(Right)

Begin in a Front Stance.

Take a step forward with your left foot in a side position by twisting your foot 90 degrees in a counter-clockwise direction. By doing so, your left foot should be perpendicular to your right foot. Lift your right knee while turning your hips towards the left in a clockwise direction so that your body is sideways. Align your left thigh with your hips. Raise your left foot level with your right knee so that your shin is horizontal and parallel with the ground. Curl the toes of your right foot and curve your ankle so that your foot is at a 90 degree angle with your leg. Extend your right leg and kick your target at a side angle. During your kick, simultaneously pivot on the ball of your left foot while twisting your hips with your kick and twist your upper body clockwise in the opposite direction as your kick. Flex your ankle and foot at the moment of impact and strike your target using the ball of your foot in a twisting and whipping motion. Return your right leg back to its original position after kicking your target. Then step back with your left leg and return back into a Front Stance.

Low

Middle

High

족술: Kicking Techniques

5. 반대 돌려차기 (하단, 중단)

선 자세에서 양 주먹을 턱 까지 올려놓고 오른쪽 발가락을 왼쪽으로 돌려 한발 앞으로 옮겨 놓으면서 중심은 오른쪽 다리에 두고 왼쪽 다리를 들어 허리를 왼쪽으로 틀면서 반대 돌려차기를 한다.

Reverse Roundhouse Kick:

(Left)

Begin in a Front Stance.

Take a step forward towards the right corner with your right leg and slightly turn your shoulders towards the right in a clockwise direction. Lift your left foot and raise it up so that your left knee is pointing towards the left and your left shin is at an angle. Arch and tilt your ankle back. Also curl your toes back and flex your foot. Extend your left leg and kick your target using the ball of your left foot by curving your body and leg towards the left while slightly twisting your body counter-clockwise into the direction of your kick. Return your left leg back to its original position after kicking your target. Then step back with your right leg and return back to a Front Stance.

Low

Middle

(Right)
Begin in a Front Stance.
Take a step forward towards the left corner with your left leg and slightly turn your shoulders towards the right in a counter-clockwise direction. Lift your right foot and raise it up so that your right knee is pointing towards the right and your right shin is at an angle. Arch and tilt your ankle back. Also curl your toes back and flex your foot. Extend your right leg and kick your target using the ball of your right foot by curving your body and leg towards the right while slightly twisting your body clockwise into the direction of your kick. Return your right leg back to its original position after kicking your target. Then step back with your left leg and return back to a Front Stance.

Low

Middle

6. 바깥 뒤축 훅 차기 (중단, 상단)

선 자세에서 양 주먹을 턱 까지 올려놓고, 오른쪽 발가락을 오른쪽 90도로 돌려 옮겨 놓으면서 중심은 오른발에 두고 왼발을 들어 왼쪽으로 바깥 뒤축 훅 돌려차기를 한다.

Heel Hook Kick:

(Left)

Begin in a Front Stance.
Take a step forward with your right foot in a side position by twisting your foot 90 degrees in a clockwise direction. By doing so, your right foot should be perpendicular to your left foot. Simultaneously, turn your hips and torso with your foot towards the right in a clockwise direction until your body is sideways. Lift your left knee and bring it in towards your stomach and align your left heel with the side of your left hip. Curve your left ankle back and tilt your foot down so that the side of your left heel is pointed and exposed to your target. Extend your left leg out slightly towards the right and then hook your foot sharply at a 90 degree angle sideways towards the left horizontally. As you hook your leg across towards the left, simultaneously twist your upper body clockwise in the opposite direction as your kick. Flex your ankle and hit your target using the back of your heel. Return your left leg back to its original position after kicking your target. Then step back with your right leg and return back to a Front Stance.

Middle

High

족술: Kicking Techniques

(Right)
Begin in a Front Stance.
Take a step forward with your left foot in a side position by twisting your foot 90 degrees in a counter-clockwise direction. By doing so, your left foot should be perpendicular to your right foot. Simultaneously, turn your hips and torso with your foot towards the left in a counter-clockwise direction until your body is sideways. Lift your left knee and bring it in towards your stomach and align your right heel with the side of your right hip. Curve your right ankle back and tilt your foot down so that the side of your right heel is pointed and exposed to your target. Extend your right leg out slightly towards the left and then hook your foot sharply at a 90 degree angle sideways towards the right horizontally. As you hook your leg across towards the right, simultaneously twist your upper body counter-clockwise in the opposite direction as your kick. Flex your ankle and hit your target using the back of your heel. Return your right leg back to its original position after kicking your target. Then step back with your left leg and return back to a Front Stance.

Middle

High

7. 앞 무릎차기

선 자세에서 양 주먹을 아래턱 까지 올려놓고 오른쪽 발가락을 앞으로 하고 한발 앞으로 옮기면서 중심은 오른발에 두고, 양손으로 상대의 어깨를 잡고 앞으로 당기면서 왼쪽 무릎으로 차기를 한다.

Forward Thrusting Knee Kick:

(Left)

Begin in a Front Stance.

Take a step forward with your right leg. Grab your with both hands. Bend your left leg and thrust your knee into your opponent using the point of your knee by driving your hips forward while simultaneously pulling your opponent into your knee using your arms and abdomen. Return your left leg back to its original position after kneeing your target. Then step back with your right leg and return back to a Front Stance.

(Right)

Begin in a Front Stance.

Take a step forward with your left leg. Grab your with both hands. Bend your right leg and thrust your knee into your opponent using the point of your knee by driving your hips forward while simultaneously pulling your opponent into your knee using your arms and abdomen. Return your right leg back to its original position after kneeing your target. Then step back with your left leg and return back to a Front Stance.

족술: Kicking Techniques

8. 뒤축 찍기

선 자세에서 양 주먹을 턱 까지 올려놓고 오른쪽 발가락을 앞으로 하고 한발 앞으로 옮기면서 중심은 오른 발에 두고 왼발을 앞으로 당겨 위로 높이들고 뒤축으로 내려찍기를 한다.

Chopping Axe Kick:

(Left)

Begin in a Front Stance.

Take a step with your left leg and lift your knee up into your chest. Raise your left foot up as high as you can. When your leg is semi straight, swing your left leg downward in a chopping manner by straightening your hips and back while swinging your leg down. Pull your foot back while flexing it and tilt your foot inward at an angle so that you come down at your target and strike it using the back corner of the heel of your foot. Once you have hit your target, take a step back and return to a Front Stance.

(Right)

Begin in a Front Stance.

Take a step with your right leg and lift your knee up into your chest. Raise your right foot up as high as you can. When your leg is semi straight, swing your right leg downward in a chopping manner by straightening your hips and back while swinging your leg down. Pull your foot back while flexing it and tilt your foot inward at an angle so that you come down at your target and strike it using the back corner of the heel of your foot. Once you have hit your target, take a step back and return to a Front Stance.

족술: Kicking Techniques

9. 이단 앞차기

선 자세에서 양 주먹을 턱 까지 올려놓고 왼쪽 발가락을 앞으로 하고 한발 앞으로 옮기면서 오른발을 위로 들었다가 바닥에 내려 닿는 순간 위로 뛰어 왼발 앞차기를 한다.

Jumping Fake Front Kick:

(Left)

Begin in a Front Stance.

Take a step forward with your right leg and lift your left knee up. Fake a left Front Kick with your left leg. Then jump off your right leg and land on your left leg while simultaneously bringing your right knee up. When you are in mid air, kick your target by extending your right leg out to your target. Pull the toes of your right foot back and flex your foot so that you hit your target using the ball of your foot. Step back and return to a Front Stance after delivering your kick.

(Right)

Begin in a Front Stance.

Take a step forward with your left leg and lift your right knee up. Fake a right Front Kick with your right leg. Then jump off your left leg and land on your right leg while simultaneously bringing your left knee up. When you are in mid air, kick your target by extending your left leg out to your target. Pull the toes of your left foot back and flex your foot so that you hit your target using the ball of your foot. Step back and return to a Front Stance after delivering your kick.

족술: Kicking Techniques

10. 가위발 앞차기

선 자세에서 양 주먹을 턱 까지 올려놓고 양 무릎을 아래로 구부렸다가 뛰면서 양발을 벌려 가위발로 앞차기를 한다.

Jumping Front Split Kick:

Begin in a Front Stance.

Take a step forward and jump up into the air. Bend your knees and raise them up to waist level when you are in mid air. When you are in the air, kick your legs out at an angle to where your legs are split from each other. Pull your toes back and flex your feet so that you hit your targets with the balls of your feet. Try to time the kick so that you hit your target when you are at the peak of your jump. After hitting your target, land with both feet and step back into a Front Stance.

11. 회전 돌려차기

선 자세에서 양 주먹을 턱 까지 올려놓고 오른쪽 발가락을 왼쪽360도로 돌려 옮겨 놓으면서 중심은 오른 발에 두고 왼발을 들어 왼쪽으로 360도 돌려 뒤축 돌려차기를 한다.

Spinning Heel Hook Kick:

(Left)

Begin in a Front Stance.

Take a step with your right leg in front of your left foot and transfer your weight into your right leg. Lift your left knee up into your stomach and spin your body towards the left in a counter-clockwise direction while pivoting on either the heel or ball of your right foot. Keep eye contact with your target by looking over your right shoulder. Continue to look over your right shoulder until you have spun your body 180degrees and until you cannot see your target. Then turn your head towards the left and glance at your target by looking over your left shoulder. Continue to spin the body in the counter-clockwise direction to increase momentum. When you have spun the body 290 degrees, extend your left leg and hook your foot horizontally across and through your target. Execute a left Heel Hook Kick while spinning the body and pivoting on your right foot. Pull the left foot back and tilt your foot downward so that when you strike, you hit your target using the back corner of your heel. If the kick is done in a smooth and balanced motion, the momentum created by the spin should help to deliver power in your kick. Continue the spin and use the momentum to help your body spin your left leg around and into a right Fight Stance. The kick is complete when your body has spun 360degrees. Then take a step back with your right leg and return to a Front Stance.

(Right)
Begin in a Front Stance.
Take a step with your left leg in front of your right foot and transfer your weight into your left leg. Lift your right knee up into your stomach and spin your body towards the right in a clockwise direction while pivoting on either the heel or ball of your left foot. Keep eye contact with your target by looking over your left shoulder. Continue to look over your left shoulder until you have spun your body 180degrees and until you cannot see your target. Then turn your head towards the right and glance at your target by looking over your right shoulder. Continue to spin the body in the clockwise direction to increase momentum. When you have spun the body 290 degrees, extend your right leg and hook your foot horizontally across and through your target. Execute a right Heel Hook Kick while spinning the body and pivoting on your left foot. Pull the right foot back and tilt your foot downward so that when you strike, you hit your target using the back corner of your heel. If the kick is done in a smooth and balanced motion, the momentum created by the spin should help to deliver power in your kick. Continue the spin and use the momentum to help your body spin your right leg around and into a left Fight Stance. The kick is complete when your body has spun 360degrees. Then take a step back with your left leg and return to a Front Stance.

12. 초승달 안찍기

선 자세에서 양 주먹을 턱 까지 올려놓고 오른쪽 발가락을 앞으로 하고 한발 앞으로 옮기면서 중심은 오른 발에 두고 왼쪽 다리를 앞으로 당겨 위로 높이들어 뒤축으로 안쪽 비스듬히 내려찍기를 한다.

Inward Crescent Kick:

(Left)

Begin in a Front Stance.

Take a step forward with your right leg. Swing your left leg up and around in an arch going clockwise. Tilt your left foot inward so that your left heel is exposed to the right side. When your foot is at the highest point of the arch, come down with your foot at an accelerating rate to your target while simultaneously straightening your back. Hit your target using the heel of your left foot. Once you have hit your target with the kick, step back and return to a Front Stance.

족술: Kicking Techniques

(Right)
Begin in a Front Stance.
Take a step forward with your left leg. Swing your right leg up and around in an arch going counter-clockwise. Tilt your right foot inward so that your right heel is exposed to the left side. When your foot is at the highest point of the arch, come down with your foot at an accelerating rate to your target while simultaneously straightening your back. Hit your target using the heel of your right foot. Once you have hit your target with the kick, step back and return to a Front Stance.

13. 초승달 밭찍기

선 자세에서 양 주먹을 턱 까지 올려놓고 오른쪽 발가락을 앞으로 하고 한발 앞으로 옮기면서 중심은 오른 발에 두고 왼쪽 다리를 앞으로 당겨 위로 높이 들어 뒤축으로 바깥 비스듬히 내려찍기를 한다.

Outward Crescent Kick:

(Left)

Begin in a Front Stance.

Take a step forward with your right leg. Swing your left leg up and around in an arch going counter-clockwise. Flex your left foot back and tilt your foot inward so that your left heel is sharp. When your foot is at the highest point of the arch, come down with your foot at an accelerating rate and hit your target using the heel of your left foot. Once you have hit your target with the kick, step back and return to a Front Stance.

(Right)
Begin in a Front Stance.
Take a step forward with your left leg. Swing your right leg up and around in an arch going clockwise. Flex your right foot back and tilt your foot inward so that your right heel is sharp. When your foot is at the highest point of the arch, come down with your foot at an accelerating rate and hit your target using the heel of your right foot. Once you have hit your target with the kick, step back and return to a Front Stance.

14. 아래 뒤축 회전차기

밑으로 앉으면서 오른손을 오른쪽으로 360도로 돌려 바닥에 집고 왼손은 왼쪽 얼굴 주먹 크기의 간격에 두고 오른쪽 무릎을 바닥에 집고 앉으면서 왼쪽 다리를 왼쪽 회전으로 상대의 무릎 및 발목에 뒤축 돌려차기를 한다.

Low Spinning Heel Hook Kick:

(Left)

Begin in a Front Stance.

Take a step with your right leg in front of your left foot and transfer your weight into your right leg. Bend your knees and crouch down on the floor while turning your body towards the left in a counter-clockwise direction. Place the palm of your right hand on the ground and lean your weight into your right arm. Sit onto your right hip and continue to turn your body in a counter-clockwise direction while looking over your left shoulder to your target. Swing your left leg around towards the left in a counter-clockwise direction and maintain your foot parallel with the ground and hover it across the floor a few inches. Flex your foot back and hit your opponent's ankle using the back of your heel. Whip your body and hips to help create more momentum for your kick during the spin. After your left leg has hit your target, spin back in a clockwise direction while standing up into a right Fight Stance.

(Right)
Begin in a Front Stance.
Take a step with your left leg in front of your right foot and transfer your weight into your left leg. Bend your knees and crouch down on the floor while turning your body towards the right in a clockwise direction. Place the palm of your left hand on the ground and lean your weight into your left arm. Sit onto your left hip and continue to turn your body in a clockwise direction while looking over your right shoulder to your target. Swing your right leg around towards the right in a clockwise direction and maintain your foot parallel with the ground and hover it across the floor a few inches. Flex your foot back and hit your opponent's ankle using the back of your heel. Whip your body and hips to help create more momentum for your kick during the spin. After your right leg has hit your target, spin back in a counter-clockwise direction while standing up into a left Fight Stance.

족술: Kicking Techniques

15. 뒤 뒤축차기

선 자세에서 두 주먹을 아래턱 까지 올려놓고 중심을 오른발에 두고 목을 왼쪽으로 틀면서 동시에 왼쪽 다리를 들어 뒤로 보면서 왼쪽 뒤축차기를 한다.

Back Heel Kick:

(Left)

Begin in a Front Stance.

Take a step forward with your right leg while simultaneously turning your body towards the left in a counter-clockwise direction. Look at your target over your right shoulder while turning your body. Then when you cannot see your target anymore, turn your head towards the left and look over your left shoulder to your target. When your back is exposed to your target, bend your left knee and touch the inner parts of your knees together. Pull your foot back and flex your foot so that the heel of your left foot is pointed. Extend your left leg straight back and kick your target using the heel of your left foot. After kicking your target with your left leg, bring your leg back in and get into a left Fight Stance.

(Right)

Begin in a Front Stance.

Take a step forward with your left leg while simultaneously turning your body towards the right in a clockwise direction. Look at your target over your left shoulder while turning your body. Then when you cannot see your target anymore, turn your head towards the right and look over your right shoulder to your target. When your back is exposed to your target, bend your right knee and touch the inner parts of your knees together. Pull your foot back and flex your foot so that the heel of your right foot is pointed. Extend your right leg straight back and kick your target using the heel of your right foot. After kicking your target with your right leg, bring your leg back in and get into a right Fight Stance.

족술: Kicking Techniques

16. 이단 한발 옆차기
선 자세에서 두 주먹을 아래턱 까지 올려놓고 양쪽 무릎을 아래로 숙였다가 위로 양발을 뛰어 왼발 옆 축으로 옆차기를 한다.

Jumping Side Kick:
(Left)

Begin in a Front stance. Take a step forward with your right leg and slightly turn towards the right. Then take a step forward with your left leg in front of your right. Bend your legs and jump up into the air. In mid air, bring your legs into your body and position them like you would for a left Side Kick. At the peak of your jump, kick your left leg straight out sideways. When kicking, flex your left foot back and tilt it downward so that your right heel is protruding. After executing the kick in mid air, bring your legs back under yourself and land while maintaining balance. Take a step backwards with your left and right leg back into your original position in a Front Stance.

(Right)
Begin in a Front stance. Take a step forward with your left leg and slightly turn towards the left. Then take a step forward with your right leg in front of your left. Bend your legs and jump up into the air. In mid air, bring your legs into your body and position them like you would for a right Side Kick. At the peak of your jump, kick your right leg straight out sideways. When kicking, flex your right foot back and tilt it downward so that your left heel is protruding. After executing the kick in mid air, bring your legs back under yourself and land while maintaining balance. Take a step backwards with your right and left leg back into your original position in a Front Stance.

족술: Kicking Techniques

17. 이단 한발 앞차기

선 자세에서 두 주먹을 아래턱 까지 올려놓고 양쪽 무릎을 아래로 숙였다가 위로 양발을 뛰어 오른 발 앞 축으로 앞차기를 한다.

Jumping Front Kick:

(Left)

Begin in a Front Stance.

Take a step with your left leg. Then jump up into the air and raise your left knee up. While in mid air, snap your left leg out and kick your target with the ball of the foot. Time your attack so that you kick when you are at the highest point of your jump. Kick your target using the ball of your left foot by curling your toes back so that the ball of the foot is exposed and flex your foot. Once you have kicked your target, bend your leg back into our body and prepare to land. After landing, take a step back with your left leg and return to the Front Stance.

(Right)
Begin in a Front Stance.
Take a step with your right leg. Then jump up into the air and raise your right knee up. While in mid air, snap your right leg out and kick your target with the ball of the foot. Time your attack so that you kick when you are at the highest point of your jump. Kick your target using the ball of your right foot by curling your toes back so that the ball of the foot is exposed and flex your foot. Once you have kicked your target, bend your leg back into our body and prepare to land. After landing, take a step back with your right leg and return to the Front Stance.

족술: Kicking Techniques

18. 이단 한발 돌려차기

선 자세에서 두 주먹을 아래턱 까지 올려놓고 양쪽 무릎을 아래로 숙였다가 몸을 위로 뛰어 왼쪽으로 돌면서 왼쪽 앞 축으로 돌려차기를 한다.

Jump Spinning Heel Hook Kick:

(Left)

Begin in a Front Stance.

Take a step with your right leg in front of your left foot and turn your right foot and body towards the left in a counter-clockwise direction. Jump into the air and spin your body counter-clockwise while looking over your left shoulder at your target. Lift your left knee into your stomach and set your leg ready to deliver a left Spinning Heel Hook Kick in mid air. Pull your foot back so that the heel of your left foot is at a sharp point. Snap your foot horizontally across and through your target while in mid air. During your kick, whip your hips and body to create more inertia to your left foot. Land on your right leg and continue to rotate your body around until your left leg swings in a full circle and you are positioned in a left Fight Stance. Take a step back and return to a Front Stance.

(Right)
Begin in a Front Stance.
Take a step with your left leg in front of your right foot and turn your left foot and body towards the right in a clockwise direction. Jump into the air and spin your body clockwise while looking over your left shoulder at your target. Lift your right knee into your stomach and set your leg ready to deliver a right Spinning Heel Hook Kick in mid air. Pull your foot back so that the heel of your right foot is at a sharp point. Snap your foot horizontally across and through your target while in mid air. During your kick, whip your hips and body to create more inertia to your right foot. Land on your left leg and continue to rotate your body around until your right leg swings in a full circle and you are positioned in a right Fight Stance. Take a step back and return to a Front Stance.

족술: Kicking Techniques

19. 이중 돌려차기:

선 자세에서 양 주먹을 아래턱 까지 올려놓고 오른쪽 다리로 앞으로 안 초승달 차기를 하고, 왼쪽다리를 오른쪽 뒤로 돌며 뒤축 돌려차기를 한다.

Jump Spinning Roundhouse Kick:

(Left)

Begin in a Front Stance.

Take a step forward with your left leg and spin your leg and body around towards the right in a clockwise direction. Lift your right knee up when you back is exposed to the front. Continue the spin until you have almost completed a full 360degree. Push off your left leg and hop into the air while whip your hips and upper body around to build momentum. As you are in mid air, simultaneously land onto your right leg while lifting and setting your left leg to kick. Deliver a left Roundhouse Kick to your target while spinning in mid air. After kicking your target, take a step forward with your left leg and get into a left Fight Stance.

(Right)
Begin in a Front Stance.
Take a step forward with your right leg and spin your leg and body around towards the left in a counter-clockwise direction. Lift your left knee up when you back is exposed to the front. Continue the spin until you have almost completed a full 360degree. Push off your left leg and hop into the air while whip your hips and upper body around to build momentum. As you are in mid air, simultaneously land onto your left leg while lifting and setting your right leg to kick. Deliver a right Roundhouse Kick to your target while spinning in mid air. After kicking your target, take a step forward with your right leg and get into a right Fight Stance.

Blocking Techniques
막 | 기 | 술

01. 하단 X 막기: Low X Block

02. 하단 옆 막기 (왼쪽, 오른쪽): Low Side Block (Left, Right)

03. 중단 옆 막기 (왼쪽, 오른쪽): Middle Side Block (Left, Right)

04. 상단 옆 막기 (왼쪽, 오른쪽): High Side Block (Left, Right)

05. 상단 X 막기: High X Block

06. 팔뚝 얼굴 막기 (왼쪽, 오른쪽): Forearm Face Block (Left, Right)

07. 얼굴 홴 막기 (왼쪽, 오른쪽): Inward Fan Block (Left, Right)

08. 하단 풍차돌려 막기 (왼쪽, 오른쪽): Low Sweep Block (Left, Right)

09. 상단 옆 양 손날 막기 (왼쪽, 오른쪽): Inward Chop Block (Left, Right)

10. 얼굴 반대 홴 막기 (왼쪽, 오른쪽): Outward Fan Block (Left, Right)

11. 하단 내려막고 옆막기 (왼쪽, 오른쪽): Low to Side Block (Left, Right)

12. 상단 옆 양 손날 막기 (왼쪽, 오른쪽): High Side Chop Block (Left, Right)

13. 이중 스탭 옆 반대 잡기 (왼쪽, 오른쪽): Step and Outward Fan Block (Left, Right)

1. 하단 X 막기

선 자세에서 양발을 어깨넓이로 벌려 중심을 양다리에 두고 양 주먹을 살짝 쥐고 양 무릎을 접으면서 기마 자세로 몸을 낮추어 양팔을 X로 만들어 아래로 내리면서 양 주먹에 힘을 주면서 앞차기 내려막기

Low X Block:

Begin in a Front Stance position.

Bend your knees and move your hips back while slightly leaning your torso forward for better balance. Extend your arms downward at a 45 degree angle with your body. Cross your arm at the forearms just above your wrists and catch an incoming front kick with your forearms. When blocking the kick, block in a manner so that you strike them on the top of their ankle with your forearms. Return back to the Front Stance after blocking.

2. 하단 옆 막기 (왼쪽, 오른쪽)

(왼쪽)

선 자세에서 양발을 어깨넓이로 벌려 중심을 양다리에 두고 양 주먹을 살짝 쥐고 왼발을 왼쪽으로 돌려 놓으면서 후방자세로 중심을 뒷다리에 두고 손가락을 모두 붙이고 양쪽 손날을 만들어 양다리를 약간 구부리고 왼쪽으로 허리를 틀어 양 손날에 힘을 주면서 바깥 하단 옆막기

Low Side Block:

(Left)

Begin in a Front Stance position.

Lean into your right leg and lift the heel of your left foot. Keep the ball of your left foot on the ground. Slightly slide your left foot in towards the right and get into a left Back Stance. Simultaneously swing your left forearm down towards your left side while turning your torso into the block in a counter-clockwise direction and deflect your opponent's incoming kick using the outer edge of your forearm. Do not completely extend your left elbow. Your right fist should follow your left forearm until it gets to the front of your waist. After executing the left Low Side Block, return to the Front Stance and back to your guard.

(오른쪽)
선 자세에서 양발을 어깨넓이로 벌려 중심을 양다리에 두고 양 주먹을 살짝 쥐고 오른발을 오른쪽으로 돌려 놓으면서 후방자세로 중심을 뒷다리에 두고 손가락을 모두 붙이고 양쪽 손날을 만들어 양다리를 약간 구부리고 오른쪽으로 허리를 틀어 양 손날에 힘을 주면서 바깥 하단 옆막기

(Right)
Begin in a Front Stance position.
Lean into your left leg and lift the heel of your right foot. Keep the ball of your right foot on the ground. Turn your torso towards the right in a clockwise direction. Slightly slide your right foot in towards the left and get into a right Back Stance. Simultaneously swing your right forearm down towards your right side while turning your torso into the block in a clockwise direction and your opponent's incoming kick using the outer edge of your forearm. Do not completely extend your right elbow. Your right fist should follow your left forearm until it gets to the front of your waist. After executing the right Low Side Block, return to the Front Stance and back to your guard.

3. 중단 옆 막기 (왼쪽, 오른쪽)

(왼쪽)

선 자세에서 양발을 어깨넓이로 벌려 중심을 양다리에 두고 양 주먹을 살짝 쥐고 왼발을 왼쪽으로 돌려 놓으면서 중방자세로 중심을 양다리에 두고 손가락을 모두 붙이고 양쪽 손날을 만들어 양다리를 약간 구부리고 왼쪽으로 허리를 틀어 양 손날에 힘을 주면서 바깥 중단 몸통막기

Middle Side Block:

(Left)

Begin in a Front Stance.

Take a step forward towards the left upper corner with your left leg while simultaneously turning your torso slightly towards the left in a counter-clockwise direction. Bend both knees and center your balance between your legs. Get into a left Middle Stance. Clench your fists and extend your left arm out at a 90degree angle towards an incoming attack and twist your wrist until the exterior part of your forearm is facing towards the left corner. Turn your body into the incoming attack and block the attack using the exterior part of your left forearm. Keep your chin down and have your left fist at eye level. Place your right fist next to the inner the part of your left elbow. After executing the Middle Side Block, return to the Front Stance.

(오른쪽)
선 자세에서 양발을 어깨넓이로 벌려 중심을 양다리에 두고 양 주먹을 살짝 쥐고 오른발을 오른쪽으로 돌려 놓으면서 중방자세로 중심을 양다리에 두고 손가락을 모두 붙이고 양쪽 손날을 만들어 양다리를 약간 구부리고 오른쪽으로 허리를 틀어 양 손날에 힘을 주면서 바깥 중단 몸통막기

(Right)
Begin in a Front Stance.
Take a step forward towards the right upper corner with your right leg while simultaneously turning your torso slightly towards the right in a clockwise direction. Bend both knees and center your balance between your legs. Get into a right Middle Stance. Clench your fists and extend your right arm out at a 90degree angle towards an incoming attack and twist your wrist until the exterior part of your forearm is facing towards the right corner. Turn your body into the incoming attack and block the attack using the exterior part of your left forearm. Keep your chin down and have your right fist at eye level. Place your left fist next to the inner the part of your right elbow. After executing the Middle Side Block, return to the Front Stance.

4. 상단 옆 막기 (왼쪽, 오른쪽)

(왼쪽)

선 자세에서 양발을 어깨넓이로 벌려 중심을 양다리에 두고 양 주먹을 살짝 쥐고 왼발을 왼쪽으로 돌려 놓으면서 전방자세로 중심을 앞다리에 두고 양쪽 주먹을 쥐고 왼쪽으로 허리를 틀어 왼쪽 주먹은 눈높이 주먹 간격으로 머리위에 띄우고 오른쪽 주먹은 주먹 간격으로 옆턱을 막고 상단 옆막기

High Side Block:

(Left)

Begin in a Front Stance.

Turn your torso to the left in a counter clockwise direction, and simultaneously step with the left leg out toward the left upper corner and get into a left Forward Stance. In the Forward Stance position, lean forward and bend your left knee so most of your weight is on the left leg. Keep your right leg aligned straight with your spine. With both fists clenched, extend your left arm up and over your head at a 45 degree angle so you are deflecting your opponent's attack coming from above your head with the outer edge of your left forearm. Keep your chin down while looking up towards your opponent and ensure that your right fist is guarding the right side of your face. After executing the left High Side Block, return to the Front Stance.

(오른쪽)
선 자세에서 양발을 어깨넓이로 벌려 중심을 양다리에 두고 양 주먹을 살짝 쥐고 오른발을 오른쪽으로 돌려 놓으면서 전방자세로 중심을 앞다리에 두고 양쪽 주먹을 쥐고 오른쪽으로 허리를 틀어 오른쪽 주먹은 눈높이 주먹 간격으로 머리위에 띄우고 왼쪽 주먹은 주먹 간격으로 옆턱을 막고 상단 옆막기

(Right)
Begin in a Front Stance.
Turn your torso to the right in a counter clockwise direction, and simultaneously step with the right leg out toward the right upper corner and get into a right Forward Stance. In the Forward Stance position, lean forward and bend your right knee so most of your weight is on the right leg. Keep your left leg aligned straight with your spine. With both fists clenched, extend your right arm up and over your head at a 45 degree angle so you are deflecting your opponent's attack coming from above your head with the outer edge of your left forearm. Keep your chin down while looking up towards your opponent and ensure that your left fist is guarding the left side of your face. After executing the right High Side Block, return to the Front Stance.

5. 상단 X 막기

선 자세에서 양발을 어깨넓이로 벌려 중심을 양다리에 두고 양 주먹을 살짝 쥐고 양 무릎을 접으면서 기마 자세로 몸을 낮추어 양발에 중심을 주고 양팔을 X로 만들어 머리 위로 올리면서 양 주먹에 힘을 주면서 상단 X 막기

High X Block:

Begin in a Front Stance position.
Bend your knees and simultaneously extend your arms over your head and meet your fists at one point. Place the outer left side of your left fist on top of the right index knuckle of your right fist. Align the knuckles of your fists. Your forearms should be at 45 degree angles and your fists should form a peak. Deflect an incoming attack coming from above the head using the outer edge of your right forearm. Use your left fist to support your right fist. After executing the High X Block, return back to your guard in a Front Stance.

막기술: Blocking Techniques

6. 팔뚝 얼굴 막기 (왼쪽, 오른쪽)

(왼쪽)

선 자세에서 양발을 어깨넓이로 벌려 중심을 양다리에 두고 양 주먹을 살짝 쥐고 양발에 중심을 주고 양주먹을 양턱에 주먹 간격으로 띄우고 오른쪽으로 허리를 틀어 왼쪽 팔뚝을 앞으로 얼굴 후려 막기

Forearm Face Block

(Left)

Begin in a Front Stance position.

Slightly lean into your left leg and dodge your body towards the left while turning your shoulders in a clockwise direction. Simultaneously, block with your left forearm across your face from left to right. Ensure that your right fist is guarding the right side your face, and keep your chin down. After executing the left Forearm Face Block, return to the Front Stance.

(오른쪽)

선 자세에서 양발을 어깨넓이로 벌려 중심을 양다리에 두고 양 주먹을 살짝 쥐고 양발에 중심을 주고 양 주먹을 양턱에 주먹 간격으로 띄우고 왼쪽으로 허리를 틀어 오른쪽 팔뚝을 앞으로 얼굴 후려 막기

(Right)

Begin in a Front Stance position.

Slightly lean into your right leg and dodge your body towards the right while turning your shoulders counter-clockwise in a counter-clockwise direction. Simultaneously, block with your right forearm across your face from right to left. Ensure that your left fist is guarding the right side your face, and keep your chin down. After executing the right Forearm Face Block, return to the Front Stance.

7. 얼굴 홴 막기 (왼쪽, 오른쪽)

(왼쪽)

선 자세에서 양발을 어깨넓이로 벌려 중심을 양다리에 두고 양 주먹을 살짝 쥐고 양발에 중심을 주고 양 주먹을 양턱에 주먹 간격으로 띄우고 손바닥을 펴고 손가락을 붙여 오른쪽으로 허리를 틀어 왼쪽 수도를 안으로 얼굴 홴 돌려막기

Inward Fan Block:

(Left)

Begin in a Front Stance position.

Slightly lean into your left leg and dodge your body towards the left while turning your shoulders in a clockwise direction. Make a Knife Hands with your left hand by locking your fingers straight and tucking your thumb inside your palm. Simultaneously time your opponent's incoming attack and intercept their arm with your left hand. The moment the outer edge of your left hand comes in contact with your opponent's arm, curve your wrist like a hook and trap their wrist. Pull their arm down to finish the Inward Fan Block and return back to a Front Stance.

(오른쪽)
선 자세에서 양발을 어깨넓이로 벌려 중심을 양다리에 두고 양 주먹을 살짝 쥐고 양발에 중심을 주고 양 주먹을 양턱에 주먹 간격으로 띄우고 손바닥을 펴고 손가락을 붙여 왼쪽으로 허리를 틀어 오른쪽 수도를 안으로 얼굴 휀 돌려막기

(Right)
Begin in a Front Stance position.
Slightly lean into your right leg and dodge your body towards the right while turning your shoulders in a counter-clockwise direction. Make a Knife Hands with your right hand by locking your fingers straight and tucking your thumb inside your palm. Simultaneously time your opponent's incoming attack and intercept their arm with your right hand. The moment the outer edge of your left hand comes in contact with your opponent's arm, curve your wrist like a hook and trap their wrist. Pull their arm down to finish the Inward Fan Block and return back to a Front Stance.

막기술: Blocking Techniques

8. 하단 풍차돌려 막기 (왼쪽, 오른쪽)

(왼쪽)

선 자세에서 양발을 어깨넓이로 벌려 중심을 양다리에 두고 양 주먹을 살짝쥐고 양발에 중심을 주고 양 주먹을 양턱에 주먹 간격으로 뛰우고 손바닥을 펴고 손가락을 붙여 중방자세에서 양쪽 손날을 만들어 오른쪽으로 허리를 틀어 왼쪽 손날에 힘을 주면서 안으로 풍차 돌려 하단 몸통 내려막기

Low Sweep Block:

(Left)

Begin in a Front Stance.

Take a step back with your right leg. Shift your weight into your right leg and scoot your hips back. Cup the palm of your left hand. Turn your body slightly towards the left while simultaneously bringing the palm of your left hand downward and sweep the hand out towards the left in a circular clockwise motion. Return your left hand back to guard once your hand has moved passed the outside of your left hip. Take a step forward with your right leg and return back to a Front Stance.

(오른쪽)
선 자세에서 양발을 어깨넓이로 벌려 중심을 양다리에 두고 양 주먹을 살짝쥐고 양발에 중심을 주고 양 주먹을 양턱에 주먹 간격으로 띄우고 손바닥을 펴고 손가락을 붙여 중방자세에서 양쪽 손날을 만들어 왼쪽으로 허리를 틀어 오른쪽 손날에 힘을 주면서 안으로 풍차 돌려 하단 몸통 내려막기

(Right)
Begin in a Front Stance.
Take a step back with your left leg. Shift your weight into your left leg and scoot your hips back. Cup the palm of your right hand. Turn your body slightly towards the right while simultaneously bringing the palm of your right hand downward and sweep the hand out towards the right in a circular counter-clockwise motion. Return your right hand back to guard once your hand has moved passed the outside of your right hip. Take a step forward with your left leg and return back to a Front Stance.

9. 상단 옆 손날 막기 (왼쪽, 오른쪽)

(왼쪽)

선 자세에서 양발을 어깨넓이로 벌려 중심을 양다리에 두고 양 주먹을 살짝 쥐고 양발에 중심을 주고 손바닥을 펴고 손가락을 붙여 중방 자세로 손날을 만들어 양다리를 약간 구부리고 오른쪽으로 허리를 틀면서 양손날에 힘을 주고 전방 상단 손날 얼굴막기

Inward Chop Block:

(Left)

Begin in a Front Stance position.

Slightly lean into your left leg and dodge your body towards the left while turning your shoulders in a clockwise direction. Make a Knife Hands with your left hand by locking your fingers straight and tucking your thumb inside your palm. Simultaneously time your opponent's incoming attack and chop the inner part of their arm just above their elbow. Ensure that your right fist is shielding the right side of your face and temple. Keep your chin down. After executing the left Inward Chop Block, return to the Front Stance.

(오른쪽)
선 자세에서 양발을 어깨넓이로 벌려 중심을 양다리에 두고 양 주먹을 살짝 쥐고 양발에 중심을 주고 손바닥을 펴고 손가락을 붙여 중방 자세로 양쪽 손날을 만들어 양다리를 약간 구부리고 왼쪽으로 허리를 틀면서 양 손날에 힘을 주면서 전방 상단 손날 얼굴막기

(Right)
Begin in a Front Stance position.
Slightly lean into your right leg and dodge your body towards the right while turning your shoulders in a counter-clockwise direction. Make a Knife Hands with your right hands by locking your fingers straight and tucking your thumb inside your palm. Simultaneously time your opponent's incoming attack and chop the inner part of their arm just above their elbow. Ensure that your left fist is shielding the left side of your face and temple. Keep your chin down. After executing the right Inward Chop Block, return to the Front Stance.

10. 얼굴 반대 핸 막기 (왼쪽, 오른쪽)

(왼쪽)

선 자세에서 양발을 어깨넓이로 벌려 중심을 양다리에 두고 양 주먹을 살짝 쥐고 양발에 중심을 주고 손바닥을 펴고 손가락을 붙여 중방 자세로 양쪽 손날을 만들어 양다리를 약간 구부리고 오른쪽으로 허리를 틀면서 왼쪽 손날에 힘을 주면서 반대로 풍차돌려 얼굴막기

Outward Fan Block:

(Left)

Begin in a Front Stance.

Lean into your right leg and dodge your body towards the right while turning your shoulders toward the left in a counter-clockwise direction. Simultaneously make a knife hand with your left hand by locking your fingers straight and tucking your thumb into your palm. Deflect an incoming attack coming at your face by blocking it away from your face toward the left. Once your hand comes into contact with your opponent's arm, curve your wrist to create a hook with your hand and trap your opponent's wrist. To complete the block, pull their hand down and return to guard.

(오른쪽)
선 자세에서 양발을 어깨넓이로 벌려 중심을 양다리에 두고 양 주먹을 살짝 쥐고 양발에 중심을 주고 손바닥을 펴고 손가락을 붙여 중방 자세로 양쪽 손날을 만들어 양다리를 약간 구부리고 왼쪽으로 허리를 틀면서 오른쪽 손날에 힘을 주면서 반대로 풍차돌려 얼굴막기

(Right)
Begin in a Front Stance.
Lean into your left leg and dodge your body towards the left while turning your shoulders toward the right in a clockwise direction. Simultaneously make a knife hand with your right hand by locking your fingers straight and tucking your thumb into your palm. Deflect an incoming attack coming at your face by blocking it away from your face toward the right. Once your hand comes into contact with your opponent's arm, curve your wrist to create a hook with your hand and trap your opponent's wrist. To complete the block, pull their hand down and return to guard.

막기술: Blocking Techniques

11. 하단 양손 내려막고 옆막기 (왼쪽, 오른쪽)

(왼쪽)

선 자세에서 양발을 어깨넓이로 벌려 중심을 양다리에 두고 양 주먹을 살짝 쥐고 양발에 중심을 주고 손바닥을 펴고 손가락을 붙여 중방 자세로 양다리를 약간 구부리고 양손바닥을 아래로 막고 오른쪽으로 허리를 틀면서 양손바닥으로 오른쪽 중단 옆막기

Low to Side Block:

(Left)

Begin in a Front Stance position.

Bend your knees and move your hips back while maintaining your balance. Block an incoming kick that is coming at you from the front using the outer edge of your left forearm and strike the top of your opponent's ankle. Then return your hands to guard take a step towards your left back corner with your left leg. Lean into your left leg and get into a right Back Stance. Simultaneously swing your right forearm down towards your right side while turning your torso into the block in a clockwise direction and deflect your opponent's incoming kick using the outer edge of your forearm. Do not completely extend your right elbow. After executing the right Low to Side Block, return to the Front Stance and back to your guard.

(오른쪽)
선 자세에서 양발을 어깨넓이로 벌려 중심을 양다리에 두고 양 주먹을 살짝 쥐고 양발에 중심을 주고 손바닥을 펴고 손가락을 붙여 중방 자세로 양다리를 약간 구부리고 양손바닥을 아래로 막고 왼쪽으로 허리를 틀면서 양손바닥으로 왼쪽 중단 옆막기

(Right)
Begin in a Front Stance position.
Bend your knees and move your hips back while maintaining your balance. Block an incoming kick that is coming at you from the front using the outer edge of your right forearm and strike the top of your opponent's ankle. Then return your hands to guard and take a step towards your right back corner with your right leg. Lean into your right leg and get into a left Back Stance. Simultaneously swing your left forearm down towards your left side while turning your torso into the block in a counter-clockwise motion and deflect your opponent's incoming kick using the outer edge of your forearm. Do not completely extend your left elbow. After executing the left Low to Side Block, return to the Front Stance and back to your guard.

막기술: Blocking Techniques

12. 상단 옆 양 손날 얼굴막기 (왼쪽, 오른쪽)

(왼쪽)

선 자세에서 양발을 어깨넓이로 벌려 중심을 양다리에 두고 양 주먹을 살짝 쥐고 양발에 중심을 주고 손바닥을 펴고 손가락을 붙여 중방자세로 양손날을 만들어 양다리를 약간 구부리고 왼쪽으로 허리를 틀면서 왼다리를 들어 왼쪽으로 돌려 놓으면서 양손날을 동시에 옆으로 돌려 왼쪽 손날은 손바닥을 아래로 눈높이로 두뼘 간격으로 뛰우고 오른쪽 손날은 손바닥을 위로 코 높이에 뛰우고 왼쪽 상단 양손날 얼굴막기

High Side Chop Block:

(Left)

Begin in a Front Stance position.

Lean into your right leg and turn your torso towards the left in a counter-clockwise direction. Lift the heel of your left foot and keep the ball of your left foot on the ground. Slightly slide your left foot in towards the right and get into a left Back Stance. Make two Knife Hands with your hands by locking your fingers straight and tucking your thumb inside your palm. Simultaneously chop your left forearm out towards the left to deflect your opponent's incoming attack. The palm of your left hand should face down and the palm of your right hand should face up. Your right Knife Hand should follow your left forearm until it gets to the right side of your face. After executing the left High Side Chop Block, return to the Front Stance and back to your guard.

(오른쪽)
선 자세에서 양발을 어깨넓이로 벌려 중심을 양다리에 두고 양 주먹을 살짝 쥐고 양발에 중심을 주고 손바닥을 펴고 손가락을 붙여 중방자세로 양손날을 만들어 양다리를 약간 구부리고 오른쪽으로 허리를 틀면서 왼다리를 들어 오른쪽으로 돌려 놓으면서 양 손날을 동시에 옆으로 돌려 오른쪽 손날은 손바닥을 아래로 눈높이로 두뼘 간격으로 뛰우고 왼쪽 손날은 손바닥 을 위로 코 높이에 뛰우고 왼쪽 상단 양손날 얼굴막기

(Right)
Begin in a Front Stance position.
Lean into your left leg and turn your torso towards the right in a clockwise direction. Lift the heel of your right foot and keep the ball of your right foot on the ground. Slightly slide your right foot in towards the left and get into a right Back Stance. Lock your fingers straight and set our hands into knife hands. Simultaneously chop your left forearm out towards the right to deflect your opponent's incoming attack. The palm of your right hand should face down and the palm of your left hand should face up. Your left Knife Hand should follow your right forearm until it gets to the right side of your face. After executing the right High Side Chop Block, return to the Front Stance and back to your guard.

막기술: Blocking Techniques

13. 이중 스탭 옆 반대 막기 (왼쪽, 오른쪽)

(왼쪽)

선 자세에서 양발을 어깨넓이로 벌려 중심을 양다리에 두고 양 주먹을 살짝 쥐고 양발에 중심을 주고 오른쪽 발가락을 왼쪽으로 돌려 한발 앞으로 바닥에 옮겨놓는 동시에 왼발을 들어 오른발 뒤로 옮기면서 중심은 왼다리에 두고 왼손으로 상대의 왼팔을 잡아채기

Step and Outward Fan Block:

(Left)

Begin in a Front Stance.

Take a step forward towards the right upper corner with your right leg. Lean into your right leg and dodge your body towards the right while turning your shoulders toward the left in a counter-clockwise direction. Simultaneously make a knife hand with your left hand by locking your fingers straight and tucking your thumb into your palm. Deflect an incoming attack coming at your face by blocking it away from your face toward the left. Once your hand comes into contact with your opponent's arm, curve your wrist to create a hook with your hand and trap your opponent's wrist. When you have trapped your opponent's wrist, swing your left leg in a counter-clockwise direction 90degrees. As you swing your left leg back, use your body's momentum and pull on your opponent's arm to take them off balance. Return to guard after completing the block and step.

(오른쪽)
선 자세에서 양발을 어깨넓이로 벌려 중심을 양다리에 두고 양 주먹을 살짝 쥐고 양발에 중심을 주고 왼쪽 발가락을 오른쪽으로 돌려 한발 앞으로 바닥에 옮겨놓는 동시에 오른발을 들어 왼른발 뒤로 옮기면서 중심은 오른다리에 두고 오른손으로 상대의 오른팔을 잡아채기

(Right)
Begin in a Front Stance.
Take a step forward towards the left upper corner with your left leg. Lean into your left leg and dodge your body towards the left while turning your shoulders toward the right in a clockwise direction. Simultaneously make a knife hand with your right hand by locking your fingers straight and tucking your thumb into your palm. Deflect an incoming attack coming at your face by blocking it away from your face toward the right. Once your hand comes into contact with your opponent's arm, curve your wrist to create a hook with your hand and trap your opponent's wrist. When you have trapped your opponent's wrist, swing your right leg in a clockwise direction 90degrees. As you swing your right leg back, use your body's momentum and pull on your opponent's arm to take them off balance. Return to guard after completing the block and step.

Basic Stance Form
기 | 본 | 자 | 세 | 형
10 | 선 | 자 | 세

01. 왼쪽 중단 지르기 "기합" (기마자세):
    Left Middle Punch "KI-Hap" (horse stance)

02. 오른쪽 중단 지르기 "기합" (기마 자세):
    Right Middle Punch "KI-Hap" (horse stance)

03. 왼쪽 팔꿈치 훅 (선자세):
    Left Elbow Hook (stand stance)

04. 오른쪽 팔꿈치 훅 (선자세):
    Right Elbow Hook (stand stance)

05. 오른쪽 양손날 하단막기 (후방자세):
    Right Low two Knife Side Block (back stance)

06. 오른쪽 양팔뚝 중단막기 (중방자세):
    Right Middle two Forearm Side Block (Middle stand)

07. 오른쪽 양팔뚝 상단막기 (전방자세):
    Right High two Forearm Side Block (front stand)

08. 왼쪽 양손날 하단막기 (후방자세):
    Left Low two Knife Side Block (back stance)

09. 왼쪽 양팔뚝 중단막기 (중방자세):
    Left Middle two Forearm Side Block (middle stance)

10. 왼쪽 양팔뚝 상단막기 (전방자세):
    Left High two Forearm Side Block (front stance)

1. 왼쪽 중단 지르기 "기합"

얼굴은 12시 정면 방향, 양주먹은 손가락을 위로 하여 양허리 띠에 대면서 양다리의 간격은 어깨넓이 1.5배 기마자세에서 중심은 양다리에 두고, 허리를 시계 방향으로 틀어 기합을 넣으며 왼쪽 주먹을 돌려 스냅으로 왼쪽 정권 중단 지르기 (기마자세)

Left Middle Punch "KI-Hap":

In a Stand Stance position facing 12:00, turn your body clockwise while pushing off with your left leg. Execute a straight left punch with your fist. Make sure your right fist is guarding your face, and keep your chin down.(Ki-Hap)

2. 오른쪽 중단 지르기 "기합"

얼굴은 12시 정면 방향, 왼쪽 중단 지르기를 한 상태에서 오른쪽 주먹은 손가락을 위로 하여 오른쪽 띠에 댄대로 양다리의 간격은 어깨넓이 1.5배 기마자세에서 중심은 양다리에 두고, 허리를 반시계 방향으로 틀어 기합을 넣으며 오른쪽 주먹을 돌려 스냅으로 오른쪽 정권 중단 지르기를 하면서 왼쪽 주먹은 왼쪽 띠에 대기 (기마자세)

Right Middle Punch "KI-Hap":

Turn your body counter-clockwise while pushing off with your right leg. Execute a straight right punch with your fist. Make sure your left fist is guarding your face, and keep your chin down. (Ki-Hap)

3. 왼쪽 팔꿈치 훅

얼굴은 12시 정면 방향, 오른쪽 중단 지르기를 한 상태에서 턱을 아래로 당겨 양주먹은 양턱에 대면서 양 다리의 간격은 어깨넓이로 세워 중심은 양다리에 두고, 왼발을 돌려 밀면서 몸을 3시 시계 방향으로 틀어 왼쪽 팔꿈치로 훅을 치고 왼쪽 어깨로 왼쪽 턱을 방어 (선자세)

Left Elbow Hook:

Push off with your left leg while turning your body clockwise, and hook your left elbow straight across. Make sure your right fist is guarding your face, and keep your chin down.

4. 오른쪽 팔꿈치 훅

얼굴은 3시 방향, 왼쪽 팔꿈치 훅을 한 상태에서 턱을 아래로 당겨 오른쪽 주먹은 오른쪽 턱을 막은대로 양다리의 간격은 어깨넓이로 세워 중심은 양다리에 두고, 오른발을 돌려 밀면서 몸을 9시 반시계 방향으로 틀어 오른쪽 팔꿈치로 훅을 치고 오른쪽 어깨로 오른쪽 턱을 방어 (선자세)

Right Elbow Hook:

Push off with your right leg while turning your body counter-clockwise, and hook your right elbow straight across. Make sure your left fist is guarding your face, and keep your chin down.

5. 오른쪽 양손날 하단막기

얼굴은 9시 방향, 오른쪽 팔꿈치 훅을 한 상태에서 턱을 아래로 당겨 양다리의 간격은 어깨넓이 몸을 시계 방향으로 돌리면서 오른발을 들어 3시 방향으로 돌려 놓으며 왼쪽 손바닥은 위로 팔뚝은 띠에 대면서 오른쪽 손바닥을 아래로 중심은 뒷다리에 두고, 오른쪽으로 허리를 틀어 동시에 양손날 하단막기 (후방자세)

Right Low two Knife Side Block:

Turn your body clockwise, and step out with your right leg towards 12:00 into a right side Back Stance. Execute a right side Low Side Block with your right forearm. Keep your left hand at belt level with your palm face up.

6. 오른쪽 양팔뚝 중단막기

얼굴은 3시 방향, 오른쪽 양손날 하단막기를 한 상태에서 턱을 아래로 당겨 양다리의 간격은 어깨넓이 오른발을 들어 4시 방향으로 옮겨 놓으며 중심은 양다리에 두고, 허리를 시계 방향으로 틀어 오른손을 손가락은 바같으로 하고 주먹을 쥐면서 돌려 어깨높이로 왼손의 손가락은 위로 주먹을 쥐며 오른쪽 팔꿈치에 대면서 오른쪽으로 양팔뚝 중단막기 (중방자세)

Right Middle two Forearm Side Block:

Step out with your right leg towards 1:00 into a right side Middle Stance, and face towards 12:00. Execute a right side Middle Side Block with your right forearm, and have your fist is at eye level. Make sure your left fist is on your inside right elbow for support, and keep your chin down.

7. 오른쪽 양팔뚝 상단막기

얼굴은 3시 방향, 오른쪽 양팔뚝 중단막기를 한 상태에서 턱을 아래로 당겨 양다리의 간격은 어깨넓이 오른발을 들어 4시 방향으로 다시 옮겨 놓으며 몸을 앞으로 밀면서 중심은 앞다리에 두고, 왼쪽 팔뚝은 왼쪽 얼굴을 막으며 오른쪽 팔뚝은 앞 얼굴을 스치면서 머리위로 올려 오른쪽으로 동시에 양팔뚝 상단막기 (전방자세)

Right High two Forearm Side Block:

Step out with your right leg towards 4:00 into a right side Forward Stance, and face towards 3:00. Execute a right side High Side Block with your right forearm, and have your arm at a 45degree angle. Make sure your left fist is guarding your face, and keep your left elbow in.

8. 왼쪽 양손날 하단막기

얼굴은 3시방향, 오른쪽 양팔뚝 상단막기를 한 상태에서 턱을 아래로 당겨 양다리의 간격은 어깨넓이 몸을 반시계 방향으로 돌리면서 왼발을 들어 9시 방향으로 돌려 놓으며 오른쪽 손바닥은 위로 팔뚝은 띠에 대면서 왼쪽 손바닥을 아래로 중심은 뒷다리에 두고, 왼쪽으로 허리를 틀어 동시에 양손날 하단막기 (후방자세)

Left Low two Knife Side Block:

Turn your body counter-clockwise and step with your left leg towards 9:00 in a left side Back Stance. Execute a left side Low Side Block with your left forearm. Keep your right hand at belt level with your palm face up.

9. 왼쪽 양팔뚝 중단막기

얼굴은 3시 방향, 왼쪽 양손날 하단막기를 한 상태에서 턱을 아래로 당겨 양다리의 간격은 어깨넓이 왼발을 들어 8시 방향으로 옮겨 놓으며 중심은 양다리에 두고, 허리를 시계 방향으로 틀어 왼손을 손가락은 바깥으로 하고 주먹을 쥐면서 돌려 어깨높이로 오른손의 손가락은 위로 주먹을 쥐며 왼쪽 팔꿈치에 대면서 왼쪽으로 양팔뚝 중단막기 (중방자세)

Left Middle two Forearm Side Block:

Step out with your left leg towards 8:00 into a left side Middle Stance, and face towards 9:00. Execute a left side Middle Side Block with your left forearm, and have your fist is at eye level. Make sure your right fist is on your inside elbow for support, and keep your chin down.

10. 왼쪽 양팔뚝 상단막기

얼굴은 9시 방향, 왼쪽 양팔뚝 중단막기를 한 상태에서 턱을 아래로 당겨 양다리의 간격은 어깨넓이 왼발을 들어 8시 방향으로 다시 옮겨 놓으며 몸을 앞으로 밀면서 중심은 앞다리에 두고, 오른쪽 팔뚝은 오른쪽 얼굴을 막으며 왼쪽 팔뚝은 앞 얼굴을 스치면서 머리위로 올려 왼쪽으로 동시에 양팔뚝 상단막기 (전방자세)

Left High two Forearm Side Block:

Step out with your left leg towards 8:00 into a left side Forward Stance, and face towards 9:00. Execute a left side High Side Block with your left forearm, and have your arm at a 45degree angle. Make sure your right fist is guarding your face, and keep your right elbow in.

16 STANCE FORM
16 | 개 | 형

01. 왼쪽 정권 직선펀치 (선 자세):
    Left Fist Straight Punch (stand stance)

02. 오른쪽 정권 직선펀치 "기합" (선 자세):
    Right Fist Straight Punch "KI-Hap" (stand stance)

03. 왼쪽 팔뚝 얼굴 안 막기 (선 자세):
    Right Low Forearm Side Block (back stance)

04. 오른쪽 팔뚝 얼굴 안 막기 (선 자세):
    Right Forearm Face Block (stand stance)

05. 오른쪽 양 손날 하단 옆막기 (후방 자세):
    Right Low two Knife Side Block (back stance)

06. 오른쪽 양 팔뚝 중단 옆막기 (중방 자세):
    Right Middle two Forearm Side Block (middle stance)

07. 오른쪽 양 팔뚝 상단 옆막기 (전방 자세):
    Right High two Forearm Side Block (front stance)

08. 왼쪽 정권 직선펀치 "기합" (선 자세):
    Left Fist Straight Punch "KI-Hap" (stand stance)

09. 왼쪽 팔꿈치 훅 (선 자세):
    Left Elbow Hook (stand stance)

10. 왼쪽 양 손날 하단 옆막기 (후방 자세):
    Left Low two Knife Side Block (back stance)

11. 왼쪽 양 팔뚝 중단 옆막기 (중방 자세):
    Left Middle two Forearm Side Block (middle stance)

12. 왼쪽 양 팔뚝 상단 옆막기 (전방 자세):
    Left High two Foream Side Block (front stance)

13. 오른쪽 정권 직선펀치 "기합" (선 자세):
    Right Fist Straight Punch "KI-Hap" (stand stance)

14. 오른쪽 팔꿈치 훅 (선 자세):
    Right Elbow Hook (stand stance)

15. 오른쪽 양 손날 하단 옆막기 (후방 자세):
    Right Low two Knife Side Block (back stance)

16. 오른쪽 양 팔뚝 중단 옆막기 (중방 자세):
    Right Middle two Forearm Side Block (middle stance)

1. 왼쪽 정권 직선펀치

얼굴은 12시 정면 방향, 상대의 눈을 주시 하면서 턱을 아래로 당겨 양 주먹은 양턱을 막으며 양다리의 간격은 어깨넓이 중심은 양다리에 두고, 왼발을 돌려 밀면서 몸을 시계 방향으로 틀어 왼쪽 주먹을 돌려 정권 직선펀치를 하면서 왼쪽 어깨로 왼쪽 턱을 방어 (선 자세)

Left Fist Straight Punch:

In a Stand Stance position facing 12:00, turn your body clockwise while pushing off with your left leg. Execute a straight left punch with your fist. Make sure your right fist is guarding your face, and keep your chin down.

2. 오른쪽 정권 직선펀치 "기합"

얼굴은 12시 정면 방향, 왼쪽 정권 직선 펀치를 한 상태에서 턱을 아래로 당겨 오른쪽 주먹은 오른쪽 턱을 막은 대로 양다리의 간격은 어깨넓이 중심은 양다리에 두고, 오른발을 돌려 밀면서 몸을 반시계 방향으로 틀어 기합을 넣으며 오른쪽 주먹을 돌려 정권 직선펀치를 하면서 왼쪽 주먹은 왼쪽 턱을 막으며 오른쪽 어깨로 오른쪽 턱을 방어. (선 자세)

Right Fist Straight Punch "KI-Hap":

Turn your body counter-clockwise while pushing off with your right leg. Execute a straight right punch with your fist. Make sure your left fist is guarding your face, and keep your chin down. (Ki-Hap)

3. 왼쪽 팔뚝 얼굴 안 막기

얼굴은 12시 정면 방향, 오른쪽 정권 직선 펀치를 한 상태에서 상대의 눈을 주시 하면서 턱을 아래로 당겨 양다리의 간격은 어깨넓이 중심은 양다리에 두고, 몸을 시계 방향으로 틀어 오른쪽 주먹은 오른쪽 턱을 막으며 왼쪽 팔뚝 안으로 얼굴막기 (선 자세)

Right Low Forearm Side Block:

Lean towards the left while blocking with your left forearm across your face. Make sure your right fist is guarding your face, and keep your chin down.

4. 오른쪽 팔꿈치 훅

얼굴은 3시 방향, 왼쪽 팔꿈치 훅을 한 상태에서 턱을 아래로 당겨 오른쪽 주먹은 오른쪽 턱을 막은대로 양다리의 간격은 어깨넓이로 세워 중심은 양다리에 두고, 오른발을 돌려 밀면서 몸을 9시 반시계 방향으로 틀어 오른쪽 팔꿈치로 훅을 치고 오른쪽 어깨로 오른쪽 턱을 방어 (선자세)

Right Forearm Face Block:

Lean towards the right while blocking with your right forearm across your face. Make sure your left fist is guarding your face, and keep your chin down.

5. 오른쪽 양 손날 하단 옆막기

얼굴은 12시 정면 방향, 오른쪽 팔뚝 얼굴 안 막기를 한 상태에서 턱을 아래로 당겨 양다리의 간격은 어깨 넓이 몸을 시계 방향으로 돌리면서 오른발을 들어 3시 방향 제자리에서 돌려 놓으며 왼쪽 손바닥은 위로 팔뚝은 띠에 대면서 오른쪽 손바닥을 아래로 중심은 뒷다리에 두고, 오른쪽으로 허리를 틀어 동시에 양손 날로 하단 옆막기 (후방자세)

Right Low two Knife Side Block:

Turn your body clockwise so you are facing towards 3:00 in a right side Back Stance. Execute a right side Low Side Block with your right forearm. Keep your left hand at belt level with your palm face up.

6. 오른쪽 양팔뚝 중단 옆막기

얼굴은 3시 방향, 오른쪽 양 손날 하단 옆막기를 한 상태에서 턱을 아래로 당겨 양다리의 간격은 어깨넓이 오른발을 들어 4시 방향으로 옮겨 놓으며 중심은 양다리에 두고, 양손은 동시에 주먹을 쥐면서 양손가락을 위로 오른손은 어깨높이에 왼손은 오른쪽 팔꿈치에 대면서 허리를 시계 방향으로 틀어 오른쪽으로 양 팔 뚝 중단 옆막기 (중방자세)

Right Middle two Forearm Side Block:

Step out with your right leg towards 4:00 into a right side Middle Stance, and face towards 3:00. Execute a right side Middle Side Block with your right forearm, and have your fist is at eye level. Make sure your left fist is on your inside right elbow for support, and keep your chin down.

7. 오른쪽 양 팔뚝 상단 옆막기

얼굴은 3시 방향, 오른쪽 양팔뚝 중단 옆막기를 한 상태에서 상대의 눈을 주시 하면서 턱을 아래로 당겨 양다리의 간격은 어깨넓이 오른발을 들어 4시 방향으로 다시 옮겨 놓으며 몸을 앞으로 밀면서 중심은 앞 다리에 두고, 왼쪽 팔뚝은 왼쪽 얼굴을 막으며 오른쪽 팔뚝은 앞 얼굴을 스치면서 머리위에 올려 오른쪽으로 동시에 양 팔뚝 상단 옆막기 (전방자세)

Right High two Forearm Side Block:

Step out with your right leg towards 4:00 into a right side Forward Stance, and face towards 3:00. Execute a right side High Side Block with your right forearm, and have your arm at a 45degree angle. Make sure your left fist is guarding your face, and keep your left elbow in.

8. 왼쪽 정권 직선펀치 "기합"

얼굴은 3시 방향, 오른쪽 양 팔뚝 상단 옆막기를 한 상태에서 상대의 눈을 주시 하면서 턱을 아래로 당겨 양다리의 간격은 어깨넓이 몸을 시계 방향으로 돌리면서 왼발을 들어 3시 방향 앞으로 한발 옮겨 놓으며 오른쪽 주먹은 오른쪽 턱을 막으며 중심은 양다리에 두고, 기합을 넣으며 왼쪽 주먹을 돌려 정권 직선펀치를 하면서 왼쪽 어깨로 왼쪽 턱을 방어 (선 자세)

Left Fist Straight Punch "KI-Hap":

Step forward with your left leg towards 3:00 while turning your body clockwise. Execute a straight left punch, and face towards 6:00. Make sure your right fist is guarding your face, and keep your chin down. (Ki-Hap)

9. 왼쪽 팔꿈치 훅

얼굴은 3시 방향, 왼쪽 정권 직선펀치를 한 상태에서 턱을 아래로 당겨 양다리의 간격은 어깨넓이 오른쪽 주먹은 오른쪽 턱을 막으며 중심은 양다리에 두고, 왼발을 돌려 밀면서 몸을 6시 시계 방향으로 틀어 왼쪽 팔꿈치로 훅치기 (선 자세)

Left Elbow Hook:
Push off with your left leg while turning your body clockwise, and hook your left elbow straight across. Make sure your right fist is guarding your face, and keep your chin down.

10. 왼쪽 양 손날 하단 옆막기

얼굴은 6시 방향, 왼쪽 팔꿈치 훅을 한 상태에서 턱을 아래로 당겨 양다리의 간격은 어깨넓이 몸을 반시계 방향으로 돌리면서 왼발을 들어 9시 방향 앞으로 한발 옮겨 놓으며 오른쪽 손바닥은 위로 팔뚝은 띠에 대면서 왼쪽 손바닥을 아래로 중심은 뒷다리에 두고 왼쪽으로 허리를 틀어 동시에 양 손날로 하단 옆막기 (후방자세)

Left Low two Knife Side Block:
Turn your body counter-clockwise and step with your left leg towards 9:00 in a left side Back Stance. Execute a left side Low Side Block with your left forearm. Keep your right hand at belt level with your palm face up.

11. 왼쪽 양 팔뚝 중단 옆막기

얼굴은 9시 방향, 왼쪽 양 손날 하단 옆막기를 한 상태에서 턱을 아래로 당겨 양다리의 간격은 어깨넓이 왼발을 들어 8시 방향으로 옮겨 놓으며 중심은 양다리에 두고, 허리를 반시계 방향으로 틀어 왼손은 주먹을 쥐면서 돌려 어깨높이로 오른손은 주먹을 쥐며 왼쪽 팔꿈치에 대면서 왼쪽으로 양 팔뚝 중단 옆막기 (중방자세)

Left Middle two Forearm Side Block:

Step out with your left leg towards 8:00 into a left side Middle Stance, and face towards 9:00. Execute a left side Middle Side Block with your left forearm, and have your fist is at eye level. Make sure your right fist is on your inside elbow for support, and keep your chin down.

12. 왼쪽 양팔뚝 상단 옆막기

얼굴은 9시 방향, 왼쪽 양 팔뚝 중단 옆막기를 한 상태에서 상대의 눈을 주시 하면서 턱을 아래로 당겨 양다리의 간격은 어깨넓이 왼발을 들어 8시 방향으로 다시 옮겨 놓으며 몸을 앞으로 밀면서 중심은 앞다리에 두고, 오른쪽 팔뚝은 오른쪽 얼굴을 막으며 왼쪽 팔뚝은 앞 얼굴을 스치면서 머리위에 올려 왼쪽으로 동시에 양 팔뚝 상단 옆막기 (전방자세)

Left High two Foream Side Block:

Step out with your left leg towards 8:00 into a left side Forward Stance, and face towards 9:00. Execute a left side High Side Block with your left forearm, and have your arm at a 45degree angle. Make sure your right fist is guarding your face, and keep your right elbow in.

13. 오른쪽 정권 직선펀치 "기합"

얼굴은 9시 방향, 왼쪽 양 팔뚝 상단 옆막기를 한 상태에서 상대의 눈을 주시 하면서 턱을 아래로 당겨 양 다리의 간격은 어깨넓이 몸을 반시계 방향으로 돌리면서 오른발을 들어 9시 방향 앞으로 한발 옮겨 놓으며 왼쪽 주먹은 왼쪽 턱을 막으며 중심은 양다리에 두고, 기합을 넣으며 오른쪽 주먹을 돌려 정권 직선펀치를 하면서 오른쪽 어깨로 오른쪽 턱을 방어 (선 자세)

Right Fist Straight Punch "KI-Hap":
Step forward with your right leg towards 9:00 while turning your body clockwise. Execute a straight right punch, and face towards 6:00. Make sure your left fist is guarding your face, and keep your chin down. (Ki-Hap)

14. 오른쪽 팔꿈치 훅

얼굴은 9시 방향, 오른쪽 정권 직선펀치를 한 상태에서 턱을 아래로 당겨 양다리의 간격은 어깨넓이 왼쪽 주먹은 왼쪽 턱을 막으며 중심은 양다리에 두고, 오른발을 돌려 밀면서 몸을 6시 반시계 방향으로 틀어 오른쪽 팔꿈치로 훅 치기 (선 자세)

Right Elbow Hook:
Push off with your right leg while turning your body counter-clockwise, and hook your right elbow straight across. Make sure your left fist is guarding your face, and keep your chin down.

15. 오른쪽 양 손날 하단 옆막기

얼굴은 6시 방향, 오른쪽 팔꿈치 훅을 한 상태에서 턱을 아래로 당겨 양다리의 간격은 어깨넓이 몸을 시계 방향으로 돌리면서 오른발을 들어 12시 방향 앞으로 한발 옮겨 놓으며 왼쪽 손바닥은 위로 팔뚝은 띠에 대면서 오른쪽 손바닥을 아래로 중심은 뒷다리에 두고, 오른쪽으로 허리를 틀어 동시에 양 손날 하단 옆막기 (후방자세)

Right Low two Knife Side Block:

Turn your body clockwise, and step out with your right leg towards 12:00 into a right side Back Stance. Execute a right side Low Side Block with your right forearm. Keep your left hand at belt level with your palm face up.

16. 오른쪽 양 팔뚝 중단 옆막기

얼굴은 12시 방향, 오른쪽 양손날 하단 옆막기를 한 상태에서 턱을 아래로 당겨 양다리의 간격은 어깨넓이 오른발을 들어 1시 방향으로 옮겨 놓으며 중심은 양다리에 두고, 허리를 시계 방향으로 틀어 오른손은 주먹을 쥐면서 돌려 어깨높이로 왼손은 주먹을 쥐며 오른쪽 팔꿈치에 대면서 오른쪽으로 양 팔뚝 중단 옆막기 (중방자세)

Right Middle two Forearm Side Block:

Step out with your right leg towards 1:00 into a right side Middle Stance, and face towards 12:00. Execute a right side Middle Side Block with your right forearm, and have your fist is at eye level. Make sure your left fist is on your inside right elbow for support, and keep your chin down.

HILL FORM
동 | 산 | 형

01. 오른쪽 정권 직선펀치 (선 자세):
    Right Fist Straight Punch (stand stance)

02. 왼쪽 정권 직선펀치 "기합" (선 자세):
    Left Fist Straight Punch "Ki-Hap" (stand stance)

03. 오른쪽 팔뚝 하단 옆막기 (선 자세):
    Right Low Forearm Side Block (back stance)

04. 오른쪽 팔뚝 중단 옆막기 (선 자세):
    Right Middle Forearm Side Block (middle stance)

05. 왼쪽 정권 직선펀치 "기합" (선 자세):
    Left Fist Straight Punch "Ki-Hap" (stand stance)

06. 왼쪽 팔꿈치 훅 (선 자세):
    Left Elbow Hook (stand stance)

07. 왼쪽 팔뚝 하단 옆막기 (선 자세):
    Left Low Forearm Side Block (stand stance)

08. 왼쪽 팔뚝 중단 옆막기 (선 자세):
    Left Middle Forearm Side Block (middle stance)

09. 오른쪽 정권 직선펀치 "기합" (선 자세):
    Right Fist Straight Punch "Ki-Hap" (stand stance)

10. 오른쪽 팔꿈치 훅 (선 자세):
    Right Elbow Hook (stand stance)

11. 오른쪽 팔뚝 하단 옆막기 (선 자세):
    Right Low Forearm Side Block (back stance)

12. 오른쪽 팔뚝 중단 옆막기 (선 자세):
    Right Middle Forearm Side Block (middle stance)

13. 왼쪽 정권 직선펀치 "기합" (선 자세):
    Left Fist Straight Punch "Ki-Hap" (stand stance)

14. 왼쪽 팔뚝 하단 옆막기 (선 자세):
    Left Low Forearm Side Block (back stance)

15. 왼쪽 팔뚝 중단 옆막기 (선 자세):
    Left Middle Forearm Side Block (middle stance)

16. 오른쪽 정권 직선펀치 "기합" (선 자세):
    Right Fist Straight Punch "Ki-Hap" (stand stance)

17. 오른쪽 팔뚝 하단 옆막기 (선 자세):
    Right Low Forearm Side Block (back stance)

18. 오른쪽 팔뚝 중단 옆막기 (선 자세):
    Right Middle Forearm Side Block (middle stance)

19. 왼쪽 손 창 수평 찌르기 "기합" (전방자세):
    Left Spear Hand "Ki-Hap" (front stance)

20. 오른쪽 상단 앞차기 (선 자세):
    Right High Front Kick to Spear Hand (stand stance)

21. 오른쪽 팔뚝 하단 옆막기 (선 자세):
    Right Low Forearm Side Block (back stance)

22. 오른쪽 팔뚝 중단 옆막기 (선 자세):
    Right Middle Forearm Side Block (middle stance)

23. 왼쪽 정권 직선펀치 "기합" (선 자세):
    Left Fist straight Punch "Ki-Hap" (stand Stance)

24. 왼쪽 팔뚝 하단 옆막기 (선 자세):
    Left Low Forearm Side Block (back stance)

25. 왼쪽 팔뚝 중단 옆막기 (선 자세):
    Left Middle Forearm Side block (middle stance)

26. 오른쪽 정권 직선펀치 "기합" (선 자세):
    Right Fist Straight Punch "Ki-Hap" (stand stance)

27. 오른쪽 팔뚝 하단 옆막기 (선 자세):
    Right Low Forearm Side Block (back stance)

28. 오른쪽 팔뚝 중단 옆막기 (선 자세):
    Right Middle Forearm Side Block (middle stance)

29. 왼쪽 손 창 수평 찌르기 "기합" (전방자세):
    Left Spear Hand "Ki-Hap" (front stance)

30. 오른쪽 상단 앞차기 (선 자세):
    Right Hight Front Kick to Spear Hand (stand stance)

31. 오른쪽 팔뚝 하단 옆막기 (선 자세):
    Right Low Forearm Side Block (back stance)

32. 오른쪽 팔뚝 중단 옆막기 (선 자세):
    Right Middle Forearm Side Block (middle stance)

1. 오른쪽 정권 직선펀치

얼굴은 12시 정면 방향, 상대의 눈을 주시 하면서 턱을 아래로 당겨 양 주먹은 양턱을 막으며 양다리의 간격은 어깨넓이 중심은 양다리에 두고, 오른발을 돌려 밀면서 몸을 반시계 방향으로 틀어 오른쪽 주먹을 돌려 정권 직선펀치를 하면서 오른쪽 어깨로 오른쪽 턱을 방어 (선 자세)

Right Fist Straight Punch:

In a Stand Stance position facing 12:00, turn your body counter-clockwise while pushing off with your right leg. Execute a straight right punch with your fist. Make sure your left fist is guarding your face, and keep your chin down.

2. 왼쪽 정권 직선펀치 "기합"

얼굴은 12시 정면 방향, 오른쪽 정권 직선펀치를 한 상태에서 턱을 아래로 당겨 왼쪽 주먹은 왼쪽 턱을 막은대로 양다리의 간격은 어깨넓이 중심은 양다리에 두고, 왼발을 돌려 밀면서 몸을 시계 방향으로 틀어 기합을 넣으며 왼쪽 주먹을 돌려 정권 직선펀치를 하면서 오른쪽 주먹은 오른쪽 턱을 막으며 왼쪽 어깨로 왼쪽 턱을 방어 (선 자세)

Left Fist Straight Punch "Ki-Hap":

Turn your body clockwise while pushing off with your left leg. Execute a straight left punch with your fist. Make sure your right fist is guarding your face, and keep your chin down.
(Ki-Hap)

3. 오른쪽 팔뚝 하단 옆막기

얼굴은 12시 정면 방향, 왼쪽 정권 직선 펀치를 한 상태에서 턱을 아래로 당겨 양다리의 간격은 어깨넓이 몸을 시계 방향으로 돌리면서 오른발을 들어 3시 방향 제자리에서 돌려놓으며 왼쪽 주먹은 왼쪽 턱을 막으며 오른쪽 주먹을 쥐면서 중심은 뒷다리에 두고, 오른쪽 팔뚝을 바같으로 돌려 하단 옆막기 (후방자세)

Right Low Forearm Side Block:

Turn your body clockwise so you are facing towards 3:00 in a right side Back Stance. Execute a right side Low Forearm Side Block with your right forearm while keeping a tight fist. Make sure your left fist is guarding your face, and keep your chin down.

4. 오른쪽 팔뚝 중단 옆막기

얼굴은 3시 방향, 오른쪽 팔뚝 하단 옆막기를 한 상태에서 턱을 아래로 당겨 양다리의 간격은 어깨넓이 왼쪽 주먹은 왼쪽 턱을 막은대로 오른쪽 주먹을 쥐면서 중심은 양다리에 두고, 허리를 반시계 방향으로 틀어 오른쪽 팔뚝을 안으로 돌려 중단 옆막기 (중방자세)

Right Middle Forearm Side Block:

Step out with your right leg towards 4:00 into a right side Middle Stance, and face towards 3:00. Execute a right side Middle Side Block with your right forearm; blocking from the outside in. Make sure your left fist is guarding your face, and keep your chin down.

동산형: Hill Form

5. 왼쪽 정권 직선펀치 "기합"

얼굴은 3시 방향, 오른쪽 팔뚝 중단 옆막기를 한 상태에서 상대의 눈을 주시 하면서 턱을 아래로 당겨 양 다리의 간격은 어깨넓이 몸을 시계 방향으로 돌리면서 왼발을 들어 3시 방향 앞으로 한발 옮겨 놓으며 오른쪽 주먹은 오른쪽 턱을 막으며 중심은 양다리에 두고, 기합을 넣으며 왼쪽 주먹을 돌려 정권 직선펀치를 하면서 왼쪽 어깨로 왼쪽 턱을 방어 (선 자세)

Left Fist Straight Punch "Ki-Hap":

Step forward with your left leg towards 3:00 while turning your body clockwise. Execute a straight left punch, and face towards 6:00. Make sure your right fist is guarding your face, and keep your chin down. (Ki-Hap)

6. 왼쪽 팔꿈치 훅

얼굴은 3시 방향, 왼쪽 정권 직선펀치를 한 상태에서 턱을 아래로 당겨 양다리의 간격은 어깨넓이 오른쪽 주먹은 오른쪽 턱을 막은대로 중심은 양다리에 두고, 왼발을 돌려 밀면서 몸을 6시 시계 방향으로 틀어 왼쪽 팔꿈치로 훅 치기 (선 자세)

Left Elbow Hook:

Push off with your left leg while turning your body clockwise, and hook your left elbow straight across. Make sure your right fist is guarding your face, and keep your chin down.

7. 왼쪽 팔뚝 하단 옆막기

얼굴은 6시 방향, 왼쪽 팔꿈치 훅을 한 상태에서 턱을 아래로 당겨 양다리의 간격은 어깨넓이 오른쪽 주먹은 오른쪽 턱을 막은대로 몸을 반시계 방향으로 돌리면서 왼발을 들어 180도로 돌려 9시 방향 앞으로 한발 옮겨 놓으며 왼쪽 주먹을 쥐면서 중심은 뒷다리에 두고, 왼쪽 팔뚝을 바깥으로 돌려 하단 옆막기 (선 자세)

Left Low Forearm Side Block:

Turn your body counter-clockwise and step with your left leg towards 9:00 in a left side Back Stance. Execute a left side Low Forearm Side Block with your left forearm while keeping a tight fist. Make sure your right fist is guarding your face, and keep your chin down.

8. 왼쪽 팔뚝 중단 옆막기

얼굴은 9시 방향, 왼쪽 팔뚝 하단 옆막기를 한 상태에서 턱을 아래로 당겨 양다리의 간격은 어깨넓이 오른쪽 주먹은 오른쪽 턱을 막은대로 왼쪽 주먹을 쥐면서 중심은 양다리에 두고, 허리를 시계 방향으로 틀어 왼쪽 팔뚝을 안으로 돌려 중단 옆막기 (중방자세)

Left Middle Forearm Side Block:

Step out with your left leg towards 8:00 into a left side Middle Stance, and face towards 9:00. Execute a left side Middle Side Block with your left forearm; blocking from the outside in. Make sure your right fist is guarding your face, and keep your chin down.

9. 오른쪽 정권 직선펀치 "기합"

얼굴은 9시 방향, 왼쪽 팔뚝 중단 옆막기를 한 상태에서 상대의 눈을 주시 하면서 턱을 아래로 당겨 양다리의 간격은 어깨넓이 몸을 반시계 방향으로 돌리면서 오른발을 들어 9시 방향 앞으로 한발 옮겨 놓으며 왼쪽 주먹은 왼쪽 턱을 막으며 중심은 양다리에 두고, 기합을 넣으며 오른쪽 주먹을 돌려 정권 직선펀치를 하면서 오른쪽 어깨로 오른쪽 턱을 방어 (선자세)

Right Fist Straight Punch "Ki-Hap":

Step forward with your right leg towards 9:00 while turning your body counter-clockwise. Execute a straight right punch, and face towards 6:00. Make sure your left fist is guarding your face, and keep your chin down. (Ki-Hap)

10. 오른쪽 팔꿈치 훅

얼굴은 9시 방향, 오른쪽 정권 직선펀치를 한 상태에서 턱을 아래로 당겨 양다리의 간격은 어깨넓이 왼쪽 주먹은 왼쪽 턱을 막은대로 중심은 양다리에 두고, 오른발을 돌려 밀면서 몸을 6시 반시계 방향으로 틀어 오른쪽 팔꿈치로 훅치기 (선자세)

Right Elbow Hook:

Push off with your right leg while turning your body counter-clockwise, and hook your right elbow straight across. Make sure your left fist is guarding your face, and keep your chin down.

11. 오른쪽 팔뚝 하단 옆막기

얼굴은 6시 방향, 오른쪽 팔꿈치 훅을 한 상태에서 턱을 아래로 당겨 양다리의 간격은 어깨넓이 왼쪽 주먹은 왼쪽 턱을 막은대로 몸을 시계 방향으로 돌리면서 오른발을 들어 270도로 돌려 6시 방향 앞으로 한발 옮겨 놓으며 오른쪽 주먹을 쥐면서 중심은 뒷다리에 두고, 오른쪽 팔뚝을 바같으로 돌려 하단 옆막기 (후방자세)

Right Low Forearm Side Block:

Turn your body clockwise and step with your right leg towards 6:00 in a right side Back Stance. Execute a right side Low Forearm Side Block with your right forearm while keeping a tight fist. Make sure your left fist is guarding your face, and keep your chin down.

12. 오른쪽 팔뚝 중단 옆막기

얼굴은 6시 방향, 오른쪽 팔뚝 하단 옆막기를 한 상태에서 턱을 아래로 당겨 양다리의 간격은 어깨넓이 왼쪽 주먹은 왼쪽 턱을 막은대로 오른쪽 주먹을 쥐면서 중심은 양다리에 두고, 허리를 반시계 방향으로 틀어 오른쪽 팔뚝을 안으로 돌려 중단 옆막기 (중방자세)

Right Middle Forearm Side Block:

Step out with your right leg towards 7:00 into a right side Middle Stance, and face towards 6:00. Execute a right side Middle Side Block with your right forearm; blocking from the outside in. Make sure your left fist is guarding your face, and keep your chin down.

13. 왼쪽 정권 직선펀치 "기합"

얼굴은 6시 방향, 오른쪽 팔뚝 중단 옆막기를 한 상태에서 상대의 눈을 주시 하면서 턱을 아래로 당겨 양 다리의 간격은 어깨넓이 몸을 시계 방향으로 돌리면서 왼발을 들어 6시 방향 앞으로 한발 옮겨 놓으며 오른쪽 주먹은 오른쪽 턱을 막으며 중심은 양다리에 두고, 기합을 넣으며 왼쪽 주먹을 돌려 정권 직선펀치를 하면서 왼쪽 어깨로 왼쪽 턱을 방어 (선자세)

Left Fist Straight Punch "Ki-Hap":

Step forward with your left leg towards 6:00 while turning your body clockwise. Execute a straight left punch, and face towards 9:00. Make sure your right fist is guarding your face, and keep your chin down. (Ki-Hap)

14. 왼쪽 팔뚝 하단 옆막기

얼굴은 6시 방향, 왼쪽 정권 직선펀치를 한 상태에서 턱을 아래로 당겨 양다리의 간격은 어깨넓이 오른쪽 주먹은 오른쪽 턱을 막은대로 몸을 반시계 방향으로 돌리면서 왼쪽 주먹을 쥐면서 중심은 뒷다리에 두고, 왼쪽 팔뚝을 바깥으로 돌려 하단 옆막기 (후방자세)

Left Low Forearm Side Block:

Lean back into a left side Back Stance. Execute a left side Low Forearm Side Block with your left forearm while keeping a tight fist. Make sure your right fist is guarding your face, and keep your chin down.

15. 왼쪽 팔뚝 중단 옆막기

얼굴은 6시 방향, 왼쪽 팔뚝 하단 옆막기를 한 상태에서 턱을 아래로 당겨 양다리의 간격은 어깨넓이 오른쪽 주먹은 오른쪽 턱을 막은대로 왼쪽 주먹을 쥐면서 중심은 양다리에 두고, 허리를 시계 방향으로 틀어 왼쪽 팔뚝을 안으로 돌려 중단 옆막기 (중방자세)

Left Middle Forearm Side Block:

Step out with your left leg towards 5:00 into a left side Middle Stance, and face towards 6:00. Execute a left side Middle Side Block with your left forearm; blocking from the outside in. Make sure your right fist is guarding your face, and keep your chin down.

16. 오른쪽 정권 직선펀치 "기합"

얼굴은 6시 방향, 왼쪽 팔뚝 중단 옆막기를 한 상태에서 상대의 눈을 주시 하면서 턱을 아래로 당겨 양다리의 간격은 어깨넓이 몸을 반시계 방향으로 돌리면서 오른발을 들어 6시 방향 앞으로 한발 옮겨 놓으며 왼쪽 주먹은 왼쪽 턱을 막으며 중심은 양다리에 두고, 기합을 넣으며 오른쪽 주먹을 돌려 정권 직선펀치를 하면서 오른쪽 어깨로 오른쪽 턱을 방어 (선자세)

Right Fist Straight Punch "Ki-Hap":

Step forward with your right leg towards 6:00 while turning your body counter-clockwise. Execute a straight right punch, and face towards 3:00. Make sure your left fist is guarding your face, and keep your chin down. <Step Right Punch> (Ki-Hap)

동산형: Hill Form

17. 오른쪽 팔뚝 하단 옆막기

얼굴은 6시 방향, 오른쪽 정권 직선펀치를 한 상태에서 턱을 아래로 당겨 양다리의 간격은 어깨넓이 왼쪽 주먹은 왼쪽 턱을 막은대로 몸을 시계 방향으로 돌리면서 오른쪽 주먹을 쥐면서 중심은 뒷다리에 두고, 오른쪽 팔뚝을 바같으로 돌려 하단 옆막기 (후방자세)

Right Low Forearm Side Block:

Lean back into a right side Back Stance. Execute a right side Low Forearm Side Block with your right forearm while keeping a tight fist. Make sure your left fist is guarding your face, and keep your chin down.

18. 오른쪽 팔뚝 중단 옆막기

얼굴은 6시 방향, 오른쪽 팔뚝 하단 옆막기를 한 상태에서 턱을 아래로 당겨 양다리의 간격은 어깨넓이 왼쪽 주먹은 왼쪽 턱을 막은대로 오른쪽 주먹을쥐면서 중심은 양다리에 두고, 허리를 반시계 반향으로 틀어 오른쪽 팔뚝을 안으로 돌려 중단 옆막기 (중방자세)

Right Middle Forearm Side Block:

Step out with your right leg towards 7:00 into a left side Middle Stance, and face towards 6:00. Execute a right side Middle Side Block with your right forearm; blocking from the outside in. Make sure your left fist is guarding your face, and keep your chin down.

19. 왼쪽 손창 수평찌르기 "기합"

얼굴은 6시 방향, 오른쪽 팔뚝 중단 옆막기를 한 상태에서 상대의 눈을 주시 하면서 턱을 아래로 당겨 양 다리의 간격은 어깨넓이 몸을 시계 방향으로 돌리면서 왼발을 들어 6시 방향 앞으로 한발 옮겨 놓으며 오른쪽 주먹은 오른쪽 턱을 막으며 중심은 앞다리에 두고, 기합을 넣으며 왼쪽 주먹을 돌려 손창을 수평으로 목젖 찌르면서 왼쪽 어깨로 왼쪽 턱을 방어 (전방자세)

Left Spear Hand "Ki-Hap":

Step forward with your left leg towards 6:00 while turning your body clockwise. Execute a straight left knife hand, and face towards 9:00. Make sure your right fist is guarding your face, and keep your chin down. (Ki-Hap)

20. 오른쪽 상단 앞차기

얼굴은 6시 방향, 왼쪽 손창 수평찌르기를 한 상태에서 턱을 아래로 당겨 양다리의 간격은 어깨넓이 오른쪽 주먹은 오른쪽 턱을 막은대로 중심은 왼쪽 다리에 두고 오른발을 들어 왼쪽 손바닥을 차고, 왼쪽 어깨로 왼쪽 턱을 방어 (선자세)

Right High Front Kick to Spear Hand:

Keep your left knife hand stationary. Pick up your right knee, and execute a right leg High Front Kick to your left knife hand. Make sure you keep your right fist guarding your face, and keep your chin down.

21. 오른쪽 팔뚝 하단 옆막기

얼굴은 6시 방향, 오른쪽 상단 앞차기를 한 상태에서 턱을 아래로 당겨 양다리의 간격은 어깨넓이 왼쪽 주먹은 왼쪽 턱을 막으며 몸을 시계 방향으로 돌리면서 오른발을 180도로 돌려 12시 방향 앞으로 한발 옮겨 놓으며 오른쪽 주먹을 쥐면서 중심은 뒷다리에 두고, 오른쪽 팔뚝을 바같으로 돌려 하단 옆막기 (후방자세)

Right Low Forearm Side Block:

Turn your body clockwise and step with your right leg towards 12:00 in a right side Back Stance. Execute a right side Low Forearm Side Block with your right forearm while keeping a tight fist. Make sure your left fist is guarding your face, and keep your chin down.

22. 오른쪽 팔뚝 중단 옆막기

얼굴은 12시 방향, 오른쪽 팔뚝 하단 옆막기를 한 상태에서 턱을 아래로 당겨 양다리의 간격은 어깨넓이 왼쪽 주먹은 왼쪽 턱을 막은대로 오른쪽 주먹을 쥐면서 중심은 양다리에 두고, 허리를 반시계 방향으로 틀어 오른쪽 팔뚝을 안으로 돌려 중단 옆막기 (중방자세)

Right Middle Forearm Side Block:

Step out with your right leg towards 1:00 into a right side Middle Stance, and face towards 12:00. Execute a right side Middle Side Block with your right forearm; blocking from the outside in. Make sure your left fist is guarding your face, and keep your chin down.

23. 왼쪽 정권 직선펀치 "기합"

얼굴은 12시 방향, 오른쪽 팔뚝 중단 옆막기를 한 상태에서 상대의 눈을 주시 하면서 턱을 아래로 당겨 양 다리의 간격은 어깨넓이 몸을 시계 방향으로 돌리면서 왼발을 들어 12시 방향 앞으로 한발 옮겨 놓으며 오른쪽 주먹은 오른쪽 턱을 막으며 중심은 양다리에 두고, 기합을 넣으며 왼쪽 주먹을 돌려 정권 직선펀치를 하면서 왼쪽 어깨로 왼쪽 턱을 방어 (선자세)

Left Fist straight Punch "Ki-Hap":

Step forward with your left leg towards 12:00 while turning your body clockwise. Execute a straight left punch, and face towards 3:00. Make sure your right fist is guarding your face, and keep your chin down. (Ki-Hap)

24. 왼쪽 팔뚝 하단 옆막기

얼굴은 12시 방향, 왼쪽 정권 직선펀치를 한 상태에서 턱을 아래로 당겨 양다리의 간격은 어깨넓이 오른쪽 주먹은 오른쪽 턱을 막은대로 몸을 반시계 방향으로 돌리면서 왼쪽 주먹을 쥐면서 중심은 뒷다리에 두고, 왼쪽 팔뚝을 바깥으로 돌려 하단 옆막기 (후방자세)

Left Low Forearm Side Block:

Lean back into a left side Back Stance. Execute a left side Low Forearm Side Block with your left forearm while keeping a tight fist. Make sure your right fist is guarding your face, and keep your chin down.

동산형: Hill Form

25. 왼쪽 팔뚝 중단 옆막기

얼굴은 12시 방향, 왼쪽 팔뚝 하단 옆막기를 한 상태에서 턱을 아래로 당겨 양다리의 간격은 어깨넓이 오른쪽 주먹은 오른쪽 턱을 막은대로 왼쪽 주먹을 쥐면서 중심은 양다리에 두고, 허리를 시계 방향으로 틀어 왼쪽 팔뚝을 안으로 돌려 중단 옆막기 (중방자세)

Left Middle Forearm Side block:

Step out with your left leg towards 11:00 into a left side Middle Stance, and face towards 12:00. Execute a left side Middle Side Block with your left forearm; blocking from the outside in. Make sure your right fist is guarding your face, and keep your chin down.

26. 오른쪽 정권 직선펀치 "기합"

얼굴은 12시 방향, 왼쪽 팔뚝 중단 옆막기를 한 상태에서 상대의 눈을 주시 하면서 턱을 아래로 당겨 양다리의 간격은 어깨넓이 몸을 반시계 방향으로 돌리면서 오른발을 들어 12시 방향 앞으로 한발 옮겨 놓으며 왼쪽 주먹은 왼쪽 턱을 막으며 중심은 양다리에 두고, 기합을 넣으며 오른쪽 주먹을 돌려 정권 직선펀치를 하면서 오른쪽 어깨로 오른쪽 턱을 방어 (선자세)

Right Fist Straight Punch "Ki-Hap":

Step forward with your right leg towards 12:00 while turning your body counter-clockwise. Execute a straight right punch, and face towards 9:00. Make sure your left fist is guarding your face, and keep your chin down. (Ki-Hap)

27. 오른쪽 팔뚝 하단 옆막기

얼굴은 12시 방향, 오른쪽 정권 직선펀치를 한 상태에서 턱을 아래로 당겨 양다리의 간격은 어깨넓이 왼쪽 주먹은 왼쪽 턱을 막은대로 몸을 시계 방향으로 돌리면서 오른쪽 주먹을 쥐면서 중심은 뒷다리에 두고, 오른쪽 팔뚝을 바깥으로 돌려 하단 옆막기 (후방자세)

Right Low Forearm Side Block:

Lean back into a right side Back Stance. Execute a right side Low Forearm Side Block with your right forearm while keeping a tight fist. Make sure your left fist is guarding your face, and keep your chin down.

28. 오른쪽 팔뚝 중단 옆막기

얼굴은 12시 방향, 오른쪽 팔뚝 하단 옆막기를 한 상태에서 턱을 아래로 당겨 양다리의 간격은 어깨넓이 왼쪽 주먹은 왼쪽 턱을 막은대로 오른쪽 주먹을 쥐면서 중심은 양다리에 두고, 허리를 반시계 방향으로 틀어 오른쪽 팔뚝을 안으로 돌려 중단 옆막기 (중방자세)

Right Middle Forearm Side Block:

Step out with your right leg towards 1:00 into a left side Middle Stance, and face towards 12:00. Execute a right side Middle Side Block with your right forearm; blocking from the outside in. Make sure your left fist is guarding your face, and keep your chin down.

29. 왼쪽 손창 수평찌르기 "기합"

얼굴은 12시 방향, 오른쪽 팔뚝 중단 옆막기를 한 상태에서 상대의 눈을 주시 하면서 턱을 아래로 당겨 양 다리의 간격은 어깨넓이 몸을시계 방향으로 돌리면서 왼발을 들어 12시 방향 앞으로 한발 옮겨 놓으며 오른쪽 주먹은 오른쪽 턱을 막으며 중심은 앞다리에 두고, 기합을 넣으며 왼쪽 주먹을 돌려 손창을 수평으로 목젖 찌르면서 왼쪽 어깨로 왼쪽 턱을 방어 (전방자세)

Left Spear Hand "Ki-Hap":

Step forward with your left leg towards 12:00 while turning your body clockwise. Execute a straight left knife hand, and face towards 3:00. Make sure your right fist is guarding your face, and keep your chin down. (Ki-Hap)

30. 오른쪽 상단 앞차기

얼굴은 12시 방향, 왼쪽 손창 수평찌르기를 한 상태에서 턱을 아래로 당겨 양다리의 간격은 어깨넓이 오른쪽 주먹은 오른쪽 턱을 막은대로 중심은 왼쪽 다리에 두고, 오른발을 들어 왼쪽 손바닥을 차고, 왼쪽 어깨로 왼쪽 턱을 방어 (선자세)

Right Hight Front Kick to Spear Hand:

Keep your left knife hand stationary. Pick up your right knee, and execute a right leg High Front Kick to your left knife hand. Make sure you keep your right fist guarding your face, and keep your chin down.

31. 오른쪽 팔뚝 하단 옆막기

얼굴은 12시 방향, 오른쪽 상단 앞차기를 한 상태에서 턱을 아래로 당겨 왼쪽 주먹은 왼쪽 턱을 막으며 몸을 시계 방향으로 돌리면서 오른발을 180도로 돌려 6시 방향 앞으로 한발 옮겨 놓으며 오른쪽 주먹을 쥐면서 중심은 뒷다리에 두고, 오른쪽 팔뚝을 바같으로 돌려 하단 옆막기 (후방자세)

Right Low Forearm Side Block:
Turn your body clockwise and step with your right leg towards 6:00 in a right side Back Stance. Execute a right side Low Forearm Side Block with your right forearm while keeping a tight fist. Make sure your left fist is guarding your face, and keep your chin down.

32. 오른쪽 팔뚝 중단 옆막기

얼굴은 6시 방향, 오른쪽 팔뚝 하단 옆막기를 한 상태에서 턱을 아래로 당겨 양다리의 간격은 어깨넓이 왼쪽 주먹은 왼쪽 턱을 막은대로 오른쪽 주먹을 쥐면서 중심은 양다리에 두고, 허리를 반시계 방향으로 틀어 오른쪽 팔뚝을 안으로 돌려 중단 옆막기 (중방자세)

Right Middle Forearm Side Block:
Step out with your right leg towards 7:00 into a right side Middle Stance, and face towards 6:00. Execute a right side Middle Side Block with your right forearm; blocking from the outside in. Make sure your left fist is guarding your face, and keep your chin down.

동산형: Hill Form

합도술

CHA-RYUK FORM
차 | 력 | 형

01. 차력 "기합" (차력자세)
    Cha Ryuk "Ki-Hap" (Cha-Ryuk stance)

02. 양손날 내려치기 "기합" (앉은자세)
    Two Knife Hand Chop "Ki-Hap" (Sit stance)

03. 오른쪽 양손날 하단 옆막기 (후방자세)
    Right Low to Knife Hand Side Block (back stance)

04. 오른쪽 양손날 상단 옆치기 "기합" (전방자세)
    Right High to Knife Hand Chop Attack "Ki-Hap" (front stance)

05. 왼쪽 정권 직선펀치 "기합" (선자세)
    Left Fist straight Punch "Ki-Hap" (stand Stance)

06. 왼쪽 팔꿈치 훅 (선자세)
    Left Elbow Hook (stand stance)

07. 왼쪽 양손날 하단 옆막기 (후방자세)
    Left Low two Knife Hand Side Block (back stance)

08. 왼쪽 양손날 상단 옆치기 "기합" (전방자세)
    Left High two Knife Hand Chop Attack "Ki-Hap" (front stance)

09. 오른쪽 정권 직선펀치 "기합" (선자세)
    Right Fist Straight Punch "Ki-Hap" (stand stance)

10. 오른쪽 팔꿈치 훅 (선자세)
    Right Elbow Hook (stand stance)

11. 오른쪽 양손날 하단 옆막기 (후방자세)
    Right Low to Knife Hand Side Block (back stance)

12. 오른쪽 양손날 상단 옆치기 "기합" (전방자세)
    Right High to Knife Hand Chop Attack "Ki-Hap" (front stance)

13. 왼쪽 정권 직선펀치 "기합" (선자세)
    Left Fist straight Punch "Ki-Hap" (stand Stance)

14. 오른쪽 손창 수평찌르기 "기합" (전방자세)
    Right Spear Hand "Ki-Hap" (front stance)

15. 왼쪽 하단 앞차기 (선자세)
    Left Low Front Kick (stand stance)

16. 오른쪽 상단 앞차기 (선자세)
    Right Hight Front Kick to Knife Hand (stand stance)

17. 왼쪽 한발 옮겨놓기 (전방자세)
    Left Step (stand stance)

18. 왼쪽 두손짚고 전방회전 낙법 (전방회전 낙법자세)
    Left Two Hand Nak-Bub (Front Nak-Bub stance)

19. 오른쪽 양손날 하단 옆막기 (후방자세)
    Right Low to Knife Hand Side Block (back stance)

20. 오른쪽 양손날 상단 옆치기 "기합" (전방자세)
    Right High two Knife Hand Chop Attack "Ki-Hap" (front stance)

21. 왼쪽 정권 직선펀치 "기합" (선자세)
    Left Fist straight Punch "Ki-Hap" (stand Stance)

22. 오른쪽 장풍지르기 "기합" (선자세)
    Right Palm Strike "Ki-Hap" (stand stance)

23. 왼쪽 한손날 옆목치기 "기합" (선자세)
    Left Knife Hand Side Chop "Ki-Hap" (stand stance)

24. 오른쪽 손창 수평찌르기 "기합" (전방자세)
    Right Spear Hand "Ki-Hap" (front stance)

25. 왼쪽 하단 앞차기 (선자세)
    Left Low Front Kick (stand stance)

26. 오른쪽 상단 앞차기 (선자세)
    Right High Front Kick to Knife Hand (stand stance)

27. 오른쪽 양손날 하단 옆막기 (후방자세)
    Right Low to Knife Hand Side Block (back stance)

28. 오른쪽 양손날 옆목치기 "기합" (전방자세)
    Right two Knife Hand Chop Attack "Ki-Hap" (front stance)

1. 차력 "기합"

얼굴은 12시 정면 방향, 허리를 똑바로 세운 선자세에서 양무릎을 약간 굽혀 양팔과 양다리의 간격은 어깨 넓이 중심은 양다리에 두고 양팔을 들어 양손날은 양눈 높이에 두며 숨을 들어 마신후 숨을 멈추고, 정신 통일로 입으로 소리와 호흡을 고르게 내면서 손, 팔, 다리, 복부에 앉은 자세까지 힘을 발육 시켜 그힘을 몰아 들고 일어나서 선자세에서 팔을 옆으로 완전히 뻗은다음 코로 숨을 천천히 들이 마시며 양팔을 아래로 내리면서 손, 팔, 다리, 복부에 힘을 이완 시킨다 (차력자세)

Cha Ryuk "Ki-Hap":

In a Cha-Ryuk Stance position facing 12:00, vocalize and exhale slowly while concentrating on developing your Ki. Bend both your legs while you vocalize until you run out of breath. Hold your breath, and come back up while focusing on transferring your Ki to different parts of your body. When reaching to the top, extend both arms out sideways while still transferring your Ki. Once you reach full extension, inhale slowly through your nose and relax your body. (Ki-Hap)

2. 양손날 내려치기 "기합"

얼굴은 12시 정면 방향, 차력을 한 상태에서 양다리의 간격은 어깨넓이 중심을 양다리에 두고, 양손날을 겨드랑이 앞에 올려놓고, 온몸에 있는 힘을 어깨에 집중시켜 양무릎을 굽혀 앉으면서 양손에 기를몰아 기합 소리를 내면서 양손날을 아래로 동시에 내려쳐 격파 (앉은자세)

Two Knife Hand Chop "Ki-Hap":

Bend both your legs, and drop down while keeping your back straight. Execute a Double Knife Hand Chop straight down. (Ki-Hap)

3. 오른쪽 양손날 하단 옆막기

얼굴은 12시 정면 방향, 양손날로 내려치기를 한 상태에서 일어나서 턱을 아래로 당겨 양다리의 간격은 어깨넓이 몸을 시계 방향으로 돌리면서 오른발을 들어 3시 방향 제자리에서 돌려 놓으며 왼쪽 손바닥은 위로 팔뚝은 띠에 대면서 오른쪽 손바닥을 아래로 중심은 뒷다리에 두고, 오른쪽으로 허리를 틀어 동시에 양손날 하단 옆막기 (후방자세)

Right Low to Knife Hand Side Block:

Turn your body clockwise so you are facing towards 3:00 in a right side Back Stance. Execute a right side Low Side Block with your right forearm. Keep your left hand at belt level with your palm face up.

4. 오른쪽 양손날 상단 옆치기 "기합"

얼굴은 3시 방향, 오른쪽 양손날 하단 옆막기를 한 상태에서 상대의 눈을 주시 하면서 턱을 아래로 당겨 양다리의 간격은 어깨넓이 왼쪽 손바닥은 위로 오른쪽 손바닥을 아래로 오른발을 들어 4시 방향으로 옮겨 놓으며 중심은 앞다리에 두고, 기합을 넣으며 오른쪽으로 양손날 상단 옆치기 (전방자세)

Right High to Knife Hand Chop Attack "Ki-Hap":

Step out with your right leg towards 3:00 and get into a right side Forward Stance. Execute a right side Chop Attack with your right knife hand. Keep your left elbow by your side with your knife hand palm up. Make sure you keep your chin down. (Ki-Hap)

5. 왼쪽 정권 직선펀치 "기합"

얼굴은 3시 방향, 오른쪽 양손날 상단 옆치기를 한 상태에서 상대의 눈을 주시 하면서 턱을 아래로 당겨 양다리의 간격은 어깨넓이 몸을 시계 방향으로 돌리면서 왼발을 들어 3시 방향 앞으로 한발 옮겨 놓으며 오른쪽 주먹은 오른쪽 턱을 막으며 중심은 양다리에 두고, 기합을 넣으며 왼쪽 주먹을 돌려 정권 직선펀치 를 하면서 왼쪽 어깨로 왼쪽 턱을 방어 (선자세)

Left Fist straight Punch "Ki-Hap":

Step forward with your left leg towards 3:00 while turning your body clockwise. Execute a straight left punch, and face towards 6:00. Make sure your right fist is guarding your face, and keep your chin down. (Ki-Hap)

6. 왼쪽 팔꿈치 훅

얼굴은 3시 방향, 왼쪽 정권 직선펀치를 한 상태에서 턱을 아래로 당겨 양다리의 간격은 어깨넓이 오른쪽 주먹은 오른쪽 턱을 막은대로 중심은 양다리에 두고, 왼발을 돌려 밀면서 몸을 6시 시계 방향으로 틀어 왼쪽 팔꿈치로 훅치기 (선자세)

Left Elbow Hook:

Push off with your left leg while turning your body clockwise, and hook your left elbow straight across. Make sure your right fist is guarding your face, and keep your chin down.

7. 왼쪽 양손날 하단 옆막기

얼굴은 6시 방향, 왼쪽 팔꿈치 훅을 한 상태에서 턱을 아래로 당겨 양다리의 간격은 어깨넓이 몸을 반시계 방향으로 돌리면서 왼발을 들어 180도로 돌려 9시 방향 앞으로 한발 옮겨 놓으며 오른쪽 손바닥은 위로 팔뚝은 띠에 대면서 왼쪽 손바닥을 아래로 중심은 뒷다리에 두고, 왼쪽으로 허리를 틀어 동시에 양손날 하단 옆막기 (후방자세)

Left Low two Knife Hand Side Block:

Turn your body counter-clockwise and step with your left leg towards 9:00 in a left side Back Stance. Execute a left side Low Side Block with your left forearm. Keep your right hand at belt level with your palm face up.

8. 왼쪽 양손날 상단 옆치기 "기합"

얼굴은 9시 방향, 왼쪽 양손날 하단 옆막기를 한 상태에서 상대의 눈을 주시 하면서 턱을 아래로 당겨 양 다리의 간격은 어깨넓이 오른쪽 손바닥은 위로 왼쪽 손바닥을 아래로 왼발을 들어 8시 방향으로 옮겨 놓 으며 중심은 앞다리에 두고, 기합을 넣으며 왼쪽으로 양손날 상단 옆치기 (전방자세)

Left High two Knife Hand Chop Attack "Ki-Hap":

Step out with your left leg towards 9:00 and get into a left side Forward Stance. Execute a left side Chop Attack with your left knife hand. Keep your right elbow by your side with your knife hand palm up. Make sure you keep your chin down. Ki-Hap)

9. 오른쪽 정권 직선펀치 "기합"

얼굴은 9시 방향, 왼쪽 양손날 상단 옆치기를 한 상태에서 상대의 눈을 주시 하면서 턱을 아래로 당겨 양 다리의 간격은 어깨넓이 몸을 반시계 방향으로 돌리면서 오른발을 들어 9시 방향 앞으로 한발 옮겨 놓으 며 왼쪽 주먹은 왼쪽 턱을 막으며 중심은 양다리에 두고, 기합을 넣으며 오른쪽 주먹을 돌려 정권 직선펀 치를 하면서 오른쪽 어깨로 오른쪽 턱을 방어 (선자세)

Right Fist Straight Punch "Ki-Hap":

TStep forward with your right leg towards 9:00 while turning your body clockwise. Execute a straight right punch, and face towards 6:00. Make sure your left fist is guarding your face, and keep your chin down. (Ki-Hap)

10. 오른쪽 팔꿈치 훅

얼굴은 9시 방향, 오른쪽 정권 직선펀치를 한 상태에서 턱을 아래로 당겨 양다리의 간격은 어깨넓이 왼쪽 주먹은 왼쪽 턱을 막은대로 중심은 양다리에 두고, 오른발을 돌려 밀면서 몸을 6시 반시계 방향으로 틀어 오른쪽 팔꿈치로 훅치기 (선자세)

Right Elbow Hook:

Push off with your right leg while turning your body counter-clockwise, and hook your right elbow straight across. Make sure your left fist is guarding your face, and keep your chin down.

11. 오른쪽 양손날 하단 옆막기

얼굴은 6시 방향, 오른쪽 팔꿈치 훅을 한 상태에서 턱을 아래로 당겨 양다리의 간격은 어깨넓이 몸을 시계 방향으로 돌리면서 오른발을 들어 270도로 돌려 6시 방향 앞으로 한발 옮겨 놓으며 왼쪽 손바닥은 위로 팔뚝은 띠에 대면서 오른쪽 손바닥을 아래로 중심은 뒷다리에 두고, 오른쪽으로 허리를 틀어 동시에 양손 날 하단 옆막기 (후방자세)

Right Low to Knife Hand Side Block:

Turn your body clockwise and step with your right leg towards 6:00 in a right side Back Stance. Execute a right side Low Side Block with your right forearm. Keep your left hand at belt level with your palm face up.

12. 오른쪽 양손날 상단 옆치기 "기합"

얼굴은 6시 방향, 오른쪽 양손날 하단 옆막기를 한 상태에서 상대의 눈을 주시 하면서 턱을 아래로 당겨 양다리의 간격은 어깨넓이 왼쪽 손바닥은 위로 오른쪽 손바닥을 아래로 오른발을 들어 7시 방향으로 옮겨 놓으며 중심은 앞다리에 두고, 기합을 넣으며 오른쪽으로 양손날 상단 옆치기 (전방자세)

Right High to Knife Hand Chop Attack "Ki-Hap":

Step out with your right leg towards 6:00 and get into a right side Forward Stance. Execute a right side Chop Attack with your right knife hand. Keep your left elbow by your side with your knife hand palm up. Make sure you keep your chin down. (Ki-Hap)

13. 왼쪽 정권 직선펀치 "기합"

얼굴은 6시 방향, 오른쪽 양손날 상단 옆치기를 한 상태에서 상대의 눈을 주시 하면서 턱을 아래로 당겨 양다리의 간격은 어깨넓이 몸을 시계 방향으로 돌리면서 왼발을 들어 6시 방향 앞으로 한발 옮겨 놓으며 오른쪽 주먹은 오른쪽 턱을 막으며 중심은 양다리에 두고, 기합을 넣으며 왼쪽 주먹을 돌려 정권 직선펀치 를 하면서 왼쪽 어깨로 왼쪽 턱을 방어 (선자세)

Left Fist straight Punch "Ki-Hap":

Step forward with your left leg towards 6:00 while turning your body clockwise. Execute a straight left punch, and face towards 9:00. Make sure your right fist is guarding your face, and keep your chin down. (Ki-Hap)

14. 오른쪽 손창 수평찌르기 "기합"

얼굴은 6시 방향, 왼쪽 정권 직선펀치를 한 상태에서 상대의 눈을 주시 하면서 턱을 아래로 당겨 양다리의 간격은 어깨넓이 몸을 반시계 방향으로 돌리면서 오른발을 들어 6시 방향 앞으로 한발 옮겨 놓으며 왼쪽 주먹은 왼쪽 턱을 막으며 중심은 앞다리에 두고, 기합을 넣으며 오른쪽 주먹을 돌려 손창을 수평으로 목젖 찌르면서 오른쪽 어깨로 오른쪽 턱을 방어 (전방자세)

Right Spear Hand "Ki-Hap":

Step forward with your right leg towards 6:00 while turning your body counter-clockwise. Execute a straight right knife hand, and face towards 3:00. Make sure your left fist is guarding your face, and keep your chin down. (Ki-Hap)

15. 왼쪽 하단 앞차기

얼굴은 6시 방향, 오른쪽 손창 수평찌르기를 한 상태에서 턱을 아래로 당겨 양다리의 간격은 어깨넓이 왼쪽 주먹은 왼쪽 턱을 막은대로 중심은 오른쪽 다리에 두고, 왼발을 들어 하단 앞차기를 하고, 오른쪽 어깨로 오른쪽 턱을 방어 (선자세)

Left Low Front Kick:

Keep your right knife hand stationary. Pick up your left knee, and execute a left leg Low Front Kick. Make sure you keep your left fist guarding your face, and keep your chin down.

차력형: Cha-Ryuk Form

16. 오른쪽 상단 앞차기

얼굴은 6시 방향, 왼쪽 하단 앞차기를 한 상태에서 턱을 아래로 당겨 양다리의 간격은 어깨넓이 왼쪽 주먹은 왼쪽 턱을 막은대로 왼발을 한발 앞으로 옮겨 놓으며 중심은 왼쪽 다리에 두고, 오른발을 들어 오른쪽 손바닥을 차고, 오른쪽 어깨로 오른쪽 턱을 방어 (선자세)

Right Hight Front Kick to Knife Hand:

Keep your right knife hand stationary. Pick up your right knee, and execute a right leg High Front Kick to your right knife hand. Make sure you keep your left fist guarding your face, and keep your chin down.

17. 왼쪽 한발 옮겨놓기

얼굴은 6시 방향, 오른쪽 상단 앞차기를 한 상태에서 오른발을 한발 앞으로 옮겨 놓으며 왼쪽 주먹은 왼쪽 턱을 막은대로 턱을 아래로 당겨 오른쪽 주먹은 오른쪽 턱을 막으며 중심은 오른쪽 다리에 두고, 왼발을 들어 6시 방향 앞으로 한발 옮겨놓기 (선자세)

Left Step:

Step forward with your left leg towards 6:00. Make sure you're keeping your guard up.

18. 왼쪽 두손짚고 전방회전 낙법

얼굴은 6시 방향, 왼쪽 한발 옮겨놓은 상태에서 몸을 엎드려 중심은 앞다리에 두고, 왼쪽 손바닥은 왼쪽 엄지 발가락 옆에 대며 오른쪽 손바닥을 바닥에 짚고, 양검지를 서로 대며 턱을 아래로 당겨 얼굴은 9시 방향으로 돌려 왼쪽 어깨 위로 몸을 넘겨 전방회전 낙법으로 돌아 오른쪽 무릎을 접어 왼쪽 발바닥과 오른쪽 손바닥을 동시에 바닥을 치면서 일어나 오른쪽 주먹은 오른쪽 턱을 막으며 왼쪽 팔뚝은 앞 얼굴을 방어 (전방회전 낙법자세)

Left Two Hand Nak-Bub:

Position your hands for a left side Nak-Bub. Tilt your head to the right and touch your right ear to your right shoulder. Fall forward while catching yourself with your hands, and tuck in your left shoulder. Roll forward. Land with your right leg tucked in and with your left leg over your right. With your right arm, slap the ground with the palm of your hand. Keep your left fist guarding your face.

19. 오른쪽 양손날 하단 옆막기

얼굴은 12시 방향, 왼쪽 두손짚고 전방회전 낙법을 한 상태에서 턱을 아래로 당겨 양다리의 간격은 어깨넓이 몸을 시계 방향으로 돌리면서 오른발을 12시 방향 제자리에서 돌려 놓으며 왼쪽 손바닥은 위로 팔뚝은 띠에 대면서 오른쪽 손바닥을 아래로 중심은 뒷다리에 두고, 오른쪽으로 허리를 틀어 동시에 양손날 하단 옆막기 (후방자세)

Right Low to Knife Hand Side Block:

Turn your body clockwise and step with your right leg towards 12:00 in a right side Back Stance. Execute a right side Low Side Block with your right forearm. Keep your left hand at belt level with your palm face up.

20. 오른쪽 양손날 상단 옆치기 "기합"

얼굴은 12시 방향, 오른쪽 양손날 하단 옆막기 상태에서 상대의 눈을 주시 하면서 턱을 아래로 당겨 양다리의 간격은 어깨넓이 왼쪽 손바닥은 위로 오른쪽 손바닥을 아래로 오른발을 들어 1시 방향으로 옮겨 놓으며 중심은 앞다리에 두고, 기합을 넣으며 오른쪽으로 양손날 상단 옆치기 (전방자세)

Right High two Knife Hand Chop Attack "Ki-Hap":

Step out with your right leg towards 12:00 and get into a right side Forward Stance. Execute a right side Chop Attack with your right knife hand. Keep your left elbow by your side with your knife hand palm up. Make sure you keep your chin down. (Ki-Hap)

21. 왼쪽 정권 직선펀치 "기합"

얼굴은 12시 방향, 오른쪽 양손날 상단 옆치기를 한 상태에서 상대의 눈을 주시 하면서 턱을 아래로 당겨 양다리의 간격은 어깨넓이 몸을 시계 방향으로 돌리면서 왼발을 들어 12시 방향 앞으로 한발 옮겨 놓으며 오른쪽 주먹은 오른쪽 턱을 막으며 중심은 양다리에 두고, 기합을 넣으며 왼쪽 주먹을 돌려 정권 직선펀치를 하면서 왼쪽 어깨로 왼쪽 턱을 방어 (선자세)

Left Fist straight Punch "Ki-Hap":

Step forward with your left leg towards 12:00 while turning your body clockwise. Execute a straight left punch, and face towards 3:00. Make sure your right fist is guarding your face, and keep your chin down. (Ki-Hap)

22. 오른쪽 장풍지르기 "기합"

얼굴은 12시 방향, 왼쪽 정권 직선펀치를 한 상태에서 상대의 눈을 주시 하면서 턱을 아래로 당겨 양다리의 간격은 어깨넓이 몸을 반시계 방향으로 돌리면서 오른발을 들어 12시 방향 앞으로 한발 옮겨 놓으며 왼쪽 주먹은 왼쪽 턱을 막으며 중심은 양다리에 두고, 기합을 넣으며 오른쪽 주먹을 돌려 장풍지르기를 하면서 오른쪽 어깨로 오른쪽 턱을 방어 (선자세)

Right Palm Strike "Ki-Hap":

Step forward with your right leg towards 12:00 while turning your body counter-clockwise. Execute a straight right palm, and face towards 9:00. Make sure your right fist is guarding your face, and keep your chin down. (Ki-Hap)

차력형: Cha-Ryuk Form

23. 왼쪽 한손날 옆목치기 "기합"

얼굴은 12시 방향, 오른쪽 장풍지르기를 한 상태에서 상대의 눈을 주시 하면서 턱을 아래로 당겨 양다리의 간격은 어깨넓이 몸을 시계 방향으로 돌리면서 왼발을 들어 12시 방향 앞으로 한발 옮겨 놓으며 오른쪽 주먹은 오른쪽 턱을 막으며 중심은 양다리에 두고, 기합을 넣으며 안으로 왼쪽 한손날로 옆목치기 (선자세)

Left Knife Hand Side Chop "Ki-Hap":

Step forward with your left leg towards 12:00 while turning your body clockwise. Execute a left chop with your knife hand. Make sure your knife hand is palm up. Face 3:00 and have your right fist guarding your face while keeping your chin down. (Ki-Hap)

24. 오른쪽 손창 수평찌르기 "기합"

얼굴은 12시 방향, 왼쪽 한손날 옆목치기를 한 상태에서 상대의 눈을 주시 하면서 턱을 아래로 당겨 양다리의 간격은 어깨넓이 몸을 반시계 방향으로 돌리면서 오른발을 들어 12시 방향 앞으로 한발 옮겨 놓으며 왼쪽 주먹은 왼쪽 턱을 막으며 중심은 앞다리에 두고, 기합을 넣으며 오른쪽 주먹을 돌려 손창을 수평으로 목젖 찌르면서 오른쪽 어깨로 오른쪽 턱을 방어 (전방자세)

Right Spear Hand "Ki-Hap":

Step forward with your right leg towards 12:00 while turning your body counter-clockwise. Execute a straight right knife hand, and face towards 9:00. Make sure your left fist is guarding your face, and keep your chin down. (Ki-Hap)

25. 왼쪽 하단 앞차기

얼굴은 12시 방향, 오른쪽 손창 수평찌르기를 한 상태에서 턱을 아래로 당겨 양다리의 간격은 어깨넓이 왼쪽 주먹은 왼쪽 턱을 막은대로 중심은 오른쪽 다리에 두고, 왼발을 들어 하단 앞차기를 하고, 오른쪽 어깨로 오른쪽 턱을 방어 (선자세)

Left Low Front Kick:

Keep your right knife hand stationary. Pick up your left knee, and execute a left
leg Low Front Kick. Make sure you keep your left fist guarding your face, and keep your chin down.

26. 오른쪽 상단 앞차기

얼굴은 12시 방향, 왼쪽 하단 앞차기를 한 상태에서 턱을 아래로 당겨 왼쪽 주먹은 왼쪽 턱을 막은대로 왼발을 한발 앞으로 옮겨 놓으며 중심은 왼쪽 다리에 두고, 오른발을 들어 오른쪽 손바닥을 차고, 오른쪽 어깨로 오른쪽 턱을 방어 (선자세)

Right High Front Kick to Knife Hand:

Keep your right knife hand stationary. Pick up your right knee, and execute a right leg High Front
Kick to your right knife hand. Make sure you keep your left fist guarding your face, and keep your
chin down.

27. 오른쪽 양손날 하단 옆막기

얼굴은 12시 방향, 오른쪽 상단 앞차기를 한 상태에서 턱을 아래로 당겨 양다리의 간격은 어깨넓이 몸을 시계 방향으로 돌리면서 오른발을 180도로 돌려 6시 방향 앞으로 한발 옮겨 놓으며 왼쪽 손바닥은 위로 팔뚝은 띠에 대면서 오른쪽 손바닥을 아래로 중심은 뒷다리에두고, 오른쪽으로 허리를 틀어 동시에 양손날 하단 옆막기 (후방자세)

Right Low to Knife Hand Side Block:

Turn your body clockwise and step with your right leg towards 6:00 in a right side Back Stance. Execute a right side Low Side Block with your right forearm. Keep your left hand at belt level with your palm face up.

28. 오른쪽 양손날 옆목치기 "기합"

얼굴은 6시 방향, 오른쪽 양손날 하단 옆막기를 한 상태에서 상대의 눈을 주시 하면서 턱을 아래로 당겨 양다리의 간격은 어깨넓이 왼쪽 손바닥은 위로 오른쪽 손바닥을 아래로 오른발을 들어 7시 방향 앞으로 한 발 옮겨 놓으며 중심은 앞다리에 두고, 기합을 넣으며 오른쪽으로 양손날 옆목치기 (전방자세)

Right two Knife Hand Chop Attack "Ki-Hap":

Step out with your right leg towards 6:00 and get into a right side Forward Stance. Execute a right side Chop Attack with your right knife hand. Keep your left elbow by your side with your knife hand palm up. Make sure you keep your chin down. (Ki-Hap)

합도술

SNOW CAP FORM
산 | 봉 | 우 | 리 | 형

01. 반달 "정신통일" (선자세):
    Half Moon (stand stance)
02. 오른쪽 손날 하단 내려막기 (선자세):
    Right Low Knife Hand Sweep (stand stance)
03. 왼쪽 손날 하단 내려막기 (선자세):
    Left Low Knife Hand Sweep (stand stance)
04. 오른쪽 손날 얼굴 안막기 (선자세):
    Right Face Knife Hand Chop Block (stand stance)
05. 왼쪽 손날 얼굴 안막기 (선자세):
    Left Face Knife Hand Chop Block (stand stance)
06. 왼쪽 정권 직선펀치 (선자세):
    Left Fist Straight Punch (stand stance)
07. 오른쪽 정권 직선펀치 "기합" (선자세):
    Right Fist Straight Punch "Ki-Hap" (stand stance)
08. 오른쪽 양손날 상단 옆막기 (후방자세):
    Right High two Knife Hand Chop Block (back stance)
09. 왼쪽 정권 직선펀치 "기합" (선자세):
    Left Fist Straight Punch "Ki-Hap" (stand stance)
10. 오른쪽 정권 직선펀치 "기합" (선자세):
    Right Fist Straight Punch "Ki-Hap" (stand stance)
11. 왼쪽 정권 어퍼컷 (선자세):
    Left Fist Uppercut (stand stance)
12. 오른쪽 정권 훅 (선자세):
    Right Fist Hook (stand stance)
13. 왼쪽 정권 쨉 (선자세):
    Left Fist Jab (stand stance)
14. 왼쪽 정권 쨉 (선자세):
    Left Fist Jab (stand stance)
15. 오른쪽 정권 직선펀치 "기합" (선자세):
    Right Fist Straight Punch "Ki-Hap" (stand stance)
16. 왼쪽 양손날 상단 옆막기 (후방자세):
    Left High two Knife Hand Chop Block (back stance)
17. 오른쪽 정권 직선펀치 "기합" (선자세):
    Right Fist Straight Punch "Ki-Hap" (stand stance)
18. 왼쪽 정권 직선펀치 "기합" (선자세):
    Left Fist Straight Punch "Ki-Hap" (stand stance)
19. 오른쪽 정권 어퍼컷 (선자세):
    Right Fist Uppercut (stand stance)
20. 왼쪽 정권 훅 (선자세):
    Left Fist Hook (stand stance)
21. 오른쪽 정권 쨉 (선자세):
    Right Fist Jab (stand stance)
22. 오른쪽 정권 쨉 (선자세):
    Right Fist Jab (stand stance)

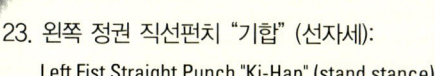

23. 왼쪽 정권 직선펀치 "기합" (선자세):
    Left Fist Straight Punch "Ki-Hap" (stand stance)
24. 오른쪽 안다리 후리기 (선자세):
    Right Inside Hook Throw (stand stance)
25. 왼쪽 안다리 후리기 (선자세):
    Left Inside Hook Throw (stand stance)
26. 오른쪽 밭다리 후리기 (선자세):
    Right Outside Hook Throw (stand stance)
27. 왼쪽 밭다리 후리기 (선자세):
    Left Outside Hook Throw (stand stance)
28. 왼쪽 정권 직선펀치 (선자세):
    Left Fist Straight Punch (stand stance)
29. 오른쪽 정권 직선펀치 "기합" (선자세):
    Right Fist straight Punch "Hi-Hap" (stand stance)
30. 오른쪽 손창 수평찌르기 "기합" (전방자세):
    Right Spear Hand "Ki-Hap" (front stance)
31. 오른쪽 상단 앞차기 (전방자세):
    Right High Front Kick to Spear Hand (front stance)
32. 왼쪽 손창 수평찌르기 "기합" (전방자세):
    Left spear Hand "Ki-Hap" (front stance)
33. 왼쪽 상단 앞차기 (전방자세):
    Left High Front Kick to Spear Hand (front stance)
34. 오른쪽 한손 짚고 왼쪽 전방회전 낙법:
    (전방회전 낙법자세)
    Left One Hand Nak-Bub (front roll nak-bub stance)
35. 오른쪽 양손날 상단 옆막기 (후방자세):
    Right High two Knife Hand Chop Block (back stance)
36. 왼손 멱살잡고 당기면서 오른쪽 정권 직선펀치 "기합" (선자세):
    Grab, Pull, and Right Fist Straight Punch "Ki-Hap" (stand stance)
37. 왼쪽 정권 직선펀치 "기합" (선자세):
    Left Fist Straight Punch "Ki-Hap" (stand stance)
38. 오른쪽 손창 수평찌르기 "기합" (전방자세):
    Right spear Hand "Ki-Hap" (front stance)
39. 오른쪽 상단 앞차기 (전방자세):
    Right High Front Kick to Spear Hand (front stance)
40. 왼쪽 손창 수평찌르기 "기합" (전방자세):
    Left Spear Hand (front stance)
41. 왼쪽 상단 앞차기 (전방자세):
    Left High Front Kick to Spear Hand (front stance)
42. 오른쪽 양손날 상단 옆막기 (후방자세):
    Right High two Knife Hand Chop Block (back stance)

1. 반달 "정신통일"

얼굴은 12시 정면 방향, 양다리의 간격은 어깨넓이 중심은 양다리에 두고, 양손날의 손등은 안으로 머리위에 세워놓고, 양검지를 서로 대며 정신통일을 하여 숨을 들어 마신후 입으로 천천히 고르게 내뿜으며 반원을 그리면서 어깨까지 내려놓기 (선자세)

Half Moon:

In a Half Moon Stance position facing 12:00, while keeping your arms at a 90degree angle, touch the tips of your hands together and slowly bring your elbows down to your sides, while exhaling slowly through your mouth and concentrating on developing your Ki.

2. 오른쪽 손날 하단 내려막기

얼굴은 12시 정면 방향, 반달을 그린 상태에서 한 상태에서 상대의 눈을 주시 하면서 턱을 아래로 당겨 양 다리의 간격은 어깨넓이 몸을 반시계 방향으로 틀어 오른쪽 손바닥을 안으로 돌려 중심은 양다리에 두고, 손날은 9시 방향으로 얼굴을 스치면서 오른쪽 손날로 하단 내려막기 (선자세)

Right Low Knife Hand Sweep:

Lean towards 9:00 while turning your body clockwise. Execute a right Low Knife Hand Sweep with your knife hand in a circular motion counter-clockwise from the right side of your face, down to your right thigh. Make sure your left hand is guarding your face, and keep your chin down.

3. 왼쪽 손날 하단 내려막기

얼굴은 12시 정면 방향, 오른쪽 손날 하단 내려막기를 한 상태에서 상대의 눈을 주시 하면서 턱을 아래로 당겨 양다리의 간격은 어깨넓이 오른쪽 주먹은 오른쪽 턱을 막으며 몸을 시계 방향으로 틀어 왼쪽 손바닥을 안으로 돌려 중심은 양다리에 두고, 손날은 3시 방향으로 얼굴을 스치면서 왼쪽 손날로 하단 내려막기 (선자세)

Left Low Knife Hand Sweep:

Lean towards 3:00 while turning your body counter-clockwise. Execute a left Low Knife Hand Sweep with your knife hand in a circular motion clockwise from the left side of your face, down to your left thigh. Make sure your right hand is guarding your face, and keep your chin down.

4. 오른쪽 손날 얼굴 안막기

얼굴은 12시 정면 방향, 왼쪽 손날 하단 내려막기를 한 상태에서 상대의 눈을 주시 하면서 턱을 아래로 당겨 양다리의 간격은 어깨넓이 왼쪽 주먹은 왼쪽 턱을 막으며 몸을 반시계 방향으로 틀어 오른쪽 손바닥을 위로 45도 각도로 중심은 양다리에 두고, 오른쪽 손날로 얼굴 안막기 (선자세)

Right Face Knife Hand Chop Block:

Lean towards 3:00 while turning your body counter-clockwise, and execute a right Chop Block with your knife hand face up. Make sure your left fist is guarding your face, and keep your chin down.

5. 왼쪽 손날 얼굴 안막기

얼굴은 12시 정면 방향, 오른쪽 손날 얼굴 안막기를 한 상태에서 상대의 눈을 주시 하면서 턱을 아래로 당겨 양다리의 간격은 어깨넓이 오른쪽 주먹은 오른쪽 턱을 막으며 몸을 시계 방향으로 틀어 왼쪽 손바닥을 위로 45도 각도로 중심은 양다리에 두고, 왼쪽 손날로 얼굴 안막기 (선자세)

Left Face Knife Hand Chop Block:

Lean towards 9:00 while turning your body clockwise, and execute a left Chop Block with your knife hand face up. Make sure your right fist is guarding your face, and keep your chin down.

6. 왼쪽 정권 직선펀치

얼굴은 12시 정면 방향, 왼쪽 손날 얼굴 안막기를 한 상태에서 상대의 눈을 주시 하면서 턱을 아래로 당겨 양다리의 간격은 어깨넓이 오른쪽 주먹은 오른쪽 턱을 막은대로 몸을 반시계 방향으로 틀어 왼발을 돌려 밀면서 중심은 양다리에 두고, 왼쪽 손날을 주먹을 쥐며 정권 직선펀치를 하면서 왼쪽 어깨로 왼쪽 턱을 방어 (선자세)

Left Fist Straight Punch:

Turn your body clockwise while pushing off with your left leg. Execute a straight left Punch with your fist. Make sure your right fist is guarding your face, and keep your chin down.

7. 오른쪽 정권 직선펀치 "기합"

얼굴은 12시 정면 방향, 왼쪽 정권 직선펀치를 한 상태에서 턱을 아래로 당겨 양다리의 간격은 어깨넓이 왼쪽 주먹은 왼쪽 턱을 막으며 오른발을 돌려 밀면서 몸을 반시계 방향으로 틀어 중심은 양다리에 두고, 기합을 넣으며 오른쪽 주먹을 돌려 정권 직선펀치를 하면서 오른쪽 어깨로 오른쪽 턱을 방어 (선자세)

Right Fist Straight Punch "Ki-Hap":

Turn your body counter-clockwise while pushing off with your right leg. Execute a straight right Punch with your fist. Make sure your left fist is guarding your face, and keep your chin down. (Ki-Hap)

산봉우리형: Snow Cap Form

8. 오른쪽 양손날 상단 옆막기

얼굴은 12시 정면 방향, 오른쪽 정권 직선펀치를 한 상태에서 턱을 아래로 당겨 양다리의 간격은 어깨넓이 몸을 시계 방향으로 돌리면서 오른발을 들어 3시 방향으로 돌려 놓으며 왼쪽 손바닥은 위로 손날은 입높이에 오른쪽 손바닥은 아래로 손날은 눈높이에 두면서 중심은 뒷다리에 두고, 오른쪽으로 양손날 상단 옆막기 (후방자세)

Right High two Knife Hand Chop Block:

Turn your body clockwise so you are facing 3:00 in a right Back Stance. Execute a right side Back Stance Chop Block with your forearm. Make sure you have your left elbow by your side, with your left palm face up.

9. 왼쪽 정권 직선펀치 "기합"

얼굴은 3시 방향, 오른쪽 양손날 상단 옆막기를 한 상태에서 상대의 눈을 주시 하면서 턱을 아래로 당겨 양다리의 간격은 어깨넓이 오른쪽 주먹은 오른쪽 턱을 막으며 몸을 시계 방향으로 돌리면서 왼발을 들어 3시 방향 앞으로 한발 옮겨 놓으며 중심은 양다리에 두고, 기합을 넣으며 왼쪽 주먹을 돌려 정권 직선펀치를 하면서 왼쪽 어깨로 왼쪽 턱을 방어 (선자세)

Left Fist Straight Punch "Ki-Hap":

Step forward with your left leg towards 3:00 while turning your body clockwise. Execute a straight left Punch, and have your chest facing towards 6:00. Make sure your right fist is guarding your face, and keep your chin down. (Ki-Hap)

10. 오른쪽 정권 직선펀치 "기합"

얼굴은 3시 방향, 왼쪽 정권 직선펀치를 한 상태에서 상대의 눈을 주시 하면서 턱을 아래로 당겨 양다리의 간격은 어깨넓이 왼쪽 주먹은 왼쪽 턱을 막으며 몸을 반시계 방향으로 돌리면서 오른발을 들어 3시 방향 앞으로 한발 옮겨 놓으며 중심은 양다리에 두고, 기합을 넣으며 오른쪽 주먹을 돌려 정권 직선펀치를 하면서 오른쪽 어깨로 오른쪽 턱을 방어 (선자세)

Right Fist Straight Punch "Ki-Hap":

Step forward with your right leg towards 3:00 while turning your body counter-clockwise. Execute a straight right Punch, and have your chest facing towards 12:00. Make sure your left fist is guarding your face, and keep your chin down. (Ki-Hap)

11. 왼쪽 정권 어퍼컷

얼굴은 3시 방향, 오른쪽 정권 직선펀치를 한 상태에서 턱을 아래로 당겨 양다리의 간격은 어깨넓이 오른쪽 주먹은 오른쪽 턱을 막으며 중심은 양다리에 두고, 양무릎을 구부렸다 일어나면서 왼쪽 주먹을 돌려 정권 어퍼컷 (선자세)

Left Fist Uppercut:

Slightly bend both your legs. Push off with your left leg so you are extending up, while turning your body clockwise so you are facing 3:00. Execute a left Fist Uppercut with your fist. Make sure your right fist is guarding the face, and keep your chin down.

산봉우리형: Snow Cap Form

12. 오른쪽 정권 훅

얼굴은 3시 방향, 왼쪽 정권 어퍼컷을 한 상태에서 턱을 아래로 당겨 양다리의 간격은 어깨넓이 왼쪽 주먹은 왼쪽 턱을 막으며 중심은 양다리에 두고, 오른발을 돌려 밀면서 몸을 9시 반시계 방향으로 틀어 오른쪽 주먹으로 훅 (선자세)

Right Fist Hook:

Push off with your right leg while turning your body counter-clockwise so you are facing 9:00, and execute a right Fist Hook straight across with your fist. Make sure your left fist is guarding your face, and keep your chin down.

13. 왼쪽 정권 쨉

얼굴은 9시 방향, 오른쪽 정권 훅을 한 상태에서 상대의 눈을 주시 하면서 턱을 아래로 당겨 양다리의 간격은 어깨넓이 오른쪽 주먹은 오른쪽 턱을 막으며 중심은 양다리에 두고, 왼쪽 주먹을 돌려 정권 쨉을 하면서 왼쪽 어깨로 왼쪽 턱을 방어하며 왼쪽 쨉을 뒤로 되튕겨 얼굴 약 25cm 앞에 두기 (선자세)

Left Fist Jab:

Turn your body counter-clockwise so your chest is facing 12:00. Execute a straight left Jab with your fist towards 9:00. Make sure your right fist is guarding your face, and keep your chin down.

14. 왼쪽 정권 쨉

얼굴은 9시 방향, 왼쪽 정권 쨉을 한 상태에서 상대의 눈을 주시 하면서 턱을 아래로 당겨 양다리의 간격은 어깨넓이 오른쪽 주먹은 오른쪽 턱을 막은대로 중심은 양다리에 두고, 왼쪽 주먹을 돌려 정권 쨉을 하면서 왼쪽 어깨로 왼쪽 턱을 방어하며 왼쪽 쨉을 뒤로 되튕겨 얼굴 약 25cm 앞에 두기 (선자세)

Left Fist Jab:

While your chest is still facing 12:00, execute another straight left Jab with your fist towards 9:00. Make sure your right fist is guarding your face, and keep your chin down.

15. 오른쪽 정권 직선펀치 "기합"

얼굴은 9시 방향, 왼쪽 정권 쨉을 한 상태에서 상대의 눈을 주시 하면서 턱을 아래로 당겨 양다리의 간격은 어깨넓이 왼쪽 주먹은 왼쪽 턱을 막으며 몸을 반시계 방향으로 돌리면서 오른발을 들어 9시 방향 앞으로 한발 옮겨 놓으며 중심은 양다리에 두고, 기합을 넣으며 오른쪽 주먹을 돌려 정권 직선펀치를 하면서 오른쪽 어깨로 오른쪽 턱을 방어 (선자세)

Right Fist Straight Punch "Ki-Hap":

Step forward with your right leg towards 9:00 while turning your body counter-clockwise so your chest is facing 6:00, and execute a straight right Punch with your fist towards 9:00. Make sure your left fist is guarding your face, and keep your chin down. (Ki-Hap)

16. 왼쪽 양손날 상단 옆막기

얼굴은 9시 방향, 오른쪽 정권 직선펀치를 한 상태에서 턱을 아래로 당겨 양다리의 간격은 어깨넓이 몸을 반시계 방향으로 돌리면서 왼발을 들어 9시 방향 앞으로 한발 옮겨 놓으며 오른쪽 손바닥은 위로 손날은 입높이에 왼쪽 손바닥을 아래로 손날은 눈높이에 두면서 중심은 뒷다리에 두고, 왼쪽으로 양손날 상단 옆막기 (후방자세)

Left High two Knife Hand Chop Block:

Step forward with your left leg towards 9:00 while turning your body clockwise so you are facing 9:00 in a right side Back Stance. Execute a left Back Stance Chop Block with your left forearm. Make sure you have your right elbow by your right side, with your right palm face up.

17. 오른쪽 정권 직선펀치 "기합"

얼굴은 9시 방향, 왼쪽 양손날 상단 옆막기를 한 상태에서 상대의 눈을 주시 하면서 턱을 아래로 당겨 양다리의 간격은 어깨넓이 왼쪽 주먹은 왼쪽 턱을 막으며 몸을 반시계 방향으로 돌리면서 오른발을 들어 9시 방향 앞으로 한발 옮겨 놓으며 중심은 양다리에 두고, 기합을 넣으며 오른쪽 주먹을 돌려 정권 직선펀치를 하면서 오른쪽 어깨로 오른쪽 턱을 방어 (선자세)

Right Fist Straight Punch "Ki-Hap":

Step forward with your right leg towards 9:00 while turning your body counter-clockwise, and execute a straight right Punch with your fist. Make sure your left fist is guarding your face, and keep your chin down. (Ki-Hap)

18. 왼쪽 정권 직선펀치 "기합"

얼굴은 9시 방향, 오른쪽 정권 직선펀치를 한 상태에서 상대의 눈을 주시 하면서 턱을 아래로 당겨 양다리의 간격은 어깨넓이 오른쪽 주먹은 오른쪽 턱을 막으며 몸을 시계 방향으로 돌리면서 왼발을 들어 9시 방향 앞으로 한발 옮겨 놓으며 중심은 양다리에 두고, 기합을 넣으며 왼쪽 주먹을 돌려 정권 직선펀치를 하면서 왼쪽 어깨로 왼쪽 턱을 방어 (선자세)

Left Fist Straight Punch "Ki-Hap":

Step forward with your left leg towards 9:00 while turning your body clockwise. Execute a straight left Punch with your fist. Make sure your right fist is guarding your face, and keep your chin down. (Ki-Hap)

19. 오른쪽 정권 어퍼컷

얼굴은 9시 방향, 왼쪽 정권 직선펀치를 한 상태에서 턱을 아래로 당겨 양다리의 간격은 어깨넓이 왼쪽 주먹은 왼쪽 턱을 막으며 중심은 양다리에 두고, 양무릎을 구부렸다 일어나면서 오른쪽 주먹을 돌려 정권 어퍼컷 (선자세)

Right Fist Uppercut:

Slightly bend both your legs. Push off with your right leg so you are extending up, while turning your body counter-clockwise so you are facing 9:00. Execute a right Fist Uppercut with your fist. Make sure your left fist is guarding the face, and keep your chin down.

산봉우리형: Snow Cap Form

20. 왼쪽 정권 훅

얼굴은 9시 방향, 오른쪽 정권 어퍼컷을 한 상태에서 턱을 아래로 당겨 양다리의 간격은 어깨넓이 오른쪽 주먹은 오른쪽 턱을 막으며 중심은 양다리에 두고, 왼발을 돌려 밀면서 몸을 3시 시계 방향으로 틀어 왼쪽 주먹으로 훅 (선자세)

Left Fist Hook:

Push off with your left leg while turning your body clockwise so you are facing 12:00, and execute a left Fist Hook straight across with your fist. Make sure your right fist is guarding your face, and keep your chin down.

21. 오른쪽 정권 쨉

얼굴은 3시 방향, 왼쪽 정권 훅을 한 상태에서 상대의 눈을 주시 하면서 턱을 아래로 당겨 양다리의 간격은 어깨넓이 왼쪽 주먹은 왼쪽 턱을 막으며 중심은 양다리에 두고, 오른쪽 주먹을 돌려 정권 쨉을 하면서 오른쪽 어깨로 오른쪽 턱을 방어하며 오른쪽 쨉을 뒤로 되튕겨 얼굴 약 25cm 앞에 두기(선자세)

Right Fist Jab:

Turn your body clockwise so your chest is facing 12:00. Execute a straight right Jab with your fist towards 3:00. Make sure your left fist is guarding your face, and keep your chin down.

22. 오른쪽 정권 잽

얼굴은 3시 방향, 오른쪽 정권 잽을 한 상태에서 상대의 눈을 주시 하면서 턱을 아래로 당겨 양다리의 간격은 어깨넓이 왼쪽 주먹은 왼쪽 턱을 막은대로 중심은 양다리에 두고, 오른쪽 주먹을 돌려 정권 잽을 하면서 오른쪽 어깨로 오른쪽 턱을 방어하며 오른쪽 잽을 뒤로 되튕겨 얼굴 약 25cm 앞에 두기 (선자세)

Right Fist Jab:

While your chest is still facing 12:00, execute another straight right Jab with your fist towards 3:00. Make sure your left fist is guarding your face, and keep your chin down.

23. 왼쪽 정권 직선펀치 "기합"

얼굴은 3시 방향, 오른쪽 정권 잽을 한 상태에서 상대의 눈을 주시 하면서 턱을 아래로 당겨 양다리의 간격은 어깨넓이 오른쪽 주먹은 오른쪽 턱을 막으며 몸을 시계 방향으로 돌리면서 왼발을 들어 3시 방향 앞으로 한발 옮겨 놓으며 중심은 양다리에 두고, 기합을 넣으며 왼쪽 주먹을 돌려 정권 직선펀치를 하면서 왼쪽 어깨로 왼쪽 턱을 방어 (선자세)

Left Fist Straight Punch "Ki-Hap":

Step forward with your left leg towards 3:00 while turning your body clockwise so your chest is facing 6:00, and execute a straight left Punch with your fist towards 3:00. Make sure your right fist is guarding your face, and keep your chin down. (Ki-Hap)

24. 오른쪽 안다리 후리기

얼굴은 3시 방향, 왼쪽 정권 직선펀치를 한 상태에서 턱을 아래로 당겨 양다리의 간격은 어깨넓이 몸을 시계 방향으로 돌리면서 왼발을 들어 6시 방향에 돌려 놓으며 양주먹은 가슴 약 18cm 앞에 놓고, 중심은 왼쪽 다리에 두고, 오른발을 들어 오른쪽 안다리 후리기 (선자세)

Right Inside Hook Throw:
While facing 6:00, execute a right leg Inside Hook Throw with the heel of your right foot in a circular counter-clockwise motion. Make sure you keep your guard up.

25. 왼쪽 안다리 후리기

얼굴은 6시 방향, 오른쪽 안다리 후리기를 한 상태에서 턱을 아래로 당겨 오른발을 제자리에 놓으며 양다리의 간격은 어깨넓이 양주먹은 가슴 약 18cm 앞에 놓고, 중심은 오른쪽 다리에 두고, 왼발을 들어 왼쪽 안다리 후리기 (선자세)

Left Inside Hook Throw:
Execute a left leg Inside Hook Throw with the heel of your left foot in a circular motion, clockwise. Make sure you keep your guard up.

26. 오른쪽 밭다리 후리기

얼굴은 6시 방향, 왼쪽 안다리 후리기를 한 상태에서 턱을 아래로 당겨 왼발을 제자리에 놓으며 양다리의 간격은 어깨넓이 양주먹은 가슴 약 18cm 앞에 놓고, 중심은 왼쪽 다리에 두고, 오른발을 들어 오른쪽 밭다리 후리기 (선자세)

Right Outside Hook Throw:

Execute a right leg Outside Hook Throw with the heel of your right foot in a circular clockwise motion.

27. 왼쪽 밭다리 후리기

얼굴은 6시 방향, 오른쪽 밭다리 후리기를 한 상태에서 턱을 아래로 당겨 오른발을 제자리에 놓으며 양다리의 간격은 어깨넓이 양주먹은 가슴 약 18cm 앞에 놓고, 중심은 오른쪽 다리에 두고, 왼발을 들어 왼쪽 밭다리 후리기 (선자세)

Left Outside Hook Throw:

Execute a left leg Outside Hook Throw with the heel of your left foot in a circular motion, counter-clockwise.

28. 왼쪽 정권 직선펀치

얼굴은 6시 방향, 왼쪽 밭다리 후리기를 한 상태에서 상대의 눈을 주 시 하면서 턱을 아래로 당겨 왼발을 제자리에 놓고, 양다리의 간격은 어깨넓이 양주먹은 양턱을 막으며 왼발을 돌려 밀면서 몸을 시계 방향으로 틀어 중심은 양다리에 두고, 왼쪽 주먹을 돌려 정권 직선펀치를 하면서 왼쪽 어깨로 왼쪽 턱을 방어 (선자세)

Left Fist Straight Punch:

Turn your body clockwise while pushing off with your left leg. Execute a straight left Punch with your fist. Make sure your right fist is guarding your face, and keep your chin down.

29. 오른쪽 정권 직선펀치 "기합"

얼굴은 6시 방향, 왼쪽 정권 직선펀치를 한 상태에서 턱을 아래로 당 겨 양다리의 간격은 어깨넓이 왼쪽 주먹은 왼쪽 턱을 막으며 오른발을 돌려 밀면서 몸을 반시계 방향으로 틀어 중심은 양다리에 두고, 기합을 넣으며 오른쪽 주먹을 돌려 정권 직선펀치를 하면서 오른쪽 주먹을 되돌려와 오른쪽 턱을 방어 (선자세)

Right Fist straight Punch "Hi-Hap":

Turn your body counter-clockwise while pushing off with your right leg. Execute a straight right Punch with your fist. Make sure your left fist is guarding your face, and keep your chin down. (Ki-Hap)

30. 오른쪽 손창 수평찌르기 "기합"

얼굴은 6시 방향, 오른쪽 정권 직선펀치를 한 상태에서 상대의 눈을 주시 하면서 턱을 아래로 당겨 양주먹은 양턱을 막은대로 몸을 반시계 방향으로 돌리면서 왼발을 들어 6시 방향 앞으로 한발 옮겨 놓으며 중심은 앞다리에 두고, 기합을 넣으며 오른쪽 주먹을 돌려 손창을 수평으로 목젖 찌르면서 오른쪽 어깨로 오른쪽 턱을 방어 (전방자세)

Right Spear Hand "Ki-Hap":

Step forward with your left leg towards 6:00. Turn your body counter-clockwise, and execute a right Knife Hand. Make sure your left fist is guarding your face. (Ki-Hap)

31. 오른쪽 상단 앞차기

얼굴은 6시 방향, 오른쪽 손창 수평찌르기를 한 상태에서 턱을 아래로 당겨 왼쪽 주먹은 왼쪽 턱을 막은대로 중심은 왼쪽 다리에 두고, 오른발을 들어 오른쪽 손바닥을 차고, 오른쪽 어깨로 오른쪽 턱을 방어 (전방자세)

Right High Front Kick to Spear Hand:

While keeping your right knife hand stationary, pick up your right knee, and execute a right leg High Front Kick to your knife hand. Make sure your left fist is guarding your face.

32. 왼쪽 손창 수평찌르기 "기합"

얼굴은 6시 방향, 오른쪽 상단 앞차기를 한 상태에서 상대의 눈을 주시 하면서 턱을 아래로 당겨 몸을 시계 방향으로 돌리면서 오른발을 들어 6시 방향 앞으로 한발 옮겨 놓으며 오른쪽 손바닥은 주먹을 쥐면서 오른쪽 턱을 막으며 중심은 앞다리에 두고, 기합을 넣으며 왼쪽 주먹을 돌려 손창을 수평으로 목젖 찌르면서 왼쪽 어깨로 왼쪽 턱을 방어 (전방자세)

Left spear Hand "Ki-Hap":

Step forward with your right leg towards 6:00. Turn your body clockwise, and execute a left Knife Hand. Make sure your right fist is guarding your face. (Ki-Hap)

33. 왼쪽 상단 앞차기

얼굴은 6시 방향, 왼쪽 손창 수평찌르기를 한 상태에서 턱을 아래로 당겨 오른쪽 주먹은 오른쪽 턱을 막은 대로 중심은 오른쪽 다리에 두고, 왼발을 들어 왼쪽 손바닥을 차고, 왼쪽 어깨로 왼쪽 턱을 방어 (전방자세)

Left High Front Kick to Spear Hand:

While keeping your left Knife Hand stationary, pick up your left knee, and execute a left leg High Front Kick to your knife hand. Make sure your right fist is guarding your face.

34. 오른쪽 한손 짚고 왼쪽 전방회전 낙법

얼굴은 6시 방향, 왼쪽 상단 앞차기를 한 상태에서 왼발을 한발 앞으로 옮겨 놓으며 몸을 엎드려 중심은 왼쪽 앞다리에 두고, 오른쪽 주먹은 손바닥으로 왼쪽 엄지 발가락옆 바닥을 짚고, 턱을 아래로 당겨 얼굴은 9시 방향으로 돌려 왼손은 들고, 왼쪽 어깨위로 몸을 360도로 돌려 전방회전 낙법으로 왼쪽 주먹은 앞 얼굴을 막으며 오른쪽 다리를 접어 왼쪽 발바닥과 오른쪽 손바닥은 동시에 바닥을 치기 (전방회전 낙법자세)

Left One Hand Nak-Bub:

Position your left hand for a left Nak-Bub. Tilt your head to the right and touch your right ear to your right shoulder. Fall forward while catching yourself with your left hand, and tuck in your left shoulder. Roll forward. Land with your right leg tucked in and with your left leg over your right. With your right arm, slap the ground with the palm of your hand. Keep your left fist guarding your face.

35. 오른쪽 양손날 상단 옆막기

얼굴은 6시 방향, 오른쪽 한손 짚고 왼쪽 전방회전 낙법을 한 상태에서 몸을 180도 시계 방향으로 돌리면서 일어나 턱을 아래로 당겨 양다리의 간격은 어깨넓이 오른발을 12시 방향으로 돌려 놓으며 왼쪽 손바닥은 위로 손날은 입높이에 오른쪽 손바닥을 아래로 손날은 눈높이에 두면서 중심은 뒷다리에 두고, 오른쪽으로 허리를 틀어 양손날 상단 옆막기 (후방자세)

Right High two Knife Hand Chop Block:

Turn your body clockwise so you are facing 12:00 in a right Back Stance. Execute a right Back Stance Chop Block with your forearm. Make sure you have your left elbow by your right side, with your left palm face up.

36. 왼손 멱살잡고 당기면서 오른쪽 정권 직선펀치 "기합"

얼굴은 12시 방향, 오른쪽 양손날 상단 옆막기를 한 상태에서 턱을 아래로 당겨 양다리의 간격은 어깨넓이 왼발을 들어 왼손으로 상대의 앞옷깃을 잡아 당기며 몸을 반시계 방향으로 틀어 왼발을 들어 12시 방향 앞으로 한발 옮겨 놓으며 중심은 양다리에 두고, 기합을 넣으며 오른쪽 손날은 주먹을 쥐면서 돌려 정권 직선펀치를 하면서 오른쪽 어깨로 오른쪽 턱을 방어 (선자세)

Grab, Pull, and Right Fist Straight Punch "Ki-Hap":
Step forward with your left leg towards 12:00. With your left hand, reach out, grab and pull towards you while turning your body counter-clockwise, and execute a straight right Punch with your fist. Make sure your left fist is guarding your face when you are punching. (Ki-Hap)

37. 왼쪽 정권 직선펀치 "기합"

얼굴은 12시 방향, 왼쪽 멱살잡고 당기면서 오른쪽 정권 직선펀치를 한 상태에서 상대의 눈을 주시 하면서 턱을 아래로 당겨 양다리의 간격은 어깨넓이 오른쪽 주먹은 오른쪽 턱을 막으며 몸을 시계 방향으로 돌리면서 오른발을 들어 12시 방향 앞으로 한발 옮겨 놓으며 중심은 양다리에 두고, 기합을 넣으며 왼쪽 주먹을 돌려 정권 직선펀치를 하면서 왼쪽 어깨로 왼쪽 턱을 방어 (선자세)

Left Fist Straight Punch "Ki-Hap":
Step forward with your right leg towards 12:00, and turn your body clockwise while executing a straight left Punch with your fist. Make sure your right fist is guarding your face. (Ki-Hap)

38. 오른쪽 손창 수평찌르기 "기합"

얼굴은 12시 방향, 왼쪽 정권 직선펀치를 한 상태에서 상대의 눈을 주시 하면서 턱을 아래로 당겨 왼쪽 주먹은 왼쪽 턱을 막으며 몸을 반시계 방향으로 돌리면서 왼발을 들어 12시 방향 앞으로 한발 옮겨 놓으며 중심은 앞다리에 두고, 기합을 넣으며 오른쪽 주먹을 돌려 손창을 수평으로 목젖 찌르면서 오른쪽 어깨로 오른쪽 턱을 방어 (전방자세)

Right spear Hand "Ki-Hap":

Step forward with your left leg towards 12:00. Turn your body counter-clockwise, and execute a right Knife Hand. Make sure your left fist is guarding your face. (Ki-Hap)

39. 오른쪽 상단 앞차기

얼굴은 12시 방향, 오른쪽 손창 수평찌르기를 한 상태에서 턱을 아래로 당겨 왼쪽 주먹은 왼쪽 턱을 막은 대로 중심은 왼쪽 다리에 두고, 오른발을 들어 오른쪽 손바닥을 차고, 오른쪽 어깨로 오른쪽 턱을 방어 (전방자세)

Right High Front Kick to Spear Hand:

While keeping your right knife hand stationary, pick up your right knee, and execute a right leg High Front Kick to your knife hand. Make sure your left fist is guarding your face.

산봉우리형: Snow Cap Form

40. 왼쪽 손창 수평찌르기 "기합"

얼굴은 12시 방향, 오른쪽 상단 앞차기를 한 상태에서 상대의 눈을 주시 하면서 턱을 아래로 당겨 몸을 시계 방향으로 돌리면서 오른발을 들어 12시 방향 앞으로 한발 옮겨 놓으며 오른쪽 손바닥은 주먹을 쥐면서 오른쪽 턱을 막으며 중심은 앞다리에 두고, 기합을 넣으며 왼쪽 주먹을 돌려 손창을 수평으로 목젖 찌르면서 왼쪽 어깨로 왼쪽 턱을 방어 (전방자세)

Left Sear Hand:

Step forward with your right leg towards 12:00. Turn your body clockwise, and execute a left Knife Hand. Make sure your right fist is guarding your face. (Ki-Hap)

41. 왼쪽 상단 앞차기

얼굴은 12시 방향, 왼쪽 손창 수평찌르기를 한 상태에서 턱을 아래로 당겨 오른쪽 주먹은 오른쪽 턱을 막은대로 중심은 오른쪽 다리에 두고, 왼발을 들어 왼쪽 손바닥을 차고, 왼쪽 어깨로 왼쪽 턱을 방어
(전방자세)

Left High Front Kick to Spear Hand:

While keeping your left knife hand stationary, pick up your left knee, and execute a left leg High Front Kick to your knife hand. Make sure your right fist is guarding your face.

42. 오른쪽 양손날 상단 옆막기

얼굴은 12시 방향, 왼쪽 상단 앞차기를 한 상대에서 턱을 아래로 당겨 왼발을 한발 앞으로 옮겨 놓으며 양 다리의 간격은 어깨넓이 몸을 시계 방향으로 돌리면서 오른발을 들어 6시 방향으로 돌려 놓으며 왼쪽 손바닥은 위로 손날은 입높이에 오른쪽 손바닥을 아래로 손날은 눈높이에 두면서 중심은 뒷 다리에 두고, 오른쪽으로 허리를 틀어 양손날 상단 옆막기 (후방자세)

Right High two Knife Hand Chop Block:

Turn your body clockwise so you are facing 6:00 in a right side Back Stance. Execute a right Back Stance Chop Block with your forearm. Make sure you have your left elbow by your side, with your left palm face up.

산봉우리형: Snow Cap Form

Universe Cap Form
우 | 주 | 형

01. 오른쪽 정권 어퍼컷 (선자세):
    Right Fist Uppercut (stand stance)

02. 왼쪽 정권 어퍼컷 (선자세):
    Left Fist Uppercut (stand stance)

03. 오른쪽 정권 훅 (선자세):
    Right Fist Hook (stand stance)

04. 왼쪽 정권 훅 (선자세):
    Left Fist Hook (stand stance)

05. 왼쪽 정권 직선펀치 (선자세):
    Left Fist Straight Punch (stand stance)

06. 오른쪽 정권 직선펀치 "기합" (선자세):
    Right Fist Straight Punch (stand stance)

07. 오른쪽 양손날 상단 옆막기 (후방자세):
    Right High two Knife Hand Chop Block (black stance)

08. 왼쪽 정권 직선펀치 "기합" (선자세):
    Left Fist Straight Punch "Ki-Hap" (stand stance)

09. 오른쪽 정권 직선펀치 "기합" (선자세):
    Right Fist Straight Punch "Ki-Hap" (stand stance)

10. 오른손 앞 옷깃잡고 당기기 (선자세):
    Right Grab and Pull (stand stance)

11. 오른쪽 팔꿈치 훅 (선자세):
    Right Elbow Hook (stand stance)

12. 오른쪽 허리걸어 던지기 (중방자세):
    Right Hip Throw (middle stance)

13. 왼쪽 한발 옮겨놓기 (선자세):
    Left Step (stand stance)

14. 오른쪽 한발 옮겨놓기 (선자세):
    Right Step (stand stance)

15. 왼쪽 양손날 상단 옆막기 (후방자세):
    Left High two Knife Hand Chop Block Step (back stance)

16. 오른쪽 정권 직선펀치 "기합" (선자세):
    Right Fist Straight Punch "Ki-Hap" Step (stand stance)

17. 왼쪽 정권 직선펀치 "기합" (선자세):
    Left Fist straight Punch "Ki-Hap" Step (stand stance)

18. 왼손 앞 옷깃잡고 당기기 (선자세):
    Left Grab and Pull (stand stance)

19. 왼쪽 팔꿈치 훅 (선자세):
    Left Elbow Hook (stand stance)

20. 왼쪽 허리걸어 던지기 (중방자세):
    Left Hip Throw (middle stance)

21. 오른쪽 한발 옮겨놓기 (선자세):
    Right Step (stand stance)

22. 왼쪽 한발 옮겨놓기 (선자세):
    Left Step (stand stance)

23. 오른쪽 안다리 후리기 (선자세):
    Right Inside Hook Throw (stand stance)

24. 왼쪽 안다리 후리기 (선자세):
    Left Inside Hook Throw (stand stance)

25. 왼쪽 한발 옮겨놓기 (선자세):
    Left Step (stand stance)

26. 오른발 뺏치기 (선자세):
    Right Leg Sweep (stand stance)

27. 왼발 뺏치기 (선자세):
    Left Leg Sweep (stand stance)

28. 왼쪽 마차바퀴 돌리기 (전방자세):
    Left Cartwheel (front stance)

29. 오른쪽 양손날 상단 옆막기 (후방자세):
    Right High two Knife Hand Chop Back (back stance)

30. 왼쪽 한발 옮겨놓기 (선자세):
    Left Step (stand stance)

31. 오른발을 뛰면서 왼발 상단 앞차기 (선자세):
    Right Jumping Left High Front Kick (stand stance)

32. 왼쪽 정권 직선펀치 (선자세):
    Left Fist Straight Punch (stand stance)

33. 오른쪽 정권 직선펀치 "기합" (선자세):
    Right Fist straight Punch "Ki-Hap" (stand stance)

34. 왼쪽 양손짚고 전방 회전낙법 (전방 회전낙법 자세):
    Left Two Hand Long Nak-Bub (front roll Nak-bub)

35. 오른쪽 양손날 상단 옆막기 (후방자세):
    Right High two Knife Hand Chop Block
    (front roll nak-bub stance)

1. 오른쪽 정권 어퍼컷

얼굴은 12시 정면 방향, 턱을 아래로 당겨 허리를 똑바로 세운 자세에서 양다리의 간격은 어깨넓이 양주먹은 양턱을 막으며 중심은 양다리에 두고, 양무릎을 구부렸다 일어나면서 오른쪽 주먹을 돌려 어퍼컷 (선자세)

Right Fist Uppercut:

In a Stand Stance position facing 12:00, bend both your legs slightly. Push off with your right leg so you are extending up, while turning your body counter-clockwise. Execute a right side fist uppercut with your fist. Make sure left fist is guarding the face, and keep your chin down.

2. 왼쪽 정권 어퍼컷

얼굴은 12시 정면 방향, 오른쪽 정권 어퍼컷을 한 상태에서 턱을 아래로 당겨 허리를 똑바로 세운 자세에서 양다리의 간격은 어깨넓이 왼쪽 주먹은 왼쪽 턱을 막은대로 중심은 양다리에 두고, 양무릎을 구부렸다 일어나면서 왼쪽 주먹을 돌려 어퍼컷을 하면서 오른쪽 주먹은 오른쪽 턱을 방어 (선자세)

Left Fist Uppercut:

Bend both your legs slightly. Push off with your left leg so you are extending up, while turning your body clockwise. Execute a left side fist uppercut with your fist. Make sure your right fist is guarding the face, and keep your chin down.

3. 오른쪽 정권 훅

얼굴은 12시 정면 방향, 왼쪽 정권 어퍼컷을 한 상태에서 턱을 아래로 당겨 양다리의 간격은 어깨넓이 오른쪽 주먹은 오른쪽 턱을 막은대로 중심은 양다리에 두고, 오른발을 돌려 밀면서 몸을 9시 반시계 방향으로 틀어 오른쪽 주먹으로 훅을 하면서 왼쪽 주먹은 왼쪽 턱을 방어 (선자세)

Right Fist Hook:

Push off with your right leg while turning your body counter-clockwise, and execute a right fist hook straight across with your fist. Make sure your left fist is guarding your face, and keep your chin down.

4. 왼쪽 정권 훅

얼굴은 12시 정면 방향, 오른쪽 정권 훅을 한 상태에서 턱을 아래로 당겨 양다리의 간격은 어깨넓이 왼쪽 주먹은 왼쪽 턱을 막은대로 중심은 양다리에 두고, 왼발을 돌려 밀면서 몸을 3시 시계 방향으로 틀어 왼쪽 주먹으로 훅을 하면서 오른쪽 주먹은 오른쪽 턱을 방어 하고, 허리를 반시계 방향으로 되돌려 왼쪽 주먹은 왼쪽 턱을 방어 (선자세)

Left Fist Hook:

Push off with your left leg while turning your body clockwise, and execute a left fist hook straight across with your fist. Make sure your right fist is guarding your face, and keep your chin down.

5. 왼쪽 정권 직선펀치

얼굴은 12시 정면 방향, 왼쪽 정권 훅을 한 상태에서 상대의 눈을 주시 하면서 턱을 아래로 당겨 양다리의 간격은 어깨넓이 양주먹은 양턱을 막으며 왼발을 돌려 밀면서 몸을 시계 방향으로 틀어 중심은 양다리에 두고, 왼쪽 주먹을 돌려 정권 직선펀치를 하면서 왼쪽 어깨로 왼쪽 턱을 방어 (선자세)

Left Fist Straight Punch:

Turn your body clockwise while pushing off with your left leg. Execute a straight left punch with your fist. Make sure your right fist is guarding your face, and keep your chin down.

6. 오른쪽 정권 직선 펀치 "기합"

얼굴은 12시 정면 방향, 왼쪽 정권 직선펀치를 한 상태에서 턱을 아래로 당겨 양다리의 간격은 어깨넓이 왼쪽 주먹은 왼쪽 턱을 막으며 오른발을 돌려 밀면서 몸을 반시계 방향으로 틀어 중심은 양다리에 두고, 기합을 넣으며 오른쪽 주먹을 돌려 정권 직선펀치를 하면서 오른쪽 어깨로 오른쪽 턱을 방어 (선자세)

Right Fist Straight Punch:

Turn your body counter-clockwise while pushing off with your right leg. Execute a straight right fist punch with your fist. Make sure your left fist is guarding your face, and keep your chin down. (Ki-Hap)

7. 오른쪽 양손날 상단 옆막기

얼굴은 12시 정면 방향, 오른쪽 정권 직선펀치를 한 상태에서 턱을 아래로 당겨 양다리의 간격은 어깨넓이 몸을 시계 방향으로 돌리면서 오른발을 들어 3시 방향에 돌려 놓으며 왼쪽 손바닥은 위로 손날은 입높이 에 오른쪽 손바닥을 아래로 손날은 눈높이에 두면서 중심은 뒷다리에 두고, 오른쪽으로 양손날 상단 옆막 기 (후방자세)

Right High two Knife Hand Chop Block:
Turn your body clockwise so you are facing 3:00 in a right Back Stance. Execute a right side back stance chop block with your forearm. Make sure you have your left elbow by your side, with your left palm face up.

8. 왼쪽 정권 직선펀치 "기합"

얼굴은 3시 방향, 오른쪽 양손날 상단 옆막기를 한 상태에서 상대의 눈을 주시 하면서 턱을 아래로 당겨 양다리의 간격은 어깨넓이 오른쪽 주먹은 오른쪽 턱을 막으며 몸을 시계 방향으로 돌리면서 왼발을 들어 3시 방향 앞으로 한발 옮겨 놓으며 중심은 양다리에 두고, 기합을 넣으며 왼쪽 주먹을 돌려 정권 직선펀치 를 하면서 왼쪽 어깨로 왼쪽 턱을 방어 (선자세)

Left Fist Straight Punch "Ki-Hap":
Step forward with your left leg towards 3:00 while turning your body clockwise. Execute a straight left punch, and face towards 6:00. Make sure your right fist is guarding your face, and keep your chin down. (Ki-Hap)

9. 오른쪽 정권 직선펀치 "기합"

얼굴은 3시 방향, 왼쪽 정권 직선 펀치를 한 상태에서 상대의 눈을 주시 하면서 턱을 아래로 당겨 양다리의 간격은 어깨넓이 왼쪽 주먹은 왼쪽 턱을 막으며 몸을 반시계 방향으로 돌리면서 오른발을 들어 3시 방향 앞으로 한발 옮겨 놓으며 중심은 양다리에 두고, 기합을 넣으며 오른쪽 주먹을 돌려 정권 직선펀치를 하면서 오른쪽 어깨로 오른쪽 턱을 방어 (선자세)

Right Fist Straight Punch "Ki-Hap":

Step forward with your right leg towards 3:00 while turning your body counter-clockwise. Execute a straight right punch, and face towards 12:00. Make sure your left fist is guarding your face, and keep your chin down. (Ki-Hap)

10. 오른손 앞 옷깃잡고 당기기

얼굴은 3시 방향, 오른쪽 정권 직선펀치를 한 상태에서 턱을 아래로 당겨 양다리의 간격은 어깨넓이 왼쪽 주먹은 왼쪽 턱을 막은대로 중심은 양다리에 두고, 오른손으로 상대의 앞 옷깃을 잡으면서 몸을 시계 방향으로 틀어 당기기 (선자세)

Right Grab and Pull:

Reach out with your right hand towards 2:00 and grab. Turn your body clockwise while pulling your right arm towards you by bringing your elbow back. Make sure your left hand is guarding your face.

11. 오른쪽 팔꿈치 훅

얼굴은 3시 방향, 오른손 앞 옷깃잡고 당기기를 한 상태에서 턱을 아래로 당겨 양다리의 간격은 어깨넓이 왼쪽 주먹은 왼쪽 턱을 막은대로 중심은 양다리에 두고, 오른발을 돌려 밀면서 몸을 12시 반시계 방향으로 틀어 오른쪽 팔꿈치로 훅치기 (선자세)

Right Elbow Hook:
Push off your right leg while turning your body counter-clockwise. Execute a right elbow hook straight across with your elbow. Make sure your left hand is guarding your face, and your chin is down.

12. 오른쪽 허리걸어 던지기

얼굴은 12시 방향, 오른쪽 팔꿈치 훅을 한 상태에서 양다리의 간격은 어깨넓이 왼손은 상대의 앞 옷깃을 잡으면서 오른발을 들어 앞으로 반발 옮겨 놓으며 오른팔로 상대의 허리를 반시계 방향으로 걸어 오른쪽 엉덩이를 상대의 사타구니에 대면서 왼발을 들어 뒤로 한발 옮겨 놓으며 얼굴은 9시 방향, 중심은 양다리에 두고, 양무릎을 굽혀 상대의 몸을 들어 올려 오른쪽으로 던지기 (중방자세)

Right Hip Throw:
Step out with your right leg towards 11:00, and hook around your opponent's waist with your right arm. Step back with your left leg towards 1:00 so both feet are square, and so you are facing 6:00. Bend both your legs and crouch slightly forward. Extend both your legs while having your right hip slightly sticking out. Turn your body counter-clockwise, and throw your opponent over your right hip while keeping your left fist guarding your face.

우주형: Universe Cap Form

13. 왼쪽 한발 옮겨놓기

얼굴은 9시 방향, 오른쪽 허리걸어 던지기를 한 상태에서 허리를 세워 양다리의 간격은 어깨넓이 양주먹은 양턱을 막으며 중심은 오른쪽 다리에 두고 왼발을 들어 9시 방향 앞으로 한발 옮겨놓기 (선자세)

Left Step:

Turn your body clockwise while stepping with your left leg towards 9:00 so you are facing 12:00. Make sure your guard is up.

14. 오른쪽 한발 옮겨놓기

얼굴은 9시 방향, 왼쪽 한발 옮겨놓기를 한 상태에서 허리를 세워 양다리의 간격은 어깨넓이 양주먹은 양턱을 막은대로 중심은 왼쪽 다리에 두고, 몸을 시계 방향으로 돌리면서 오른발을 들어 180도로 돌려 9시 방향 앞으로 한발 옮겨놓기 (선자세)

Right Step:

Turn your body clockwise while stepping back with your right leg towards 9:00 so you are facing 6:00. Make sure your guard is up.

15. 왼쪽 양손날 상단 옆막기

얼굴은 9시 방향, 오른쪽 한발 옮겨놓기를 한 상태에서 턱을 아래로 당겨 양다리의 간격은 어깨넓이 몸을 반시계 방향으로 돌리면서 왼팔을 들어 9시 방향 앞으로 한발 옮겨 놓으며 오른쪽 손바닥은 위로 손날은 입높이에 왼쪽 손바닥을 아래로 손날은 눈높이에 두면서 중심은 뒷다리에 두고, 왼쪽으로 양손날 상단 옆막기 (후방자세)

Left High two Knife Hand Chop Block Step:

Turn your body clockwise while stepping with your left leg towards 9:00 into a left side Back Stance. Execute a left side back stance chop block with your forearm. Make sure you have your right elbow by your side, with your right palm face up.

16. 오른쪽 정권 직선펀치 "기합"

얼굴은 9시 방향, 왼쪽 양손날 상단 옆막기를 한 상태에서 상대의 눈을 주시 하면서 턱을 아래로 당겨 양다리의 간격은 어깨넓이 왼쪽 주먹은 왼쪽 턱을 막으며 몸을 반시계 방향으로 돌리면서 오른발을 들어 9시 방향 앞으로 한발 옮겨 놓으며 중심은 양다리에 두고, 기합을 넣으며 오른쪽 주먹을 돌려 정권 직선펀치를 하면서 오른쪽 어깨로 오른쪽 턱을 방어 (선자세)

Right Fist Straight Punch "Ki-Hap" Step:

Step forward with your right leg towards 9:00 while turning your body counter-clockwise. Execute a straight right punch, and face towards 6:00. Make sure your left fist is guarding your face, and keep your chin down. (Ki-Hap)

17. 왼쪽 정권 직선펀치 "기합"

얼굴은 9시 방향, 오른쪽 정권 직선펀치를 한 상태에서 상대의 눈을 주시 하면서 턱을 아래로 당겨 양다리의 간격은 어깨넓이 오른쪽 주먹은 오른쪽 턱을 막으며 몸을 시계 방향으로 돌리면서 왼발을 들어 9시 방향 앞으로 한발 옮겨 놓으며 중심은 양다리에 두고, 기합을 넣으며 왼쪽 주먹을 돌려 정권 직선펀치를 하면서 왼쪽 어깨로 왼쪽 턱을 방어 (선자세)

Left Fist straight Punch "Ki-Hap" Step:

Step forward with your left leg towards 9:00 while turning your body clockwise. Execute a straight left punch, and face towards 12:00. Make sure your right fist is guarding your face, and keep your chin down. (Ki-Hap)

18. 왼손 앞 옷깃잡고 당기기

얼굴은 9시 방향, 왼쪽 정권 직선펀치를 한 상태에서 턱을 아래로 당겨 양다리의 간격은 어깨넓이 오른쪽 주먹은 오른쪽 턱을 막은대로 중심은 양다리에 두고, 왼손으로 상대의 앞 옷깃을 잡으면서 몸을 반시계 방향으로 틀어 당기기 (선자세)

Left Grab and Pull:

Reach out with your left hand towards 10:00 and grab. Turn your body counter-clockwise while pulling your left arm towards you by bringing your elbow back. Make sure your right hand is guarding your face.

19. 왼쪽 팔꿈치 훅

얼굴은 9시 방향, 왼손 앞 옷깃잡고 당기기를 한 상태에서 턱을 아래로 당겨 양다리의 간격은 어깨넓이 오른쪽 주먹은 오른쪽 턱을 막은대로 중심은 양다리에 두고, 왼발을 돌려 밀면서 몸을 12시 시계 방향으로 틀어 왼쪽 팔꿈치로 훅치기 (선자세)

Left Elbow Hook:

Push off your left leg while turning your body clockwise. Execute a left elbow hook straight across with your elbow. Make sure your right hand is guarding your face, and your chin is down.

20. 왼쪽 허리걸어 던지기

얼굴은 12시 정면 방향, 왼쪽 팔꿈치 훅을 한 상태에서 양다리의 간격은 어깨넓이 오른손은 상대의 앞 옷깃을 잡으면서 왼발을 들어 앞으로 반발 옮겨 놓으며 왼팔로 상대의 허리를 시계 방향으로 걸어 왼쪽 엉덩이를 상대의 사타구니에 대면서 오른발을 들어 뒤로 한발 옮겨 놓으며 얼굴은 3시 방향, 중심은 양다리에 두고, 양무릎을 굽혀 상대의 몸을 들어 올려 왼쪽으로 던지기 (중방자세)

Left Hip Throw:

Step out with your left leg towards 1:00, and hook around your opponent's waist with your left arm. Step back with your right leg towards 11:00 so both feet are square, and so you are facing 6:00. Bend both your legs and crouch slightly forward. Extend both your legs while having your left hip slightly sticking out. Turn your body clockwise, and throw your opponent over your left hip while keeping your right fist guarding your face.

우주형: Universe Cap Form

21. 오른쪽 한발 옮겨놓기

얼굴은 3시 방향, 왼쪽 허리걸어 던지기를 한 상태에서 허리를 세워 양다리의 간격은 어깨넓이 양주먹은 양턱을 막으며 중심은 왼쪽 다리에 두고, 오른발을 들어 반시계 방향으로 3시 방향 앞으로 한발 옮겨놓기 (선자세)

Right Step:

Turn your body counter-clockwise while stepping with your right leg towards 3:00 so you are facing 12:00. Make sure your guard is up.

22. 왼쪽 한발 옮겨놓기

얼굴은 3시 방향, 오른쪽 한발 옮겨놓기를 한 상태에서 허리를 세워 양다리의 간격은 어깨넓이 양주먹은 양턱을 막으며 중심은 오른쪽 다리에 두고, 왼발을 들어 반시계 방향으로 180도를 돌려 3시 방향 앞으로 한발 옮겨 놓으며 얼굴과 발은 6시 방향 (선자세)

Left Step:

Turn your body counter-clockwise while stepping back with your left leg towards 3:00 so you are facing 6:00. Make sure your guard is up.

23. 오른쪽 안다리 후리기

얼굴은 6시 방향, 왼쪽 한발 옮겨놓기를 한 상태에서 턱을 아래로 당겨 양다리의 간격은 어깨넓이 양주먹은 가슴 약 18cm 앞에 놓고, 중심은 왼쪽 다리에 두고, 오른발을 들어 오른쪽 안다리 후리기 (선자세)

Right Inside Hook Throw:

While facing 6:00, execute a right leg inside hook throw with your heel in a circular motion, from the outside in. Make sure you keep your guard up.

24. 왼쪽 안다리 후리기

얼굴은 6시 방향, 오른쪽 안다리 후리기를 한 상태에서 턱을 아래로 당겨 오른발을 제자리에 놓고, 양다리의 간격은 어깨넓이 몸을 반시계 양주먹은 가슴 약 18cm 앞에 놓고, 중심은 오른쪽 다리에 두고, 왼발을 들어 왼쪽 안다리 후리기 (선자세)

Left Inside Hook Throw:

While facing 6:00, execute a right leg inside hook throw with your heel in a circular motion, from the outside in. Make sure you keep your guard up.

25. 왼쪽 한발 옮겨놓기

얼굴은 6시 방향, 왼쪽 안다리 후리기를 한 상태에서 왼발을 제자리에 놓고, 허리를 세워 양다리의 간격은 어깨넓이 양주먹은 양턱을 막으며 중심은 오른쪽 다리에 두고, 왼발을 들어 6시 방향 앞으로 한발 옮겨놓기 (선저세)

Left Step

Turn your body clockwise while stepping forward with your left leg towards 6:00 so you are facing 9:00. Make sure you keep your guard up.

26. 오른발 뺏치기

얼굴은 6시 방향, 왼쪽 한발 옮겨놓기를 한 상태에서 양다리의 간격은 어깨넓이 왼손은 상대의 오른쪽 옷깃을 잡고, 오른손은 상대의 왼쪽 옷깃을 잡고, 중심은 왼쪽 다리에 두고, 왼손을 밀면서 오른손은 앞으로 당겨 몸을 반시계 방향으로 틀어 오른발로 뺏치기 (선자세)

Right Leg Sweep:

Turn your body counter-clockwise while sweeping your inside right foot towards 6:00 so you are now facing 3:00.

27. 왼발 뺏치기

얼굴은 6시 방향, 오른발 뺏치기를 한 상태에서 양다리의 간격은 어깨넓이 오른손은 상대의 왼쪽 옷깃을 잡고, 왼손은 상대의 오른쪽 옷깃을 잡고, 중심은 오른쪽 다리에 두고, 오른손을 밀면서 왼손은 앞으로 당겨 몸을 시계 방향으로 틀어 왼쪽발로 뺏치기 (선자세)

Left Leg Sweep:

Turn your body clockwise while sweeping your inside left foot towards 6:00 so you are now facing 9:00.

28. 왼쪽 마차바퀴 돌리기

얼굴은 6시 방향, 왼발 뺏치기를 한 상태에서 양다리의 간격은 어깨넓이 몸을 왼쪽으로 기울려 왼쪽 손바닥은 바닥을 짚고, 몸을 6시 방향으로 돌려 양다리를 똑바로 펴고 마차바퀴 돌리기 (전방자세)

Left Cartwheel:

Push off with your right leg and place your left hand flat on the floor. Execute a left side cartwheel. Try to keep your body as straight as possible.

29. 오른쪽 양손날 상단 옆막기

얼굴은 12시 방향, 왼쪽 마차바퀴 돌리기를 한 상태에서 몸을 일으켜 세워 턱을 아래로 당겨 양다리의 간격은 어깨넓이 몸을 시계 방향으로 돌리면서 오른발을 12시 방향에 돌려 놓으며 왼쪽 손바닥은 위로 손날은 입높이에 오른쪽 손바닥을 아래로 손날은 눈높이에 두면서 중심은 뒷다리에 두고, 오른쪽으로 양손날 상단 옆막기 (후방자세)

Right High two Knife Hand Chop Back:
Turn your body clockwise so you are facing 12:00 in a right side Back Stance. Execute a right side back stance chop block with your forearm. Make sure you have your left elbow by your side, with your left palm face up.

30 왼쪽 한발 옮겨놓기

얼굴은 12시 방향, 오른쪽 양손날 상단 옆막기를 한 상태에서 양주먹은 양턱을 막으며 중심은 오른쪽 다리에 두고, 왼발을 들어 12시 방향 앞으로 한발 옮겨놓기 (선자세)

Left Step:
Step forward with your left leg towards 12:00. Make sure your guard is up.

31. 오른발을 뛰면서 왼발 상단 앞차기

얼굴은 12시 방향, 양다리의 간격은 어깨 넓이, 양주먹은 양턱을 막음대로 오른쪽 한발을 뛰면서 턱은 아래로 당기고 왼발 상단 앞차기 (선자세)

Left Jumping Double Front Kick:

Pick up your right knee at about belt level. Jump with your left leg and bring your right leg back down as you bring up your left knee. Extend your left leg and execute a jumping double front kick. Make sure your guard is up.

32. 왼쪽 정권 직선펀치

얼굴은 12시 방향, 뛰어 왼발 상단 앞차기를 하고 양발이 바닥에 닿는 순간 오른쪽 주먹은 오른쪽 턱을 막은 상태에서 몸을 시계방향으로 틀어 중심을 양다리에 두고 왼쪽 정권 직선 펀치 (선자세)

Left Fist Straight Punch:

Turn your body clockwise and execute a straight left punch with your fist. Make sure your right fist is guarding your face, and keep your chin down.

33. 오른쪽 정권 직선펀치 "기합"

얼굴은 12시 방향, 왼쪽 정권 직선펀치를 한 상태에서 턱을 아래로 당기고 양다리의 간격은 어깨넓이, 왼쪽 주먹은 왼쪽 턱을 막으면서 오른발을 밀면서 몸을 반시계 방향으로 틀어 중심은 양다리에 두고, 기합을 넣으면서 오른쪽 주먹을 돌려 정권 직선펀치를 하면서 오른쪽 어깨로 오른쪽 턱을 방어 (선자세)

Right Fist straight Punch "Ki-Hap":

Turn your body counter-clockwise and execute a straight right punch with your fist. Make sure your left fist is guarding your face, and keep your chin down. (Ki-Hap)

34. 왼쪽 양손짚고 전방 회전낙법

얼굴은 12시 방향, 오른쪽 정권 직선펀치를 한 상태에서 몸을 앞으로 엎드리면서 중심은 앞다리에 두고, 양 손바닥을 동시에 바닥에 짚고, 양 검지를 서로 대면 턱을 아래로 당겨 얼굴은 3시 방향으로 돌리고, 왼쪽 어깨위로 몸을 넘겨 전방회전 낙법을 하고, 오른쪽 다리와 왼쪽 발바닥과 오른쪽 손바닥을 동시에 바닥을 치고, 오른쪽 손바닥을 밀어 일어나면서 왼쪽 주먹은 앞 몸통 막기 (전방회전낙법 자세)

Left Two Hand Long Nak-Bub:

Position your hands for a left side Nak-Bub. Tilt your head to the right and touch your right ear to your right shoulder. Dive forward as far as you can and catch yourself with your hands while tucking in your left shoulder. Roll forward. Land with your right leg tucked in and with your left leg over your right. With your right arm, slap the ground with the palm of your hand. Keep your left fist guarding your face.

35. 오른쪽 양손날 상단 옆막기

얼굴은 12시 방향 전방회전 낙법에서 일어나면서 왼쪽 양손날을 들어올려 턱을 아래로 당기고, 몸을 시계 방향으로 돌려 오른발을 들어 앞으로 한발 옮겨 놓으면서 왼쪽 손바닥은 위로 오른쪽 손바닥은 밑으로 양손날 상단 옆막기 (후방자세)

Right High two Knife Hand Chop Block :

Turn your body clockwise so you are facing 6:00 in a right side Back Stance. Execute a right side back stance chop block with your forearm. Make sure you have your left elbow by your side, with your left palm face up.

WING FORM
날 | 개 | 형

01. 양손날 기발육 "기합" (선자세):
    Vocalize willpower (stand stance)

02. 오른쪽 손창 45도 수직찌르기 (선자세):
    Right Spear (stand stance)

03. 왼쪽 손창 45도 수직찌르기 (선자세):
    Left Spear (stand stance)

04. 정면 양손창 수평찌르기 "기합" (선자세):
    Two Spear Hand "Ki-Hap" (stand stance)

05. 오른쪽 뒷정권 치기 (선자세):
    Right Back Fist (stand stance)

06. 왼쪽 뒷정권 치기 (선자세):
    Left Back Fist (stand stance)

07. 오른쪽 양손날 하단 옆막기 (후방자세):
    Right Low Two Knife hand Side Block (back stance)

08. 오른쪽 양팔뚝 중단 옆막기 (중방자세):
    Right Middle two Forearm side Block (middle stance)

09. 왼쪽 정권 직선펀치 "기합" (선자세):
    Left Fist straight Punch "Ki-Hap" (stand stance)

10. 오른쪽 정권 어퍼컷 (선자세):
    Right Fist Uppercut (stand stance)

11. 오른쪽 정권 훅 (선자세):
    Right fist Hook (stand stance)

12. 오른쪽 상단 옆차기 (옆방자세):
    Right high Side kick (side stance)

13. 오른발 비꼬아놓기 (선자세):
    Right Step (stand stance)

14. 왼쪽 양손날 하단 옆막기 (후방자세):
    Left Low two Knife Hand Side Block (back stance)

15. 왼쪽 양팔뚝 중단 옆막기 (중방자세):
    Left Middle two Forearm Side Block (middle stance)

16. 오른쪽 정권 직선펀치 (선자세):
    Right Fist Straight Punch (stand stance)

17. 왼쪽 정권 어퍼컷 (선자세):
    Left Fist Uppercut (stand stance)

18. 왼쪽 정권 훅 (선자세):
    Left Fist Hook (stand stance)

19. 왼쪽 상단 옆차기 (옆방자세):
    Left High Side Kick (side stance)

20. 왼발 비꼬아놓기 (선자세):
    Left Step (stand stance)

21. 오른쪽 한발 옮겨놓기 (선자세):
    Right Step (stand stance)

22. 오른쪽 안다리 후리기 (선자세):
    Right Inside Hook Throw (stand stance)

23. 왼쪽 안다리 후리기 (선자세):
    Left Inside Hook Throw (stand stance)

24. 오른쪽 양팔뚝 중단 옆막기 (중방자세):
    Right Middle two Forearm Side Block (middle stance)

25. 왼쪽 양팔뚝 중단 옆막기 (중방자세):
    Left Middle two Forearm Side Block (middle stance)

26. 오른쪽 양팔뚝 상단 옆막기 (전방자세):
    Right High two Forearm Side Block (front stance)

27. 왼쪽 양팔뚝 상단 옆막기 (전방자세):
    Lift High two Forearm Side Block (front stance)

28. 왼쪽 양정권 직선펀치 "기합" (선자세):
    Lift two Fist Straight Punch "Ki-Hap" (stand stance)

29. 오른쪽 중단 앞차기 (선자세):
    Right Middle Front Kick (stand stance)

30. 오른쪽 양정권 직선펀치 "기합" (선자세):
    Right two Fist Straight Punch "KI-Hap" (stand stance)

31. 왼쪽 중단 앞차기 (선자세):
    Left Middle Front Kick (stand stance)

32. 왼쪽 긴 전방 회전낙법 (전방회전 낙법자세):
    Left Two Hand Long Nak-bub
    (front roll nak-bub stance)

33. 오른쪽 양팔뚝 중단 옆막기 (중방자세):
    Right Middle two Forearm Side Block (middle stance)

1. 양손날 기발육 "기합"

얼굴은 12시 정면 방향, 허리를 똑바로 세운 선자세에서 양무릎을 약간 굽혀 양팔과 양다리의 간격은 어깨 넓이 중심은 양다리에 두고, 양손을 가슴앞에 두고, 숨을 들어 마신후 숨을 멈추고, 단전에 힘을넣어 양뒷축을 들었다가 내리면서 단전의 힘으로 양손날에 기를 몰아 순간 짧게 아얏 소리를 지르며 양손가락을 쥐면서 턱밑까지 들어 올리기 (선자세)

Vocalize Willpower:

In a Vocalize Willpower Stance, Vocalize while thrusting both knife hands downward. Bend elbows so your thumbs are pointed up, and explode upward. (Ki-Hap)

2. 오른쪽 손창 45도 수직찌르기

얼굴은 12시 정면 방향, 양손날 기발육을 한 상태에서 상대의 눈을 주시 하면서 턱을 아래로 당겨 양다리의 간격은 어깨넓이 왼쪽 주먹은 왼쪽 턱을 막으며 오른발을 돌려 밀면서 몸을 반시계 방향으로 틀어 중심은 양다리에 두고, 오른쪽 손바닥을 위로 하여 오른쪽 손창으로 목젖을 45도 각도로 수직찌르기 (선자세)

Right Spear:

Turn your body counter-clockwise while pushing off with your right leg. Execute a right hand spear to your opponent's neck. Make sure your right palm is face up, and your left fist is guarding your face.

3. 왼쪽 손창 45도 수직찌르기

얼굴은 12시 정면 방향, 오른쪽 손창 45도 수직찌르기를 한 상태에서 턱을 아래로 당겨 양다리의 간격은 어깨넓이 오른쪽 주먹은 오른쪽 턱을 막으며 왼발을 돌려 밀면서 몸을 시계 방향으로 틀어 중심은 양다리에 두고, 왼쪽 손바닥을 위로 하여 왼쪽 손창으로 목젖을 45도 각도로 수직 찌르기 (선자세)

Left Spear:

Turn your body clockwise while pushing off with your left leg. Execute a left hand spear to your opponent's neck. Make sure your left palm is face up, and your right fist is guarding your face.

날개형: Wing Form

4. 정면 양손창 수평찌르기 "기합"

얼굴은 12시 정면 방향, 왼쪽 손창 45도 수직 찌르기를 한 상태에서 턱을 아래로 당겨 양다리의 간격은 어깨넓이 중심은 양다리에 두고, 양무릎을 굽혀 양손을 턱앞까지 당겨 다시 양무릎을 세우면서 양손바닥을 아래로 돌려 기합을 넣으며 양손창 수평으로 목젖을 찌르기 (선자세)

Two Spear Hand "Ki-Hap":

While leaning forward, execute a double knife hand to your opponent's throat. Make sure both your palms are face down. (Ki-Hap)

5. 오른쪽 뒷정권 치기

얼굴은 12시 정면 방향, 정면 양손창 수평찌르기를 한 상태에서 턱을 아래로 당겨 양다리의 간격은 어깨넓이 중심은 양다리에 두고, 오른쪽 뒷정권을 돌려 인중을 치기 (선자세)

Right Back Fist:

Turn your body counter-clockwise while pushing off with your right leg. Execute a right hand back fist with your back knuckles. Make sure your left fist is guarding your face.

6. 왼쪽 뒷정권 치기

얼굴은 12시 정면 방향, 오른쪽 뒷정권 치기를 한 상태에서 턱을 아래로 당겨 양다리의 간격은 어깨넓이 중심은 양다리에 두고, 왼쪽 뒷정권을 돌려 인중을 치기 (선자세)

Left Back Fist:

Turn your body clockwise while pushing off with your left leg. Execute a left hand back fist with your back knuckles. Make sure your right fist is guarding your face.

7. 오른쪽 양손날 하단 옆막기

얼굴은 12시 정면 방향, 왼쪽 뒷정권 치기를 한 상태에서 턱을 아래로 당겨 양다리의 간격은 어깨넓이 몸을 시계 방향으로 돌리면서 오른발을 들어 3시 방향 제자리에서 돌려 놓으며 왼쪽 손바닥은 위로 팔뚝은 띠에 대면서 오른쪽 손바닥을 아래로 중심은 뒷다리에 두고, 오른쪽으로 허리를 틀어 동시에 양손날로 하단 옆막기 (후방자세)

Right Low Two Knife hand Side Block:

Turn your body clockwise so you are facing towards 3:00 in a right side Back Stance. Execute a right side Low Side Block with your right forearm. Keep your left hand at belt level with your palm face up.

8. 오른쪽 양팔뚝 중단 옆막기

얼굴은 3시 방향, 오른쪽 양손날 하단 옆막기를 한 상태에서 턱을 아래로 당겨 양다리의 간격은 어깨넓이 오른발을 들어 4시 방향으로 옮겨 놓으며 중심은 양다리에 두고, 양손은 동시에 주먹을 쥐면서 양손가락을 위로 오른손은 어깨높이에 왼손은 오른쪽 팔꿈치에 대면서 허리를 시계 방향으로 틀어 오른쪽으로 양팔뚝 중단 옆막기 (중방자세)

Right Middle two Forearm side Block:

Step out with your right leg towards 4:00 into a right side Middle Stance, and face towards 3:00. Execute a right side Middle Side Block with your right forearm, and have your fist is at eye level. Make sure your left fist is on your inside right elbow for support, and keep your chin down.

9. 왼쪽 정권 직선펀치 "기합"

얼굴은 3시 방향, 오른쪽 양팔뚝 중단 옆막기를 한 상태에서 상대의 눈을 주시 하면서 턱을 아래로 당겨 양다리의 간격은 어깨넓이 오른쪽 주먹은 오른쪽 턱을 막으며 몸을 시계 방향으로 돌리면서 왼발을 들어 3시 방향 앞으로 한발 옮겨 놓으며 중심은 양다리애 두고, 기합을 넣으며 왼쪽 주먹을 돌려 정권 직선펀치 를 하면서 왼쪽 어깨로 왼쪽 턱을 방어 (선자세)

Left Fist straight Punch "Ki-Hap":

Step forward with your left leg towards 3:00 while turning your body clockwise. Execute a straight left punch, and face towards 6:00. Make sure your right fist is guarding your face, and keep your chin down. (Ki-Hap)

10. 오른쪽 정권 어퍼컷

얼굴은 3시 방향, 왼쪽 정권 직선펀치를 한 상태에서 턱을 아래로 당겨 허리를 똑바로 세운 자세에서 양다리의 간격은 어깨넓이 왼쪽 주먹은 왼쪽 턱을 막으며 중심은 양다리에 두고, 양무릎을 구부렸다 일어나면서 오른쪽 주먹을 돌려 정권 어퍼컷 (선자세)

Right Fist Uppercut:

Bend both your legs slightly. Push off with your right leg so you are extending up, while turning your body counter-clockwise so you are facing 3:00. Execute a right side fist uppercut with your fist. Make sure your left fist is guarding the face, and keep your chin down.

11. 오른쪽 정권 훅

얼굴은 3시 방향, 오른쪽 정권 어퍼컷을 한 상태에서 턱을 아래로 당겨 양다리의 간격은 어깨넓이 왼쪽 주먹은 왼쪽 턱을 막으며 중심은 양다리에 두고, 오른발을 돌려 밀면서 몸을 12시 반시계 방향으로 틀어 오른쪽 주먹으로 훅 (선자세)

Right Fist Hook:

Push off with your right leg while turning your body counter-clockwise so you are facing 3:00, and execute a right fist hook straight across with your fist. Make sure your left fist is guarding your face, and keep your chin down.

날개형: Wing Form

12. 오른쪽 상단 옆차기

얼굴은 3시 방향, 오른쪽 정권 훅을 한 상태에서 턱을 아래로 당겨 양다리의 간격은 어깨넓이 왼쪽 주먹은 왼쪽 턱을 막은대로 중심은 왼쪽 다리에 두고, 왼발을 들어 12시 방향으로 돌려 놓으며 몸을 9시 방향으로 기울려 얼굴은 3시 방향으로 돌리고, 오른발을 들어 3시 방향으로 상단 옆차기 (옆방자세)

Right High Side Kick:

Pivot your left foot so your toes are facing 12:00. Pick up your right leg, and bring in your right knee. Execute a right leg high side kick towards 3:00. Make sure your back is straight when kicking, and your guard is up.

13. 오른발 비꼬아놓기

얼굴은 3시 방향, 오른쪽 상단 옆차기를 한 상태에서 오른발을 반시계 방향으로 돌려 9시에 비꼬아 놓으며 얼굴은 9시로 돌려 허리를 세워 왼쪽 주먹은 왼쪽 턱을 막은대로 오른쪽 주먹은 오른쪽 턱을 막으며 중심은 양다리에 두고, 비꼬아서기 (선자세)

Right Step:

Turn your body counter-clockwise while stepping with your right leg towards 9:00 so you are facing 6:00. Make sure you keep your guard up.

14. 왼쪽 양손날 하단 옆막기

얼굴은 9시 방향, 오른발을 비꼬아 놓기를 한 상태에서 턱을 아래로 당겨 몸을 반시계 방향으로 돌리면서 왼발을 들어 9시 방향 앞으로 한발 옮겨 놓으며 오른쪽 손바닥은 위로 팔뚝은 띠에 대면서 왼쪽 손바닥을 아래로 중심은 뒷다리에 두고, 왼쪽으로 허리를 틀어 동시에 양손날 하단 옆막기 (후방자세)

Left Low two Knife Hand Side Block:

Turn your body clockwise while stepping with your left leg towards 9:00 into a left side Back Stance. Execute a left side Low Side Block with your left forearm. Keep your right hand at belt level with your palm face up.

15. 왼쪽 양팔뚝 중단 옆막기

얼굴은 9시 방향, 왼쪽 양손날 하단 옆막기를 한 상태에서 턱을 아래로 당겨 양다리의 간격은 어깨넓이 왼발을 들어 8시 방향으로 옮겨 놓으며 중심은 양다리에 두고, 양손은 동시에 주먹을 쥐면서 양손가락을 위로 왼손은 어깨높이에 오른손은 왼쪽 팔꿈치에 대면서 허리를 반시계 방향으로 틀어 왼쪽으로 양팔뚝 중단 옆막기 (중방자세)

Left Middle two Forearm Side Block:

Step out with your left leg towards 8:00 into a left side Middle Stance, and face towards 9:00. Execute a left side Middle Side Block with your left forearm, and have your fist is at eye level. Make sure your right fist is on your inside elbow for support, and keep your chin down.

날개형: Wing Form

16. 오른쪽 정권 직선펀치

얼굴은 9시 방향, 왼쪽 양팔뚝 중단 옆막기를 한 상태에서 상대의 눈을 주시 하면서 턱을 아래로 당겨 양다리의 간격은 어깨넓이 왼쪽 주먹은 왼쪽 턱을 막으며 몸을 반시계 방향으로 돌리면서 오른발을 들어 9시 방향 앞으로 한발 옮겨 놓으며 중심은 양다리에 두고, 오른쪽 주먹을 돌려 정권 직선펀치를 하면서 오른쪽 어깨로 오른쪽 턱을 방어 (선저세)

Right Fist Straight Punch:
Step forward with your right leg towards 9:00 while turning your body clockwise. Execute a straight right punch, and face towards 6:00. Make sure your left fist is guarding your face, and keep your chin down. (Ki-Hap)

17. 왼쪽 정권 어퍼컷

얼굴은 9시 방향, 오른쪽 정권 직선펀치를 한 상태에서 턱을 아래로 당겨 허리를 똑바로 세운 자세에서 양다리의 간격은 어깨넓이 오른쪽 주먹은 오른쪽 턱을 막으며 중심은 양다리에 두고, 양무릎을 구부렸다 일어나면서 왼쪽 주먹을 돌려 정권 어퍼컷 (선자세)

Left Fist Uppercut:
Bend both your legs slightly. Push off with your left leg so you are extending up, while turning your body clockwise so you are facing 9:00. Execute a left side fist uppercut with your fist. Make sure your right fist is guarding the face, and keep your chin down.

18. 왼쪽 정권 훅

얼굴은 9시 방향, 왼쪽 정권 어퍼컷을 한 상태에서 턱을 아래로 당겨 양다리의 간격은 어깨넓이 오른쪽 주먹은 오른쪽 턱을 막으며 중심은 양다리에 두고, 왼발을 돌려 밀면서 몸을 12시 시계 방향으로 틀어 왼쪽 주먹으로 훅(선자세)

Left Fist Hook:

Push off with your left leg while turning your body clockwise so you are facing 9:00, and execute a left fist hook straight across with your fist. Make sure your right fist is guarding your face, and keep your chin down.

19. 왼쪽 상단 옆차기

얼굴은 9시 방향, 왼쪽 정권 훅을 한 상태에서 턱을 아래로 당겨 양다리의 간격은 어깨넓이 오른쪽 주먹은 오른쪽 턱을 막은대로 중심은 오른쪽 다리에 두고, 오른발을 들어 12시 방향으로 돌려 놓으며 몸을 3시 방향으로 기울려 얼굴은 9시 방향으로 돌리고, 왼발을 들어 9시 방향으로 상단 옆차기 (옆방자세)

Left High Side Kick:

Pivot your right foot so your toes are facing 12:00. Pick up your left leg, and bring in your left knee. Execute a left leg high side kick towards 9:00. Make sure your back is straight when kicking, and your guard is up.

날개형: Wing Form

20. 왼발 비꼬아놓기

얼굴은 9시 방향, 왼쪽 상단 옆차기를 한 상태에서 왼발을 시계 방향으로 돌려 3시에 비꼬아 놓으며 얼굴은 3시로 돌려 허리를 세워 오른쪽 주먹은 오른쪽 턱을 막은대로 왼쪽 주먹은 왼쪽 턱을 막으며 중심은 양다리에 두고, 비꼬아서기 (선자세)

Left Step:
Turn your body clockwise while stepping with your left leg towards 3:00 so you are facing 6:00. Make sure you keep your guard up.

21. 오른쪽 한발 옮겨놓기

얼굴은 9시 방향, 왼발 비꼬아놓기를 한 상태에서 허리를 세워 양다리의 간격은 어깨넓이 양주먹은 양턱을 막은대로 중심은 왼쪽 다리에 두고, 오른발을 들어 12시 방향으로 얼굴과 오른발을 돌려 3시 방향 한발 옮겨놓기 (선자세)

Right Step:
Turn your body counter-clockwise while stepping with your right leg towards 3:00 so you are facing 12:00. Make sure you keep your guard up.

22. 오른쪽 안다리 후리기

얼굴은 12시 방향, 오른쪽 한발 옮겨놓기를 한 상태에서 턱을 아래로 당겨 양다리의 간격은 어깨넓이 양주먹은 가슴 약 18cm 앞에 놓고, 중심은 왼쪽 다리에 두고, 오른발을 들어 오른쪽 안다리 후리기 (선자세)

Right Inside Hook Throw:

While facing 12:00, execute a right leg inside hook throw with your heel in a circular motion, from the outside in. Make sure you keep your guard up.

23. 왼쪽 안다리 후리기

얼굴은 12시 방향, 오른쪽 안다리 후리기를 한 상태에서 턱을 아래로 당겨 오른발을 제자리에 놓고, 양다리의 간격은 어깨넓이 양주먹은 가슴 약 18cm 앞에 놓고, 중심은 오른쪽 다리에 두고, 왼발을 들어 왼쪽 안다리 후리기 (선자세)

Left Inside Hook Throw:

Execute a left leg inside hook throw with your heel in a circular motion, from the outside in. Make sure you keep your guard up.

24. 오른쪽 양팔뚝 중단 옆막기

얼굴은 12시 방향, 왼쪽 안다리 후리기를 한 상태에서 턱을 아래로 당겨 왼발을 제자리에 놓고, 양다리의 간격은 어깨넓이 오른발을 들어 1시 방향으로 옮겨 놓으며 중심은 양다리에 두고, 양손은 동시에 주먹을 쥐면서 양손가락을 위로 오른손은 어깨높이에 왼손은 오른쪽 팔꿈치에 대면서 허리를 시계 방향으로 틀어 오른쪽으로 양팔뚝 중단 옆막기 (중방자세)

Right Middle two Forearm Side Block:

Step out with your right leg towards 2:00 into a right side Middle Stance, and face towards 1:00. Execute a right side Middle Side Block with your right forearm, and have your fist is at eye level. Make sure your left fist is on your inside right elbow for support, and keep your chin down.

25. 왼쪽 양팔뚝 중단 옆막기

얼굴은 1시 방향, 오른쪽 양팔뚝 중단 옆막기를 한 상태에서 턱을 아래로 당겨 양다리의 간격은 어깨넓이 왼발을 들어 11시 방향으로 옮겨 놓으며 중심은 양다리에 두고, 양손은 동시에 주먹을 쥐면서 양손가락을 위로 왼손은 어깨높이에 오른손은 왼쪽 팔꿈치에 대면서 허리를 반시계 방향으로 틀어 왼쪽으로 양팔뚝 중단 옆막기 (중방자세)

Left Middle two Forearm Side Block:

Step out with your left leg towards 10:00 into a left side Middle Stance, and face towards 11:00. Execute a left side Middle Side Block with your left forearm, and have your fist is at eye level. Make sure your right fist is on your inside left elbow for support, and keep your chin down.

26. 오른쪽 양팔뚝 상단 옆막기

얼굴은 11시 방향, 왼쪽 양팔뚝 중단 옆막기를 한 상태에서 상대의 눈을 주시 하면서 턱을 아래로 당겨 양다리의 간격은 어깨넓이 오른발을 들어 1시 방향으로 다시 옮겨 놓으며 몸을 앞으로 밀면서 중심은 앞다리에 두고, 왼쪽 팔뚝은 왼쪽 얼굴을 막으며 오른쪽 팔뚝은 앞 얼굴을 스치면서 머리위에 올려 오른쪽으로 동시에 양팔뚝 상단 옆막기 (전방자세)

Right High two Forearm Side Block:

Step out with your right leg towards 2:00 into a right side Forward Stance, and face towards 1:00. Execute a right side High Side Block with your right forearm, and have your arm at a 45degree angle. Make sure your left fist is guarding your face, and keep your left elbow in.

27. 왼쪽 양팔뚝 상단 옆막기

얼굴은 1시 방향, 오른쪽 양팔뚝 상단 옆막기를 한 상태에서 턱을 아래로 당겨 양다리의 간격은 어깨넓이 왼발을 들어 11시 방향으로 다시 옮겨 놓으며 몸을 앞으로 밀면서 중심은 앞다리에 두고, 오른쪽 팔뚝은 오른쪽 얼굴을 막으며 왼쪽 팔뚝은 앞 얼굴을 스치면서 머리위에 올려 왼쪽으로 동시에 양팔뚝 상단 옆막기 (전방자세)

Lift High two Forearm Side Block:

Step out with your left leg towards 10:00 into a left side Forward Stance, and face towards 11:00. Execute a left side High Side Block with your left forearm, and have your arm at a 45degree angle. Make sure your right fist is guarding your face, and keep your right elbow in.

28. 왼쪽 양정권 직선펀치 "기합"

얼굴은 11시 방향, 왼쪽 양팔뚝 상단 옆막기를 한 상태에서 상대의 눈을 주시 하면서 턱을 아래로 당겨 양 다리의 간격은 어깨넓이 오른발을 들어 8시 방향 뒤로 한발 옮겨 놓으며 중심은 양다리에 두고, 기합을 넣으며 4시 방향으로 양주먹을 동시에 앞턱 직선펀치 (선자세)

Lift two Fist Straight Punch "Ki-Hap":

Turn your body clockwise while sliding your right leg backward behind your left leg towards 11:00, and keep your left leg planted. Execute a double punch with both your fists towards 5:00. (Ki-Hap)

29. 오른쪽 중단 앞차기

얼굴은 4시 방향 양정권 직선펀치를 한 상태에서 턱을 아래로 당겨 양다리의 간격은 어깨넓이 중심은 왼쪽 다리에 두고, 오른발을 들어 앞턱을 차면서 양주먹은 양턱을 방어 (선자세)

Right Middle Front Kick:

Pick up your right leg, and execute a right leg middle front kick with the ball of your foot towards 5:00.

30. 오른쪽 양정권 직선펀치 "기합"

얼굴은 4시 방향, 오른쪽 상단 앞차기를 한 상태에서 상대의 눈을 주시 하면서 턱을 아래로 당겨 양다리의 간격은 어깨넓이 오른발을 들어 1시 방향 뒤로 한발 옮겨 놓으며 중심은 양다리에 두고, 기합을 넣으며 8시 방향으로 양주먹을 동시에 앞턱 직선펀치 (선자세)

Right two Fist Straight Punch "KI-Hap":

Step out with your right leg towards 7:00. Execute a double punch with both your fists towards 7:00. (Ki-Hap)

31. 왼쪽 중단 앞차기

얼굴은 8시 방향, 양정권 직선펀치를 한 상태에서 턱을 아래로 당겨 양다리의 간격은 어깨넓이 중심은 오른쪽 다리에 두고, 왼발을 들어 앞턱을 차면서 양주먹은 양턱을 방어 (선자세)

Left Middle Front Kick:

Pick up your left leg, and execute a left leg middle front kick with the ball of your foot towards 7:00.

날개형: Wing Form

32. 왼쪽 긴 전방 회전낙법

얼굴은 8시 방향, 왼쪽 상단 앞차기를 한 상태에서 왼발을 한발 앞으로 옮겨 놓으며 몸을 엎드려 중심은 앞다리에 두고, 몸을 6시 방향 앞으로 뛰면서 양손바닥을 바닥에 짚고, 왼쪽 어깨위로 몸을 360도로 돌려 긴 전방 회전 낙법으로 왼쪽 주먹은 앞 얼굴을 막으며 오른쪽 다리를 접어 왼쪽 발바닥과 오른쪽 손바닥은 동시에 바닥을 치면서 몸을 12시 방향으로 돌려 일어나기 (전방회전 낙법자세)

Left Two Hand Long Nak-bub:
While facing 6:00, execute a left side long nak-bub towards 6:00.

33. 오른쪽 양팔뚝 중단 옆막기

얼굴은 12시 방향, 왼쪽 긴 전방 회전낙법을 한 상태에서 턱을 아래로 당겨 양다리의 간격은 어깨넓이 오른발을 들어 1시 방향으로 옮겨 놓으며 중심은 양다리에 두고, 양손은 동시에 주먹을 쥐면서 양손가락을 위로 오른손은 어깨높이에 왼손은 오른쪽 팔꿈치에 대면서 허리를 시계 방향으로 틀어 오른쪽으로 양팔뚝 중단 옆막기 (중방자세)

Right Middle two Forearm Side Block:

Step out with your right leg towards 1:00 into a right side Middle Stance, and face towards 12:00. Execute a right side Middle Side Block with your right forearm, and have your fist is at eye level. Make sure your left fist is on your inside right elbow for support, and keep your chin down.

날개형: Wing Form

LIGHTNING FORM
번 | 개 | 형

01. 차력 "기합" (선자세):
     Cha Ryuk "KI-Hap" (stand stance)
02. 오른쪽 정권 어퍼컷 (선자세):
     Right Fist Uppercut (stand stance)
03. 오른쪽 정권 훅 (선자세):
     Right Fist Hook (stand stance)
04. 왼쪽 정권 어퍼컷 (선자세):
     Left Fist Uppercut (stand stance)
05. 왼쪽 정권 훅 (선자세):
     Left Fist Hook (stand stance)
06. 왼쪽 정권 직선펀치 (선자세):
     Left Fist straight Punch (stand stance)
07. 오른쪽 정권 직선펀치 "기합" (선자세):
     Right Fist straight Punch (stand stance)
08. 오른쪽 양손난 하단 옆막기 (후방자세):
     Right Low to Knife Hand Side Block
     (back stance)
09. 오른쪽 양팔뚝 중단 옆막기 (중방자세):
     Right Middle two Forearm Side Block
     (middle stance)
10. 오른쪽 양팔뚝 상단 옆막기 (전방자세):
     Right High two Forearm Side Block
     (front stance)
11. 왼쪽 정권 직선펀치 "기합" (선자세):
     Left Fist straight Punch "KI-Hap"
     (stand stance)
12. 오른쪽 안다리 후리기 (선자세):
     Right Inside Hook Throw (stand stance)
13. 오른쪽 상단 옆차기 (옆방자세):
     Right High Side Kick (stand stance)
14. 오른쪽 어깨걸어 던지기 (중방자세):
     Right Shoulder Throw (middle stance)
15. 왼쪽 한발 옮겨놓기 (선자세):
     Left Step (stand stance)
16. 오른쪽 한발 옮겨놓기 (선자세):
     Right Step (stand stance)
17. 왼쪽 양손날 하단 옆막기 (후방자세):
     Left Low two Knife Hand Side Block
     (back stance)
18. 왼쪽 양팔뚝 중단 옆막기 (중방자세):
     Left Middle two Forearm Side Block
     (middle stance)
19. 왼쪽 양팔뚝 상단 옆막기 (전방자세):
     Left High two Forearm Side Block (front stance)
20. 오른쪽 정권 직선펀치 "기합" (선자세):
     Right Fist straight Punch (stand stance)
21. 왼쪽 안다리 후리기 (선자세):
     Left Inside Hook Throw (stand stance)
22. 왼쪽 상단 옆차기 (옆방자세):
     Left High Side Kick (side stance)

23. 왼쪽 어깨걸어 던지기 (중방자세):
    Left Shoulder Throw (middle stance)
24. 오른쪽 한발 옮겨놓기 (선자세):
    Right Step (stand stance)
25. 왼쪽 한발 옮겨놓기 (선자세):
    Left Step (stand stance)
26. 오른쪽 안다리 후리기 (선자세):
    Right Inside Hook Throw (stand stance)
27. 왼쪽 안다리 후리기 (선자세):
    Left Inside Hook Throw (stand stance)
28. 오른쪽 팔뚝 얼굴 안막기 (선자세):
    Right Forearm Face Block
29. 왼쪽 팔뚝 얼굴 안막기 (선자세):
    Left Forearm Face Block (back stance)
30. 왼쪽 뒷정권 치기 "기합" (전방자세):
    Left Back Fist (front stance)
31. 왼쪽 손창 수직찌르기 (전방자세):
    Left Sideways Spear Hand (front stance)
32. 오른쪽 안으로 반달차기 (선자세):
    Right Inside Crescent Kick (stand stance)
33. 오른쪽 뒷정권 치기 "기합" (전방자세):
    Right Back Fist (front stance)
34. 오른쪽 손창 수직찌르기 (전방자세):
    Right Sideways Spear Hand (front stance)
35. 왼쪽 안으로 반달차기 (선자세):
    Left Inside Crescent Kick (stand stance)
36. 왼쪽 뒷정권 치기 "기합" (전방자세):
    Left Back Fist "KI-Hap" (front stance)
37. 왼쪽 손창 수직찌르기 (전방자세):
    Left Sideways Spear Hand (front stance)
38. 왼쪽 마차바퀴 돌리기 (전방자세):
    Left Cartwheel (front stance)
39. 오른쪽 양손날 상단 찍어막기 (전방자세):
    Right Forward stance Chop Block (front stance)
40. 왼쪽 한발 옮겨놓기 (선자세):
    Left Step (stand stance)
41. 오른쪽 한발 들고 왼쪽 상단 앞차기 (선자세):
    Right Leg Up Left Hight Front Kick (stand stance)
42. 왼쪽 정권 직선펀치 (선자세):
    Left Fist straight Punch (stand stance)
43. 오른쪽 정권 직선펀치 "기합" (선자세):
    Right Fist straight Punch "KI-Hap" (stand stance)
44. 양손 바닥 짚고 도립 (도립자세):
    Front two Hand Spring (handspring stance)
45. 상단 X 막기 (선자세):
    High X Block (stand stance)
46. 양손창 수평찌르기 "기합" (선자세):
    Two Spear Hand "KI-Hap" (front stance)
47. 양손창 45도 수직 찌르기 "기합" (전방자세):
    Two Under Hand Spear "KI-Hap" (front stance)

1. 차력 아!--- (전신 힘발육) "기합"

얼굴은 12시 정면 방향, 똑바로 허리를세워 선자세에서 양팔을 들고 양눈 높이로 올려놓고 호흡을 들어 마시고, 양손가락을 펴서 손가락 끝에서부터 발가락 끝까지 온 몸에 기를넣어 숨을 천천히 고르게 입으로 내뿜으면서 힘을 발육시켜 천천히 앉으면서 숨을 완전히 내뱉은후에 숨을 멈추고 발육한 기를 양손에 몰아 양주먹을 양턱에까지 들어올려 양주먹을 옆으로 끝까지 벌린다음 숨을 내보내면서 몸을 이완 시킨다. (선자세)

Cha Ryuk:

In a Cha-Ryuk Stance position facing 12:00, vocalize and exhale slowly while concentrating on developing your Ki. Bend both your legs while you vocalize until you run out of breath. Hold your breath, and come back up while focusing on transferring your Ki to different parts of your body. When reaching to the top, extend both arms out sideways while still transferring your Ki. Once you reach full extension, inhale slowly through your nose and relax your body. (Ki-Hap)

2. 오른쪽 정권 어퍼컷

얼굴은 12시 정면 방향, 차력을 한 상태에서 턱을 아래로 당겨 허리를 똑바로 세운 자세에서 양다리의 간격은 어깨넓이 양주먹은 양턱을 막으며 중심은 양다리에 두고, 양무릎을 구부렸다 일어나면서 오른쪽 주먹을 안으로 돌려 어퍼컷 (선자세)

Right Fist Uppercut:

In a Stand Stance position facing 12:00, bend both your legs slightly. Push off with your right leg so you are extending up, while turning your body counter-clockwise. Execute a right side fist uppercut with your fist. Make sure left fist is guarding the face, and keep your chin down.

3. 오른쪽 정권 훅

얼굴은 12시 정면 방향, 오른쪽 정권 어퍼컷을 한 상태에서 턱을 아래로 당겨 양다리의 간격은 어깨넓이 왼쪽 주먹은 왼쪽 턱을 막은대로 중심은 양다리에 두고, 오른쪽 주먹을 되돌려 오른쪽 턱을 막고 오른발을 돌려 밀면서 몸을 9시 반시계 방향으로 틀어 오른쪽 주먹으로 훅을 치며 오른쪽 어깨로 오른쪽 턱을 방어 (선자세)

Right Fist Hook:

Push off with your right leg while turning your body counter-clockwise, and execute a right fist hook straight across with your fist. Make sure your left fist is guarding your face, and keep your chin down.

번개형: Lifhtning Form

4. 왼쪽 정권 어퍼컷

얼굴은 12시 정면 방향, 오른쪽 정권 훅을 한 상태에서 턱을 아래로 당겨 허리를 똑바로 세운 자세에서 양 다리의 간격은 어깨넓이 왼쪽 주먹은 왼쪽 턱을 막은대로 중심은 양다리에 두고, 양무릎을 구부렸다 일어나면서 왼쪽 주먹을 안으로 돌려 어퍼컷을 하면서 오른쪽 주먹은 오른쪽 턱을 방어 (선자세)

Left Fist Uppercut:

Bend both your legs slightly. Push off with your left leg so you are extending up, while turning your body clockwise. Execute a left side fist uppercut with your fist. Make sure your right fist is guarding the face, and keep your chin down.

5. 왼쪽 정권 훅

얼굴은 12시 정면 방향, 왼쪽 정권 어퍼컷을 한 상태에서 턱을 아래로 당겨 양다리의 간격은 어깨넓이 오른쪽 주먹은 오른쪽 턱을 막은대로 중심은 양다리에 두고, 왼쪽 주먹을 되돌려 왼쪽 턱을 막고, 왼발을 돌려 밀면서 몸을 3시 시계 방향으로 틀어 왼쪽 주먹으로 훅을 치며 왼쪽 어깨로 왼쪽 턱을 방어 (선자세)

Left Fist Hook:

Push off with your left leg while turning your body clockwise, and execute a left fist hook straight across with your fist. Make sure your right fist is guarding your face, and keep your chin down.

6. 왼쪽 정권 직선펀치

얼굴은 12시 정면 방향, 왼쪽 정권 훅을 한 상태에서 왼쪽 주먹을 되돌려 왼쪽 턱을 막고, 상대의 눈을 주시 하면서 턱을 아래로 당겨 양다리의 간격은 어깨넓이 양주먹은 양턱을 막으며 왼발을 돌려 밀면서 몸을 시계 방향으로 틀어 중심은 양다리에 두고, 왼쪽 주먹을 돌려 정권 직선펀치를 하면서 왼쪽 어깨로 왼쪽 턱을 방어 (선자세)

Left Fist straight Punch:

Turn your body clockwise while pushing off with your left leg. Execute a straight left punch with your fist. Make sure your right fist is guarding your face, and keep your chin down.

7. 오른쪽 정권 직선펀치 "기합"

얼굴은 12시 정면 방향, 왼쪽 정권 직선펀치를 한 상태에서 턱을 아래로 당겨 양다리의 간격은 어깨넓이 왼쪽 주먹을 되돌려 오며 오른발을 돌려 밀면서 몸을 반시계 방향으로 틀어 중심은 양다리에 두고, 기합을 넣으며 오른쪽 주먹을 돌려 정권 직선펀치를 하면서 왼쪽 주먹은 왼쪽 턱을 막으며 오른쪽 어깨로 오른쪽 턱을 방어 (선자세)

Right Fist straight Punch:

Turn your body counter-clockwise while pushing off with your right leg. Execute a straight right punch with your fist. Make sure your left fist is guarding your face, and keep your chin down. (Ki-Hap)

8. 오른쪽 양손날 하단 옆막기

얼굴은 12시 정면 방향, 오른쪽 정권 직선펀치를 한 상태에서 턱을 아래로 당겨 양다리의 간격은 어깨넓이 몸을 시계 방향으로 돌리면서 오른발을 들어 3시 방향 제자리에 돌려 놓으며 왼쪽 손바닥은 위로 팔뚝은 띠에 대면서 오른쪽 손바닥을 아래로 중심은 뒷다리에 두고, 오른쪽으로 허리를 틀어 동시에 양손날로 하단 옆막기 (후방자세)

Right Low to Knife Hand Side Block:
Turn your body clockwise so you are facing towards 3:00 in a right side Back Stance. Execute a right side Low Side Block with your right forearm. Keep your left hand at belt level with your palm face up.

9. 오른쪽 양팔뚝 중단 옆막기

얼굴은 3시 방향, 오른쪽 양손날 하단 옆막기를 한 상태에서 턱을 아래로 당겨 양다리의 간격은 어깨넓이 오른발을 들어 4시 방향으로 옮겨 놓으며 중심은 양다리에 두고, 양손은 동시에 주먹을 쥐면서 양손가락을 위로 오른손은 어깨높이에 왼손은 오른쪽 팔꿈치에 대면서 허리를 시계 방향으로 틀어 오른쪽으로 양팔뚝 중단 옆막기 (중방자세)

Right Middle two Forearm Side Block:
Step out with your right leg towards 4:00 into a right side Middle Stance, and face towards 3:00. Execute a right side Middle Side Block with your right forearm, and have your fist is at eye level. Make sure your left fist is on your inside right elbow for support, and keep your chin down.

10. 오른쪽 양팔뚝 상단 옆막기

얼굴은 3시 방향, 오른쪽 양팔뚝 중단 옆막기를 한 상태에서 상대의 눈을 주시 하면서 턱을 아래로 당겨 양다리의 간격은 어깨넓이 오른발을 들어 4시 방향으로 다시 옮겨 놓으며 몸을 앞으로 밀면서 중심은 앞 다리에 두고, 왼쪽 팔뚝은 왼쪽 얼굴을 막으며 오른쪽 팔뚝은 앞 얼굴을 스치면서 머리위에 올려 오른쪽으로 동시에 양팔뚝 상단 옆막기 (전방자세)

Right High two Forearm Side Block:

Step out with your right leg towards 4:00 into a right side Forward Stance, and face towards 3:00. Execute a right side High Side Block with your right forearm, and have your arm at a 45degree angle. Make sure your left fist is guarding your face, and keep your left elbow in.

11. 왼쪽 정권 직선펀치 "기합"

얼굴은 3시 방향, 오른쪽 양팔뚝 상단 옆막기를 한 상태에서 상대의 눈을 주시 하면서 턱을 아래로 당겨 양다리의 간격은 어깨넓이 오른쪽 주먹은 오른쪽 턱을 막으며 몸을 시계 방향으로 돌리면서 왼발을 들어 3시 방향 앞으로 한발 옮겨 놓으며 중심은 양다리에 두고, 기합을 넣으며 왼쪽 주먹을 돌려 정권 직선펀치를 하면서 왼쪽 어깨로 왼쪽 턱을 방어 (선자세)

Left Fist straight Punch "KI-Hap":

Step forward with your left leg towards 3:00 while turning your body clockwise. Execute a straight left punch, and face towards 6:00. Make sure your right fist is guarding your face, and keep your chin down. (Ki-Hap)

12. 오른쪽 안다리 후리기

얼굴은 3시 방향, 왼쪽 정권 직선펀치를 한 상태에서 턱을 아래로 당겨 양다리의 간격은 어깨넓이 양주먹은 양턱을 막으며 허리를 똑바로 세워 왼발을 12시 방향으로 돌려놓고, 중심은 왼쪽 다리에 두고, 오른발을 들어 오른쪽 안다리 후리기 (선자세)

Right Inside Hook Throw:

Position your left foot so it's facing 12:00.Then pick up your right leg, and execute a right leg inside hook throw. Make sure your guard is up, and you hook with the heel of the foot.

13. 오른쪽 상단 옆차기

얼굴은 3시 방향, 오른쪽 안다리 후리기를 하고 오른발을 들은 상태에서 턱을 아래로 당겨 양주먹은 양턱을 막은대로 중심은 왼≠ 다리에 두고, 몸을 9시 방향으로 기울려 오른발을 3시 방향으로 상단 옆차기 (옆방자세)

Right High Side Kick:

Bring your right knee in, and keep your back straight. Execute a right leg high sidekick. Make sure you kick with the knife-edge heel of the foot, and keep your guards up.

14. 오른쪽 어깨걸어 던지기

얼굴은 3시 방향, 오른쪽 상단 옆차기를 한 상태에서 오른발을 9시 방향 앞으로 한발 옮겨 놓고, 양다리의 간격은 어깨넓이 왼손은 상대의 앞 옷깃을 잡아 당기면서 오른쪽 엉덩이를 상대의 사타구니에 대고 오른쪽 팔꿉치를 상대의 오른쪽 겨드랑이 밑으로 반시계 방향으로 걸어 왼발을 들어 뒤로 반발 옮기며 얼굴은 9시 방향, 중심은 양다리에 두고, 양무릎을 굽혀 얼굴을 6시 방향으로 돌리면서 오른쪽 어깨걸어 던지기 (중방자세)

Right Shoulder Throw:

Step with your right foot towards 11:00 while grabbing your opponent's lapel with both hands. Then step back with your left leg towards 1:00, and bend your legs. Bring your right elbow in so your shoulder is caught under your opponent's lapels, and pick up your opponent with your legs. Turn your shoulders counter-clockwise, and throw your opponent over your right shoulder.

15. 왼쪽 한발 옮겨놓기

얼굴은 6시 방향, 오른쪽 어깨걸어 던지기를 한 상태에서 허리를 세워 양다리의 간격은 어깨넓이 양주먹은 양턱을 막으며 중심은 오른쪽 다리에 두고, 왼발을 들어 9시 방향 앞으로 한발 옮겨놓기 (선자세)

Left Step:

Turn your body clockwise while stepping with your left leg towards 9:00 so you are facing 12:00. Make sure your guard is up.

16. 오른쪽 한발 옮겨놓기
얼굴은 9시 방향, 왼쪽 한발 옮겨놓기를 한 상태에서 양주먹은 양턱을 막은대로 중심은 왼쪽 다리에 두고, 오른발을 들어 9시 방향 앞으로 한발 옮겨 놓기 (선자세)

Right Step:
Turn your body clockwise while stepping back with your right leg towards 9:00 so you are facing 6:00. Make sure your guard is up.

17. 왼쪽 양손날 하단 옆막기
얼굴은 9시 방향, 오른쪽 한발 옮겨놓기를 한 상태에서 턱을 아래로 당겨 양다리의 간격은 어깨넓이 몸을 반시계 방향으로 돌리면서 왼발을 들어 9시 방향 한발 옮겨 놓으며 오른쪽 손바닥은 위로 팔뚝은 띠에 대면서 왼쪽 손바닥을 아래로 중심은 뒷다리에 두고, 왼쪽으로 허리를 틀어 동시에 양손날로 하단 옆막기 (후방자세)

Left Low two Knife Hand Side Block:
Turn your body clockwise, and step with your left leg towards 9:00 in a left side Back Stance. Execute a left side Low Side Block with your left forearm. Keep your right hand at belt level with your palm face up.

18. 왼쪽 양팔뚝 중단 옆막기

얼굴은 9시 방향, 왼쪽 양손날 하단 옆막기를 한 상태에서 턱을 아래로 당겨 양다리의 간격은 어깨넓이 왼발을 들어 8시 방향으로 옮겨 놓으며 중심은 양다리에 두고, 양손은 동시에 주먹을 쥐면서 양손가락을 위로 왼손은 어깨높이에 오른손은 왼쪽 팔꿈치에 대면서 허리를 반시계 방향으로 틀어 왼쪽으로 양팔뚝 중단 옆막기 (중방자세)

Left Middle two Forearm Side Block:

Step out with your left leg towards 8:00 into a left side Middle Stance, and face towards 9:00. Execute a left side Middle Side Block with your left forearm, and have your fist is at eye level. Make sure your right fist is on your inside elbow for support, and keep your chin down.

19. 왼쪽 양팔뚝 상단 옆막기

얼굴은 9시 방향, 왼쪽 양팔뚝 중단 옆막기를 한 상태에서 상대의 눈을 주시 하면서 턱을 아래로 당겨 양다리의 간격은 어깨넓이 왼발을 들어 8시 방향으로 다시 옮겨 놓으며 몸을 앞으로 밀면서 중심은 앞다리에 두고, 오른쪽 팔뚝은 오른쪽 얼굴을 막으며 왼쪽 팔뚝은 앞 얼굴을 스치면서 머리위에 올려 왼쪽으로 동시에 양팔뚝 상단 옆막기 (전방자세)

Left High two Forearm Side Block:

Step out with your left leg towards 8:00 into a left side Forward Stance, and face towards 9:00. Execute a left side High Side Block with your left forearm, and have your arm at a 45degree angle. Make sure your right fist is guarding your face, and keep your right elbow in.

20. 오른쪽 정권 직선펀치 "기합"

얼굴은 9시 방향, 왼쪽 양팔뚝 상단 옆막기를 한 상태에서 상대의 눈을 주시 하면서 턱을 아래로 당겨 양 다리의 간격은 어깨넓이 왼쪽 주먹은 왼쪽 턱을 막으며 몸을 반시계 방향으로 돌리면서 오른발을 들어 9시 방향 앞으로 한발 옮겨 놓으며 중심은 양다리에 두고, 기합을 넣으며 오른쪽 주먹을 돌려 정권 직선펀치를 하면서 오른쪽 어깨로 오른쪽 턱을 방어 (선자세)

Right Fist straight Punch:

Step forward with your right leg towards 9:00 while turning your body clockwise. Execute a straight right punch, and face towards 6:00. Make sure your left fist is guarding your face, and keep your chin down. (Ki-Hap)

21 왼쪽 안다리 후리기

얼굴은 9시 방향, 오른쪽 정권 직선펀치를 한 상태에서 턱을 아래로 당겨 양다리의 간격은 어깨넓이 양주먹은 양턱을 막으며 허리를 똑바로 세워 오른발을 12시 방향으로 돌려 놓고, 중심은 오른쪽 다리에 두고, 왼발을 들어 왼쪽 안다리 후리기 (선자세)

Left Inside Hook Throw:

Position your right foot so it's facing 12:00. Then pick up your left leg, and execute a left leg inside hook throw. Make sure your guard is up, and you hook with the heel of the foot.

22. 왼쪽 상단 옆차기

얼굴은 9시 방향, 왼쪽 안다리 후리기를 하고 왼발을 들은 상태에서 턱을 아래로 당겨 양주먹은 양턱을 막은대로 중심은 오른쪽 다리에 두고, 몸을 3시 방향으로 기울려 왼발을 9시 방향으로 상단 옆차기 (옆방자세)

Left High Side Kick:

Bring your left knee in, and keep your back straight. Execute a left leg high sidekick. Make sure you kick with the knife-edge heel of the foot, and keep your guards up.

23. 왼쪽 어깨걸어 던지기

얼굴은 9시 방향, 왼쪽 상단 옆차기를 한 상태에서 왼발을 3시 방향 앞으로 한발 옮겨 놓고, 양다리의 간격은 어깨넓이 오른손은 상대의 앞 옷깃을 잡아 당기면서 왼쪽 엉덩이를 상대의 사타구니에 대고 왼쪽 팔꿈치를 상대의 왼쪽 겨드랑이 밑으로 시계 방향으로 걸어 오른발을 들어 뒤로 반발 옮기며 얼굴은 3시 방향, 중심은 양다리에 두고, 양무릎을 굽혀 얼굴을 6시 방향으로 돌리면서 왼쪽 어깨걸어 던지기 (중방자세)

Left Shoulder Throw:

Step with your left foot towards 1:00 while grabbing your opponent's lapel with both hands. Then step back with your right leg towards 11:00, and bend your legs. Bring your left elbow in so your shoulder is caught under your opponent's lapels, and pick up your opponent with your legs. Turn your shoulders clockwise, and throw your opponent over your left shoulder.

24. 오른쪽 한발 옮겨놓기

얼굴은 6시 방향, 왼쪽 어깨걸어 던지기를 한 상태에서 허리를 세워 양다리의 간격은 어깨넓이 양주먹은 양턱을 막으며 중심은 왼쪽 다리에 두고, 오른발을 들어 3시 방향 앞으로 한발 옮겨놓기 (선자세)

Right Step:

Turn your body counter-clockwise while stepping with your right leg towards 3:00 so you are facing 12:00. Make sure your guard is up.

25. 왼쪽 한발 옮겨놓기

얼굴은 3시 방향, 오른쪽 한발 옮겨놓기를 한 상태에서 양주먹은 양턱을 막은대로 중심은 오른쪽 다리에 두고, 왼발을 들어 3시 방향 앞으로 한발 옮겨 놓기 (선자세)

Left Step:

Turn your body counter-clockwise while stepping back with your left leg towards 3:00 so you are facing 6:00. Make sure your guard is up.

26. 오른쪽 안다리 후리기

얼굴은 6시 방향, 왼쪽 한발 옮겨놓기를 한 상태에서 턱을 아래로 당겨 양다리의 간격은 어깨넓이 양주먹은 양턱을 막으며 허리를 똑바로 세워 중심은 왼쪽 다리에 두고, 오른발을 들어 오른쪽 안다리 후리기 (선자세)

Right Inside Hook Throw:
While facing 6:00, execute a right leg inside hook throw with your heel in a circular motion, from the outside in. Make sure you keep your guard up.

27. 왼쪽 안다리 후리기

얼굴은 6시 방향, 오른쪽 안다리 후리기를 한 상태에서 턱을 아래로 당겨 오른발을 제자리에 놓고, 양다리의 간격은 어깨넓이 양주먹은 양턱을 막으며 허리를 똑바로 세워 중심은 오른쪽 다리에 두고, 왼발을 들어 왼쪽 안다리 후리기 (선자세)

Left Inside Hook Throw:
Execute a left leg inside hook throw with your heel in a circular motion, from the outside in. Make sure you keep your guard up.

28. 오른쪽 팔뚝 얼굴 안막기

얼굴은 6시 방향 왼쪽 안다리 후리기를 한 상태에서 상대의 눈을 주시 하면서 턱을 아래로 당겨 왼발을 제 자리에 놓고, 양다리의 간격은 어깨넓이 중심은 양다리에 두고, 양주먹은 양턱을 막은대로 몸을 반시계 방향으로 틀어 오른쪽 팔뚝을 안으로 돌려 얼굴막기 (선자세)

Right Forearm Face Block:

Lean towards the right while blocking with your right forearm across your face. Make sure your left fist is guarding your face, and keep your chin down.

29. 왼쪽 팔뚝 얼굴 안막기

얼굴은 6시 방향 오른쪽 팔뚝 얼굴 안막기를 한 상태에서 상대의 눈을 주시 하면서 턱을 아래로 당겨 양다리의 간격은 어깨넓이 중심은 양다리에 두고, 왼쪽 주먹은 왼쪽 턱을 막은대로 몸을 시계 방향으로 틀어 오른쪽 주먹을 되돌려 오른쪽 턱을 막으며 왼쪽 팔뚝을 안으로 돌려 얼굴막기 (선자세)

Left Forearm Face Block:

Lean towards the left while blocking with your left forearm across your face. Make sure your right fist is guarding your face, and keep your chin down.

30. 왼쪽 뒷정권 치기 "기합"

얼굴은 6시 방향, 왼쪽 팔뚝 얼굴 안막기를 한 상태에서 턱을 아래로 당겨 양다리의 간격은 어깨넓이 오른쪽 주먹은 오른쪽 턱을 막은대로 왼발을 들어 앞으로 한발 옮겨 놓으며 중심은 왼쪽 다리에 두고, 기합을 넣으며 왼쪽 뒷정권으로 인중을 치기 (전방자세)

Left Back Fist:

Step forward with your left leg towards 6:00, and execute a left-hand back fist towards 6:00. Have your right fist guarding your face, and keep your chin down. (Ki-Hap)

31. 왼쪽 손창 수직찌르기

얼굴은 6시 방향, 왼쪽 뒷정권 치기를 한 상태에서 상대의 눈을 주시 하면서 턱을 아래로 당겨 양다리의 간격은 어깨넓이 오른쪽 주먹은 오른쪽 턱을 막은대로 중심은 왼쪽 다리에 두고, 왼쪽 주먹을 되돌려 다시 왼쪽 손창으로 수직찌르기를 하면서 왼쪽 어깨로 왼쪽 턱을 방어 (전방자세)

Left Sideways Spear Hand:

Lean slightly back, and thrust your body forward while executing a left sideways knife hand towards 6:00. Have your left palm facing 9:00, and have your right fist guarding your face.

번개형: Lithtning Form

32. 오른쪽 안으로 반달차기

얼굴은 6시 방향, 왼쪽 손창 수직찌르기를 한 상태에서 턱을 아래로 당겨 양다리의 간격은 어깨넓이 오른쪽 주먹은 오른쪽 턱을 막은대로 중심은 왼쪽 다리에 두고, 오른발을 들어 왼쪽 손바닥을 안으로 반달차기 (선자세)

Right Inside Crescent Kick:

While keeping your left knife hand stationary pick up your right knee, and execute a right inside crescent kick to your knife hand. Make sure you kick with the knife-edge heel of your foot, and keep your left fist guarding face.

33. 오른쪽 뒷정권 치기 "기합"

얼굴은 6시 방향, 오른쪽 안으로 반달차기를 한 상태에서 오른발을 앞으로 한발 옮겨 놓으며 턱을 아래로 당겨 양다리의 간격은 어깨넓이 왼쪽 손바닥은 주먹을 쥐며 왼쪽 턱을 막으며 중심은 앞다리에 두고, 기합을 넣으며 오른쪽 뒷정권 치기 (전방자세)

Right Back Fist:

While facing 3:00, step forward with your right leg towards 6:00, and execute a right hand back fist towards 6:00. Have your left fist guarding your face, and keep your chin down. (Ki-Hap)

34. 오른쪽 손창 수직찌르기

얼굴은 6시 방향, 오른쪽 뒷정권 치기를 한 상태에서 상대의 눈을 주시 하면서 턱을 아래로 당겨 양다리의 간격은 어깨넓이 왼쪽 주먹은 왼쪽 턱을 막은대로 중심은 오른쪽 다리에 두고, 오른쪽 주먹을 되돌려 다시 오른쪽 손창으로 수직찌르기를 하면서 오른쪽 어깨로 오른쪽 턱을 방어 (전방자세)

Right Sideways Spear Hand:

Lean slightly back, and thrust your body forward while executing a right sideways knife hand towards 6:00. Have your right palm facing 9:00, and have your left fist guarding your face.

35. 왼쪽 안으로 반달차기

얼굴은 6시 방향, 오른쪽 손창 수직찌르기를 한 상태에서 턱을 아래로 당겨 양다리의 간격은 어깨넓이 왼쪽 주먹은 왼쪽 턱을 막은대로 중심은 오른쪽다리에 두고, 왼발을 들어 오른쪽 손바닥을 안으로 반달차기 (선자세)

Left Inside Crescent Kick:

While keeping your right knife hand stationary pick up your left knee, and execute a left inside crescent kick to your knife hand. Make sure you kick with the knife-edge heel of your foot, and keep your right fist guarding face.

번개형: Lihtning Form

36. 왼쪽 뒷정권 치기 "기합"

얼굴은 6시 방향, 왼쪽 안으로 반달차기를 한 상태에서 왼발을 앞으로 한발 옮겨 놓으며 턱을 아래로 당겨 양다리의 간격은 어깨넓이 오른쪽 손바닥은 주먹을 쥐면서 오른쪽 턱을 막으며 중심은 앞다리에 두고, 기합을 넣으며 왼쪽 뒷정권 치기 (전방자세)

Left Back Fist:

While facing 9:00, step forward with your left leg towards 6:00, and execute a left-hand back fist towards 6:00. Have your right fist guarding your face, and keep your chin down. (Ki-Hap)

37. 왼쪽 손창 수직찌르기

얼굴은 6시 방향, 왼쪽 뒷정권 치기를 한 상태에서 상대의 눈을 주시 하면서 턱을 아래로 당겨 양다리의 간격은 어깨넓이 오른쪽 주먹은 오른쪽 턱을 막은대로 중심은 왼쪽 다리에 두고, 왼쪽 주먹을 되돌려 다시 왼쪽 손창으로 수직찌르기를 하면서 왼쪽 어깨로 왼쪽 턱을 방어 (전방자세)

Left Sideways Spear Hand:

Lean slightly back, and thrust your body forward while executing a left sideways knife hand towards 6:00. Have your left palm facing 9:00, and have your right fist guarding your face.

38. 왼쪽 마차바퀴 돌리기

얼굴은 6시 방향, 왼쪽 손창 수직찌르기를 한 상태에서 양다리의 간격은 어깨넓이 몸을 왼쪽으로 기울려 중심은 왼쪽 다리에 두고, 왼쪽 손바닥은 바닥을 짚고, 몸을 6시 방향으로 돌려 양다리를 똑바로 세워 마차바퀴 돌리기 (전방자세)

Left Cartwheel:

Push off with your right leg and place your left hand flat on the floor. Execute a left side cartwheel. Try to keep your body as straight as possible.

39. 오른쪽 양손날 상단 찍어막기

얼굴은 12시 방향, 왼쪽 마차바퀴 돌리기를 한 상태에서 상대의 눈을 주시 하면서 턱을 아래로 당겨 양다리의 간격은 어깨넓이 몸을 시계 방향으로 틀어 왼쪽 손바닥은 위로 손날은 입높이 오른쪽 손바닥을 아래로 손날은 눈높이 중심은 오른쪽 다리에 두고, 오른쪽으로 양손날 상단 찍어막기 (전방자세)

Right Forward Stance Chop Block:

Turn your body clockwise so you are facing 12:00 in a right side Forward Stance. Execute a right side forward chop block with your forearm. Make sure you have your left elbow by your side, with your left palm face up.

40. 왼쪽 한발 옮겨놓기

얼굴은 12시 방향, 오른쪽 양손날 상단 찍어막기를 한 상태에서 허리를 세워 양다리의 간격은 어깨넓이 양 주먹은 양턱을 막으며 중심은 오른쪽 다리에 두고, 왼발을 들어 12시 방향 앞으로 한발 옮겨놓기 (선자세)

Left Step:

Step forward with your left leg towards 12:00. Make sure your guard is up.

41. 오른쪽 한발 들고 왼쪽 상단 앞차기

얼굴은 12시 방향 상대의 눈을 주시하면서 턱을 아래로 당겨 양다리의 간격은 어깨넓이 양무릎을 구부려 중심은 왼쪽 다리에 두고 양주먹은 양턱을 막은대로 오른쪽 한발을 들면서 몸을 위로 뛰어 왼쪽 상단 앞차기 (선자세)

Right Leg Up Left Hight Front Kick:

Pick up your right knee at about belt level. Jump with your left leg and bring your right leg back down as you bring up your left knee. Extend your left leg and execute a jumping double front kick. Make sure your guard is up.

42. 왼쪽 정권 직선펀치

얼굴은 12시 방향, 왼쪽 상단 공중 앞차기를 한 상태에서 상대의 눈을 주시 하면서 턱을 아래로 당겨 양다리의 간격은 어깨넓이 양주먹은 양턱을 막은대로 몸을 시계 방향으로 틀어 중심은 앞다리에 두고, 왼쪽 주먹을 돌려 정권 직선펀치를 하면서 왼쪽 어깨로 왼쪽 턱을 방어 (선자세)

Left Fist straight Punch:

Turn your body clockwise and execute a straight left punch with your fist. Make sure your right fist is guarding your face, and keep your chin down.

43. 오른쪽 정권 직선펀치 "기합"

얼굴은 12시 방향, 왼쪽 정권 직선펀치를 한 상태에서 턱을 아래로 당겨 양다리의 간격은 어깨넓이 왼쪽 주먹을 되돌려 왼쪽 턱을 막으며 오른발을 돌려 밀면서 몸을 반시계 방향으로 틀어 중심은 양다리에 두고, 기합을 넣으며 오른쪽 주먹을 돌려 정권 직선펀치를 하면서 왼쪽 주먹은 왼쪽 턱을 막으며오른쪽 어깨로 오른쪽 턱을 방어 (선자세)

Right Fist straight Punch "KI-Hap":

Turn your body counter-clockwise and execute a straight right punch with your fist. Make sure your left fist is guarding your face, and keep your chin down. (Ki-Hap)

44. 양손 바닥짚고 도립

얼굴은 12시 방향, 오른쪽 정권 직선펀치를 한 상태에서 몸을 엎드려 양손바닥은 어깨넓이로 양손가락은 앞으로 하여 바닥을 짚고 양무릎을 접어 튕겨서 도립 (도립자세)

Front two Hand Spring:

Place both hands on the floor about should width apart. Have your arms slightly bent, and kick your legs over your head while pushing off with your arms so you are executing a front handspring. Make sure you land with your feet square.

45. 상단 X 막기

얼굴은 12시 방향, 양손 바닥짚고 도립한 상태에서 양다리의 간격은 어깨넓이 허리를 똑바로 세워 일어나면서 중심은 양다리에 두고, 양팔뚝으로 상단 X 막기 (선자세)

High X Block:

Slightly bend both your leg and execute a high-x-block, blocking over your head. Make sure you're your fists are crossed, and your knuckles are next to each other.

46. 양손창 수평찌르기 "기합"

얼굴은 12시 방향, 상단 X 막기를 한 상태에서 턱을 아래로 당겨 양다리의 간격은 어깨넓이 중심은 왼쪽 다리에 두고, 왼발을 들어 12시 방향 앞으로 한발 옮겨 놓으며 양손바닥을 아래로 돌려 기합을 넣으며 양손창 수평 찌르기 (전방자세)

Two Spear Hand "KI-Hap":

Step forward towards 12:00 with your right leg into a forward stance. Execute a double knife hand to your opponent's throat. Make sure your chin is down, and your both your knife hands are facing down. (Ki-Hap)

47. 양손창 45도 수직찌르기 "기합"

얼굴은 12시 방향, 양손창 수평찌르기를 한 상태에서 턱을 아래로 당겨 양다리의 간격은 어깨넓이 중심은 왼쪽 앞다리에 두고, 단전의 기를 몰아 양손가락 끝에 힘을 넣어 기합과 동시에 양손창으로 45도 수직 찌르기 (전방자세)

Two Under Hand Spear "KI-Hap":

Bring both your arms back, and thrust both knife hands under your opponent's ribs executing an under hand double knife hand. Make sure your elbows are out, and your knife hands are pointed in with both your knife hands are facing up. (Ki-Hap)

Tumbling Techniques
공│중│제│비│술

1. 양손 짚고 앞으로 구르기: Forward Rolling Somersault
2. 양손 짚고 마차바퀴 (왼쪽, 오른쪽): Two Hand Cartwheel (Left, Right)
3. 양손 짚고 전방 도립: Front Hand Spring
4. 양손 짚고 전방 회전도립: Front Flip

1. 양손 짚고 앞으로 구르기

몸을 앞으로 숙이면서 양손은 바닥을 짚고 양 팔굽을 굽혔다가 세우면서 양발을 뛰어 머리 뒤로 넘겨 양발이 바닥에 닿는 순간 몸을 위로 세우기

Forward Somersault:

Begin in a Front Stance. Take a step forward with your left leg. Then take a step forward with your right leg next to your left leg. Bend your knees and crouch forward. Place the palm of your hands on the floor at a distance wider than shoulder span. Do not place your hands too far out in front of you. Extend your knees and lift your hips into the air while tucking your chin into your chest. Bend your arms, curve your back forward, and roll forward by kicking your body over with your legs. Roll smoothly onto your back and do not touch your head on the ground during your roll. During your roll, keep your body tucked tightly into a ball and keep your knees bent. After rolling on your back, tuck your heels under your hips and stand back up onto your feet. You should finish standing into a Front Stance.

2. 양손 짚고 마차바퀴 (왼쪽, 오른쪽)

왼발을 한발 앞으로 옮겨 몸을 옆으로 숙이면서 왼손은 바닥을 짚고 오른손은 한발 간격을 띄어 바닥을 짚으면서 양다리를 수직으로 돌리면서 양발이 각각 바닥에 닿는 순간 몸을 위로 세우기

Two Hand Cartwheel:

(Left)

Begin by standing sideways with your left leg forward and your right leg back. Extend your arms out to your sides. Lean sideways towards your left side while shifting your weight into your left leg. Slightly bend your left knee and place the palm of your left hand on the floor next to your left foot. Simultaneously kick off the ground with your right leg and build sideways momentum. Bring your legs up from the side. Keep your back and hips straight while you are in a handstand position. Spread your legs apart and keep them semi straight. During the cartwheel, keep your body straight and your hands and feet should be set on the ground aligned from each other. Once your body has turned over and your legs are dropping, land your right foot on the ground next to your right hand. Then land your left foot next to your right leg. Finish into a left Fight Stance.

(Right)
Begin by standing sideways with your right leg forward and your left leg back. Extend your arms out to your sides. Lean sideways towards your right side while shifting your weight into your right leg. Slightly bend your right knee and place the palm of your right hand on the floor next to your right foot. Simultaneously kick off the ground with your left leg and build sideways momentum. Bring your legs up from the side. Keep your back and hips straight while you are in a handstand position. Spread your legs apart and keep them semi straight. During the cartwheel, keep your body straight and your hands and feet should be set on the ground aligned from each other. Once your body has turned over and your legs are dropping, land your left foot on the ground next to your left hand. Then land your right foot next to your left leg. Finish into a right Fight Stance.

3. 양손 짚고 전방 도립

몸을 앞으로 숙이면서 양손은 바닥을 짚고 양 팔굽을 굽혔다가 세우면서 양발을 뛰어 머리 뒤로 넘겨 양발이 바닥에 닿는 순간 몸을 위로 세우기

Front Hand Spring:

Begin in a Front Stance. Take a step forward with your left leg and lean forward. Bend your left knee and place the palm of your hands at shoulder span on the ground in front of you. Keep your arms semi straight and post them on the ground. Kick your right leg back over your head. Immediately after, kick your left leg over your head and follow your right leg. At the same time your body flips over from the momentum of your kick, arch your back backwards, extend your arms, and bend your legs. Bring your feet underneath you and keep them apart at a distance slightly wider than shoulder span. Land onto your feet in a Front Stance while maintaining balance.

공중제비술: Tumbling Techniques

4. 양손 짚고 전방 회전도립

몸을 앞으로 숙이면서 손을 안 짚고 양발을 뛰어 머리 뒤로 넘겨 양발이 바닥에 닿는 순간 몸을 위로 세우기

Front Flip:

Get a running start. Build some momentum forward. Lift your arms into the air. Then push off the ground with your legs and leap into the air while simultaneously swing your arms down and flipping your body forward. In mid air, bring tuck your legs and body into itself while flipping forward. You should have created enough inertia for your entire body to flip completely over. Once you have done one full rotation, extend your legs and body. Land onto your feet and absorb the landing impact with your legs. Try to land into a Front stance and balanced.

공중제비술: Tumbling Techniques

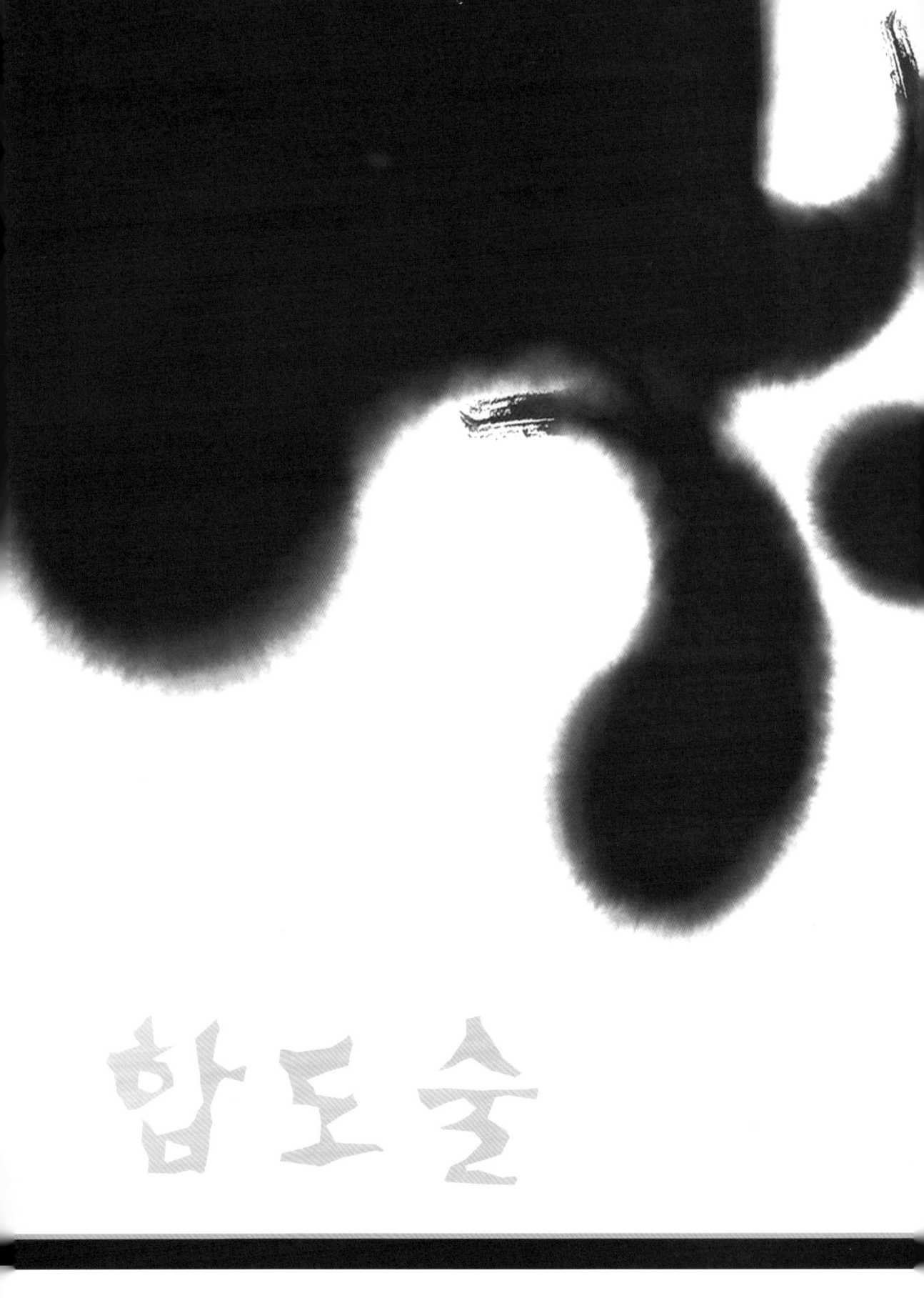

Nakbub Techniques
낙 | 법 | 술

01. 한손 측방낙법 (왼쪽, 오른쪽):
    One hand touch side nakbub (L. R.)

02. 공중 한손 측방낙법 (왼쪽, 오른쪽):
    Flying one hand touch side nakbub (L. R.)

03. 양손대고 전방낙법:
    Hands touch front nakbub

04. 한손대고 전방낙법:
    One hand touch front nakbub

05. 긴 전방낙법:
    Front long nakbub

06. 높이 전방낙법:
    Front high nakbub

07. 공중 전방낙법:
    Front no hand touch nakbub

08. 후방낙법 공중제비:
    Back nakbub hand spring

09. 후방낙법 무릎 밀기:
    Back nakbub Knee push

10. 공중 후방낙법 손안대고 공중제비:
    No hand spring Flying back nakbub

1. 한손 측방낙법 (왼쪽, 오른쪽)

(왼쪽)
옆으로 누워 머리를 들고 턱을 앞으로 숙이고, 왼팔은 45도 벌려 손바닥은 바닥에 대고, 왼다리는 45도 무릎은 90도로 접어 바닥에 대고, 오른발은 왼발을 넘겨 45도 바닥에 대고, 오른팔은 오른쪽 겨드랑이에 붙여 손바닥은 허벅지에 대고, 몸을 반대로 돌리면서 어깨 엉덩이 손바닥이 공중에서 아래로 동시에 떨어지면서 오른쪽 손바닥은 바닥을 친다.

Side Nakbub:

(Left) Begin by lying on the floor so that you are on your right side and hip. Extend your right arm out to side towards the right so that your arm forms a 45degree angle with your body. Rotate your right hand so that your right palm is face down. Keep your right leg straight and cross your left leg over your right leg while slightly bending your left knee and keeping it up. Place the sole of your left foot on the ground by your right knee. Guard your face with your left hand and elevate your head above the floor while keeping the rest of your body relaxed.

Lift your legs and hips off the floor while flipping your body over towards the left. Twist your hips and cross your right leg over your left while straightening your left leg. Slightly bend your right knee. As you flip your body to your left side, bring your right hand in to guard your face and extend your left arm out towards the left side. As soon as you flip your body completely over to your left side, drop your legs to the ground and simultaneously land on the sole of your right foot and left hip. Do not let the inner part of your right ankle and knee touch the floor. Time your flip so that, on the exact moment your left hip comes into contact with the floor, you simultaneously slap the ground with the palm of your left hand next to your left hip and exhale quickly while tensing the body at the moment of exhale. When slapping the ground with the palm of your left hand, extend your left arm out and bring it down so that your arm is at a 45degree with your body when it hits the ground. You must slap the ground at the same time your left hip impacts the floor. When exhaling, exhale only about 50% of your air while simultaneously tensing your abdominals and neck. This is to brace your body for impact and it must be done at the instantaneous moment of impact. Do not hit the ground with your elbow and keep your head elevated at all times.

(오른쪽)
옆으로 누워 머리를 들고 턱을 앞으로 숙이고, 오른팔은 45도 벌려 손바닥은 바닥에 대고, 오른다리는 45도 무릎은 90도로 접어 바닥에 대고, 왼발은 오른발을 넘겨 45도 바닥에 대고, 왼팔은 왼쪽 겨드랑이에 붙여 손바닥은 허벅지에 대고, 몸을 반대로 돌리면서 어깨, 엉덩이, 손바닥이 공중에서 아래로 동시에, 떨어지면서 왼쪽 손바닥은 바닥을 친다.

(Right) Begin by lying on the floor so that you are on your left side and hip. Extend your left arm out to side towards the left so that your arm forms a 45degree angle with your body. Rotate your left hand so that your left palm is face down. Keep your left leg straight and cross your right leg over your left leg while slightly bending your right knee and keeping it up. Place the sole of your right foot on the ground by your left knee. Guard your face with your right hand and elevate your head above the floor while keeping the rest of your body relaxed.

Lift your legs and hips off the floor while flipping your body over towards the right. Twist your hips and cross your left leg over your right while straightening your right leg. Slightly bend your left knee. As you flip your body to your right side, bring your left hand in to guard your face and extend your right arm out towards the right side. As soon as you flip your body completely over to your right side, drop your legs to the ground and simultaneously land on the sole of your left foot and right hip. Do not let the inner part of your left ankle and knee touch the floor. Time your flip so that, on the exact moment your right hip comes into contact with the floor, you simultaneously slap the ground with the palm of your right hand next to your right hip and exhale quickly while tensing the body at the moment of exhale. When slapping the ground with the palm of your right hand, extend your right arm out and bring it down so that your arm is at a 45degree with your body when it hits the ground. You must slap the ground at the same time your right hip impacts the floor. When exhaling, exhale only about 50% of your air while simultaneously tensing your abdominals and neck. This is to brace your body for impact and it must be done at the instantaneous moment of impact. Do not hit the ground with your elbow and keep your head elevated at all times.

낙법술: Nakbub Techniques

2. 공중 한손 측방낙법 (왼쪽, 오른쪽)

(왼쪽)
옆으로 누워 머리를 들고 턱을 앞으로 숙이고, 왼팔은 45도 벌려 손바닥은 바닥에 대고, 왼다리는 45도 무릎은 90도로 접어 바닥에 대고, 오른발은 왼발을 넘겨 45도 바닥에 대고, 오른팔은 오른쪽 겨드랑이에 붙여 손바닥은 허벅지에 대고, 몸을 튕겨 반대로 돌리면서 어깨, 엉덩이, 손바닥이 공중에서 아래로 동시에 떨어지면서 오른쪽 손바닥은 바닥을 친다.

Flying Side Nakbub:

(Left)Begin by lying on the floor so that you are on your right side and hip. Extend your right arm out to side towards the right so that your arm forms a 45degree angle with your body. Rotate your right hand so that your right palm is face down. Keep your right leg straight and cross your left leg over your right leg while slightly bending your left knee and keeping it up. Place the sole of your left foot on the ground by your right knee. Guard your face with your left hand and elevate your head above the floor while keeping the rest of your body relaxed.

Lift your legs and hips off the ground. Bend your legs and bring your knees into your body. Kick your legs up and out and try to pop your shoulders from off the ground. Once your shoulders are off the ground, twist your hips and flip your body onto your left side. Cross your right leg over your left during the twist and keep your left leg semi straight. As soon as you flip your body completely over to your left side, drop your legs to the ground and simultaneously land on the sole of your right foot and left hip. Try to land flat onto your left side. Do not let the inner part of your right ankle and knee touch the floor. Time your flip so that, on the exact moment your left hip lands on the ground, you simultaneously slap the ground with the palm of your left hand next to your left hip and exhale quickly while tensing the body at the moment of exhale. When slapping the ground with the palm of your left hand, extend your left arm out and bring it down so that your arm is at a 45degree with your body when it hits the ground. You must slap the ground at the same time your left hip impacts the floor. When exhaling, exhale only about 50% of your air while simultaneously tensing your abdominals and neck. This is to brace your body for impact and it must be done at the instantaneous moment of impact. Do not hit the ground with your elbow and keep your head elevated at all times.

(오른쪽)
옆으로 누워 머리를 들고 턱을 앞으로 숙이고, 오른팔은 45도 벌려 손바닥은 바닥에 대고, 오른다리는 45도 무릎은 90도로 접어 바닥에 대고, 왼발은 오른발을 넘겨 45도 바닥에 대고, 왼팔은 왼쪽 겨드랑이에 붙여 손바닥은 허벅지에 대고, 몸을 튕겨 반대로 돌리면서 어깨, 엉덩이, 손바닥이 공중에서 아래로 동시에 떨어지면서 왼쪽 손바닥은 바닥을 친다.

(Right)Begin by lying on the floor so that you are on your left side and hip. Extend your left arm out to side towards the left so that your arm forms a 45degree angle with your body. Rotate your left hand so that your left palm is face down. Keep your left leg straight and cross your right leg over your left leg while slightly bending your right knee and keeping it up. Place the sole of your right foot on the ground by your left knee. Guard your face with your right hand and elevate your head above the floor while keeping the rest of your body relaxed.

Lift your legs and hips off the ground. Bend your legs and bring your knees into your body. Kick your legs up and out and try to pop your shoulders from off the ground. Once your shoulders are off the ground, twist your hips and flip your body onto your right side. Cross your left leg over your right during the twist and keep your right leg semi straight. As soon as you flip your body completely over to your right side, drop your legs to the ground and simultaneously land on the sole of your left foot and right hip. Try to land flat onto your right side. Do not let the inner part of your right ankle and knee touch the floor. Time your flip so that, on the exact moment your left hip lands on the ground, you simultaneously slap the ground with the palm of your right hand next to your right hip and exhale quickly while tensing the body at the moment of exhale. When slapping the ground with the palm of your right hand, extend your right arm out and bring it down so that your arm is at a 45degree with your body when it hits the ground. You must slap the ground at the same time your right hip impacts the floor. When exhaling, exhale only about 50% of your air while simultaneously tensing your abdominals and neck. This is to brace your body for impact and it must be done at the instantaneous moment of impact. Do not hit the ground with your elbow and keep your head elevated at all times.

낙법술: Nakbub Techniques

3. 양손대고 전방낙법 (왼쪽, 오른쪽)

(왼쪽)
선 자세에서 양발을 어깨넓이로 벌려 왼발을 중앙 한발 앞에 놓고, 왼쪽 손가락을 오른쪽으로 돌려 왼쪽 엄지발가락 위 바닥에 대고, 오른쪽 손바닥 검지는 왼손 검지에 대고, 목을 오른쪽으로 돌려 턱을 숙이고, 왼쪽 어깨가 바닥에 닿지 않게 굴러 오른쪽 무릎을 90도로 접어 바닥에 대고, 오른쪽 손바닥은 바닥을 치면서 왼쪽 발바닥은 오른쪽 발목위 바닥에 대고, 일어나면서 왼쪽 주먹을 앞으로 올려 얼굴을 방어 하면서 오른쪽 주먹은 오른쪽 턱을 방어한다.

Two Handed Forward Rolling Nakbub:

(Left) Begin by standing with your left leg forward and your right leg back.

Place your hands out in front of you with your palms facing out and extend your arms until your elbows are semi straight. Tilt your left hand sideways towards the right so that your hand is horizontal and keep your right hand vertical. Position your hands so that the tips of your left index and middle finger are touching the tips of your right index and middle finger. Your hands should now form 90 degree angle. Then slightly separate your hands apart from each other. Relax your shoulders and tilt your head towards the right while bringing your right ear to your right shoulder. Lean forward and dive into the ground at an angle. As you are falling forward, place the palms of your hands on the floor and catch yourself with your arms. When your left shoulder gets close to the ground, tuck your left shoulder and elbow into your body. When tucking, curve your back forward and compact your entire upper body into a ball. When rolling, exhale quickly and tighten your body while rolling over your left shoulder without letting it come into contact with the ground. Smoothly roll onto your left shoulder blade and down your back. As you roll, bend your legs and tuck your right foot behind your left knee. Your goal should be to roll over your left shoulder and through your right hip. Do not turn or twist your body during the roll. Slap the ground next to your right hip with the palm of your right hand as your feet come into contact with the ground. Simultaneously land onto the sole of your left foot and keep your right foot tucked tightly until your upper body is leaning forward. Let the momentum carry your body up as you lean into your left leg and stand up. Place your right foot on the ground as you stand into a left Fight Stance.

(오른쪽)
선 자세에서 양발을 어깨넓이로 벌려 오른발을 중앙 한발 앞에 놓고, 오른쪽 손가락을 왼쪽으로 돌려 오른쪽 엄지발가락 위 바닥에 대고, 왼쪽 손바닥 검지는 오른손 검지에 대고, 목을 왼쪽으로 돌려 턱을 숙이고, 오른쪽 어깨가 바닥에 닿지 않게 굴러 왼쪽 무릎을 90도로 접어 바닥에 대고, 왼쪽 손바닥은 바닥을 치면서 오른쪽 발바닥은 왼쪽 발목위 바닥에 대고, 일어나면서 오른쪽 주먹을 앞으로 올려 얼굴을 방어 하면서 왼쪽 주먹은 왼쪽 턱을 방어한다.

(Right) Begin by standing with your right leg forward and your left leg back.
Place your hands out in front of you with your palms facing out and extend your arms until your elbows are semi straight. Tilt your right hand sideways towards the left so that your hand is horizontal and keep your left hand vertical. Position your hands so that the tips of your right index and middle finger are touching the tips of your left index and middle finger. Your hands should now form 90 degree angle. Then slightly separate your hands apart from each other. Relax your shoulders and tilt your head towards the left while bringing your left ear to your left shoulder. Lean forward and dive into the ground at an angle. As you are falling forward, place the palms of your hands on the floor and catch yourself with your arms. When your right shoulder gets close to the ground, tuck your right shoulder and elbow into your body. When tucking, curve your back forward and compact your entire upper body into a ball. When rolling, exhale quickly and tighten your body while rolling over your right shoulder without letting it come into contact with the ground. Smoothly roll onto your right shoulder blade and down your back. As you roll, bend your legs and tuck your left foot behind your right knee. Your goal should be to roll over your right shoulder and through your left hip. Do not turn or twist your body during the roll. Slap the ground next to your left hip with the palm of your left hand as your feet come into contact with the ground. Simultaneously land onto the sole of your right foot and keep your left foot tucked tightly until your upper body is leaning forward. Let the momentum carry your body up as you lean into your right leg and stand up. Place your left foot on the ground as you stand into a right Fight Stance.

낙법술: Nakbub Techniques

4. 한손대고 전방낙법 (왼쪽, 오른쪽)

(왼쪽)
선 자세에서 양발을 어깨넓이로 벌려 왼발을 중앙 한발 앞에 놓고, 오른쪽 손가락을 앞으로 왼쪽 엄지발가락과 한뼘 간격으로 일직선 되게 손목을 세워 바닥에 짚고, 왼손을 왼발과 오른손 가운데로 뻣쳐 밀어 넣으면서, 왼쪽 어깨가 바닥에 닿지 않게 굴러 오른쪽 무릎을 90도로 접어 바닥에 대고, 오른쪽 손바닥은 바닥을 치면서 왼쪽 발바닥은 오른쪽 발목위 바닥에 대고, 일어나면서 왼쪽 주먹을 앞으로 올려 얼굴을 방어 하면서 오른쪽 주먹은 오른쪽 턱을 방어한다.

One Handed Forward Rolling Nakbub:

(Left) Begin by standing with your left leg forward and your right leg back.
Place your left hand out in front of you with your palm facing out and extend your left arm until your elbow is semi straight. Tilt your left hand sideways towards the right so that your hand is horizontal. Relax your shoulders and tilt your head towards the right while bringing your right ear to your right shoulder. Lean forward and dive into the ground at an angle. As you are falling forward, place the palm of your left hand on the floor and catch yourself with your left arm. When your left shoulder gets close to the ground, tuck your left shoulder and elbow into your body. When tucking, curve your back forward and compact your entire upper body into a ball. When rolling, exhale quickly and tighten your body while rolling over your left shoulder without letting it come into contact with the ground. Smoothly roll onto your left shoulder blade and down your back. As you roll, bend your legs and tuck your right foot behind your left knee. Your goal should be to roll over your left shoulder and through your right hip. Do not turn or twist your body during the roll. Slap the ground next to your right hip with the palm of your right hand as your feet come into contact with the ground. Simultaneously land onto the sole of your left foot and keep your right foot tucked tightly until your upper body is leaning forward. Let the momentum carry your body up as you lean into your left leg and stand up. Place your right foot on the ground as you stand into a left Fight Stance.

(오른쪽)
선 자세에서 양발을 어깨넓이로 벌려 오른발을 중앙 한발 앞에 놓고, 왼쪽 손가락을 앞으로 오른쪽 엄지발가락 과 한뼘 간격으로 일직선 되게 손목을 세워 바닥에 짚고, 오른손을 오른발과 왼손 가운데로 뻣쳐 밀어 넣으면서, 오른쪽 어깨가 바닥에 닿지 않게 굴러 왼쪽 무릎을 90도로 접어 바닥에 대고, 왼쪽 손바닥은 바닥을 치면서 오른쪽 발바닥은 왼쪽 발목 위 바닥에 대고, 일어나면서 오른쪽 주먹을 앞으로 올려 얼굴을 방어 하면서 왼쪽 주먹은 왼쪽 턱을 방어한다.

(Right) Begin by standing with your right leg forward and your left leg back.
Place your right hand out in front of you with your palm facing out and extend your right arm until your elbow is semi straight. Tilt your right hand sideways towards the left so that your hand is horizontal. Relax your shoulders and tilt your head towards the left while bringing your left ear to your left shoulder. Lean forward and dive into the ground at an angle. As you are falling forward, place the palm of your right hand on the floor and catch yourself with your right arm. When your right shoulder gets close to the ground, tuck your right shoulder and elbow into your body. When tucking, curve your back forward and compact your entire upper body into a ball. When rolling, exhale quickly and tighten your body while rolling over your right shoulder without letting it come into contact with the ground. Smoothly roll onto your right shoulder blade and down your back. As you roll, bend your legs and tuck your left foot behind your right knee. Your goal should be to roll over your right shoulder and through your left hip. Do not turn or twist your body during the roll. Slap the ground next to your left hip with the palm of your left hand as your feet come into contact with the ground. Simultaneously land onto the sole of your right foot and keep your left foot tucked tightly until your upper body is leaning forward. Let the momentum carry your body up as you lean into your right leg and stand up. Place your left foot on the ground as you stand into a right Fight Stance.

낙법술: Nakbub Techniques

5. 긴 전방낙법 (왼쪽, 오른쪽)

(왼쪽)

선 자세에서 양발을 어깨넓이로 벌려 왼발을 중앙 한발 앞에 놓고, 양손을 앞으로 하고 앞으로 멀리 뛰면서 목을 오른쪽으로 돌리고, 왼쪽 손바닥의 손가락 끝은 오른쪽으로 오른쪽 손바닥의 손가락 끝을 앞으로, 양 손가락의 검지를 서로 붙이게 하면서 바닥을 동시에 짚고, 왼쪽 어깨가 바닥에 닿지 않게 굴러 오른쪽 무릎을 90도로 접어 바닥에 대고, 오른쪽 손바닥은 바닥을 치면서 왼쪽 발바닥은 오른쪽 발목 위 바닥에 대고, 일어나면서 왼쪽 주먹을 앞으로 올려 얼굴을 방어 하면서 오른쪽 주먹은 오른쪽 턱을 방어한다.

Two Handed Forward Rolling Long Nakbub:

(Left) Begin in a Front Stance.

Take a step with your left leg and direct your momentum forward. Place your hands out in front of you with your palms facing out and extend your arms until your elbows are semi straight. Tilt your left hand sideways towards the right so that your hand is horizontal and keep your right hand vertical. Position your hands so that the tips of your left index and middle finger are touching the tips of your right index and middle finger. Your hands should now form 90 degree angle. Then slightly separate your hands apart from each other. Relax your shoulders and tilt your head towards the right while bringing your right ear to your right shoulder. Leap up and forward into the air as far as you can and dive into the ground at an angle on the decline. As you are falling forward, place the palms of your hands on the floor and catch yourself with your arms. When your left shoulder gets close to the ground, tuck your left shoulder and elbow into your body. Timing is very important. Tuck and roll with the same speed as your fall. When tucking, curve your back forward and compact your entire upper body into a ball. When rolling, exhale quickly and tighten your body while rolling over your left shoulder without letting it come into contact with the ground. Smoothly roll onto your left shoulder blade and down your back. As you roll, bend your legs and tuck your right foot behind your left knee. Your goal should be to roll over your left shoulder and through your right hip. Do not turn or twist your body during the roll. Slap the ground next to your right hip with the palm of your right hand as your feet come into contact with the ground. Simultaneously land onto the sole of your left foot and keep your right foot tucked tightly until your upper body is leaning forward. Let the momentum carry your body up as you lean into your left leg and stand up. Place your right foot on the ground as you stand into a left Fight Stance.

(오른쪽)
선 자세에서 양발을 어깨넓이로 벌려 오른발을 중앙 한발 앞에 놓고, 양손을 앞으로 하고 앞으로 멀리 뛰면서 목을 왼쪽으로 돌리고, 오른쪽 손바닥의 손가락 끝은 왼쪽으로 왼쪽 손바닥의 손가락 끝은 앞으로, 양손가락의 검지를 서로 붙이게 하면서 바닥을 동시에 짚고, 오른쪽 어깨가 바닥에 닿지 않게 굴러 왼쪽 무릎을 90도로 접어 바닥에 대고, 왼쪽 손바닥은 바닥을 치면서 오른쪽 발바닥은 왼쪽 발목 위 바닥에 대고, 일어나면서 오른쪽 주먹을 앞으로 올려 얼굴을 방어 하면서 왼쪽 주먹은 오른쪽 턱을 방어한다.

(Right) Begin in a Front Stance.
Take a step with your right leg and direct your momentum forward. Place your hands out in front of you with your palms facing out and extend your arms until your elbows are semi straight. Tilt your right hand sideways towards the left so that your hand is horizontal and keep your left hand vertical. Position your hands so that the tips of your right index and middle finger are touching the tips of your left index and middle finger. Your hands should now form 90 degree angle. Then slightly separate your hands apart from each other. Relax your shoulders and tilt your head towards the left while bringing your left ear to your left shoulder. Leap up and forward into the air as far as you can and dive into the ground at an angle on the decline. As you are falling forward, place the palms of your hands on the floor and catch yourself with your arms. When your right shoulder gets close to the ground, tuck your right shoulder and elbow into your body. Timing is very important. Tuck and roll with the same speed of your fall. When tucking, curve your back forward and compact your entire upper body into a ball. When rolling, exhale quickly and tighten your body while rolling over your right shoulder without letting it come into contact with the ground. Smoothly roll onto your right shoulder blade and down your back. As you roll, bend your legs and tuck your left foot behind your right knee. Your goal should be to roll over your right shoulder and through your left hip. Do not turn or twist your body during the roll. Slap the ground next to your left hip with the palm of your left hand as your feet come into contact with the ground. Simultaneously land onto the sole of your right foot and keep your left foot tucked tightly until your upper body is leaning forward. Let the momentum carry your body up as you lean into your right leg and stand up. Place your left foot on the ground as you stand into a right Fight Stance.

낙법술: Nakbub Techniques

6. 높이 전방낙법 (왼쪽, 오른쪽)

(왼쪽)
선 자세에서 양발을 어깨넓이로 벌려 왼발을 중앙 한발 앞에 놓고, 양손을 앞으로 하고 앞으로 높이 뛰면서 목을 오른쪽으로 돌리고, 왼쪽 손바닥의 손가락 끝은 오른쪽으로 오른쪽 손바닥의 손가락 끝은 앞으로, 양 손가락의 검지를 서로 붙이게 하면서 바닥을 동시에 짚고, 왼쪽 어깨가 바닥에 닿지 않게 굴러 오른쪽 무릎을 90도로 접어 바닥에 대고, 오른쪽 손바닥은 바닥을 치면서 왼쪽 발바닥은 오른쪽 발목 위 바닥에 대고, 일어나면서 왼쪽 주먹을 앞으로 올려 얼굴을 방어 하면서 오른쪽 주먹은 오른쪽 턱을 방어한다.

Two Handed Forward Rolling High Nakbub:

(Left) Begin in a Front Stance.
Take a step with your left leg and direct your momentum forward. Place your hands out in front of you with your palms facing out and extend your arms until your elbows are semi straight. Tilt your left hand sideways towards the right so that your hand is horizontal and keep your right hand vertical. Position your hands so that the tips of your left index and middle finger are touching the tips of your right index and middle finger. Your hands should now form 90 degree angle. Then slightly separate your hands apart from each other. Relax your shoulders and tilt your head towards the right while bringing your right ear to your right shoulder. Leap up into the air as high as you can and dive into the ground at an angle on the decline. As you are falling forward, place the palms of your hands on the floor and catch yourself with your arms. When your left shoulder gets close to the ground, tuck your left shoulder and elbow into your body. Timing is very important. Tuck and roll with the same speed as your fall. When tucking, curve your back forward and compact your entire upper body into a ball. When rolling, exhale quickly and tighten your body while rolling over your left shoulder without letting it come into contact with the ground. Smoothly roll onto your left shoulder blade and down your back. As you roll, bend your legs and tuck your right foot behind your left knee. Your goal should be to roll over your left shoulder and through your right hip. Do not turn or twist your body during the roll. Slap the ground next to your right hip with the palm of your right hand as your feet come into contact with the ground. Simultaneously land onto the sole of your left foot and keep your right foot tucked tightly until your upper body is leaning forward. Let the momentum carry your body up as you lean into your left leg and stand up. Place your right foot on the ground as you stand into a left Fight Stance.

합도술

(오른쪽)
선 자세에서 양발을 어깨넓이로 벌려 오른발을 중앙 한발 앞에 놓고, 양손을 앞으로 하고 앞으로 높이 뛰면서 목을 왼쪽으로 돌리고, 오른쪽 손바닥의 손가락 끝은 왼쪽으로 왼쪽 손바닥의 손가락 끝을 앞으로, 양손가락의 검지를 서로 붙이게 하면서 바닥을 동시에 짚고, 오른쪽 어깨가 바닥에 닿지 않게 굴러 왼쪽 무릎을 90도로 접어 바닥에 대고, 왼쪽 손바닥은 바닥을 치면서 오른쪽 발바닥은 왼쪽 발목위 바닥에 대고, 일어나면서 오른쪽 주먹을 앞으로 올려 얼굴을 방어 하면서 왼쪽 주먹은 오른쪽 턱을 방어한다.

(Right) Begin in a Front Stance.
Take a step with your right leg and direct your momentum forward. Place your hands out in front of you with your palms facing out and extend your arms until your elbows are semi straight. Tilt your right hand sideways towards the left so that your hand is horizontal and keep your left hand vertical. Position your hands so that the tips of your right index and middle finger are touching the tips of your left index and middle finger. Your hands should now form 90 degree angle. Then slightly separate your hands apart from each other. Relax your shoulders and tilt your head towards the left while bringing your left ear to your left shoulder. Leap up into the air as high as you can and dive into the ground at an angle on the decline. As you are falling forward, place the palms of your hands on the floor and catch yourself with your arms. When your right shoulder gets close to the ground, tuck your right shoulder and elbow into your body. Timing is very important. Tuck and roll with the same speed of your fall. When tucking, curve your back forward and compact your entire upper body into a ball. When rolling, exhale quickly and tighten your body while rolling over your right shoulder without letting it come into contact with the ground. Smoothly roll onto your right shoulder blade and down your back. As you roll, bend your legs and tuck your left foot behind your right knee. Your goal should be to roll over your right shoulder and through your left hip. Do not turn or twist your body during the roll. Slap the ground next to your left hip with the palm of your left hand as your feet come into contact with the ground. Simultaneously land onto the sole of your right foot and keep your left foot tucked tightly until your upper body is leaning forward. Let the momentum carry your body up as you lean into your right leg and stand up. Place your left foot on the ground as you stand into a right Fight Stance.

낙법술: Nakbub Techniques

7. 공중 전방낙법 (왼쪽, 오른쪽)

(왼쪽)
선 자세에서 양발을 어깨넓이로 벌려 왼발을 중앙 한발 앞에 놓고, 왼쪽 손바닥으로 허공을 아래로 내려치며, 왼쪽 어깨가 바닥에 닿지 않게 굴러 오른쪽 무릎을 90도로 접어 바닥에 대고, 오른쪽 손바닥은 바닥을 치면서 왼쪽 발바닥은 오른쪽 발목위 바닥에 대고, 일어나면서 왼쪽 주먹을 앞으로 올려 얼굴을 방어 하면서 오른쪽 주먹은 오른쪽 턱을 방어한다.

Forward Rolling Nakbub with No Hands:

(Left) Begin by standing with your left leg forward and your right leg back.
Relax your shoulders and tilt your head towards the right while bringing your right ear to your right shoulder. Lean forward and fall into the ground at an angle. As you are falling forward, tuck your left shoulder in towards your right hip. When your left shoulder gets close to the ground, tuck your left shoulder and elbow into your body tightly. When tucking, curve your back forward and compact your entire upper body into a ball. When rolling, exhale quickly and tighten your body while rolling over your left shoulder without letting it come into contact with the ground. Smoothly roll onto your left shoulder blade and down your back. As you roll, bend your legs and tuck your right foot behind your left knee. Your goal should be to roll over your left shoulder and through your right hip. Do not turn or twist your body during the roll. Slap the ground next to your right hip with the palm of your right hand as your feet come into contact with the ground. Simultaneously land onto the sole of your left foot and keep your right foot tucked tightly until your upper body is leaning forward. Let the momentum carry your body up as you lean into your left leg and stand up. Place your right foot on the ground as you stand into a left Fight Stance.

(오른쪽)
선 자세에서 양발을 어깨넓이로 벌려 오른발을 중앙 한발 앞에 놓고, 오른쪽 손바닥으로 허공을 아래로 내려치며, 오른쪽 어깨가 바닥에 닿지 않게 굴러 왼쪽 무릎을 90도로 접어 바닥에 대고, 왼쪽 손바닥은 바닥을 치면서 오른쪽 발바닥은 왼쪽 발목위 바닥에 대고, 일어나면서 오른쪽 주먹을 앞으로 올려 얼굴을 방어하면서 왼쪽 주먹은 왼쪽 턱을 방어한다.

(Right) Begin by standing with your left leg forward and your right leg back. Relax your shoulders and tilt your head towards the left while bringing your left ear to your left shoulder. Lean forward and fall into the ground at an angle. As you are falling forward, tuck your right shoulder in towards your left hip. When your right shoulder gets close to the ground, tuck your right shoulder and elbow into your body tightly. When tucking, curve your back forward and compact your entire upper body into a ball. When rolling, exhale quickly and tighten your body while rolling over your right shoulder without letting it come into contact with the ground. Smoothly roll onto your right shoulder blade and down your back. As you roll, bend your legs and tuck your left foot behind your right knee. Your goal should be to roll over your right shoulder and through your left hip. Do not turn or twist your body during the roll. Slap the ground next to your left hip with the palm of your left hand as your feet come into contact with the ground. Simultaneously land onto the sole of your right foot and keep your left foot tucked tightly until your upper body is leaning forward. Let the momentum carry your body up as you lean into your right leg and stand up. Place your left foot on the ground as you stand into a right Fight Stance.

낙법술: Nakbub Techniques

8. 후방낙법 손치고 일어나기

선 자세에서 양발을 어깨넓이로 벌리고, 목을 앞으로 숙여 턱을 당겨 붙이고 양손을 가슴 높이에 두고, 무릎을 접어 뒤로 누우면서 등이 바닥에 닿는 순간, 양팔을 45도 벌려 양 손바닥을 바닥을 치고, 양발바닥을 아래로 내려 스냅으로 바닥 에 대고 양손을 바닥을 치며 일어나기.

Rolling Back Nakbub and Rock Up:

Begin by standing with your feet parallel from each other in a Front Stance. Bend your legs. Curve your spine forward, tuck your chin into your chest and roll backwards. The moment the center of your back comes into contact with the ground, exhale your breath quickly while flexing your stomach and neck muscles while also slapping the ground with the palm of your hands. Slap the ground by extending your arms out at about a 45degree angle to your body. When you slap the ground, your arms should be flat. The purpose of this technique is to practice on timing your fall with a slap. The slap is to break your fall and disperse the impacting force throughout your entire body in contrast to letting the force be concentrated at one point. Once you have slapped the ground, keep your legs bent and rock your body up. Tuck your heels underneath you and use that momentum to help bring your body back up onto your feet. Once you are back onto your feet, stand into a Front Stance.

9. 후방낙법 공중제비

선 자세에서 양발을 어깨넓이로 벌려, 목을 앞으로 숙여 턱을 당겨 붙이고 양손을 가슴 높이에 두고, 무릎을 접으면서 위로 높이 뛰어 등이 바닥에 닿는 순간, 양팔을 45도 벌려 양 손바닥으로 바닥을 치고, 양다리를 머리 뒤로 넘겨 다시 양손을 동시에 목 아래 바닥을 짚고, 양손으로 밀어 양다리로 훅을 하면서 일어나기.

Falling Back Nakbub and Hand Spring Up:

Begin by standing with your feet parallel from each other in a Front Stance. Keep your back straight. Bend your legs and lean back. Fall backwards and land flat onto your back. The moment your body hits the ground, simultaneously slap the ground with the palm of your hands to break your fall, tuck your chin into your chest, quickly exhale your breath, and flex your stomach and neck muscles to brace your body for impact. When you slap the ground, your intent should be to disperse the impacting force throughout your entire body. Do not land on your elbows and do not let your head hit the ground. Then to spring your body back up onto your feet, bend your legs and bring your knees into your chest. Bend your arms and place your hands on the floor above your shoulders and lift your hips and lower back off the ground. Coil your body into your arms and shoulders. Kick your legs out while arching your back and bend your legs while bringing your feet underneath your body. Push off the ground using your hands to assist popping your body up. Use the momentum to pull your body up and land onto your feet so that you return back to a Front Stance.

낙법술: Nakbub Techniques

10. 후방낙법 무릎 밀기

선 자세에서 양발을 어깨넓이로 벌리고, 목을 앞으로 숙여 턱을 당겨 붙이고 양손을 가슴 높이에 두고, 무릎을 접으면서 뒤로 누워 등이 바닥에 닿는 순간, 양팔을 45도 벌려 양 손바닥으로 바닥을 치고, 양다리를 머리 뒤로 넘겨 양손으로 양 무릎을 밀면서, 양다리로 훅을 하며 일어나기.

Jumping Back Nakbub and Spring Up by Pushing Off the Legs:

Begin by standing with your feet parallel from each other in a Front Stance. Keep your back straight and bend your legs. Jump and fall backwards and land flat onto your back. The moment your body hits the ground, simultaneously slap the ground with the palm of your hands to break your fall, tuck your chin into your chest, quickly exhale your breath, and flex your stomach and neck muscles to brace your body for impact. When you slap the ground, your intent should be to disperse the impacting force throughout your entire body. Do not land on your elbows and do not let your head hit the ground. Then to spring your body back up onto your feet, bend your legs and bring your knees into your chest. Place your hands on your thighs. Lift your hips and lower back off the ground and coil your body and legs into your shoulders. Kick your legs out and push off your thighs with your hands while arching your back. Bend your legs while bringing your feet underneath body. Use the momentum to pull your body up and land onto your feet so that you return back to a Front Stance.

11. 공중 후방낙법 손안대고 공중제비

선 자세에서 양발을 어깨넓이로 벌리고, 목을 앞으로 숙여 턱을 당겨 붙이고 양손을 가슴 높이에 두고, 무릎을 접으면서 위로 높이 뛰어 등이 바닥에 닿는 순간, 양팔을 45도 벌려 양 손바닥으로 바닥을 치고, 양다리를 머리위로 올렸다가 양다리를 아래로 내리면서 스냅으로 훅을 하면서 일어나기.

Jumping Back Nakbub and Spring Up Using No Hands:

Begin by standing with your feet parallel from each other in a Front Stance. Keep your back straight and bend your legs. Jump and fall backwards and land flat onto your back. The moment your body hits the ground, simultaneously slap the ground with the palm of your hands to break your fall, tuck your chin into your chest, quickly exhale your breath, and flex your stomach and neck muscles to brace your body for impact. When you slap the ground, your intent should be to disperse the impacting force throughout your entire body. Do not land on your elbows and do not let your head hit the ground. Then to spring your body back up onto your feet, bend your legs and bring your knees into your chest. Lift your hips and lower back off the ground and coil your body and legs into your shoulders. Kick your legs out and arch your back. Kick your legs out hard enough to pop your shoulders off the ground and to create enough momentum to whip the rest of your body up. Bend your legs while bringing your feet underneath body. Use that momentum to help you land back onto your feet and return back to a Front Stance.

낙법술: Nakbub Techniques

Yu Sool Technique
던 | 지 | 기 | 술

01. 옷깃잡고 밭다리 후려던지기:
    Lapel Grab Outside Hook Throw

02. 옷깃잡고 안다리 후려던지기:
    Lapel Grab Inside Hook Throw

03. 허리걸어 던지기:
    Waist Grab Hip Throw

04. 옷깃잡고 뺏쳐 던지기:
    Lapel Grab Sweep Throw

05. 옷깃잡고 허리걸어 던지기:
    Lapel Grab Hip Throw

06. 옷깃잡고 풍차 던지기:
    Lapel Grab Windmill Throw

07. 목걸고 허리걸어 던지기:
    One Arm Neck Hold Hip Throw

08. 옷깃잡고 어깨걸어 던지기:
    Lapel Grab Shoulder Throw

09. 한다리들고 밭다리 후려던지기:
    One Leg Hold Outside Hook Throw

10. 한다리들고 안다리 후려던지기:
    One Leg Hold Inside Hook Throw

11. 겨드랑이걸어 어깨 던지기:
    Underarm Lock Shoulder Throw

12. 허리걸고 가랑이들어 던지기:
    Waist Lock Thigh Lift Body Drop

13. 목졸라 허리걸어 던지기:
    Two Arm Headlock Hip Throw

14. 안팔굽걸고 다리뻗어 던지기:
    Inside Elbow Hold Leg Throw

15. 뒷옷깃잡고 발등풍차 던지기:
    Back Collar Grab Instep Windmill Throw

16. 뒷목걸고 무릎풍차 던지기:
    Reverse Head Lock Knee Windmill Throw

1. 옷깃잡고 밭다리 후려던지기

선 자세에서 상대의 양 옷깃을 잡고 대치하다가 왼발을 들어 상대의 오른발 옆으로 한발 옮겨 놓으며 중심은 왼발에 두고 왼손은 상대의 오른쪽 옷깃을 잡아 당겨 오른발을 들어 상대의 오른쪽 장딴지를 걸어 당기면서 오른손은 상대의 왼쪽 옷깃을 동시에 밀어 왼쪽으로 넘어뜨리기.

Lapel Grab Outside Hook Throw:

Step out with your left leg towards the outside of your opponent's right leg. Lean slightly forward while pulling your opponent's right lapel straight down with your left arm so all of your opponent's weight is shifted onto their right leg. Push your opponent's left lapel with your right arm so your opponent's shoulders are turned counter-clockwise and your opponent is off balance. Hook the back of your opponent's right ankle clockwise with the knife-edge heel of your right foot, and take your opponent down to the floor.

2. 옷깃잡고 안다리 후려던지기

선 자세에서 상대의 양 옷깃을 잡고 대치하다가 오른발을 들어 상대의 양다리 사이에 앞으로 한발 옮겨 놓으며 중심은 오른발에 두고 왼발을 들어 상대의 오른쪽 장딴지를 걸어 당기면서 동시에 양 옷깃을 잡은 손으로 상대를 밀면서 뒤로 넘어뜨리기.

Lapel Grab Inside Hook Throw:

Step out with your right leg in between your opponent's legs. Lean slightly forward while pulling your opponent's right lapel straight down with your left arm so all of your opponent's weight is shifted onto their right leg. Push your opponent's left lapel with your right arm so your opponent's shoulders are turned counter-clockwise and your opponent is off balance. Hook the back of your opponent's right leg clockwise with the knife-edge heel of your left foot, and take your opponent down to the floor.

3. 허리걸어 던지기

선 자세에서 상대의 양 옷깃을 잡고 대치하다가 오른발을 들어 상대의 양다리 사이에 180도로 돌려 앞으로 한발 옮겨 놓으며 중심은 양다리에 두고 오른팔로 상대의 허리를 감아 걸어 엉덩이를 상대의 가랑이 사이에 붙여 왼발을 들어 뒤로 한발 옮겨 놓으며 양 무릎을 굽혀 상대의 엉덩이를 업어 양 무릎을 세우면서 오른쪽으로 넘어뜨리기.

Waist Grab Hip Throw:

Step across with your right leg towards the outside of your opponent's right foot while hooking your right arm around your opponent's waist. Step back with your left leg towards the inside of your opponent's left foot, and bend both your legs so your waist is below your opponent's waist. Catch your opponent's right armpit with your right elbow while slightly sticking your right hip out. Slightly crouch over, extend both your legs, and pick up your opponent. Turn your body clockwise and throw your opponent over your right hip.

4. 옷깃잡고 뺏쳐 던지기

선 자세에서 상대의 양 옷깃을 잡고 대치하다가 왼발을 들어 상대의 양다리사이에 앞으로 한발 옮겨 놓으며 중심은 왼발에 두고 왼손으로 상대의 오른쪽 옷깃을 밀면서 오른손은 상대의 왼쪽 옷깃을 앞으로 당겨 오른발을 들어 상대의 왼쪽 바깥 복사뼈를 동시에 뺏치면서 오른쪽으로 넘어뜨리기.

Lapel Grab Sweep Throw:

Step out with your left leg towards the outside of your opponent's right foot. Pull your opponent's left lapel down and towards you with your right arm so all your opponent's weight is shifted onto their left leg. At the same time, push your opponent's right lapel with your left arm back so your opponent's shoulders are turned clockwise and your opponent is off balance. Then shift your weight to your left leg, and catch your opponent's outside left ankle with the inside of your right foot, sweeping your opponent to the ground sideways.

5. 옷깃잡고 허리걸어 던지기

선 자세에서 상대의 양 옷깃을 잡고 대치하다가 양손을 앞으로 당기면서 오른발을 들어 상대의 양다리 사이에 180도로 돌려 앞으로 한발 옮겨 놓으며 양 무릎을 굽혀 오른쪽 엉덩이를 상대의 가랑이 사이에 붙여 중심은 오른쪽 다리에 두고 왼쪽으로 몸을 기울여 왼발을 들어 뒤로 한발 옮겨 놓으며 양손을 앞으로 당겨 양 무릎을 세우면서 엉덩이를 들어 올려 오른쪽으로 넘어뜨리기.

Lapel Grab Hip Throw:

Step across with your right leg towards the outside of your opponent's right foot while bending your right arm and tucking your right elbow in towards your left. Step back with your left leg towards the inside of your opponent's left foot, and bend both your legs so your waist is below your opponent's waist. Catch your opponent's right armpit with your right elbow while slightly sticking your right hip out. Slightly crouch over, extend your legs, and pick up your opponent. Turn your body clockwise and throw your opponent over your right hip.

6. 옷깃잡고 풍차 던지기

선 자세에서 상대의 양 옷깃을 잡고 대치하다가 상대가 앞으로 밀면 양손을 아래로 당기면서 자세를 낮추어 중심은 왼쪽 다리에 두고 앉으면서 몸을 뒤로 굴려 오른발을 상대의 복부에 대고 오른쪽 다리를 위로 뻗으면서 머리위로 넘겨뜨리기.

Lapel Grab Windmill Throw:

As your opponent is pushing you, slightly step forward with your left leg. Then drop your body down while pulling your opponent's lapel straight down. Place your right foot on your opponent's chest while rolling backwards and launching your opponent over your head with your right leg.

7. 목걸고 허리걸어 던지기

선 자세에서 상대의 양 옷깃을 잡고 대치하다가 오른발을 들어 상대의 양다리 사이에 180도로 돌려 앞으로 한발 옮겨 놓으며 오른팔로 상대의 목을 돌려 감고 왼발을 들어 뒤로 한발 옮겨 놓으며 양 무릎을 약간 굽혀 오른쪽 엉덩이로 상대의 가랑이 사이에 붙여 중심은 오른쪽 다리에 두고 왼쪽으로 몸을 기울여 상대의 목을 앞으로 당겨 양 무릎을 세우면서 엉덩이를 들어 올려 오른쪽으로 넘어뜨리기.

One Arm Neck Hold Hip Throw:

Step across with your right leg towards the outside of your opponent's right leg while hooking your right arm around the back of your opponent's neck. Step back with your left leg towards the inside of your opponent's left foot and bend both your legs so your waist is lower than your opponent's waist. Slightly stick your right hip out, crouch slightly forward and extend both your legs so you are lifting your opponent off the ground. Turn your body clockwise and throw your opponent over your right hip.

8. 옷깃잡고 어깨걸어 던지기

선 자세에서 상대의 양 옷깃을 잡고 대치하다가 오른발을 들어 상대의 양다리 사이에 180도로 돌려 앞으로 한발 옮겨 놓으며 중심은 오른쪽 다리에 두고 양 무릎을 굽혀 상대의 가슴아래에 어깨를 붙여 왼발을 들어 뒤로 한발 옮겨 놓으며 양손을 아래로 당기며 엉덩이를 들어 올려 오른쪽으로 넘어뜨리기.

Lapel Grab Shoulder Throw:

Step across with your right leg towards the outside of your opponent's right foot. Bend your elbow and tuck it in towards your left. Step back with your left leg towards the front of your opponent's left foot while bending your legs, and dropping your waist below your opponent's waist. Crouch over and extend both of your legs, so you are lifting your opponent's heels off the ground while turning your body clockwise, and dipping your right shoulder down so that you are throwing your opponent over your right shoulder.

9. 한다리 들고 밭다리 후려던지기

선 자세에서 상대의 양 옷깃을 잡고 대치하다가 오른발을 들어 상대의 양다리 사이로 한발 옮겨 놓으며 허리를 똑바로 세워 양 무릎을 굽혀 오른팔로 상대의 왼쪽 다리를 들어 오른쪽 옆구리에 끼고 무릎과 허리를 똑바로 세워 중심은 오른쪽 다리에 두고 왼발을 들어 상대의 다리 사이로 발을 넣어 상대의 오른쪽 다리를 바깥으로 걸어 당기면서 동시에 왼손으로 상대의 오른쪽 옷깃을 밀면서 뒤로 넘어뜨리기.

One Leg Hold Outside Hook Throw:

Step forward with your right leg in-between your opponent's legs. Then hook and grab your opponent's left thigh with your right arm. While leaning slightly forward shift your weight to your right leg and hook the back of your opponent's right ankle counter-clockwise with the knife edge heel of your left foot.

10. 한다리잡고 안다리 후려던지기

선 자세에서 상대의 양 옷깃을 잡고 대치하다가 오른발을 들어 상대의 양다리 사이로 한발 옮겨 놓으며 허리를 똑바로 세워 양 무릎을 굽혀 오른팔로 상대의 왼쪽 다리를 들어 오른쪽 옆구리에 끼고 무릎과 허리를 똑바로 세워 중심은 오른쪽 다리에 두고 왼발을 들어 상대의 오른쪽 뒷다리를 바깥에서 안으로 걸어 당기면서 동시에 왼손으로 상대의 오른쪽 옷깃을 밀면서 뒤로 넘어뜨리기.

One Leg Hold Inside Hook Throw:

Step forward with right leg in-between your opponent's legs. Then hook and grab your opponent's left thigh with your right arm. While leaning slightly forward, shift your weight to your right leg, and hook the back of your opponent's right ankle clockwise with the knife-edge heel of your left foot.

던지기술:Yu Sool Technique

11. 겨드랑이걸어 어깨 던지기

선 자세에서 상대의 양 옷깃을 잡고 대치하다가 오른발을 들어 상대의 오른발 앞으로 180도로 돌려 앞으로 한발 옮겨 놓으며 왼손으로 상대의 오른쪽 팔뚝을 잡으면서 오른쪽 팔로 상대의 오른쪽 겨드랑이 밑으로 팔뚝을 고정시켜 팔을 들어 올리면서 왼발을 들어 한발 뒤로 옮겨 놓으며 중심은 왼쪽 다리에 두고 몸을 왼쪽으로 기울여 오른쪽 어깨를 들어 올려 넘어뜨리기.

Underarm Lock Shoulder Throw:

Step across with your right leg towards the outside of your opponent's right foot. Grab your opponent's right arm with your left hand and place your right shoulder underneath your opponent's right armpit while grabbing your opponent's right shoulder with your right hand. Step back with your left leg towards the inside of your opponent's left foot. Bend both your legs so that your waist is lower than your opponent's waist. Crouch over and extend both your legs so you're lifting your opponent up. Turn your body clockwise while slightly dipping your right shoulder, and throwing your opponent over your right shoulder.

12. 허리걸고 가랑이들어 던지기

선 자세에서 상대의 양 옷깃을 잡고 대치하다가 오른발을 들어 상대의 양다리 사이에 앞으로 한발 옮겨 놓으며 오른팔로 상대의 허리를 돌려 감아 앞으로 당겨 왼손으로 상대의 오른쪽 허벅지를 잡고 왼발을 들어 오른발 뒤꿈치에 대고 중심은 왼쪽 다리에 두고 몸을 뒤로 기울이면서 오른쪽 허벅지로 상대를 들어 올려 왼손으로 상대의 오른쪽 허벅지를 치면서 왼쪽으로 몸을 기울여 넘어뜨리기.

Waist Lock Thigh Lift Body Drop:

Step forward with your right leg in-between your opponent's legs. Then hook your opponent's waist with your right arm. Slightly slide your left foot forward while raising your right knee. Then lean slightly back and lift your opponent up. Slap the outside of your opponent's right thigh with your left hand so their leg is tucked in. Turn your body and pivot off your left foot counter- clockwise and slam your opponent to the floor.

던지기술: Yu Sool Technique

13. 목졸라 허리걸어 던지기

선 자세에서 상대의 양 옷깃을 잡고 대치하다가 오른발을 들어 상대의 오른발 앞으로 180도로 돌려 앞으로 한발 옮겨 놓으며 오른팔로 상대의 목을 돌려 감고 왼손으로 자신의 오른쪽 손목을 잡아 앞으로 당겨 상대의 목을 조르면서 오른쪽 엉덩이를 상대의 가랑이 사이에 붙여 왼발을 들어 뒤로 한발 옮겨 놓으며 중심은 오른쪽 다리에 두고 오른쪽으로 넘어뜨리기.

Two Arm Headlock Hip Throw:

Step across with your right leg towards the outside of your opponent's right leg while hooking the back of your opponent's neck with your right arm. Then clasp both your hands together, and head lock your opponent. Step back with your left leg towards the inside of your opponents left foot, and bend both your legs so your waist lower than your opponents waist while keeping your right hip slightly sticking out. Crouch slightly forward and extend both your legs so you are lifting your opponent off the ground. Turn your body clockwise and throw your opponent over your right hip.

14. 안팔굽걸고 다리뻗어 던지기

선 자세에서 상대의 양 옷깃을 잡고 대치하다가 왼손으로 상대의 오른쪽 소매를 잡아 당겨 오른발을 들어 상대의 왼발 옆에 90도로 돌려 한발 앞으로 옮겨 뻗어 놓고 오른쪽 팔뚝을 상대의 오른쪽 안팔굽에 붙여 왼발을 들어 뒤로 한발 옮겨 놓으면서 오른쪽 엉덩이를 상대의 가랑이에 붙여 왼쪽 다리를 약간 굽혀 엉덩이를 들어 올려 중심은 왼쪽 다리에 두고 오른쪽 다리를 상대의 오른쪽 다리에 대고 팅기면서 왼손을 당겨 오른쪽 팔굽을 누르면서 허리를 오른쪽으로 틀어 넘어뜨리기.

Inside Elbow Hold Leg Throw:

Grab your opponent's right wrist with your left hand. Then place your right forearm in the crook of your opponent's right arm. Turn your body counter-clockwise while stepping back with your left leg. Step across with your right leg towards the back of your opponent's outside right ankle. Slightly bend and lean towards your left leg while extending your right leg. Apply pressure to the crook of your opponent's arm, and turn your body counter-clockwise so you are throwing your opponent over your right leg.

15. 뒷옷깃잡고 발등풍차 던지기

선 자세에서 상대의 양 옷깃을 잡고 대치하다가 오른발을 들어 상대의 양발 사이에 앞으로 한발 옮겨 놓으며 오른손으로 상대의 뒷옷깃을 잡고 앞으로 당기면서 양 무릎을 굽혀 중심은 왼쪽 다리에 두고 오른쪽 발등으로 상대의 가랑이 사이를 차며 뒤로 누우면서 머리위로 넘겨뜨리기.

Back Collar Grab Instep Windmill Throw:

While your opponent is pushing against you, step forward with your left leg. Reach over your opponent's right shoulder with your right arm, and grab the back of your opponent's collar. Bend both your legs and roll backwards while kicking your opponent in the groin with your right instep and launching your opponent over your right shoulder.

16. 뒷목걸고 무릎풍차 던지기

선 자세에서 상대의 양 옷깃을 잡고 대치하다가 오른발을 들어 상대의 양발 사이에 앞으로 한발 옮겨 놓으며 오른팔로 상대의 목을 뒤로 돌려 감아 왼손으로 자신의 오른쪽 손목을 잡고 목을 조르면서 아래로 당겨 양 무릎을 굽혀 중심은 왼쪽 다리에 두고 오른쪽 무릎으로 상대의 가랑이 사이를 차며 뒤로 누우면서 머리위로 넘겨뜨리기.

Reverse Head Lock Knee Windmill Throw:

While your opponent is pushing against you, step forward with your left leg. Reach over your opponent's your opponent's right shoulder with your right arm, and hook the back of your opponent's neck. Clasp both your hands underneath your opponent's chin, and apply a reverse headlock. Bend both your legs and roll backwards while kneeing your opponent in the groin with your right knee and launching your opponent over your right shoulder.

던지기술: Yu Sool Technique

Go Jung Sool Technique
고 | 정 | 술

01. 가위다리로 한쪽허벅지 고정시켜 목조르기:
    One Leg Scissor Lock, Head and Arm Choke

02. 가위다리로 양허벅지 고정시켜 양옷깃잡고 팔뚝척골로 목조르기:
    Two Leg Grape Vine Lock, Cross Forearm Collar Choke

03. 가위다리로 한쪽팔뚝 잠그고 팔뚝 및 손가락 꺾기:
    One Arm Scissor Lock, Arm Bar and Finger Break

04. 가위다리로 허리잠그고 한쪽팔꿈치 접어 양손으로 손목잡고 목뒤로
    팔을돌려 목조르기:
    Two Leg Grape Vine Lock, Reverse Arm Lock and Choke

05. 가위다리로 한쪽허벅지 고정시켜 한쪽 손목잡고 팔을 목뒤로
    감아 예풍 누르기:
    One Leg Scissor Lock, Arm Lock and Trunk Twist with Pressure Point

06. 가위다리로 허리를 고정시켜 한쪽 손목잡고 팔을 상대의 목뒤로
    감아 양손으로 상대의 한쪽손목을 잡아당겨 목조르기:
    Solar Plex Scissor Lock, Arm Lock and Trunk Twist

07. 가위다리로 등뒤 허리잠그고 겨드랑이 아래로 팔을넣어 목뒤로
    양손 깍지끼고 양팔들어올리기:
    Waist Scissor Lock, Full Nelson

08. 가위다리로 등뒤 양다리로 허리잠그고 한쪽팔은 목을돌려 팔뚝잡고
    다른손은 머리눌러 목조르기:
    Waist Scissor Lock, Bicep Choke

1. 가위다리로 한쪽허벅지 고정시켜 목조르기

가위다리로 상대의 한쪽 허벅다리를 고정시키고, 상대의 오른팔을 머리위로 올려놓고, 오른쪽 어깨로 상대의 턱 아래 목젖에 붙이면서 목뒤로 팔을돌려 요골로 목 흉쇄유돌근에 붙여 본인의 왼쪽 팔꿈치를 뒤로 뻗어 바닥에 고정시키고 몸을 바닥에 납작하게 엎드려 중심을 잡고, 목을 돌린 오른쪽 손목을 반대의 왼손으로 잡아 당기면서 오른팔에 기를 넣어 머리로 상대의 오른쪽 팔뚝을 밀면서 오른쪽 요골로 상대의 왼쪽 흉쇄유돌근을 누르면서 목조르기를 하여 질식케 한다.

One Leg Scissor Lock, Head and Arm Choke:

Lay next to your opponent's right side, and slide your left leg underneath your opponent's right thigh. Bring your right leg over your opponent's right thigh, and interlock your ankles. Execute a scissors lock to your opponent's right thigh. Make sure your opponent is lying down on his back with his right arm straight up over his head. While lying on your left side, bring your right arm over, and around your opponent's neck. Make sure the right side of your opponent's neck is flesh against the crook of your right arm. Bring your left elbow out sideways, and clasp both your hands. Place your head next to your opponent's outside right arm. Execute a head and arm lock while pushing against your opponent's right arm with your head. Drop your right shoulder straight down underneath your opponent's chin, and sink your shoulder straight down into their throat so you are choking them.

2. 가위다리로 양허벅지 고정시켜 양옷깃잡고 팔뚝척골로 목조르기

가위다리로 상대의 양 허벅다리를 고정시키고, 오른손으로 상대의 뒷 옷깃을 잡고, 왼손은 상대의 턱밑 왼쪽 옷깃을 잡아 당기면서 목뒤 옷깃을 잡은 오른쪽 팔뚝에 기를 넣어 오른쪽 척골로 상대의 목 흉쇄유돌근을 누르면서 목조르기를 하여 질식케 한다.

Two Leg Grape Vine Lock, Cross Forearm Collar Choke:

While your opponent is lying on their back, mount your opponent. Wrap your legs under their hamstrings from the outside in, and lock your ankles over their shins. Sink your hips down, and extend your legs while spreading them out in opposite direction. Reach across your opponent's chest with your right hand, and grab your opponent's right collar from high up. Place your right forearm across your opponent's neck, and grab your opponent's left collar with your left hand underneath your right arm. Pull their left collar tightly towards you with your left hand while applying pressure to their neck with your right forearm by pulling their right collar across their neck, and bending your right elbow while twisting your forearm into their throat. Make sure to lean your weight on your right forearm.

3. 가위다리로 한쪽팔뚝을 잠그고 장지 손가락 꺾기

가위다리로 상대의 오른쪽 팔뚝을 고정시키고, 양다리에 기를 넣어 양 무릎으로 상대의 팔뚝을 조르면서 왼손으로 상대의 손목을 잡아 본인의 검지(식지) 손가락과 장지(중지) 손가락 사이에 상대의 장지손가락을 끼어 뒤로 제쳐 꺾기를 한다.

One Arm Scissor Lock, Arm Bar and Finger Break:

Lay on your back with your feet towards your opponent so you are perpendicular with your opponent. Place your opponent's right arm between your legs. Interlock your ankle, and execute a scissors lock to your opponent's right shoulder. Grab your opponent's right wrist with your left hand. Grab your opponent's middle finger with your index and middle finger. Place their right arm over your right thigh so their elbow is rested on your right thigh, and place their right wrist next to your right side. Lay flat on your back, and lift your hip off the ground while grabbing hold of their wrist. At the same time, squeeze your right hand and pull your opponent's finger back so you are breaking their finger.

4. 가위다리로 허리잠그고 한쪽 팔꿈치접어 양손으로 손목잡고 목뒤로 팔을돌려 목조르기

가위다리로 상대의 양 허벅다리를 고정시키고, 왼손으로 상대의 오른쪽 손목을 잡아 팔꿈치를 접어 본인의 오른팔을 상대의 목뒤로 돌려 양손으로 상대의 오른쪽 손목을 잡고, 상대의 오른쪽 팔뚝을 오른쪽 뺨에 붙여 본인의 머리로 상대의 팔뚝을 밀면서 오른쪽 어깨로 기를 넣어 상대의 목젖을 눌러 질식케 한다.

Two Leg Grape Vine Lock, Reverse Arm Lock and Choke:

While your opponent is lying on their back, mount your opponent. Wrap your legs under their hamstrings from the outside in, and lock your ankles over their shins. Sink your hips down, and extend your legs while spreading them out in opposite direction. Make sure your opponent's right arm is bent with his elbow pointed straight up. Reach over with your right arm around your opponent's neck, and grab your opponent's right wrist with your right hand. Grab your opponent's right wrist with our left hand, and with have your left elbow sticking out sideways. Place your head next to their outside right arm. Push your head against their right arm. Drop your right shoulder underneath their chin, and sink your shoulder straight down and up into their throat so you are choking them. At the same time, pull in your opponent's right wrist and drive your opponent's right elbow up.

5. 가위다리로 한쪽허벅지 고정시켜 한쪽 손목잡고 팔을 목뒤로 감아 예풍 누르기

가위다리로 상대의 오른쪽 허벅다리를 고정시키고, 상대의 오른팔을 상대의 턱밑으로 목을 돌려 손목을 잡고, 오른손으로 상대의 목옆 옷깃을 잡아 양다리에 기를 넣어 옷깃을 잡은 엄지손가락으로 상대의 귓밥 뒤 오목한 부위 예풍을 눌러 항복을 시킨다.

One Leg Scissor Lock, Arm Lock and Trunk Twist with Pressure Point:

Lay next to your opponent's right side, and slide your left leg, underneath your opponent's right thigh. Bring your right leg over your opponent's right thigh, and interlock your ankles. Execute a scissors lock to your opponent's right thigh. Make sure your opponent's right arm is across their neck. Grab your opponent's right wrist from under your opponent's left ear. Place your right hand on your opponent's right shoulder and grab the back of your opponent's collar. Place the tip of your right thumb in the back of your opponent's right ear lobe, and apply pressure by pushing in. Extend your right arm and pull their right arm tight with your left arm. Turn your body counter-clockwise so you are twisting your opponent's body counter-clockwise.

6. 가위다리로 허리를 고정시켜 한쪽 손목잡고 팔을 상대의 목뒤로 감아 양손으로 상대의 한쪽손목을 잡아당겨 목조르기

가위다리로 상대의 허리를 고정시키고, 상대의 한쪽 손목을 잡아 상대의 목뒤로 돌려 본인의 양손으로 상대의 한쪽 손목을 잡고, 양다리에 기를 넣어 허리를 뻗으면서 상대의 손목을 앞으로 당겨 목을 졸라 기절케 한다.

Solar Plex Scissor Lock, Arm Lock and Trunk Twist:

Place your left leg underneath your opponent's back. Bring your right leg over, and across your opponent's solarplex. Interlock your ankles, and execute a scissors lock to your opponent's solarplex. Make sure your opponent's right arm is across their neck. Grab your opponent's right wrist from under your opponent's left ear with both your hands. Pull your opponent's right arm tight with both your arms so you are twisting your opponent's body counter-clockwise. Make sure your opponent is flat on their back and you have applied a secure scissors lock across their solarplex before turning their shoulders.

7. 가위다리로 등뒤 허리 잠그고 겨드랑이 아래로 팔을넣어 목뒤로 양손깍지를 끼고 양팔 들어올리기

가위다리로 상대의 허리를 고정시키고, 양팔을 상대의 양 겨드랑이 밑으로 돌려 목뒤에서 양 손깍지를 끼고 양다리에 기를 넣어 양 팔뚝으로 목뒤에서 빗장을 만들어 위로 들어 올려 목뒤를 눌러 항복케 한다.

Waist Scissor Lock, Full Nelson:

While your opponent is sitting up, wrap both your legs around their waist from behind. Interlock your ankles, and execute a scissors lock to your opponent's waist. Bring both your arms under your opponent's armpits, and interlock your finger behind your opponent's head. Lock your legs tight while leaning back. Raise your opponent's elbows up. Extend both your arms up while pushing your opponent's head straight down by rotating your wrists away from you.

8. 가위다리로 등뒤 양다리로 허리잠그고 한쪽팔은 목을돌려 팔뚝잡고 다른손은 머리눌러 목조르기

가위다리로 등 뒤에서 허리를 고정시키고, 왼팔을 상대의 턱밑으로 목을 돌려 왼손으로 오른쪽 팔뚝 이두박근을 잡고, 잡힌 팔뚝의 손을 상대의 목뒤로 돌려 뒷머리에 손바닥을 대고 앞으로 밀면서 양다리에 기를 넣어 허리를 뻗으면서 턱밑으로 목을 돌린 왼쪽 팔뚝의 요골로 상대의 목젖을 누르면서 목을 졸라 질식케 한다.

Waist Scissor Lock, Bicep Choke:

While your opponent is sitting up, wrap both your legs around their waist from behind. Interlock your ankles, and execute a scissors lock to your opponent's waist. Bring your left arm around your opponent's neck underneath their chin. Grab hold of your right bicep with your left hand. Bring your right hand behind your opponent's head with your palm against their head. Lock your legs tight while squeezing their neck with your left arm, and pushing their head straight down with your right hand.

Ho Shin Sool Technique
호 | 신 | 술

01. 오른손으로 띠 위에서 아래로 잡혔을때:
    팔꿈치 눌러 팔꿈치꺾기
    Over-Hand Belt Grab: Arm Bar

02. 오른손으로 띠 아래에서 위로 잡혔을때:
    팔꿈치 들어올려 팔꿈치 꺾기
    Under-Hand Grab": Reverse Arm Bar

03. 오른손으로 앞 양옷깃잡고 당길때:
    팔꿈치로 앞턱 치고 던지기
    Two Lapel Grab Pull: Elbow Hook and Outside Hook Throw

04. 오른손으로 왼쪽 손목 잡혔을때:
    손목 비틀어 손목 꺾기
    One Wrist Grab: Wrist Twist

05. 오른손으로 앞 양옷깃 잡고 밀때:
    안팔뚝으로 팔꿈치 눌러 꺾기
    Two Lapel Grab Push: Arm Bar

06. 오른손으로 오른쪽 앞 옷깃잡고 밀때:
    겨드랑이 걸어 업어치고 무릎 늑골치기
    One Lapel Grab Push: Underarm Hip Throw and Knee Drop to RibsDoubles

07. 오른손으로 왼쪽 손목 잡혔을때:
    팔뚝잡고, 손목 들어올려 팔꿈치
    One Wrist Grab: Reverse Arm Bar

08. 오른손으로 왼쪽 팔뚝을 잡혔을때:
    한쪽 팔끼고 손목 관절꺾기
    Upper Arm Grab: Outside Wrist Lock

09. 오른손으로 왼쪽 손목 잡혔을 때:
    팔뚝 아래로 들어가 뒤로 돌려서 팔꿈치 꺾기
    One Wrist Grab: Arm and Shoulder Twist

10. 오른손으로 왼쪽 손목 잡혔을때:
    왼쪽 팔뚝으로 엄지손가락 접어 팔뚝 눌러 팔꿈치 꺾기
    One Wrist Grab: Wrist and Arm Lock

11. 오른손으로 멱살잡고 당길때:
    오른쪽 무릎 사타구니 찍기
    Two Lapel Grab Pull: Inside Hooking Throw

12. 오른손으로 왼쪽 옷깃잡고 밀때:
    손목잡고 안팔굽에 팔꿈치 대고 팔꿈치 꺾기
    One Lapel Grab Push: Inside Elbow and Leg Throw

13. 오른손으로 뒤에서 옷깃 잡혔을때:
    다리걸어 던져 이마 정면 박치기
    Two Hand Back Collar Grab: Inside Elbow Throw and Head Butt

14. 오른손으로 뒤에서 옷깃 잡혔을때:
    팔뚝 뒤로 걸어 팔꿈치 꺾기
    Two back collar grab: Outside arm bar

15. 양손으로 양상완 이두근을 잡혔을때:
    수도로 안팔뚝치고 정면 박치기
    Both arm grab: Front head butt

16. 오른손으로 머리 카락을 잡혔을때:
    손목안 눌러 틀어 팔꿈치 꺾기
    Front hair grab: Arm bar

1. 오른손으로 띠 위에서 아래로 잡혔을때: 팔꿈치 눌러 팔꿈치 꺾기

왼발을 들어 상대의 오른발 옆으로 한발 옮겨 놓으며 오른손으로 상대의 오른쪽 손목을 위에서 아래로 잡고, 왼쪽 안팔뚝으로 상대의 오른쪽 팔뚝을 위에서 아래로 대면서 오른발을 들어 자신의 왼발 뒤로 한발 옮겨 놓으며 중심은 오른쪽 다리에 두고, 오른손으로 상대의 오른쪽 손목을 잡아당겨 지렛대로 왼팔을 들어 올리면서 오른쪽 팔뚝을 아래로 눌러 팔꿈치 인대 꺾기

Over-Hand Belt Grab: Arm Bar

Start: Opponent over hand grabs the front of your belt with their right hand.

Description: Step to the outside of your opponent's right foot with your left leg while grabbing your opponent's right wrist with your right hand. Then step back with your right leg so that you are standing next to your opponent; both facing the same direction, and having your bodies aligned with each other. While stepping back with your right leg, slightly twist your opponent's right arm clockwise so that your opponent's right elbow is pointed up. Place your left inner forearm securely against your opponent's right elbow, creating an arm bar. Step out towards the right with your right leg and slightly bend your leg, shifting your weight to your right leg. At the same time, turn your shoulders clockwise, and applying pressure down to your opponent's right elbow with your left forearm. Make sure you are keeping their right wrist up with your right hand, and you are applying pressure to their right elbow downward while you are taking your opponent down to the floor.

2. 오른손으로 띠 아래에서 위로 잡혔을때: 팔꿈치 들어올려 팔꿈치 꺾기

왼발을 들어 상대의 오른발 옆으로 한발 옮겨 놓으며 오른손으로 상대의 오른쪽 손목을 아래에서 위로 잡고, 왼쪽 안팔굽으로 상대의 오른쪽 팔꿈치에 대면서 오른발을 들어 자신의 왼발 뒤로 한발 옮겨 놓으며 중심은 오른쪽 다리에 두고, 오른손으로 상대의 오른쪽 손목을 잡아당겨 지렛대로 왼팔을 들어 올리며 오른쪽 팔뚝을 아래로 눌러 팔꿈치 인대 꺾기

Under-Hand Grab":Reverse Arm Bar

Start: Opponent under hand grabs the front of your belt with their right hand.

Description: Step to the outside of your opponent's right foot with your left leg while grabbing your opponent's right wrist with your right hand. Then step back with your right leg so that you are standing next to your opponent, you both are facing the same direction, and your bodies are aligned with each other. While stepping back with your right leg, hold on to your opponent's right wrist with your right hand. Hook your opponent's right elbow from underneath with the crook of your arm locking their elbow, and creating an arm bar. Lift your right arm up, and push your opponent's right wrist down with your left hand while shifting your hips towards the left, and leaning your body slightly towards the right so you are cranking your opponent's right elbow.

3. 오른손으로 앞 양옷깃잡고 당길때: 팔꿈치로 앞턱 치고 던지기

왼손으로 상대의 오른쪽 팔뚝을 잡으면서 왼발을 들어 앞으로 한발 상대의 오른쪽 다리 옆으로 옮겨 놓으며 중심은 왼쪽 다리에 두고, 오른쪽 팔꿈치로 상대의 앞턱을 치고 오른손으로 상대의 앞 옷깃을 잡으면서 밭다리 후리기로 넘어 뜨리고 오른쪽 무릎으로 상대의 오른쪽 정권 치기

Two Lapel Grab Pull: Elbow Hook and Outside Hook Throw

Start: Opponent grabs both lapels with their right hand.

Description: As your opponent pulls you with their right hand, step to the outside of your opponent's right foot with your left leg. Grab your opponent's right sleeve with your left hand. Shift your weight to your left leg, and slightly lean forward. Execute an elbow hook to your opponent's chin with your right elbow while pulling your opponent's right sleeve down with your left hand. Then hook the back of your opponent's right ankle with the knife-edge heel of your right foot in a circular motion clockwise. After taking your opponent to the floor, drop all your weight down with your right knee to your opponent's right rib cage.

4. 오른손으로 왼쪽 손목 잡혔을때: 손목 비틀어 손목 꺾기

왼쪽 손가락을 펴서 왼쪽으로 틀면서 들어올려 오른손으로 상대의 오른쪽 손목을 아래로 넣어 손바닥 단모지외전근을 잡고, 왼손을 오른쪽으로 틀어빼고, 왼쪽 한발을 뒤로 옮겨 놓으면서 왼쪽 손바닥으로 상대의 오른쪽 손등위를 치면서 눌러 손목인대 꺾기

One Wrist Grab: Wrist Twist

Start: Opponent grabs your left wrist with their right hand.

Description: Step out towards the outside of your opponent's right foot with your left leg while turning your wrist inward counter-clockwise, and flipping your hand so your palm is facing up. Reach underneath your opponent's right hand with your right hand, and grab the thumb side of your opponent's right palm with your four fingers. Place your right thumb on the back of your opponent's right hand for support. Break the grip of your opponent's right hand with your four fingers, and release your left hand from the hold. Then step back behind your left foot with your right leg while slightly turning your body clockwise. Turn your opponent's right hand counter-clockwise with your right hand, and place the palm of your left hand on the pinky side of your opponent's right hand. Apply pressure to the wrist by turning their wrist counter-clockwise with your right hand, and pushing the side of their hand diagonally out towards the left with your left palm.

5. 오른손으로 앞 양옷깃 잡고 밀때: 안팔뚝으로 팔꿈치 눌러 꺾기

오른손으로 상대의 오른쪽 손등을 눌러잡고, 오른발을 들어 뒤로 한발 옮겨 놓으며 몸을 오른쪽으로 틀어 왼팔 안팔뚝으로 상대의 오른쪽 팔꿈치에 대고, 중심은 왼쪽 다리에 두고, 오른손으로 상대의 손목을 잡아 당기면서 들어 올려 지렛대로 왼쪽 안팔뚝으로 상대의 오른쪽 팔꿈치에 기를 넣어 눌러 팔꿈치 인대 꺾기

Two Lapel Grab Push: Arm Bar

Start: Opponent grabs both your lapel with their right hand.

Description: As your opponent pushes you with their right arm, step back behind your left foot with your right leg, turn your body clockwise, and grab your opponent's right wrist with your right hand. Place the inner forearm of your left arm on your opponent's right elbow. Slightly step straight back with your right leg, and slightly bend your right knee while shifting your weight to your right leg. Turn your body clockwise, and dip your left shoulder while applying pressure to your opponent's elbow. Make sure to keep your opponent's right wrist up while you apply pressure downward into their elbow downward.

6. 오른손으로 오른쪽 앞 옷깃잡고 밀때: 겨드랑이 걸어 업어치고 무릎 늑골치기

몸을 왼쪽으로 틀어 오른발을 들어 앞으로 한발 옮겨 놓으며 오른팔을 상대의 오른쪽 겨드랑이 밑으로 넣어 팔뚝을 걸어 잠그고 왼발을 들어 뒤로 한발 옮겨 놓으며 몸을 왼쪽으로 기울이면서 중심은 왼쪽 다리에 두고, 오른쪽 업어치기로 상대를 넘어 뜨려 오른쪽 무릎으로 상대의 오른쪽 늑골 찍기

One Lapel Grab Push: Underarm Hip Throw and Knee Drop to RibsDoubles

Start: Opponent grabs your left lapel with their right hand.

Description: As your opponent pushes you with their right hand, turn your body counter-clockwise. Grab their right wrist with your left hand, and pull their right arm while stepping forward with your right leg towards the outside of your opponent's right foot. Under hook your opponent's right arm with your right arm, and catch your opponent's armpit with your right shoulder. Step back with your left leg, and bend both your legs so your waist is below your opponent's waist. Slightly crouch over, and extend both your legs while your right hip is slightly sticking out so you are picking up your opponent. Turn your body counter-clockwise, and throw your opponent over your right hip. Then drop your right knee down on your opponent's right ribs. Make sure to drop all your weight down to your right knee.

호신술: Ho Shin Sool Technique

7. 오른손으로 왼쪽 손목 잡혔을때: 팔뚝잡고, 손목 들어올려 팔꿈치

왼손에 기를 넣어 손가락을 펴며 오른발을 들어 상대의 오른발 옆으로 한발 옮겨 놓으며 오른팔로 상대의 오른쪽 팔의 상완 이두근을 잡아 고정시키고, 왼쪽 손목을 틀어 상대의 오른쪽 손목을 잡아 위로 올리면서 중심은 오른쪽 다리에 두고, 왼발을 들어 상대의 뒤로 돌면서 왼쪽 팔꿈치 인대 꺾기

One Wrist Grab: Reverse Arm Bar

Start: Opponent grabs your left wrist with their right hand.
Description: Flip your left wrist counter-clockwise so the palm of your hand is facing up. Then grab your opponent's right wrist with your left hand. Make sure your left palm is still facing up. Step behind your opponent's right ankle with your right leg. Hook and lock your opponent's right elbow with the crook of your right arm. Apply pressure to your opponent's right elbow by pushing your opponent's right wrist backwards while keeping your opponent's right elbow locked. By doing this, you should be hyper extending your opponent's right elbow.

8. 오른손으로 왼쪽 팔뚝을 잡혔을때: 한쪽 팔끼고 손목 관절꺾기

오른손으로 상대의 오른쪽 손목을 눌러잡고, 오른발을 뒤로 한발 옮겨 놓으며 오른쪽 어깨를 오른쪽으로 돌리면서 잡힌 오른팔을 높이 위로 들어 오른쪽으로 돌려 상대의 손목을 겨드랑이에 끼고, 상대의 오른쪽 손목을 잡아 고정시키고, 겨드랑이에 낀 왼팔을 아래로 눌러 손목관절 꺾기

Upper Arm Grab: Outside Wrist Lock

Start: Opponent grabs your left bicep with their right hand.
Description: Reach across your chest with your right hand and grab your opponent's right wrist. Step forward with your right leg towards the outside of your opponent's right foot. Hold your opponent's right hand on your left bicep, and bring your left arm straight up and over your opponent's right wrist. Lock your opponent's right wrist with your left armpit. Place your left inner forearm on top of their wrist. Apply pressure to their wrist by turning your left forearm into their wrist downward while slightly leaning your body towards them.

9. 오른손으로 왼쪽 손목 잡혔을 때: 팔뚝 아래로 들어가 뒤로 돌려서 팔꿈치 꺾기

왼쪽 손목을 바깥쪽으로 들어 올리면서 오른손으로 상대의 오른쪽 안팔굽에 대면서 오른발을 들어 상대의 오른팔 아래로 한발 옮겨 놓으며 몸을 돌려 앉으면서 오른쪽 무릎을 바닥에 대고, 중심은 오른쪽 무릎에 두고, 왼손을 비틀어 상대의 오른쪽 손목을 잡아 지렛대로 왼손을 들어 올리면서 오른팔을 아래로 당겨 손은 안팔굽을 잡아 지렛대로 아래로 눌러 상대의 오른쪽 팔굽 인대를 꺾으면서 넘어뜨리기

One Wrist Grab: Arm and Shoulder Twist

Start: Opponent grabs your left wrist with their right hand.

Description: Flip your wrist counter-clockwise so your palm is facing up. Grab your opponent's right wrist with your left hand. Step forward with your right leg, and kneel down to your right knee. Place your right forearm in the crook of your opponent's right elbow. Go under your opponent's right arm while turning your body counter-clockwise. Once you have gone under the arm, bring your left leg back behind your opponent. Then pop your opponent's right wrist over their shoulder while holding on to their elbow with your right hand.

10. 오른손으로 왼쪽 손목 잡혔을때: 왼쪽 팔뚝으로 엄지 손가락 접어 팔뚝 눌러 팔꿈치 꺾기

오른손으로 상대의 손등을 잡고, 왼팔을 위로 올려 팔뚝으로 상대의 오른쪽 엄지를 아래로 눌러 꺾으면서 왼쪽 안 팔뚝을 옆으로 돌려 상대의 오른쪽 팔꿈치에 대고, 오른손으로 상대의 손목을 잡아당기면서 위로 올려 중심은 왼쪽 다리에 두고, 기를 넣어 지렛대로 왼쪽 안 팔뚝을 눌러 팔꿈치 인대 꺾기

One Wrist Grab: Wrist and Arm Lock

Start: Opponent grabs your left wrist with their right hand.

Description: Step to the outside of your opponent's right foot with your left leg while raising your left arm up above your head, and twisting your left wrist clockwise so your palm, is facing towards the left. With your right hand, reach over your opponent's right hand and grab the pinky side of your opponent's palm with your four-fingers, and place your thumb on the back of their hand for support. Step back with your right leg so that you are standing next to your opponent, you both are facing the same direction, and your bodies aligned with each other. At the same time, bend your opponent's right thumb back with your left wrist so you can slip your left hand free from your opponent's grasp. Twist your opponent's right wrist clockwise with your right hand. Then slide your left forearm down your opponent's arm, and place your left inner forearm securely against your opponent's right elbow, creating an arm bar. Slightly bend your right knee, and extend your left while pulling your opponent's right arm with your left, and taking them to the floor. Apply pressure by pushing down on your opponent's right elbow with your left inner forearm, and dipping your left shoulder down while keeping your opponent's right wrist up.

11. 오른손으로 멱살잡고 당길때: 오른쪽 무릎 사타구니 찍기

오른발을 들어 상대의 양다리 사이로 한발 옮겨 놓으며 양손으로 상대의 양팔뚝을 잡으면서 이마로 상대의 앞턱을 치면서 왼발을 들어 상대의 오른쪽 안다리 후리기로 넘어뜨리고, 왼발을 들어 앞으로 한발 옮겨 놓으며 몸을 낮추면서 오른쪽 무릎으로 상대의 사타구니 찍기

Two Lapel Grab Pull: Inside Hooking Throw

Start: Opponent grabs both lapels with their right hand.

Description: As your opponent pulls you with their right hand, step forward in between their legs with your right leg. With your left hand, grab your opponent's right sleeve, and pull it straight down so that your opponent is leaning on their right leg. Slightly bend your right knee, and extend your left leg. Then grab your opponent's left collar with your right hand, and elbow hook your opponent's chin with your right elbow. At the same time, lean slightly forward while hooking the back of your opponent's right ankle clockwise with the knife-edge heel of your left foot. After taking your opponent to the floor, drop all of your weight down with your right knee in to your opponent's groin.

12. 오른손으로 왼쪽 옷깃잡고 밀때: 손목잡고 안팔굽에 팔꿈치 대고 팔꿈치 꺾기

몸을 왼쪽으로 틀면서 왼손을 상대의 오른쪽 손목을 잡고, 오른발을 들어 상대의 오른다리를 걸어 바닥에 넘어 뜨리고 상대의 오른팔을 바닥에 깔고, 엉덩이로 상대의 오른쪽 엉덩이에 붙여 고정시키고, 오른쪽 팔 뚝을 상대의 안 팔굽에 대고 왼손에 기를 넣어 왼손으로 상대의 손목을 눌러 상대의 팔꿈치 인대 꺾기

One Lapel Grab Push: Inside Elbow and Leg Throw

Start: Opponent grabs both lapels with their right hand.

Description: As your opponent pushes you with their right hand, turn your body counter-clockwise, and grab your opponent's right wrist with your left hand. Place your right forearm in the crook of your opponent's right elbow. Step back with your left leg towards 5:00, and step behind the outside of your opponent's right outside ankle with your right leg at the same time. Extend your right leg while shifting your weight to your left leg. Slightly bend your left leg, and apply pressure to the inside elbow, and turn your body counter-clockwise so your opponent is tripping over your right leg. After your opponent is taken to the floor, kneel next to your opponent.   Apply pressure to the crook of their right elbow by extending their right arm with your left hand, and leaning all of your weight in the inside of their elbow with your right forearm. Then with your left hand, grab your opponent's right wrist and bring their wrist in towards their chest.

13. 오른손으로 뒤에서 옷깃 잡혔을때: 다리걸어 던져 이마 정면 박치기

몸을 오른쪽으로 돌려 왼손으로 상대의 오른쪽 손목을 잡고, 오른팔을 위로 들어 올려 상대의 오른쪽 안 팔굽에 대고 오른발을 들어 상대의 오른발 옆에 옮겨 놓으며 몸을 왼쪽으로 기울이면서 오른팔을 아래로 눌러 다리 걸어 던지기로 상대를 바닥에 던지고, 오른쪽 무릎을 바닥에 대면서 오른쪽 이마로 상대의 정면 얼굴 박치기

Two Hand Back Collar Grab: Inside Elbow Throw and Head Butt

Start: Opponent's stands behind you, and grabs the back of your collar with both their hands.
Description: Turn your body clockwise towards your opponent. Reach across your chest with your left hand, and grab your opponent's right wrist. At the same time, step behind the outside of your opponent's right ankle with your right leg. Bend your left knee and extend your right leg. Place your right forearm in the crook of your opponent's right arm. Apply pressure to the inside elbow, and lean your body to your left while turning your body counter-clockwise so your opponent is tripping over your right leg. After your opponent's is taken to the floor, kneel next to your opponent, and apply pressure to the crook of their right arm by extending their right arm with your left hand, and leaning all of your weight on their right inside elbow with your right forearm. Then with your left hand, grab your opponent's right wrist and bring their wrist in towards his chest while executing a head butt with your forehead to your opponent's chin.

14. 오른손으로 뒤에서 옷깃 잡혔을때: 팔뚝 뒤로 걸어 팔꿈치 꺾기

몸을 왼쪽으로 돌려 오른발을 들어 본인의 왼발 뒤에 옮겨 놓으며 왼발을 90도로 돌려놓으면서 오른손으로 상대의 오른쪽 손목을 잡으면서 왼팔로 상대의 왼쪽 팔꿈치에 대면서 오른발을 오른쪽으로 돌려 왼발 뒤 한 발 옮겨 놓으면서 오른팔에 기를 넣어 상대의 팔꿈치를 지렛대로 누르면서 중심은 오른쪽 다리에 두고, 앞으로 당겨 상대의 오른쪽 팔꿈치 인대 꺾기

Two back collar grab: Outside arm bar

Start: Opponent stands behind you, and grabs the back of your collar with both their hands.
Description: Turn your body counter-clockwise towards your opponent. At the same time, step across your left leg behind your right foot, and step across with your right leg to where your left foot was. Reach across your chest with your right hand and grab your opponent's right wrist. Place your left forearm on their extended right elbow. Then step with your right leg while turning your body clockwise 180 degrees so that both you and your opponent are facing the same direction and are almost aligned with each other. Slightly bend your right knee, and extend your left leg. Shift your weight to your right leg, and slightly pull your opponent with your right arm. Apply pressure to their elbow with your left forearm while twisting your body clockwise, and dipping your left shoulder down.

15. 양손으로 양 상완 이두근을 잡혔을때: 수도로 안 팔뚝치고 정면 박치기

왼발을 들어 한발 앞으로 옮겨 놓으며 중심은 왼쪽 다리에 두고, 양수도로 상대의 양팔 상안 이두근을 치면서 동시에 앞이마로 상대의 인중을 정면 박치기 아래턱을 닫으면서 양손으로 상대의 양팔 상완 이두근을 잡으면서 오른발을 들어 상대의 왼쪽 다리를 안다리 후리기를 하여 뒤로 넘어뜨리기

Both arm grab: Front head butt

Start: When your arms are at your sides, opponent grabs your outside biceps with both their hands.
Description: Step forward with your left leg towards your opponent. Bring your arms up between your opponent's arms, and extend your forearms outwards, popping your opponent's hands off your arms. At the same time, push off with your right leg, and slightly bend your lefty knee while leaning slightly forward. Head butt your opponent by driving the top of your forehead to the bridge of your opponent's nose.

16. 오른손으로 머리카락을 잡혔을때: 손목 안 눌러 틀어 팔꿈치 꺾기

양손으로 상대의 오른쪽 손등을 위에서 아래로 눌러 잡고, 왼발을 들어 상대의 오른발 옆에 옮겨 놓으며 양 엄지손가락으로 상대의 손목 인대를 누르면서 오른발을 들어 뒤로 한발 옮겨 놓고, 몸을 오른쪽으로 틀어 중심은 왼쪽 다리에 두고, 왼쪽 안팔뚝 척골로 상대의 오른쪽 팔꿈치에 대고 누르면서 양손으로 손목을 잡아 지렛대로 들어 올리면서 오른쪽 팔꿈치 인대 꺾기

Front hair grab: Arm bar

Start: Opponent grabs the front of your hair with their right hand.

Description: Grab your opponent's right wrist with both your hands, and hold your opponent's right hand to your head. Place the tips of your thumbs at the pressure point located underneath the wrist at the center. Step forward towards the outside of your opponent's right leg with your left leg. Apply pressure to the pressure point by digging the tip of your thumbs into their wrist. At the same time, step slightly back with your right leg, and turn your body clockwise while dipping your head down, and raising your left elbow up. Twist your opponent's right wrist clockwise with both your hands, and place your left elbow securely on your opponent's right elbow. Apply pressure to their elbow by pushing down on it with your left elbow, and leaning your weight backwards on the elbow while keeping their right wrist up above their head.

Yoga Sool Technique
기 | 공 | 요 | 가 | 술

01. 목 교량: Neek Bridge
02. 양팔 올린 목 교량 : Two Arm Raise Neck Bridge
03. 엉덩이 뻗어올린 연결교량: Extended Bridge Hip Raise
04. 한다리 올려 엉덩이 들기: One Leg Extended Hip Raise
05. 목과 어깨 교량: Neek and Shoulder Bridge
06. 교량: Bridge
07. 한다리 교량: One Leg Bridge
08. 한팔 교량: One Arm Bridge
09. 허리잡고 어깨 서기: Shoulder Stand Waist Hold
10. 허리잡고 거꾸로 45도:
    45-Degree Over the Top Waist Hold
11. 양팔 뻗고 거꾸로 45도:
    45-Degree Over the Top Arms Spread
12. 팔뻗고 거꾸로 무릎대기:
    Over the Top Knee Touch and Arms Spread
13. 양다리 45도 들기: 45-Degree Leg Raise
14. 45도 V 에너지: 45-Degree Power V
15. 45도 복부단련: 45-Degree Abdomen Crunch
16. 코브라: Cobra
17. 꼬리감긴 코브라: Coiled Cobra
18. 슈퍼맨: Superman
19. 날으는 백조: Flying Swan
20. 등뒤 90도 양팔들기:
    Behind the Back 90-Degree Arms Raise
21. 활자세: Bow Pose
22. 전갈: Scorpion
23. 양무릎대고 삼각대: Knees Down Tri-Pod
24. 양다리뻗은 삼각대: Extended Legs Tri-Pod
25. 한다리 뻗기: Single Leg Stretch
26. 양다리 뻗기: Double Legs Stretch
27. 복부에 발 붙이기: Foot to Abdomen
28. 앞으로 다리벌리기: Front Splits
29. 거꾸로 앞으로 다리벌리기: Reverse Front Splits
30. 옆으로 다리벌리기: Side Splits
31. 수직나비: Vertical Butterfly
32. 수평선나비: Horizontal Butterfly
33. 갈매기날개: Sea Gull Wings

34. 거꾸로 갈매기날개: Reverse Sea Gull Wings

35. 다리 90도자세: 90-Degree Leg Pose

36. 주걱자세: Spatula Pose

37. 목뒤에 발걸기: Foot Behind the Neck

38. 90도무릎에 팔꿈치대기: 90-Degree Elbow to Knee

39. 팔다리 90도뻗기: 90-Degree Arm & Leg Extension

40. 부처자세: Buddha Pose

41. 앞으로 긴걸음: Front Lunge

42. 앉아서 거꾸로 팔뻗기: Sitting Reverse Arm Stretch

43. 서서 거꾸로 팔뻗기 : Standing Reverse Arm Stretch

44. 매력 자세 : Glamour Pose

45. 소화전: Fire Hydrant

46. 거꾸로 등 아치: Reverse Back Arch

47. 양팔 거꾸로 등아치: Two Arm Reverse Back Arch

48. 본체 틀기: Trunk Twist

49. 잭 자세: Jack Pose

50. 머리대고 삼각 물구나무서기: 3-Point Head Stand

51. 이마대고 팔꿈치 삼각 물구나무서기: Triangle Head Stand

52. 머리들고 팔꿈치 삼각 물구나무서기: Triangle Hand Stand

53. 수평 공작새: Horizontal Peacock

54. 수직 공작새: Vertical Peacock

55. 물구나무서기: Hand Stand

56. 거위자세 : Goose Pose

57. 가슴에 무릎대기: Knee to Chest

58. 수닭자세: Cock Pose

59. 핀셋자세: Pincette Pose

60. 거꾸로 핀셋자세 : Reverse Pincette Pose

61. 양다리 접어뻗기 : Double Quad Stretch

62. 앞에 붙인 양손 : Front Sealed Hands

63. 앞에 거꾸로 붙인 양손 : Reverse Front Sealed Hands

64. 뒤에 붙인 양손 : Back Sealed Hands

65. 뒤에 거꾸로 붙인 양손 : Reverse Back Sealed Hands

*편안한 몸과 마음으로 호흡조절을 해가며 기공 요가를 해야 더 큰 효력을 볼 수가 있을 것입니다.

*You have to maintain a steady breath control and a clear mind when practicing Qi Yoga for it to be effective.

기공(氣孔) 요가술 (Qigong Yoga Techniques)

인간은 누구나 건강하게 오래살수 있기를 원하나 항상 외부의 적으로부터 미세한 세균에 이르기 까지도 위협과 공격을 받고 있는 현실입니다. 기공 요가의 기본은 호흡 조절과 단전에 기를 모아 혈액 순환을 촉진시켜 힘을 발육시켜 초인간의 힘을 만들어 그 힘을 사용하게 하는 것입니다. 조금도 쉴새 없이 지속적으로 몸속에서 돌고 있는 혈액으로 파장을 만들어 열을 내게 하여 힘을 발육 시키게 하는 것입니다.

쉴새없이(continuously) 심장을 박동시켜 혈액 순환이 돌고 있는 심장에 기를 넣어 혈액 순환을 촉진 시켜 단전에 기를 모아 발육시켜 사용하는 연습을 하는 동안 폐의 활량이 커지면서 힘이 발육 되어 초인간의 힘을 만들 수 있는 것입니다.

사람의 몸속에 혈액 순환과 호흡 조절로 각 장기의 기능을 강화시키고, 호흡으로 인하여 대기 중에서 유입되는 수많은 세균을 몸속의 혈액순환으로 이어지는 과정에서 백혈구가 세균을 박멸시켜 사람의 몸을 정상으로 유지되게 하고, 인간의 건강을 공격해오는 수많은 적대적인 세균을 적절하게 방어 할수 있는 방법을 인체 과학자 들은 심도 있게 연구 중이며, 본인의 경우도 東, 西洋 의학을 공부하고 각종 무술들의 기예를 터득한 후 많은 실제 경험들이 축적된 지금에 와서 더욱 절실한 깨우침을 얻게 되었습니다.

인간은 호흡과 혈액순환 조절로 인하여 기를 발육시키고 자신의 병과 마음을 통제 및 제어 할 수 있다고 지금에 와서 더욱 확고하게 알게 되었습니다. 합도술을 1968년 4월 19일에 세상에 공개하면서 처음엔 뭉친 근육을 풀어주는 방법으로 요가를 하였다가 이제는 기공 요가의 필요성을 절실히 알게 되었으며, 굳어진 근육을 이완(relaxation) 시키고 관절(joint), 힘줄(tendon) 인대(ligament)를 조정(adjustment)시켜 호흡을 이용하여 혈액의 파장(blood of the wavelength)과 혈액순환(circulation of the blood), 호흡조절(breath of the control)을 조화(harmonizing) 시켜 정신수양(mental improvement)으로 몸과 마음을 단련시켜 건강관리(health control)를 합리적으로 증진시키며, 사람은 일단 병에 걸리면 서양 의학에서는 증상(symptom) 치료를 하게 되고, 동양 의학에서는 기능(function) 치료를 하게 됩니다.

이 모두를 조절하는 것은 자기 스스로 할 수 있다고 결론을 가지게 되었으며, 모든 혈관이 open 되어 있을 때는 원활한 혈액순환으로 인하여 몸속에 구석구석 모든 곳을 백혈구가 돌다가 작은 균들까지 쉽게 찾아 박멸시킬 수 있게 됩니다. 순차적으로 계속해서 백혈구가 싸워 이기도록 길을 열어 주어야하는 과제는 자기 스스로 해결해야 하며 강한 백혈구가 만들어 질 수 있도록 하는 것도 자신이 해야 합니다.

누구나 어떠한 병에 걸리든 혈액순환이 정상일 때 는 자연 치유 되지만 대사과정에서 어느 한 기능이라도 비정상일 때 는 중심이 깨어져 병이 생기게 되는 것입니다. 우리 다 같이 건강한 삶을 유지 하려면 정상적인 신진대사에 주력을 해야 합니다. 원칙을 알고 관리를 하면 결코 어려운 과제가 아니며 누구나 자신의 몸을 돌볼 수 있는 의사가 되고, 또한 자기의 가족들 나아가선 궁극적으로 남을 도우며 건강하게 장수를 누릴 수 있을 것입니다.

무술이 자기 몸의 기능 조절과 자기방어 건강관리 및 정신수양을 하는 데는 의술보다 더욱 효율적이라고 할 수 있으며, 다음 기회에 미국인 골수암 환자와 갑상선 환자들을 기공요가 술과 동양의술로 완치한 임상 실험 결과를 자세한 내용으로 소개하겠습니다. 인간의 구조는 동양의 陰陽五行(음양오행)에 원칙에서 우리 몸속에 있는 장기들로 몸을 조절하는 기공요가 술로 인하여 신체의 균형을 조절하며 모든 자기의 병을 치료하고 신체를 강화시켜 건강하게 할 수 있도록 간추려 만들어 놓은 기공요가 술 을 소개합니다.

많은 요가 술이 있으나 중요한 자세(Pose)만 간추려 만들어 놓은 순서로 건강한 몸으로 장수 할 수 있도록 하루 한 시간을 자신에게 귀중한 시간으로 생각하시고 활용 할 수 있도록 그동안 50년이 넘도록 연구 개발하여 임상 경험과 국내외 학생들을 직접 지도했든 기공(氣孔) 요가술 65가지를 소개하오니 실행하여서 건강하시고 보람된 행복한 삶이 될 수 있도록 열심히 수련 하시기를 요망합니다.

1. 목 교량

시작: 양다리를 붙이고 무릎을 약간 접어 뒤로 눕는다.

취하기: 목을 뒤로 제쳐 양다리와 목에 기를 연결하여 양손은 양허벅지 위에 붙여 놓고 몸을 위로 들어 올려 중심은 머리와 양다리에 두고, 무릎을 펴고 허리에 힘을 넣어 허리를 똑바로 세워 올려 호흡조절을 한다. 꼭 양 무릎을 똑바로 뻗는다.

Neck Bridge:

Start: Lay flat on your back. Place your hands on your thighs and slightly bend both of your legs. Base your feet against the ground at a shoulder width apart.

Description: Push off the ground with your feet and raise your hips off the floor. Extend both of your legs and roll onto the top of your head while arching your neck back and balancing on your head and feet. Lock your body and legs straight and keep your hands on your thighs.

2. 양팔올린 목 교량

시작: 양다리를 붙이고 무릎을 약간 접어 뒤로 눕는다.

취하기: 목을 뒤로 제쳐 양다리와 목에 기를 연결하여 양손은 양허벅지에 붙여 몸을 위로 들어 올려 중심을 머리와 양다리에 두고, 허리에 힘을 넣어 허리를 똑바로 세워 양팔을 위로 똑바로 뻗어 올려 호흡조절을 한다. 꼭 양 무릎을 똑바로 뻗는다.

Two Arm Raise Neck Bridge:

Start: Lay flat on your back. Place your hands on your thighs and slightly bend both of your legs. Base your feet against the ground at a shoulder width apart.

Description: Push off the ground with your feet and raise your hips off the floor. Extend both of your legs and roll onto the top of your head while arching your neck back and balancing on your head and feet. Lock your body and legs straight. Then raise both of your arms straight up vertically.

3. 엉덩이 뻗어 올린 연결교량

시작: 양발을 붙이고 양팔을 뒤로 뻗어 바닥을 짚고 앉는다.

취하기: 양발을 붙이고 양팔을 똑바로 뒤로하여 양손바닥은 바닥을 짚고 머리를 뒤로 제쳐 양다리와 양팔에 기를 연결하여 중심을 양발과 양 손에 두고, 엉덩이에 힘을 넣어 허리를 세워 호흡 조절을 한다. 꼭 양 무릎을 똑바로 뻗는다.

Extended Bridge Hip Raise:

Start: Sit up with both of your legs together and straight out in front of you. Place your palms on the floor behind your hips and lean back into your arms.

Description: Lock your arms and legs straight. Lift your hips off the ground until your waist is straight with your body and legs. Balance yourself on your hands and feet. Relax your neck and let your head hang back.

4. 한 다리 올려 엉덩이 들기

시작: 양다리를 뻗고 앉는다.

취하기: 양팔을 뒤로 돌려 양손바닥을 바닥에 짚고 한 다리를 바닥에 대고 다른 다리는 무릎을 펴고 엉덩이를 바닥에서 들어 올려 중심을 양팔과 한 다리에 두고 무릎에 기를 넣어 몸을 45도 각도로 세워 허리를 위로 똑바로 들어 올려 양 팔꿈치를 똑바로 펴고 호흡조절을 한다. 꼭 발목을 앞으로 뻗는다

One Leg Extended Hip Raise:

Start: Sit up with both of your legs straight out in front of you. Place your palms on the floor behind your hips and lean back into your arms.

Description: Lock your arms and legs straight. Lift your hips off the ground until your waist is straight with your body and legs. Balance yourself on your hands and feet. Relax your neck and let your head hang back. Then lean into one leg and raise the other leg at a 45-degree angle. Balance on your arms and one leg.

5. 목과 어깨교량

시작: 양다리를 접어 뒤로 눕는다.

취하기: 양 무릎을 구부려 양발을 어깨넓이로 벌려 양손은 허리에 붙여 엉덩 이를 들어 허리를 세워 기를 넣어 호흡 조절을 한다. 꼭 양발 뒤축을 들어 올린다.

Neck and Shoulder Bridge:
Start: Lay flat on your back and bend both of your legs.
Description: Base the balls of your feet on the floor and lift your hips and heels off the ground. Arch your back and put your chin into your chest so that you are up on your shoulders. Post your hands on your lower back to support your waist.

6. 교량

시작: 양다리를 접어 뒤로 눕는다.

취하기: 양 무릎을 구부려 양발을 어깨넓이로 벌려 양손은 어깨넓이로 뒤로 돌려 바닥에 짚고 허리를 위로 휘여 활 모양으로 뻗어 올려놓고 호흡 조절을 한다. 꼭 목을 뒤로 제친다.

Bridge:
Start: Lay flat on your back and bend both of your legs. Bend your arms up and over your head and place your palms on the floor behind your shoulders so that your thumbs are by your ears.
Description: Base the balls of your feet on the floor. Push off the floor with your hands and feet and lift your body and head off the ground. Arch your back and relax your neck.

7. 한 다리 교량

시작: 양다리를 접어 뒤로 눕는다.

취하기: 양발을 약간 벌리고 양팔을 뒤로 돌려 양손을 바닥에 짚고 허리를 휘여 활 모양으로 위로 뻗어 올려 한쪽 다리를 직선으로 뻗어 올려 놓고 호흡조절을 한다. 꼭 무릎을 펴서 180도 각도로 세운다.

One Leg Bridge:

Start: Lay flat on your back and bend both of your legs. Bend your arms up and over your head and place your palms on the floor behind your shoulders so that your thumbs are by your ears.

Description: Base the balls of your feet on the floor. Push off the floor with your hands and feet and lift your body and head off the ground. Arch your back and relax your neck. Then lean most of your weight into one leg. Next, raise the other leg vertically in the air and balance yourself on your arms and one leg.

8. 한팔 교량

시작: 양다리를 접어 뒤로 눕는다.

취하기: 양발을 약간 벌리고 양팔을 뒤로 돌려 양손을 바닥에 짚고 허리를 휘여 활 모양으로 위로 뻗어 올려 한쪽 팔을 직선으로 뻗어 올려 놓고 호흡조절을 한다. 꼭 팔꿈치를 펴서 180도 각도로 세운다.

One Arm Bridge:

Start: Lay flat on your back and bend both of your legs. Bend your arms up and over your head and place your palms on the floor behind your shoulders so that your thumbs are by your ears.

Description: Base the balls of your feet on the floor. Push off the floor with your hands and feet and lift your body and head off the ground. Arch your back and relax your neck. Then lean most of your weight into one arm. Next, raise the other arm vertically in the air and balance yourself on one arm and your legs.

9. 허리잡고 어깨서기

시작: 양다리를 접어 뒤로 눕는다

취하기: 양손을 허리에 대고 양다리를 들어 올려 엉덩이를 들어 무릎을 펴고 180도로 세워 양어깨를 바닥에 붙이고 몸을 일직선으로 세워 호흡 조절을 한다. 꼭 양발을 붙인다.

Shoulder Stand Waist Hold:

Start: Lay flat on your back.

Description: Bend your knees into your chest and rock your body into your shoulders. Raise your hips off the ground. Post your elbows on the ground and support you back with your hands for stability. Straighten your waist and legs and balance your body vertically on your shoulders. Point your feet and keep your legs together.

10. 허리잡고 거꾸로 45도

시작: 양다리를 접어 뒤로 눕는다.

취하기: 양손을 허리에 대고 양팔꿈치를 바닥에 붙이고, 양무릎을 펴서 양다리를 같이 붙여 머리위로 무릎을 넘겨 양발의 발가락을 뒤로 제쳐 바닥에 붙여 호흡조절을 한다. 꼭 양 무릎을 45도 각도로 세운다.

45-Degree Over the Top Waist Hold:

Start: Lay flat on your back.

Description: Bend your knees into your chest and rock your body into your shoulders. Raise your hips off the ground. Post your elbows against the ground and support you back with your hands for stability. Straighten your waist and legs and balance your body vertically on your shoulders. Point your feet and keep your legs together. Then lower your legs over your head with control until your feet touch the ground and keep your legs straight. Support your back with your hands.

11. 양 팔 뻗어 거꾸로 45도

시작: 양다리를 접어 뒤로 눕는다.

취하기: 양다리를 붙이고, 발가락을 곧게 뻗어 양다리와 엉덩이를 올리면서 양손바닥을 바닥에 붙이며 양팔을 뒤로하여 바닥에 어깨넓이로 벌려 팔꿈치를 뻗어 손바닥을 펴고 중심은 양발가락과 양손가락에 두고 양 무릎을 펴서 양다리를 머리위로 넘겨 발가락을 뒤로 제쳐 바닥에 붙여 호흡조절을 한다. 꼭 양다리를 붙여 무릎은 45도 각도로 세운다.

45-Degree Over the Top Arms Spread:

Start: Lay flat on your back with your arms at your sides.

Description: Post your arms flat against the ground. Bend your knees into your chest and rock your body into your shoulders. Raise your hips off the ground and straighten your waist and legs. Balance your body vertically on your shoulders and use your arms to stabilize yourself. Point your feet and keep your legs together. Then lower your legs over your head with control until your feet touch the ground.

12. 팔 뻗어 거꾸로 무릎대기

시작: 양다리를 접어 뒤로 눕는다.

취하기: 양다리를 붙이고 발가락을 곧게 뻗으며 양다리와 엉덩이를 올리면서 양팔을 벌려 엉덩이 밑에 놓고 팔꿈치를 뻗어 바닥에 붙여 양손바 닥을 펴고 바닥에 붙여 양어깨에 중심을 두고 양다리를 머리위로 넘겨 양 무릎을 접어 바닥에 붙여 양어깨와 손가락에 기를 넣어 호흡조절을 한다.

Over the Top Knee Touch and Arms Spread:

Start: Lay flat on your back.

Description: Raise your hips and both your legs straight up. Keep your legs together and your toes pointed up towards the ceiling. Place your arms under your hips with both your arms and palms flat on the ground for support. Then bring your legs over your head and bend your legs. Try to touch the ground with your knees. Place your shins and the tops of your feet flat on the floor.

13. 양다리 45도 들기

시작: 등을 바닥에 대고 누워 양팔을 몸에서 45도를 벌려 양손바닥을 바닥에 붙인다.

취하기: 양다리를 붙여 양 무릎을 똑바로 펴고 어깨 견갑골을 바닥에 붙여 양다리를 45도로 올려 양팔을 약간 벌려 팔꿈치와 손바닥을 바닥에 대고 머리를 들어 올려 단전에 기를 넣어 호흡조절을 한다. 꼭 머리를 들어 턱을 앞으로 당긴다.

45-Degree Leg Raise:

Start: Lay flat on your back with your arms straight out at a 45-dergree angle with your body and both your arms and palms flat on the ground.

Description: Keep your legs straight and your feet together. Raise your legs up about a 45-degree angle from the ground. Lift your head off the ground, but make sure your shoulder blades are still flat on the ground.

14. 45도 V 에너지

시작: 앞으로 다리를 벌리고 앉는다.

취하기: 양다리를 붙이고 무릎을 똑바로 펴서 양다리와 몸을 45도 각도를 만들어 양손바닥을 무릎 옆에 올려놓고 양팔을 바닥에서 수평으로 앞으로 똑바로 뻗어 놓으며 단전에 기를 넣어 호흡조절을 한다. 꼭 양발을 위로 뻗어 올린다.

45-Degree Power V:

Start: Lay flat on your back.

Description: Keep your legs straight. Raise your legs and body up to form a 45-degree angle. Keep your arms straight out so your hands are next to your knees. Your arms should be parallel with the ground.

15. 45도 복부단련

시작: 등을 바닥에 대고 눕는다.

취하기: 양다리를 붙이고 양 무릎을 똑바로 펴고 양팔을 머리 뒤로 돌려 손깍지를 끼고 어깨를 45도 각도로 들어 올려 단전에 기를 넣어 호흡조절을 한다. 꼭 양 무릎은 똑바로 펴서 바닥에 붙인다.

45-Degree Abdomen Crunch:

Start: Lay flat on the ground with your legs together and your hands behind your head.

Description: Lift your body up at a 45-degree angle with the ground. Make sure your legs are straight.

16. 코브라

시작: 배를 바닥에 대고 납작하게 엎드린다.

취하기: 양 무릎을 똑바로 펴고 양손을 바닥에 짚고 팔꿈치를 펴서 머리를 위로 들어 등 뒤로 넘겨 어깨와 허리를 휘어지도록 들어 올려 호흡조절을 한다. 꼭 목을 뒤로 제친다.

Cobra:

Start: Lay flat on your stomach with you're your arms bent and your hands at your side. Place your palms flat on the ground, and keep your legs straight with your feet together.

Description: Extend your arms and arch your back backwards. Make sure your waist is flat on the ground and your head is arched back as well.

17. 꼬리감긴 코브라

시작: 엎드려 양팔을 바닥에 대고 허리를 세운다.

취하기: 양손을 바닥에 짚고 팔꿈치를 뻗어 올리고 허리를 들어 뒤로 구부려 고개를 뒤로 제치고 양다리를 위로 들어 머리에 붙이고 호흡조절을 한다.

Coiled Cobra:

Start: Lay flat on your stomach with your arms bent and your hands at your side. Keep your legs straight and your feet together.

Description: Extend your arms and arch your back backwards. Make sure your waist is flat on the ground and your head is arched back as well. Then bend your legs and try to touch your feet to your head. Make sure your feet are together.

18. 슈퍼맨

시작: 배를 바닥에 대고 똑바로 엎드린다.

취하기: 가슴과 허벅지를 들어 올려 허리를 뒤로 제치며 양다리를 밀고 양팔을 앞으로 뻗어 몸을 길게 늘리면서 호흡조절을 한다. 꼭 양 무릎과 양 팔꿈치를 똑바로 뻗는다.

Superman:

Start: Lay flat on your stomach with your arms straight up over your head and your legs straight with your feet together.

Description: Lift your chest and thighs off the ground. Arch your back backwards and raise both your arms and legs up while keeping them straight. Arch your head back, and look towards the ceiling.

19. 날으는 백조

시작: 배를 바닥에 대고 똑바로 엎드린다.

취하기: 가슴과 허벅지를 들어 올려 허리를 뒤로 제치며 양다리를 밀고 양팔을 뒤로 뻗어 들어 올리며 몸을 길게 늘리면서 호흡조절을 한다. 꼭 목을 위로 올려 앞으로 뻗는다.

Flying Swan:

Start: Lay flat on your stomach with your arms at your side and your legs straight with your feet together.

Description: Lift your chest and thighs off the ground. Arch your back backwards, and lift both your legs up while keeping them straight. Pull both your arms straight back behind you.

20. 등 뒤 90도 양 팔 들기

시작: 배를 바닥에 대고 몸을 납작하게 엎드린다.

취하기: 양다리를 똑바로 붙이고 턱을 바닥에 대고 양팔을 등 뒤 위로 90도 각도로 들어 올려 양손가락은 깍지를 낀다. 꼭 턱을 바닥에 댄다.

Behind the Back 90-Degree Arms Raise:

Start: Lay flat on your stomach with your legs straight and your feet together. Interlock your fingers behind your back.

Description: Raise your arms straight up at a 90-degree angle with your body. Make sure to keep your fingers interlock behind your back.

21. 활자세

시작: 배를 바닥에 대고 엎드린다.

취하기: 가슴과 대퇴를 바닥에서 들어 허리를 뒤로 제쳐 머리를 들고 양손은 양발목을 잡고 몸을 활모양 휘어지게 만들면서 중심은 배에두고 기를 허리에 넣어 호흡조절을 한다. 꼭 목을 위로 들어 올려 힘을 준다.

Bow Pose:

Start: Lay flat on your stomach. Grab both your outside ankles from behind with your hand.

Description: Lift your chest and thighs off the ground. Arch your back backwards and look up.

22. 전갈

시작: 손바닥과 무릎을 바닥에 대고 엎드린다.

취하기: 양팔을 어깨 넓이로 벌려 양손바닥으로 바닥을 짚고 양 팔꿈치를 세워 한 다리는 무릎을 펴고 위로 45도 각도로 들어 올리면서 머리를 들어 중심을 한쪽 무릎에 두고 한쪽 엉덩이에 기를 넣으면서 호흡 조절을 한다.

Scorpio:

Start: Stand up on your hands and knees.

Description: Extend one leg straight up and keep your leg is straight. Make sure your arms and your back is straight with your head up.

23. 양 무릎대고 삼각대

시작: 양 무릎과 머리를 바닥에 댄다.
취하기: 양 무릎과 머리를 바닥에 대고 양팔을 등뒤로 돌려 손깍지를 끼고 양팔꿈치를 펴서 양팔을 머리위로 올리며 중심은 양다리와 목에 두고 목에 기를 넣어 호흡조절을 한다. 꼭 머리정수리를 바닥에 댄다.

Knees Down Tri-Pod:

Start: Stand on your knees so your knees are at shoulder width apart with your fingers interlocked behind your back.
Description: Place the top of your head on the ground with your knees bent at a 90-degree angle. Raise your arms over your head and keep your arms straight. Try to get as close to the ground as you can with your hands.

24. 양 다리 뻗은 삼각대

시작: 양 무릎과 머리를 바닥에 댄다
취하기: 양팔을 등 뒤로 돌려 양 손깍지를 끼고 머리를 바닥에 대고 양다리를 들어 올려 무릎을 똑바로 펴서 세우고 양팔을 똑바로 뻗어 머리위로 넘겨서 중심은 양다리와 목에 두고 목에 기를 넣어 호흡조절을 한다. 꼭 머리정수리를 바닥에 댄다.

Extended Legs Tri-Pod:

Start: Stand on your knees so your knees are at shoulder width apart with your fingers interlocked behind your back.
Description: Place the top of your head on the ground with your legs extended and your feet wider then the width of your shoulders. Raise your arms over your head and keep your arms straight. Try to get as close to the ground as you can with your hands.

가공요가술: Yoga Sool Technique

25. 한 다리 뻗기

시작: 다리를 뻗고 앉는다.

취하기: 한 다리를 앞으로 똑바로 무릎을 뻗고 발가락을 앞으로 일직선으로 하고 다른 다리를 접어 뒤로 빼고 양손은 발목을 잡고 앞으로 당겨 가슴을 양 허벅다리에 대면서 기를 무릎에 넣고 호흡조절을 한다. 꼭 양 팔꿈치를 바닥에 닿게 한다.

Single Leg Stretch:

Start: Sit up with one leg extended out sideways and the other leg bent back behind you with your knee pulled back.

Description: Lean toward the extended leg and grab your ankle. Point your toes forward and try to touch your chest to your knee. Make sure you keep the extended leg straight.

26. 양다리 뻗기

시작: 양다리를 뻗고 앉는다.

취하기: 양 무릎을 앞으로 똑바로 펴서 양 발목을 앞으로 뻗고 양손으로 양발목을 잡고 앞으로 당기면서 가슴을 양 허벅다리에 대고 이마를 양정강이에 붙이고 기를 양다리에 넣어 호흡조절을 한다. 꼭 양 무릎을 바닥에 댄다.

Double Leg Stretch:

Start: Sit up with both your legs straight out in front of you. Keep your legs straight and together.
Description: Pull your toes toward you. Lean your body forward and try to touch your chest to your knees. Make sure your legs are straight.

27. 복부에 발붙이기

시작: 등을 바닥에 대고 눕는다.

취하기: 한 다리는 무릎과 발목을 앞으로 뻗고 다른 다리는 발목을 잡고 위로 들어 올렸다가 단전에 대고 몸을 뒤로 누워 고개를 들고 단전에 기를 넣어 호흡조절을 한다. 꼭 무릎을 펴서 바닥에 댄다.

Foot to Abdomen:

Start: Sit up with one leg extended straight out in front of you. Bend your other leg, and grab your foot.
Description: Touch the inside of your ankle to your abdomen. Keep your other leg extended. Lay back while holding your foot to your abdomen.

28. 앞으로 다리 벌리기

시자: 다리를 옆으로 벌리고 앉는다.

취하기: 양 무릎을 펴고 양다리를 옆으로 벌려 양손으로 한 발목을 잡고 당겨 가슴을 허벅다리에 붙이고 가랑이를 벌려 양 무릎에 기를 넣어 호흡조절을 한다. 꼭 이마를 정강이뼈에 붙인다.

Front Splits:

Start: Stand up with your feet pointed in the same direction sideways.
Description: While keeping your legs straight, spread your legs apart in opposite directions. Your front leg on your heel, and your back leg on your instep. Try to sink your hips to the ground. Lean forward and touch your chest to your front leg. Make sure to keep your legs straight out sideways.

29. 거꾸로 앞으로 다리 벌리기

시작: 뒤로 눕는다.

취하기: 누워서 한 다리는 무릎을 뻗어 똑바로 아래로 펴고 다른 다리를 위로 무릎을 뻗어 똑바로 펴고 양손으로 허벅지를 잡고 아래로 눌러 가랑이 벌리기를 하면서 기를 양다리에 넣으면서 호흡조절을 한다.

Reverse Front Splits:

Start: Lay flat on your back.

Description: Keep your legs straight. Raise one leg straight up and grab your leg with both your hands. Pull your extended leg towards you and try to touch your knee to your shoulder while keeping the other leg flat on the floor.

30. 옆으로 다리 벌리기

시작: 다리를 옆으로 벌리고 앉는다.

취하기: 양 무릎을 펴고 양다리를 옆으로 벌려 양팔꿈치를 앞의 바닥에 대고 몸을 앞으로 구부려 가슴을 바닥에 붙여 가랑이를 옆으로 벌려 양무릎에 기를 넣어 호흡조절을 한다. 꼭 턱을 바닥에 붙인다.

Side Splits:

Start: Stand up with your feet pointed towards the front.

Description: While keeping your legs straight, spread your legs out in opposite direction. Try to sink your hips to the ground. Lean forwards and lay your chest flat on the ground in front of you.

31. 수직나비

시작: 허리를 세워 똑바로 앉는다.

취하기: 양손바닥을 안쪽 무릎위에 올려놓으며 양 무릎은 바닥에 대고 양발바닥을 같이 붙이고 엉덩이를 들고 허리를 똑바로 세워 기를 양손에 넣어 호흡조절을 한다. 꼭 똑바로 앉아서 턱을 아래로 당긴다.

Vertical Butterfly:

Start: Sit up with your back straight. Bend your knees and touch your feet together.

Description: Place the palm of your hand on your knees. Push your knees to the floor with your hands, and elevate your hips up off the ground. Make sure your feet are together, and keep your back straight.

32. 수평선나비

시작: 양발바닥을 붙이고 앉는다.

취하기: 양발바닥을 붙이고 양손으로 양쪽 발등을 잡아 손깍지를 끼고 뒤로 누우면서 양발을 당겨 위로 올려붙여 호흡조절을 한다. 꼭 양 무릎을 수평으로 한다.

Horizontal Butterfly:

Start: Sit up with your knees bent and your feet together. Grab your feet with both your hands from underneath.

Description: Lay back and pull your feet in towards you.

33. 갈매기날개

시작: 양다리를 옆으로 벌리고 눕는다.

취하기: 양다리를 옆으로 벌려 누워 양손으로 양 무릎 안을 잡고 아래로 누르면서 고개를 들고 양발가락을 뒤로 제쳐 바닥에 대고 양손에 기를 넣어 아래로 눌러 가랑이를 벌리면서 호흡조절을 한다. 꼭 턱을 앞으로 당긴다.

Sea Gull Wings:

Start: Lay flat on your back with your legs straight up. Place your hands in the inner thighs of your legs.

Description: While keeping your legs straight, spread your legs apart in opposite direction. Use your hands to help pull your legs further apart. Try to touch your toes to the ground.

34. 거꾸로 갈매기날개

시작: 다리를 벌려 위로 올리고 드러눕는다.

취하기: 양어깨를 바닥에 대고 양다리를 위로 올려 가랑이를 벌려 양손을 양무릎안쪽 다리에 대고 옆으로 밀어 가랑이를 벌리면서 양발가락을 뒤로 제쳐 바닥에 대고 호흡조절을 한다. 꼭 양무릎을 뻗는다.

Reverse Sea Gull Wings:

Start: Lay flat on your back with your legs straight up in the air. Place your hands in the inner thigh of your legs.

Description: Bring your legs over your head and split them in opposite direction. Touch your feet to the ground. Use your hands to help pull them further apart. You should be up on your shoulders.

35. 다리 90도 자세

시작: 등을 바닥에 대고 다리를 뻗고 눕는다.

취하기: 등을 바닥에 대고 반드시 누워서 한 다리를 똑바로 아래로 뻗고 다른 다리는 옆으로 올려 다리와 다리사이를 90도로 되게 하고 양팔을 옆으로 똑바로 벌려 바닥에 대고 한 팔과 한 다리를 평행으로 하고 기를 양다리에 넣고 호흡조절을 한다.

90-Degree Leg Pose:

Start: Lay flat on your back.

Description: Raise one leg straight up. Then lower your leg down sideways so your leg is at a 90-degree angle with your other leg. Place your arms straight out sideways. Your leg and arm should be parallel. Keep your other leg straight.

36. 주걱자세

시작: 뒤로 반드시 눕는다.

취하기: 한다리를 똑바로 뻗고 다른다리는 위로 올려 무릎을 접어 위로 올려 팔뚝을 발목 아래에서 위로 걸어 올려 잡고 팔꿈치를 위로 접어 올려 무릎에 기를 넣으며 호흡조절을 한다.

Spatula Pose:

Start: Lay flat on your back.

Description: Bend one leg, and place your foot on the side of your head on the same side as your bent leg. Grab your bent leg to help pull it closer to the side of your head. Keep your other leg straight.l

37. 목뒤에 발걸기

시작: 등을 바닥에 대고 눕는다.

취하기: 한무릎을 접어 한손으로 발뒤축을 잡고 목뒤로 돌려 걸고 다른 다리는 아래로 일직선으로 뻗어 바닥에 대고 호흡조절을 한다. 꼭 무릎을 뻗어 바닥에 붙인다.

Foot Behind the Neck:

Start: Sit straight up with your legs straight out in front of you.

Description: Grab your foot with your arms and place it behind your head. Keep your head up. Lay flat on your back with your other leg completely straight.

38. 90도 무릎에 팔꿈치대기

시작: 누워서 다리를 든다

취하기: 누워서 양다리를 90도로 올려 세우고 양손은 뒷머리를 잡고 양팔꿈치는 양 무릎에 대며 무릎을 똑바로 뻗고 단전에 기를 넣으며 호흡조절을 한다. 꼭 양 무릎을 붙인다.

90-Degree Elbow to Knee:

Start: Lay flat on your back with your legs straight and your feet together. Place your hands behind your head.

Description: Raise your legs straight up so your legs are at a 90-degree with the ground. Then lift your body up and touch your elbows to your knees.

39. 팔다리 90도 뻗기

시작: 누워서 다리를 든다.

취하기: 양다리를 똑바로 바닥에서 90도로 올리고 양팔과 몸을 똑바로 올려 양팔과 양다리를 평행으로 하여 양손바닥과 양발바닥을 직선으로 뻗어 올려 양무릎을 직선으로 펴고 단전에 기를 넣어 호흡조절을 한다 꼭 어깨를 들어 올려야 한다.

90-Degree Arm and Leg Extension:

Start: Lay flat on your back with your legs straight and your feet together. Place your arms straight over your head. Your body should be straight from your feet to your hands.

Description: Raise your legs straight up so your legs are at a 90-degree with the ground. Then elevate your arms and your body straight up, including your head. Your arms should be parallel with your legs.

40. 부처자세

시작: 다리를 꼬아 허리를 세워 똑바로 앉는다.

취하기: 한 다리를 구부리고 한 발은 다른 다리 허벅지 안에 대고 또 다른다리를 구부리면서 그 발은 다른 다리 안쪽 정강이 위에 올려놓고 허리를 세워 양손을 안쪽 무릎에 대며 양손바닥을 위로 향하게 하여 양손의 가운데 장지 끝과 엄지 끝을 서로 붙이고 허리를 똑바로 펴고 어깨에 힘을 빼면서 편안한 마음으로 전신의 긴장을 풀고 호흡조절을 한다. 꼭 호흡조절을 하면서 몸을 움직이지 말아야 한다.

Lotus Pose:

Start: Sit straight up.

Description: Bend one leg in towards you, and place your foot on the thigh of your other leg. Then bend your other leg and place your foot over your shin. Keep your back straight. Place both of your hands on your knees with your palms face up. Then touch the tip of your middle and thumb fingers together.

41. 앞으로 긴 걸음

시작: 한 다리를 뒤로 빼고 다른 다리는 세워 앉는다.

취하기: 한 다리는 무릎을 세우고 다른 다리를 뒤로 45도로 똑바로 뻗고 양팔을 몸 아래로 내려 양손바닥은 바닥을 짚고 목을 뒤로 제치면서 중심은 앞다리에 두고 허벅다리에 기를 넣어 호흡조절을 한다. 꼭 양어깨를 세운다.

Front Lunge:

Start: Stand straight up with your feet at shoulder width apart.

Description: Step out with one leg and bend your knee. Extend your other leg. Place your arms down at your sides and touch the ground with your hands. Arch your head back and sink your hips down.

42. 앉아서 거꾸로 팔 뻗기

시작: 양다리를 뻗고 앉는다.

취하기: 양다리는 양 무릎을 펴고 앞으로 똑바로 앉아 양팔을 등 뒤로 돌려 양손은 서로 손깍지를 끼고 위로 뻗어 올리면서 무릎과 팔꿈치를 똑바로 펴고 양어깨에 기를 넣어 호흡조절을 한다. 꼭 양 무릎을 펴고 바닥에 붙인다.

Sitting Reverse Arm Stretch:

Start: Sit up with both of your legs straight out in front of you. Keep your legs straight and your legs together. Interlock your fingers behind your back.

Description: Lean forward and elevate your arms up. Make sure your arms and legs are straight.

43. 서서 거꾸로 팔 뻗기

시작: 다리는 어깨넓이의 2배로 벌려 선다.

취하기: 기마 자세에서 양 무릎을 뻗어 세우고 양팔을 등 뒤로 양손을 붙여 깎지를 끼고 양팔을 머리위로 올리면서 허리를 아래로 구부려 목을 뒤로 들어 올리고 양어깨에 기를 넣어 호흡 조절을 한다. 꼭 머리를 바닥에 닿지 않게 한다.

Standing Reverse Arm Stretch:

Start: Stand up with your legs spread far apart. Keep your legs straight. Interlock your fingers behind your back.

Description: Bend over forward and elevate your arms over your head trying to touch the floor with your hands. Make sure to keep your arms straight.

44. 마법자세

시작: 뒤로 눕는다.

취하기: 한 다리는 무릎을 뻗고 바닥에 대고 다른 다리는 무릎을 구부리고 들어 올려 반대 팔을 구부려 뒷목을 손으로 걸어 팔꿈치로 무릎에 대고 다른 팔은 똑바로 아래로 뻗어 손바닥을 펴서 바닥에 대고 단전에 기를 넣어 호흡조절을 한다.

Glamour Pose:

Start: Lay flat on your back.

Description: Raise and bend one leg. Place the opposite side hand behind your head. Turn your body, and touch your elbow to your bent knee. Make sure your other leg is straight and your other arm is straight out sideways at a 45-degree angle.

45. 소화전

시작: 양팔을 어깨넓이로 벌려 손바닥은 바닥을 짚고 무릎을 꿇어 엉덩이를 들고 앉는다.

취하기: 한쪽 무릎을 펴고 발을 앞으로 뻗어 90도 각도로 옆으로 벌려 다시 앞으로 45도 각도로 뻗으면서 엉덩이에 기를 넣어 호흡조절을 한다. 꼭 양팔을 똑바로 뻗는다.

Fire Hydrant:

Start: Stand on your hands and knees.

Description: Lift up one knee sideways. Then extend your leg straight out sideways so your foot is level with your head. Make sure to keep your head up and your arms straight.

46. 거꾸로 등 아치

시작: 양 무릎을 세우고 앉는다.

취하기: 양 무릎을 세우고 앉아 양손으로 양 발목을 잡고 양 팔굽을 뻗어 단전에 기를 넣어 복부를 앞으로 나오게 밀면서 호흡조절을 한다. 꼭 목을 뒤로 제친다.

Reverse Back Arch:

Start: Stand on your knees.

Description: Place your hands on your ankles. Stick your hip straight out and arch your back and neck backwards.

47. 양팔 거꾸로 등 아치

시작: 양 무릎을 세워 앉는다.

취하기: 양발가락을 제쳐 무릎을 꿇어앉아 허리를 뒤로 제쳐 양팔을 똑바로 90도 각도로 올려서 머리를 뒤로 넘겨 바닥으로 내리면서 허리에 기를 넣어 호흡조절을 한다.

Two Arm Reverse Back Arch:

Start: Stand on your knees.

Description: Arch your back backward. Raise your arms straight up and lower your head as close to the floor as possible without touching the ground.

48. 본체틀기

시작: 양다리를 앞으로 뻗고 앉는다.

취하기: 한 다리는 무릎을 펴고 앉고 다른 다리를 접어 반대의 다리위에 꼬아 올려놓고 팔꿈치를 반대다리에 엇갈리게 걸어놓고 다른 팔을 뒤로 돌려 바닥에 놓고 기를 넣어 팔을 밀면서 허리를 90도로 틀어 척추를 교정 시키면서 호흡조절을 한다. 꼭 척추에 무리가 없을 만큼 허리를 틀어야 한다.

Trunk Twist:

Start: Sit up with one leg straight out in front of you. Bend and cross the other leg over the knee of your extended leg. Place the opposite side elbow of your bent knee on your bent knee. Then place your other arm back behind you.

Description: Turn your trunk towards the arm that is behind you. Use your elbow to push off your knee and help twist your trunk.

Chapter 49~52

49. 잭 자세

시작: 팔꿈치를 접어 삼각대를 만들어 엎드린다.

취하기: 양 팔꿈치를 바닥에 대고 손바닥을 펴고 양 엄지와 양 검지를 서로 붙여 삼각형을 만들어 이마를 양 엄지와 양 검지를 붙인 삼각형 위에 대고 한 다리를 바닥에서 45도 각도로 세우고 다른 다리는 위로 들어 올려 허리에 중심을 잡아 190도 각도를 만들어 척추에 기를 넣어 호흡조절을 한다.

Jack Pose:

Start: Place your elbows on the ground at shoulder width apart. Touch your index and thumb fingers to form a triangle. Place the palm of your hands flat on the floor.

Description: Place the top of your forehead in between your index and thumb fingers inside the triangle. Raise one leg straight up in the air and plant your other leg on the ground. Make sure to extend the leg that's planted and to keep the leg in the air straight. Use your elbows and head to support your body.

50. 머리대고 삼각 물구나무서기

시작: 양손과 머리를 바닥에 대고 삼각대를 만들어 엎드린다.

취하기: 머리정수리를 바닥에 대고 양손바닥을 바닥에 삼각대를 만들어 몸을 똑바로 세워 허리에 기를 넣어 호흡조절을 한다.

3-Point Head Stand:

Start: Place your hands on the ground at shoulder width apart.

Description: Place the top of your head on the floor just above your hands. Bend your arms to form a 90-degree angle and use them to support your body. Place your knees on your elbows and slowly extend both your legs straight up. Make sure your legs are straight and together.

51. 머리대고 팔꿈치 삼각 물구나무서기

시작: 양팔은 삼각대를 만들어 이마를 손바닥 위에 올려놓고 엎드린다

취하기: 이마를 양 엄지와 양 검지를 붙인 삼각형 손바닥 위에대고 양다리를 붙여서 똑바로 위로 뻗어 올려 허리에 기를 넣어 호흡조절을 한다. 꼭 양 발목을 위로 뻗는다.

Triangle Head Stand:

Start: Place your elbows on the ground at shoulder width apart. Touch your index and thumb fingers to form a triangle. Place your palms flat on the floor.

Description: Place the top of your forehead in between your index and thumb fingers inside the triangle. Raise both your legs straight up. Make sure your legs are straight and together. Use your elbows and head to support your body.

52. 머리 들고 팔꿈치 삼각 물구나무서기

시작: 양팔을 삼각대를 만들어 손바닥을 바닥에 대고 엎드린다.

취하기: 양 팔꿈치는 삼각대를 만들어 다리를 붙여 똑바로 위로 뻗어 올려 목을 뒤로 제쳐서 머리를 올려 중심은 양 팔꿈치에 두고 몸을 똑바로 세워 허리에 기를 넣어 호흡조절을 한다.

Triangle Hand Stand:

Start: Place your elbows on the ground at shoulder width apart. Touch your index and thumb fingers to form a triangle. Place the palm of your hands flat on the floor.

Description: Raise both your legs straight up. Make sure your legs are straight and together. Keep your head up off the ground by arching your head back and looking up. Use your elbows and forearm to support your body.l

53. 수평공작새

시작: 양손바닥을 바닥에 대고 엎드린다.

취하기: 양손가락을 옆으로 벌려 양 팔꿈치를 양옆구리에 붙여 양다리를 뻗어 위로 올려 중심은 양손에 두고 몸을 약간 앞으로 구부리면서 목을 들어 몸의 중심은 평행을 이루어 허리에 기를 넣어 호흡조절을 한다.

Horizontal Peacock:

Start: Place the pal of your hands flat on the ground with your fingers pointed outward in opposite direction. Touch both your wrist and elbows together.

Description: Rest your abdomen on your elbows and lean forward to raise your legs off the ground. Make sure your legs are completely straight with your body and you are parallel with the floor.

54. 수직공작새

시작: 양손바닥을 바닥에 대고 허리를 구부린다.

취하기: 양손과 이마를 바닥에 대고 삼각대를 만들어 양발을 붙이고 양 무릎을 뻗어 물구나무서기를 하여 허리에 기를 넣어 호흡조절을 한다.

Vertical Peacock:

Start: Place your hands on the ground with your fingers pointed in opposite direction. Touch both your wrist and elbows together.

Description: Lean forward and place your forehead on the ground in front of you. Then elevate your legs straight up. Use your hands and head to support your body.

55. 물구나무서기

시작: 양손바닥을 어깨넓이로 바닥에 짚는다.

취하기: 양손가락을 위로 벌려 양 팔뚝을 똑바로 뻗어 중심은 양손에 두고 양다리를 위로 똑바로 뻗으면서 허리에 기를 넣어 호흡조절을 한다. 꼭 목을 들어 올려 중심을 조절 한다.

Hand Stand:

Start: Place your hands on the ground at shoulder width apart.

Description: Raise your legs straight up so only your arms support your body. Make sure to keep your legs aligned with your back and keep your feet together.

56. 거위자세

시작: 양손바닥을 어깨넓이로 바닥에 대고 앉는다.

취하기: 양 팔꿈치를 접어 양 무릎을 팔꿈치위에 올려놓고 목을 뒤로 들어중심을 잡고 양팔에 기를 넣어 중심을 잡아 호흡조절을 한다.

Goose Pose:

Start: Place your hands on the floor at shoulder width apart.

Description: Bend your arms to a 90-degree angle. Lean slightly forward and place your knees on your elbows. Only your arms should support your body.

57. 가슴에 무릎대기

시작: 등을 바닥에 대고 눕는다.

취하기: 한 다리를 아래로 똑바로 뻗고 다른 다리는 무릎을 접어 구부려 양손으로 정강이를 잡아 가슴에 대고 기를 넣어 누르면서 호흡조절을 한다. 꼭 양 발목을 아래로 뻗는다.

Knee to Chest:

Start: Lay flat on your back.

Description: Bend and raise one knee. Grab your knee with your arms and pull it to your chest. Make sure your other leg is extended.

58. 수탉 자세

시작: 양 무릎을 접어 앉는다.

취하기: 허리를 세워 똑바로 앉아 양다리를 접어 한팔은 가운데 다리 안에 넣고 다른 팔은 바깥 대퇴 옆에 놓고 중심은 양손에 두고 엉덩이를 들어 올린다.

Cock Pose:

Start: Sit up straight with both your legs out in front of you. Bend one leg in, and place your foot securely on the thigh of your other leg. Then lift your other leg up and on top of the shin of your other bent leg.

Description: Place one arm in between your legs and put the palm of your hand flat on the ground. Then place your other arm next to your hip and put the palm of your hand flat on the ground. Elevate and lift your whole body up off the ground with both your arms. Your arms should be the only things supporting your body.

59. 핀셋자세

시작: 양다리를 꼬아 엮어 바닥에 엎드린다.

취하기: 양다리를 엇갈리게 꼬아 엮어 바닥에 사타구니를 닿게 눌러 엎드리고 양팔을 위로 뻗어 올려 양손바닥을 바닥에 대고 편안한 마음으로 전신의 근육을 이완시키면서 호흡조절을 한다.

Pincette Pose:

Start: Sit up straight with both your legs out in front of you. Bend one leg in, and place your foot securely on the thigh of your other leg. Then lift your other leg up and on top of the shin of your other bent leg.

Description: While keeping your legs weaved, lay flat on your stomach with both your arms straight up over your head. Your arms should be straight with your palms flat on the floor. Try to sink your hips to the ground.

60. 거꾸로 핀셋자세

시작: 양다리를 꼬아 엮어 등을 바닥에 대고 눕는다.

취하기: 양다리를 꼬아 엮어 드러누워 양팔을 몸에서 45도로 벌려 놓고 양팔을 똑바로 하면서 양손바닥은 바닥을 짚으며 양 무릎을 바닥에 대고 편안한 마음으로 전신의 근육을 이완시키면서 호흡조절을 한다.

Reverse Pincette Pose:

Start: Sit up straight with both your legs out in front of you. Bend one leg in, and place your foot securely on the thigh of your other leg. Then lift your other leg up and on top of the shin of your other bent leg.

Description: Lay backwards so you are lying flat on your back. Place your arms at a 45-degree angle with your body. Keep your arms straight and your palms flat on the ground. Try to touch your knees to the floor.

15

Chapter 61~63

61. 양다리 접어뻗기

시작: 양 무릎을 접고 뒤로 드러눕는다.

취하기: 양 무릎을 접고 뒤로 바닥에 납작하게 누워 양팔을 몸에서 30도에 똑바로 벌려 놓고 양손바닥은 바닥을 짚으며 엉덩이를 바닥에서 들어 올려 편안한 마음으로 허리의 근육을 이완시키면서 호흡조절을 한다.

Double Quad Stretch:

Start: Stand on your knees with your toes pointed so your insteps are flat on the floor.

Description: Lay backwards so you are laying flat on your back. Place your arms at a 45-degree angle with your body. Keep your arms straight and your palms flat on the ground.

62. 앞에 붙인 양손

시작: 무릎을 접어 앉는다.

취하기: 양 손가락 끝을 붙이고 양손바닥을 납작하게 붙여서 양손가락이 위를 향하게 하며 양팔꿈치를 올려서 양손바닥 아래 부분과 평행이 되게 올려 목과 허리를 똑바로 세워 편안한 마음으로 정신의 긴장을 풀고 양어깨에 기를 넣어 호흡조절을 한다.

Front Sealed Hands:

Start: Sit up straight with your leg out in front of you. Bend one leg in, and place your foot securely on the thigh of your other leg. Then lift your other leg up and on top of the shin of your other bent leg.

Description: Place the tips of your fingers together so both your palms are flat against each other. Make sure your fingers are pointed upward. Bring your elbows up so they are level with the bottom on your palms and keep your back straight.

63. 앞에 거꾸로 붙인 양손

시작: 양 무릎을 접어 앉는다.

취하기: 양다리를 접어 꼬아 앉아 양 손가락 끝을 붙이고 양손바닥을 납작하게 붙여서 양손가락이 밑을 향하게 돌려 허리를 똑바로 세워 양손목과 팔꿈치가 일직선이 되게 양팔꿈치에 기를 넣어 아래로 당겨 평행을 만들고 편안한 마음으로 긴장을 풀고 호흡조절을 한다.

Reverse Front Sealed Hands:

Start: Sit up straight with your leg out in front of you. Bend one leg in, and place your foot securely on the thigh of your other leg. Then lift your other leg up and on top of the shin of your other bent leg. Description: Place the tips of your fingers together so both your palms are flat against each other and your fingers are pointed upward. Then turn your wrists inward towards your body. Keep turning until your fingers are pointed downwards. Make sure your elbows are level with the bottom of your palms. Make sure to keep your back straight.

64. 뒤에 붙인 양손

시작: 양 무릎을 접어 앉는다.

취하기: 양다리를 접어 꼬아 앉아 양손바닥을 허리 뒤에서 납작하게 손바닥을 붙여서 양손가락을 위로 향하게 하고 목과 허리를 똑바로 세워 편안한 마음으로 전신의 긴장을 풀고 호흡조절을 한다.

Back Sealed Hands:

Start: Sit up straight with your leg out in front of you. Bend one leg in, and place your foot securely on the thigh of your other leg. Then lift your other leg up and on top of the shin of your other bent leg.
Description: Bring your hands behind your back and place the tips of your fingers together so our palms are flat against each other. Make sure your fingers are pointed upward.

65. 뒤에 거꾸로 붙인 양손

시작: 양 무릎을 접어 앉는다.

취하기: 양다리를 접어 꼬아 앉아 양손바닥을 머리 뒤에서 납작하게 붙여 양손가락 끝을 아래로 향하게 하고 허리를 똑바로 세워 양손목과 팔꿈치가 일직선이 되게 양 팔꿈치에 기를 넣어 밑으로 당겨 평행을 만들고 편안한 마음으로 긴장을 풀고 호흡조절을 한다.

Reverse Back Sealed Hands:

Start: Sit up straight with your leg out in front of you. Bend one leg in, and place your foot securely on the thigh of your other leg. Then lift your other leg up and on top of the shin of your other bent leg. Description: Bring your hands behind your head and place the tips of your fingers together so our palms are flat against each other. Make sure your fingers are pointed downward.

Acupressure Technique
지 | 압 | 술

01. 백회 (百會): Baik-Hoi (독맥: Du Channel)

02. 사신총 (四神聰): Sa-Shin-Chong (특별한 점: Special Point)

03. 인당 (印堂): Yin-Dang (특별한 점: Special Point)

04. 어요 (魚腰): Eu-Yo (특별한 점: Special Point)

05. 태양 (太陽): Tai-Yang (특별한 점: Special Point)

06. 풍지 (風池): Poong-Jee (담경: Gallbladder Channel)

07. 견정 (肩井): Gyun-Jung (담경: Gallbladder Channel)

08. 합곡 (合谷): Hab-Gok (대장경: Large Intestine Channel)

09. 곡지 (曲池): Gork-Jee (대장경: Large Intestine Channel)

10. 수삼리 (手三里): Soo-Sarm-Lee (대장경: Large Intestine Channel)

11. 태충 (太沖): Tai-Choong (간경: Liver Channel)

12. 족삼리 (足三里): Jork-Sam-Lee (위경: Stomach Channel)

13. 용천 (涌泉): Yong-Chun (신경: Kidney Channel)

14. 풍시 (諷示): Poong-Shi (담경: Gallbladder Channel)

15. 귀 신문 (耳神門): Ear Shin-Moon (Special Point)

16. 관원 (關元): Gwan-One (임맥: 관원 또는 단전 (丹田): Ren Channel)

1. 백회(百會)-독맥

위치: 양 귀첨 연결선 중앙부위.
병증: 두통, 어지럼증, 정신질환, 귀울림, 안구질환, 불면증, 혈액순환, 변비, 치질, 반신불수, 중풍, 직장탈출 등.

Baik-Hoi Du-Channel:

Location: Midpoint of the line connecting the apexes of the two auricles.
Indication: headache, dizziness, mental disorders, tinnitus, blurring of vision, insomnia, circulation, constipation, hemorrhoids, hemiplegia, apoplexy, prolapse of rectum, etc.

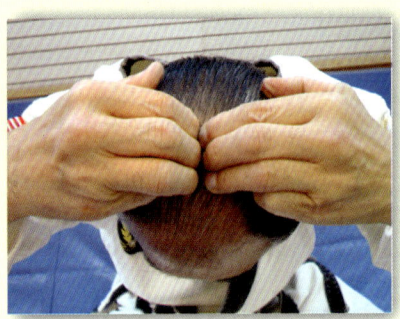

2. 사신총(四神聰)-특별한 점

위치: 머리의 중앙에서 백회 전후좌우 각 약 2.5cm.
병증: 두통, 현기증, 불면증, 기억력 감퇴, 간질.

Sa-Shin-Chong Special Point:

Location: A group of 4 points at the vertex about 2.5cm respectively posterior, anterior and lateral to BaikHoi(Du 20)
Indications: Headache, dizziness, insomnia, poor memory epilepsy

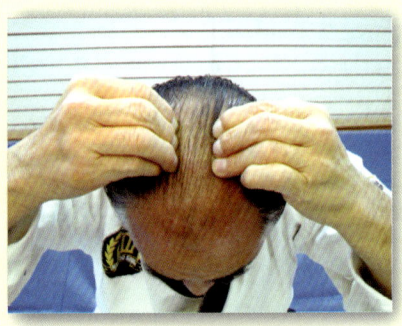

3. 인당(印堂)—특별한 점

위치: 앞 양눈썹 사이의 정가운데.

병증: 소아의 경기, 전두통, 콧물 등.

Yin-Dang Special Point:

Loction: Midway between the medial ends of the two eyebrows.

Indications: Infantile conulsion, frontal headache, rhinorrhea

4. 어요(魚腰)—특별한 점

위치: 눈썹 정가운데.

병증; 각막흐림, 눈꺼풀 떨림, 눈 충혈 붓고 아픔, 눈위 통증 등.

Eu-Yo Special Point:

Location: In the middle of the eyebrow.

Indications: Cloudiness of the cornea, twitching of eyelids, redness swelling and pain of the eye, pain in the supraorbital region.

지압술: Acuqressure Technique

5. 태양(太陽)-특별한 점

위치: 눈꼬리 윗쪽 오목한 부위 (관자놀이)
병증: 편두통, 어지럼증, 두통, 눈질환 등.

Tai-Yang Special Point:

Location: Lateral end of the eyebrow and the outer canthus.
Indications: migraine, dizziness, headache, redness swelling and pain of the eye, ete.

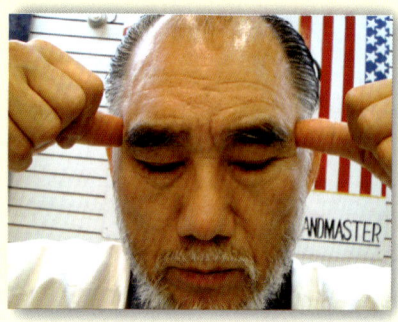

6. 풍지(風池)-담경

위치: 뒷머리 가운데 양옆 오목한 부위.
병증: 감기, 두통, 불면, 어지럼증, 발열, 등 어깨 통, 목의 뻣뻣함과 아픔, 눈질환, 콧물, 고혈압, 귀울림, 코 점막의 염증 등.

Poong-Jee Gallbladder channel:

Location: In the posterior aspect of the neck, below the occipital bone.
Indication: common cold, headache, insomnia, dizziness, febrile diseases, pain in the shoulder and back, pain and stiffness of the neck, red and painful eyes, rhinorrhea, hypertension, tinnitus, rhinitis, etc.

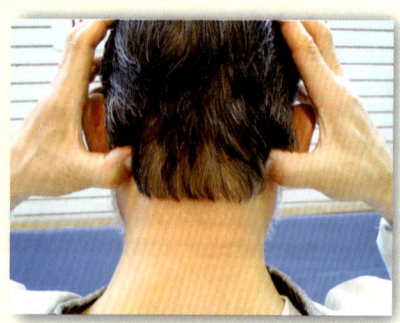

7. 견정(肩井)-담경

위치: 어깨 쇄골의 높은곳과 대추혈을 이은 선의 중간.

병증: 등 어깨통, 두통, 손 팔통, 유방염, 목 뻣뻣함, 중풍 등.

Gyun-Jung Gallbladder channel:

Location: Midway between "DeaChu" and the acromion, at the highes point of the shoulder.

Indications: Pain in the shoulder and back, headache, motor impairment of the hand and arm, mastitis, neck rigidity, apoplexy, ete.

8. 합곡(合谷)-대장경

위치: 엄지와 검지손가락 뼈사이 부위.

병증: 두통, 복부통, 치통, 인후통, 변비, 무월경, 발한, 이질, 발열, 눈질환, 손가락 질환, 안면마비, 열증과 무땀, 코피, 안면의 종창 등.

Hab-Gok Large Intestine Channel:

Location: Between the 1st and 2nd metacarpus bones.

Indications: headache, abdominal pain, toothache, sore throat, constipation, amenorrhea, hidrosis, dysentery, febrile, redness with swelling and pain of the eye, contracture of fingers, facial paralysis, febrile diseases with anahidrosiss, epistaxis, facial swelling, ete.

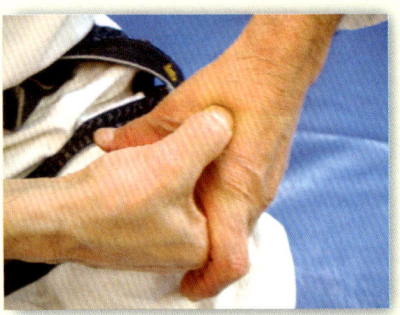

9. 곡지(曲池)-대장경

위치: 접은 팔꿈치 오목한 부위.

병증: 구토, 설사, 인후통, 이질, 발열, 복통, 팔과 팔꿈치통, 나력(연주창), 담마진(피부 가려움), 치통, 반신불수, 피부염, 두통 등.

Gork-Jee Large Intestin Channel:

Location: When the elbow is flexed, the point is in the depression at the lateral end of the transvers cubital crease, the lateral epicondyle of the humerus.

Indications: vomiting, diarrhea, sore throat, dysentery, febrile diseases, abdominal pain, pain of the elbow and arm, scrofula, urticaria, toothache, hemiplegia dermatitis, headache, ete.

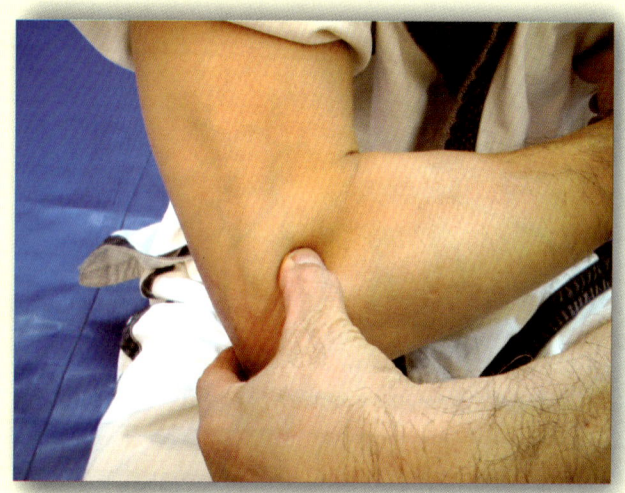

10. 수삼리(手三里)-대장경

위치: 곡지 약 5cm 아래.

병증: 알러지, 구토, 설사, 복통, 어깨통, 치통, 안면마비, 통증조절 등.

Soo-Sarm-Lee Large Intestine Channel:

Location: about 5cm below gorkJee.

Indications: allege, vomiting, diarrhea, abdominal pain, pain in the shoulder, toothache, facial paralysis, pain control, ete.

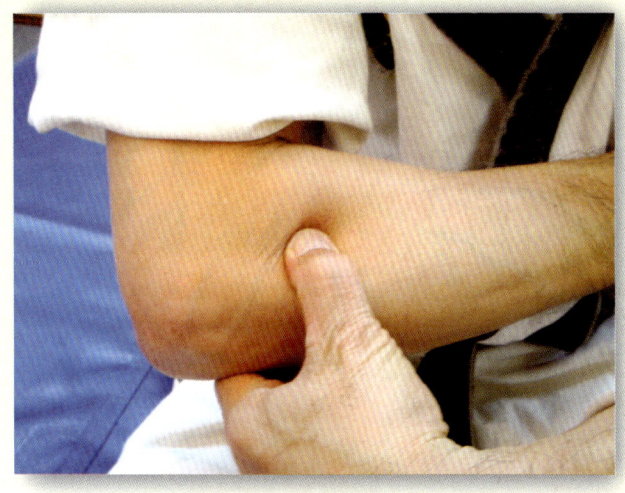

11. 태충(太沖)-간경

위치: 첫째와 둘째 발가락 뼈사이.

병증: 안면마비, 소아경기, 간질, 두통, 불면, 자궁출혈, 어지러움, 오줌곤란, 오줌정체, 족통, 간증, 엄지통, 눈충혈, 황달, 속메스꺼움, 기절, 황달 등.

Tai-Choong Liver Channel:

Locations: In the depression distal to the junction of the 1st and 2nd metatarsal bones.

Indications: deviation of mouth, infantile convulsion, epilepsy, headache, insomnia, uterine bleeding, vertigo, enuresis, retention of urine, foot pain liver disease, thumb pain, red eyes, nausea, fainting, jaundice, ete.

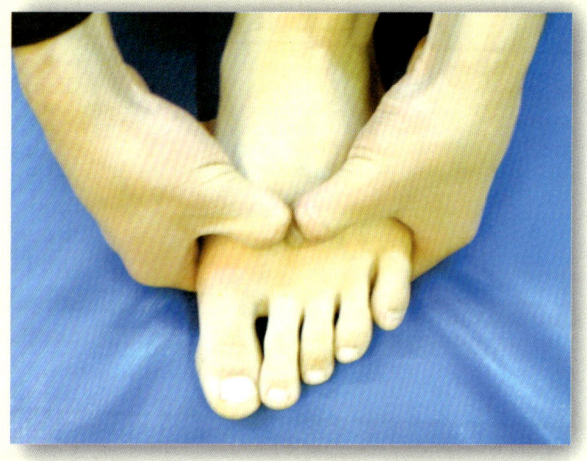

12. 족삼리(足三里)-위경

위치: 무릎아래 약 7.5cm 부위.

병증: 복부팽만, 설사, 이질, 변비, 유방염, 반신불수, 어지럼증, 각기, 위통, 구토, 정신질환, 소화불량, 복명, 소화기질환, 통증조절, 월경곤란, 좌골신경통, 무릎관절과 다리통 등.

Jork-Sam-Lee Stomach Channel:

Location: about 7.5cm below knee.

Indications: abdominal distension, diarrhea, dysentery, constipation, mastitis, hemiplegia, dizziness, beriberi, gastric pain, vomiting, mental disorders, indigestion, borborygmus, digestive organ disease, pain control, dysmenorrhea, sciatica, aching of the knee joint and leg, ete.

13. 용천(涌泉)-신경

위치: 발바닥 앞부분의 오목한부위.

병증: 두정통, 소변곤란, 어지러움, 인후통, 배변 곤란, 안과질환, 실성증, 소아의경기, 혼수, 실신, 두통, 고혈압, 요통, 긴급조치 등.

Yong-Chun Kidney Channel:

Location: Approximately at the junction of the anterior and middle third of the sole.

Indications: pain in the vertex, dysuria, dizziness, sore throst, dyschezia, biurring of vision, aphonia, infantile convulsion, loss of consciousness, cyncope, headache, hypertension, lumbago, emergency care, ete.

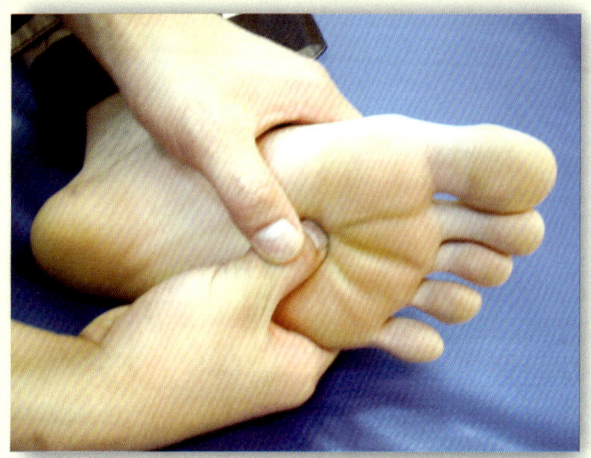

14. 풍시(風市)-담경

위치: 대퇴 외측에서 손을 바로 내려서 장지끝이 닿는곳.
병증: 소양증(피부가려움), 하체의 마비, 반신불수, 근육의 위축.

Poong-Shi Gallbladder Channel:

Location: When the patient is standing erect with the hands close to the sides, the point is where the tip of the middle finger touches.

Indications: General pruritus, motor impairment and pain of the loxer extremities, hemiplegia, muscular atrophy.

15. 귀 신문(耳 神門)

위치: 귀의 위쪽 대이륜 각과 아래쪽 대이륜 각 두갈래로 갈라진 곳.
병증: 염증, 불면증, 아픔, 정신조절, 잠을 방해하는 꿈 등.

Ear Shin-moon Ear point:

Location: At bifurcating point of superior antihelix crus and inferior antihelix crus.
Indications: Inflammation, insomnia, pain, mond control, dream-disturbed sleep.

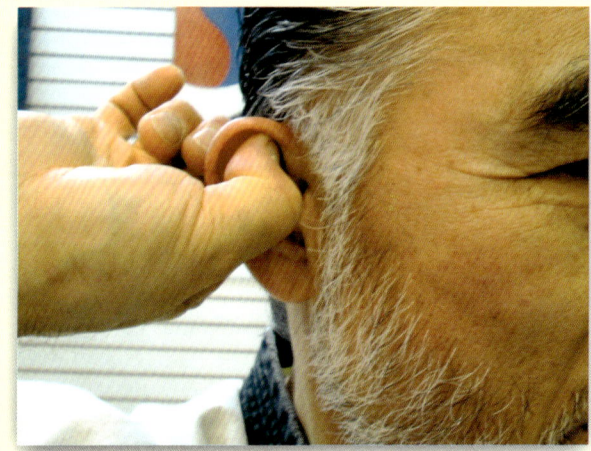

16. 관원(關元)-임맥: (관원(關元) 또는 단전(丹田)

위치: 배꼽 아래 약 7.5cm 부위.

병증: 육체적인 힘발육, 원기, 아랫배의 통증, 소변정체, 오줌곤란, 무의식적 정액 방출, 불규칙월경, 월경곤란, 무월경, 백대하, 설사, 자궁출혈, 자궁탈출, 분만후 출혈, 몽정, 허로, 발기부전, 당뇨병 등.

Gwan-One Ren Channel: (GwanOne or DanJun)

Location: On the midline of the abdomen about 7.5cm below the umbilicus.

Indications: developmental physical power, energy, lower abdominal pain, retention of urine, enuresis, seminal emission, irregular menstruation, dysmenorrhea, amenorrhea, leukorrhea, diarrhea, uterine bleeding, prolapse of uterus, postpartum hemorrhage, nocturnal emission, body fatigue, impotence, diabetes, ete.

COMBINED MARTIAL ART

실전무예
합도술 교본

2009년 1월 25일 초판 1쇄 발행

저 자 : 곽 웅 쾌
발행인 : 김 중 영
발행처 : 오성출판사

서울시 영등포구 영등포동6가 147-7
TEL : (02) 2635-5667~8
FAX : (02) 835-5550

출판등록 : 1973년 3월 2일 제13-27호
ISBN 978-89-7336-733-7
www.osungbook.com

값 38,000원

※파본은 교환해 드립니다.
※독창적인 내용의 무단 전재, 복제를 절대 금합니다.